The Postcolonial
Low Countries

The Postcolonial Low Countries

Literature, Colonialism, and Multiculturalism

Edited by
Elleke Boehmer
and
Sarah De Mul

LEXINGTON BOOKS
Lanham • Boulder • New York • Toronto • Plymouth, UK

Published by Lexington Books
A wholly owned subsidiary of The Rowman & Littlefield Publishing Group, Inc.
4501 Forbes Boulevard, Suite 200, Lanham, Maryland 20706
www.rowman.com

10 Thornbury Road, Plymouth PL6 7PP, United Kingdom

British Library Cataloguing in Publication Information Available

Library of Congress Cataloging-in-Publication Data

The postcolonial Low Countries : literature, colonialism, and multiculturalism / edited
by Elleke Boehmer and Sarah De Mul.
    p.   cm.
  Includes bibliographical references and index.
  ISBN 978-0-7391-6428-0 (cloth : alk. paper) — ISBN 978-0-7391-6430-3 (electronic)
  1. Dutch literature—History and criticism. 2. Postcolonialism in literature. 3. Benelux
countries—Social conditions. 4. Netherlands—Civilization—Foreign influences. I.
Boehmer, Elleke, 1961– II. Mul, Sarah de.
  PT5073.P67 2012
  839.3'109—dc23
                                                                2012009359

∞™ The paper used in this publication meets the minimum requirements of American
National Standard for Information Sciences—Permanence of Paper for Printed Library
Materials, ANSI/NISO Z39.48-1992.

Printed in the United States of America

Contents

SECTION III: LITERATURE AND MULTICULTURALISM

Chapter One

Introduction

Postcolonialism and the Low Countries

Elleke Boehmer and Sarah De Mul

In the novel *On Black Sisters' Street* by the Nigerian-Belgian writer Chika Unigwe, four African women respond to the lure of a better life in Europe and end up as sex workers in the red-light district of the Flemish-Belgian city of Antwerp.[1] The novel centres on the experiences of these women, who are usually observed from the outside, as sexualized spectacles sitting under red spotlights behind the windows of the *Schipperskwartier*-borough of Antwerp. Yet it is not so much a novel about four African diasporic sex workers but, rather, about how four protagonists *become* African diasporic sex workers on their arrival in Antwerp. The success the women achieve largely depends on the extent to which they can transform themselves to conform to general, if not stereotypical, ideas about hypererotic and exotic black womanhood that exist in the minds of their clientele. But by focusing on the perspectives and voices of these four women, the novel also explores more subtle and complex portrayals of the women and the community they share.

While narrating their family histories to each other, the women, the novel suggests, attempt to wrest control of how their bodies are constructed away from the distorted views and values of the dominant culture. The sense of social control they experience is spatially reinforced by the image of the house on Zwartzusterstraat (Black Sisters' Street) where they live together, with their fake passports withheld by their Madam, who keeps them under close surveillance. The street name "Zwartzusterstraat" refers to the renowned Roman Catholic religious order of the Black Sisters, in this way singling out the geographical location of the port-city of Antwerp, its local Catholic history and possibly also the minor role women play in this history. Additionally, *On Black Sisters' Street* of course alludes to the possibilities of black diasporic womanhood and community formation—"black sisterhood"—in Europe that is thematised in the novel. Zwartzusterstraat is also the location where in

May 2006 the 18–year-old Flemish man Hans Van Temssche assassinated the Malinese nanny Oulematou Niangadou and her two-year-old Belgian charge shortly after shooting a Turkish woman. The events, occurring one year preceding the publication of the Dutch language edition of Unigwe's novel, led to the first prosecution in Belgian history that officially considered racist motives.

Chika Unigwe's debut novel *De feniks* (*The Phoenix*) was heralded when it was published in 2005 as the first book written by a Flemish author of African origin and welcomed as a promising trendsetter for more ethnic minority writing based in Flanders. At the same time, Unigwe's cultural and linguistic background (Nigerian-born, speaking Igbo and English and using Dutch only as third language) may also have disrupted the conventional paradigms of literature in Dutch. Unigwe's bilingual oeuvre is characterised by complex linguistic transfers between Dutch and English language texts.[2] *De feniks* certainly confused a number of reviewers in Flanders: the novel was based on an English language manuscript, and in 2004 Unigwe had been shortlisted for the Britain-based Caine Prize for African literature.

Challenging conventional definitions of literature in Dutch and its concomitant notions of language, culture and race, Unigwe's oeuvre is situated within multiple, interconnected literary contexts that reach beyond its immediate locale of Flanders-Belgium. There are indeed reasons to suggest that Unigwe's writing supports Rebecca Walkowitz's idea that literature of migration "reflects a shift from nation-based paradigms to new ways of understanding community and belonging and to transnational models emphasizing a global space of ongoing travel and interconnection."[3] On the one hand, Unigwe's work relates to a localised body of literature, including other texts pertaining to multicultural Flanders such as Tom Naegel's *Los* (2005), Tom Lanoye's *Het derde huwelijk* (2006) or Rachida Lamrabet's *Vrouwland* (2007), work that reflects and contributes to the heightened discursivity of multiculturalism in Flemish society in transition across the past two decades, in ways comparable to developments in Netherlands writing also, as this book observes. But, on the other hand, Unigwe's texts also circulate in an anglophone global book market, where they are shelved under black, African, Nigerian or African diasporic writing. They belong to a new generation of Nigerian (diasporic) writing that also embraces authors such as the anglophone Chimamanda Ngozi Adichie and Helen Oyeyemi.[4]

Writings like Unigwe's are part of a wider body of texts that document as much as shape the transnational formations through which the study of literatures in Dutch—or Netherlands and Flemish—is currently being challenged. There are plentiful examples of texts asking the discipline to abandon its traditional focus on Dutch language material read and interpreted as only pertaining to what is happening within the national boundaries of the Nether-lands and the Dutch speaking part of Belgium, Flanders. For example, Moses Isegawa's *Abyssinian Chronicles* about 1970s and 1980s Uganda was first published in the Netherlands in 1998, as *Abessijnse kronieken*, though origi-nally written in English.[5] And novels such as Abdelkader Benali's *Bruiloft aan zee*, Rachida Lamrabet's *Vrouwland* and many others deal in the Netherlands' and Belgium's post-World War II histories of labour migration and their inter-twinements with Italy, Morocco and Turkey.[6] Going further back, traditions of travel writing in the Dutch or Netherlands language, too, have pointed to the permeable nature of cultural and national boundaries. A related perspective has been provided by the large and still growing body of fiction documenting the former Dutch-language colonial settlements and their legacies in Indone-sia, the Caribbean and South Africa as well as the Congo under King Leop-old II's and then Belgian state rule. Taken together, these texts explore and interrogate how metropolitan cultures of the Low Countries are not, nor have ever been self-sufficient entities, but rather form part of a complex network of interconnected Netherlands language or neerlandophone spaces, regions and countries.[7] If this latter point is to be taken seriously, however, it entails nothing less than a reassessment of literary criticism's Dutch metropolitan focus and calls for a research agenda which is transnational and postcolonial in scope. The recent growth of scholarly interest in colonial, postcolonial and multicultural literatures in Dutch, as brought together in this book, bears wit-ness to precisely such attempts to widen and re-think the scope of the field.

POSTCOLONIAL THEORY
AND CONTINENTAL EUROPEAN PERSPECTIVES

The Postcolonial Low Countries seeks to consolidate the many piecemeal interventions in recent years that have sought to make connections between international, often largely anglophone postcolonial debates on the one hand, and explicitly neerlandophone perspectives on the other. Together, these have given rise to what recently has been called "the postcolonial turn in Dutch literary criticism."[8] Establishing an encounter between postcolonial theoreti-cal discourses both from within and without the region, and the cultures and literatures of the Low Countries, the contributors aim to put under pressure certain of the definitive concepts of postcolonial studies in its anglophone formation, as well as perceptions of the Low Countries, Belgium and the Netherlands as lying outside or to the side of the postcolonial domain.

The overarching objective of this at once postcolonial and Low Coun-tries located book therefore is two-fold, theoretical/methodological as well as historical. In effect, it explores the oxymoron it posits, of a postcolonial Netherlands and a postcolonial Flanders-Belgium. First, the book develops postcolonial concepts that are pertinent for a critical understanding of the relations between literature, colonialism and multicultural contexts in the Low Countries. Second, it reflects on historical and contemporary shifts and transformations in national literatures, identities and histories from a neerlandophone postcolonial perspective. In so doing, the volume situates itself within the interstices of two areas of inquiry—postcolonial studies and literary criticism of literatures in Dutch—and has a significant dialogic contribution to make to both of these.

As this implies, *The Postcolonial Low Countries* is the first book to theorise and bring together approaches that might be collected under the title "neerlandophone Postcolonial Studies." It aspires to engage with some of the most interesting postcolonial interventions that have been made in recent years by various scholars of modern language materials, including Charles Forsdick and David Murray, whose work has already exposed the ineffectiveness and indeed redundancy of mostly anglocentric attempts to divide postcolonialisms along language-specific lines. Attention has increasingly moved to addressing the heuristic costs of this predominant focus on anglophone, and to a lesser extent francophone, texts and contexts. This observation is not a criticism of a field which has always been subjected to intense self-interrogation, but does express some constructive disenchantment with the direction in which the discipline has evolved to date. Moreover, this anglocentrism has exacerbated the derivative way in which postcolonial concepts have often been taken up in the Low Countries, where these are seen as emanating always from elsewhere, not from within. Though the Netherlands has until recently enjoyed a long-established reputation as a progressive and proactive country in relation to migration policies and ideas, at stake is what might be termed the Dutch "dependency mentality" in relation to theory, including postcolonial theory, which is elaborated further below.

From the outset postcolonial innovation outside its anglophone homelands has been hampered by the relatively limited comparative scope of the field—a comparative scope which, as the editors of *Comparing Postcolonial Diasporas* rightly point out, has always been "posited as essential, but its realization is perpetually deferred."[9] It is indeed the case that Ashcroft, Griffiths and Tiffin, authors of one of the seminal textbooks of postcolonial studies *The Empire Writes Back*, envisioned that "the strength of post-colonial theory may well lie in its inherently comparative methodology and the hybridized and syncretic view of the modern world which this implies."[10] In practice, however, this comparatism has not delivered on that early promise, perhaps because it conventionally operates in relation to europhone and hence formerly colonial languages, in relation to which properly postcolonial compara-tive and translational perspectives are more difficult to introduce. To date, postcolonial theories of literary and cultural production in the europhone languages have predictably tended to focus on the legacies of colonialism in order to create fissures in dominant narratives of national literatures and histories, rather than to interrogate the methodologies and cultural biases involved, as Gayatri Spivak begins to do in her *Death of a Discipline* in her discussion of Tayeb Salih.[11]

These constraints notwithstanding, postcolonial studies has travelled and taken root in many non-anglophone cultural and linguistic contexts, includ-ing in continental Europe. In particular, the self-conscious field-construction of "francophone postcolonial studies" has significantly contributed to the creation of comparative links between postcolonial debates in different lan-guages.[12] In Germany, Italy and Central and Eastern Europe, responses to postcolonial studies have emerged, while important postcolonial publications have appeared which expressly deploy comparative, transcolonial and cross-linguistic perspectives.[13] These newer variants of postcolonial studies have led to a branching and fragmentation of the field's already scattered objects and methods of inquiry, but it has also given substance to the emergence of a new trans-linguistic consciousness and the need to engage with other colonial trajectories and their contemporary legacies, though a focus on europhone spaces and languages still remains predominant.

The reception of postcolonial studies in other parts of the European world, as elsewhere, has of course been shaped by the respective theoretical tradi-tions, cultural memories and colonial histories existing in these different locations. In the Low Countries, local issues concerning multiculturalism and colonial belatedness have raised important questions about the possible grounds on which postcolonial critical concepts might be not only translated but generated out of these paradoxically new contexts. When brought to bear on new Low Countries materials, postcolonial concepts and perspectives are often transferred and reproduced without attention to how postcolonial frame-works might be produced from within.

Netherlands and Belgium were colonial powers with extensive overseas possessions and economies heavily dependent on colonial inputs and trade. From the colonial period onwards, contentious debates over migration, mul-ticulturalism and hybridity/"allochtony" have radically affected and divided Belgian and Dutch cultures.[14] The postcolonial Low Countries and their his-torical contingencies invite us to re-think and reconstruct as adaptatively as possible the theoretical assumptions that arose from anglophone colonial his-tory and literatures. For a properly analytical and historicized understanding of the mixed-race colonial elite in the history and literature of the Dutch East

Indies, for example, conventional postcolonial ideas about "the coloniser" and "hybridity" have to be re-calibrated and elaborated.[15] The Belgian context, for its part, insists upon an approach to questions of imperialism and its aftermath that considers the relation of this aftermath to subnational tensions among the different, often divided language communities and the difficult development of the federal nation-state.[16] In both the Dutch and the Belgian contexts, there also exists a historical disconnect between colonialism and a post-world war history of migration from Italy, Morocco and Turkey, which is very different from the British context where migrants have tended to come from the former empire. The postcolonial examination of such previously unconsidered specificities in the Low Countries demands a careful rearticulation of such postcolonial "readymades" as hybridity, accommodation and creolization.

TOWARDS A NEERLANDOPHONE POSTCOLONIAL STUDIES

Although a number of scholars have contributed to the development of neerlandophone postcolonial studies, the genealogy of the emerging field has not been without interruption. To begin with, the pertinence or appropriateness of postcolonial concepts brought from elsewhere to the Low Countries contexts has not always been widely accepted. The consequent sense of crisis which has marked postcolonial studies in the region virtually from its inception has further been reinforced by the absence of a shared frame through which scholars in Belgium and the Netherlands could situate their different though interrelated theories and strategies.

How postcolonial then are the Low Countries? This question has either implicitly or explicitly subtended the preceding paragraphs. If the essays collected here are anything to go by, then the answer to this question must be: to a significant degree, at least in experiential terms. Yet, at a conceptual level, the answer is rather different, especially if we are considering the postcolonial as something emanating from, and intricately involved with, the fabric of the regional and local cultures to which it is ascribed. The postcolonial, the Netherlands and Flanders academy is rather ready to conclude, arrived in the Netherlands and Flanders from without, in the main from Anglo-American academic contexts. It came as a cultural and theoretical import that, as Theo D'haen recognizes in these pages, could therefore conveniently be written off both as coming too early and at the same time as belated relative to elsewhere, to other spaces where it was previously applied—though this in a field that, it should be noted, has from the outset been beset by announcements of its imminent demise.

As our wording suggests, such answers to the question of Dutch postcoloniality have begun increasingly to sound like convenient excuses, especially where they permit Netherlands and Flanders critics and academics to pass over the postcolonial as insufficiently related to the contexts they inhabit and therefore as not worth dealing with, either now or in the future. There is no point bothering with the postcolonial, such conservative conclusions imply, especially if its critical purchase elsewhere is receding—yet this at a time when the social, cultural and political pertinence of such approaches in the Low Countries cannot be denied.

Across the decades, when scholars working in the Netherlands and Flanders introduced cultural studies and postcolonial approaches, responses to their work repeatedly included the assertion that the postcolonial was inadequate methodologically or theoretically. This presumption was connected to the idea that the postcolonial was from elsewhere and hence "new" to the Low Countries—that is, new in comparison to established interpretative literary traditions including biographical, literary historical, text-immanent or reception-oriented approaches. So it is suggestive that literary historical approaches to colonial and postcolonial literatures, such as in *Europa Buitengaats* (2002), have been more readily accepted, though that legacy has also now been obscured by the importation of postcolonial theory from elsewhere. The persistent focus on the new has also been reinforced by postcolonial theorists themselves, eager, perhaps, to put the postcolonial on the Low Countries' institutional academic map, and to open up space for a cultural or literary analysis which has so far not received the academic scrutiny it deserves in the criticism of literatures in Dutch.

In 1991, when the volume *De canon onder vuur* (*The Canon Contested*) was published, the editors Ernst van Alphen and Maaike Meijer wrote that they sought to challenge "the dominant interpretative tradition that tends to persist indefinitely"[17] by studying the political and socio-historical dimensions of canonical works in Dutch. The volume includes, for example, a study of racial, sexist and homophobic elements in E. DuPerron's *Het land van herkomst* or Couperus's ornamental literary style and the aestheticisation of slavery in his work. Scrutinizing the imbrications of canonical texts with unbalanced racial, gender or class relations in society, the editors robustly defend their post-Marxist, postcolonial approach against the anticipated charge that deconstruction would only be concerned with noncommittal word play and jouissance, and hence be unserious and unscientific. Yet, approximately ten years later, when the 2002 benchmark volume *Cultural Studies: Een inleiding*, edited by Jan Baetens en Ginette Verstraete, introduced the discipline of Cultural Studies (including postcolonial approaches) to the Dutch academy, one detractor fiercely named Cultural Studies a "fake-discipline," charging its defenders and their critical practices with impulsiveness, inconsistency, and political correctness. The implicit contrast was with more traditional strands of literary theory, connoting respectability and seriousness. Despite its relentless association with the new, the postcolonial, we conclude from these examples, has been repeatedly introduced in the academy in the Low Countries, though under different names, "ideology critique" or "cultural studies." With every re-introduction of the postcolonial, however, the connotation of newness has been related to notions of inadequacy and unscientificity, assertions which become powerful arguments to sideline the postcolonial, certainly in current times when universities, particularly Modern Languages departments, are under pressure to make cuts rather than expand.

This writing off, as our use of the word *elsewhere* implies, is predicated on postcolonial concepts being taken as in some sense "foreign," borrowed or non-native, something that doesn't suit us, or, alternatively, that we don't adequately do, or aren't equal to. This too-ready Dutch acceptance of belatedness vis-à-vis the postcolonial, at times with an almost audible exclamation of relief, is a situation which paradoxically invites description as postcolonial, as a characteristic expression of late colonial or postcolonial unreadiness or dependency. Ah, the resolutely non-postcolonial Dutch culture critic sighs, we don't need to be bothering with that colonial-type business after all. It is past its sell-by date. The debate has moved on to questions of the global, the transnational, of fundamentalist Islam and multicultural (non)-integration, currently of greater relevance to ourselves.[18]

Yet, as would-be Dutch postcolonial critics, we might here remember that the postcolonial when viewed from any metropolitan perspective—which includes perspectives directed from Amsterdam or Brussels, Rotterdam or Antwerp—will always seem to be an expression of something out of joint with the contemporary, whether it be deemed too late or too early. Over time, in other cultural spaces, this has proved to be a time-tested strategy with which social and cultural authorities in ex-colonial spaces have attempted to deflect the always potentially pertinent edge of postcolonial critique away from those whom it might most cogently serve.

The postcolonial, let us not forget, emerged out of situations of resistance to colonial inequality, its core concepts born out of anti-colonial struggle. And though our times may appear superficially post-postcolonial, unequal conditions analogous to those under empire, or stemming from them, continue to pertain in ex-colonizing countries like the Netherlands and Belgium today. All the more reason then to ignore postcolonialism's Dutch detractors and to draw postcolonial critical perspectives out of Low Countries' conditions themselves, to find them immanent or emergent in people's lived lives, both in the so-called metropole and on its local margins, the outlying districts of Amsterdam, for example.

To be clear, what we are saying here is not that our primary objective should be to translate such perspectives across from other contexts, whereby Dutch postcolonial conditions become locked into an almost-but-not-quite situation such as famously described in Homi Bhabha's essay on colonial mimicry.[19] While we concede that such situations of postcolonial transference and adaptation are in many ways unavoidable and can be fruitful, the primary objective in "post-colonizing" the Low Countries academy, to coin a phrase, is to generate such perspectives from within. Aydemir does as much in his essay in this book, when he speaks of discrimination among different minorities (sexual, religious) in the unevenly liberal Netherlands (chapter 10). So, too, do Boehmer and Gouda, with their discussion of colonial amnesia in respect to the Dutch East Indies' experience, even though the Netherlands' deep experience of governance over a predominantly Muslim population carries powerful relevance in the present-day (chapter 2).

In short, the Low Countries is not only ripe for lively postcolonial critique and debate, in intellectual contexts as in the culture at large, it is also potentially rich in generating innovative postcolonial critique. To illustrate, think only of the cultural event represented by the feature film *Sonny Boy* in the summer of 2010. This film, based on the eponymous fictional history of *Sonny Boy*, by prominent Dutch writer Annejet van der Zijl, first published in 2004, was directed by Maria Peters and screened across the Low Countries.[20] Its audiences often outstripped those watching more conventionally popular Hollywood films. What brought the audiences flocking, the exotic background of the young male hero from Paramaribo, the salacious circumstances of his affair with a married Dutch woman, the sad tale of their mixed-race child, their own experience of working in the Dutch resistance and falling foul of the Nazi authorities? It was probably all these factors combined, many of which bear colonial or postcolonial facets.

Sonny Boy is the affecting story of a 1930s Dutch-Surinamese love affair between a Dutch mother of four in Scheveningen, Rika van der Lans, and her Surinamese lodger, Waldemar Nods, of the discrimination and social suspicion they and their mixed-race child suffered, and of the strength of their feeling for one another, which sustained them through their work for the Dutch resistance during the German occupation. Despite the crusading quality of the novel and of the film, both championing the love and the idealism of the couple—a tale, wrote one critic, that outdoes even Romeo and Juliet's—the narrative is interestingly, perhaps even predictably, laden with colonial clichés: modern industrializing Holland, though with its conservative backwaters, is set against a steaming primitive Suriname. In a twenty-first century novel, the conventionality of such constructions alone would be worth some thoroughgoing critical attention drawing on paradigms familiar from postcolonial theory.

But where the book and the film become more interesting, and more closely related to the idea of postcolonial critique generated from within, is in the area of their reception, where, in anti-immigration fortress Nederland, their central construction of the man from without who becomes, effectively, an unsung national hero, has spoken to a broad majority of Netherlanders. What does this mean? In increasingly more right-wing Holland, do such tales operate in a compensatory way, allaying liberal guilt? Or does multicultural heterogeneity represent a way of holding out against authoritarianism, which is therefore to be salvaged as a value? Certainly the figure of Rika's mixed-race child "Sonny Boy," with his African American sobriquet, Waldy, unable across his life to confront and write out the story of his parents in such a way as to give him psychological release, represents a poignantly postcolonial figure who speaks directly if also in contradictory ways to the Netherlands' misrecognition of its own postcoloniality.

In an important 2004 essay, Isabel Hoving distinguished at least two "postcolonial" traditions that have operated in research schools and academic circuits in the Low Countries.[21] The first group of scholars, its point of gravity at the University of Leiden, was rooted in the philological study of non-Western languages and literature. The second group, younger and less historically embedded, was trained in women's or gender studies and influenced by Anglo-American strands within cultural studies, including postcolonial studies. In her historical outline of the field, Hoving observed that the two research traditions were "as opposed as the members of different football teams," but also conceded that scholars existed who were interested in combining these approaches and bridging the gap between the two.[22] In the early 1990s, for example, Theo D'haen, former Chair of English and American literature at Leiden University, founded the interdisciplinary research group "Koloniale en Postkoloniale Literaturen" together with a range of historians, literary theorists and scholars of Indonesian, Caribbean, Dutch and French literature.[23] Such cross-border research activities including traditional, philological, or anglophone postcolonial traditions have proved particularly fruitful for the elaboration of a postcolonial studies perspective directed from the Low Countries, though the concept of a postcolonialism that might be generated *from within* has taken more time to evolve.

Today the contours of the two research traditions outlined by Hoving remain discernible, but the field has also developed and diversified to a considerable degree.[24] These developments, many of which are reflected in this book, have taken place against the background of turbulent times for the Low Countries in which issues of national citizenship, identity, religion, and immigration have become increasingly controversial.[25] Hugo Brems' important recent literary history of literatures in Dutch, *Altijd weer vogels die nesten beginnen* (2006), discusses the diverse and historically evolving colonial and postcolonial literary traditions of the Dutch East Indies, Suriname, the Dutch Antilles and the Congo within one "exotic" chapter of a literary history largely focused on developments and histories of the metropolitan Low Countries.[26] But signs are also emerging that colonial and postcolonial literary studies in the region are slowly on their way to becoming integrated in the curricula of Dutch literature programmes. In the course of 2000s, three new chairs, in South African literature, Caribbean literature and Migrant Literature, were added to the already existing Chairs in Colonial and Postcolonial literature (with focus on the Dutch East Indies) to the Dutch Language and Culture course programmes at the University of Amsterdam. In most universities in Flanders and the Netherlands, scholars of literatures in Dutch are also increasingly collaborating with, and joining cultural studies research schools. At present, however, the institutional space for neerlandophone postcolonial studies is relatively insignificant in the region, certainly in comparison to the established position of postcolonial studies in English.[27] In most taught course programmes in literatures in Dutch, the presence of postcolonial theoretical perspectives depends on the personal interests of individual scholars. This situation can only change once such perspectives are properly generated from within Dutch cultural spaces and seen to have relevance for Dutch language communities today.

Scholars working in Dutch departments in the world outside the Low Countries (including Jeroen De Wulf and Henriette Louwerse) have generally speaking made greater efforts than their counterparts in the Netherlands and Belgium to open their courses and research activities to non-metropolitan neerlandophone cultures and literatures, perhaps because, from outside, the postcoloniality of the region is cast into critical relief. Relatedly, scholars working in non-Dutch departments in the Netherlands and Flanders, too, have dealt with the postcolonial to a relatively higher degree than their Dutch colleagues.[28] This situation resonates with the Italian academy, where Ian Chambers observes an engagement with postcolonial studies in many modern language departments except for the Italian, or in his terms "in an academic framework of an elsewhere and an other. [. . .] As such, the other remains the object of the academic gaze, an inert item seemingly incapable of disturbing the unilateral mechanisms of cultural incorporation and the silent hegemony of an apparently 'neutral' knowledge."[29] Such engagement depends, then, on the individual efforts of scholars working in these non-Dutch and non-Low Countries departments to transgress the linguistic boundaries of their primary field, as many of the contributors here—Ieme van der Poel, Elleke Boehmer, Mireille Rosello or Theo D'haen among them—effectively do.

SECTION I: TOWARDS A
NEERLANDOPHONE POSTCOLONIAL STUDIES

The concept or spectre of the postcolonial Low Countries is what all the contributors to this volume have embraced in their analyses. Although diverse in their contexts and theorizations, they all bring together postcolonial concepts and approaches with Netherlands texts and cultural phenomena. Each chapter engages with approaches to pressing issues which tentatively may be described as neerlandophone postcolonial perspectives. The book is structured in three sections that are each integrated around a coherent central theme. The first section, "Towards a Neerlandophone Postcolonial Studies," explores the (im)possibility of the encounter between postcolonial theory and the literatures and cultures of the Low Countries. The second section, "Postcolonial Memory," addresses the question of literature as memory-work making a bridge to the colonial past so as to build a creolized future. The third section, "Literature and Multiculturalism," centres on issues of migration and multiculturalism in neerlandophone texts and contexts. This structure has been deliberately chosen to correspond to much debated postcolonial issues in the international arena and will enable readers clearly to see the differently angled contributions neerlandophone theorisations and case studies bring to the international and postcolonial table.

The first section addresses the question of how to find new ways of thinking about the postcolonial Low Countries. Although concerned with different cultural and political issues, the four chapters by respectively Elleke Boehmer and Frances Gouda, Isabel Hoving, Theo D'haen, and Sarah Bracke and Nadia Fadil all convey the pertinence of postcolonial perspectives for the Low Countries. In "Postcolonial Studies in the Context of the 'Diasporic' Netherlands," Elleke Boehmer and Frances Gouda explore the postcolonial pedagogic landscape at the tertiary level in the "diasporic" Netherlands, approaching this through a discussion of Netherlands' colonial legacies, and of how the postcolonial is interpreted in the Dutch present-day. Boehmer and Gouda find that postcolonial practice in this pedagogical context should be concerned to construct colonial histories not merely as a subsidiary national and transnational backdrop to the study of literary texts. Rather, they suggest, a postcolonial perspective would see colonial history as formative in the making of imaginative literature, and to the construction of critical readings of that literature.

Isabel Hoving's essay "Polderpoko: Why It Cannot Exist" suggests some reasons for the awkward relations that exist between neerlandophone literary studies and postcolonial theory. Hoving observes that postcolonial theorizing in the Dutch context is being caught in a condition of untimeliness; it is both too early and too late; it exists in a context which is not yet ready to address postcolonial issues, yet already seems past these issues. Hoving explores two case studies: one centring on the relation between Ajax, Amsterdam's star football team, and the Amsterdam Jewish community; the other relating to several art projects that aim at recreating the (Dutch) forest in a non-exclusionary, non-nationalist way. These examples, Hoving argues, suggest how postcolonial theory might address contemporary public debates on modernity and multiculturalization, despite Dutch resistance to postcolonial terms and concepts.

While Boehmer and Gouda as well as Hoving focus on responses to the postcolonial in the Low Countries, Theo D'haen brings in the global so as to open up a neerlandophone-postcolonial dialogue. Taking his cues from David Scott, he asks what the goal or end of postcolonialism is, at a time when the achievements of postcolonial approaches and institutional practices are being reconsidered. More specifically, D'haen explores the extent to which the postcolonial paradigm is currently on the defensive against globalization studies and raises the question of whether postcolonialism has not exhausted its avowed "end" or "ends" with specific reference to the Low Countries context. To this, one response might be that if the postcolonial is considered a critical position and a politics, and not just one theoretical stance amongst others, its purchase vis-à-vis the global can be seen as powerful and combative, not defensive. Moreover, announcements of the demise of the postcolonial form an important constituent of its position.

In the final essay of this section, Sarah Bracke and Nadia Fadil shift the discussion to the question of how postcolonial critical insights on gender, religion and agency can be effectively translated into a cultural critique of the headscarf ban in Belgium. Bracke and Fadil reflect on their roles as scholars and engaged intellectuals in Belgium who are regularly invited to take part in public discussions and conversations about gender and multiculturalism, particularly those centring on the headscarf. They reflect on the performative effect of the question around which many of these debates are structured—*Is the headscarf oppressive or emancipatory?*—and ask what it reproduces, what kinds of discussion it enables and what kind of imaginary, speech and action it renders impossible. Oscillating between scholarly critique and deconstruction on the one hand, and political participation and action on the other, Bracke and Fadil's positioning is all but comfortable. Yet, as they argue, it is potentially productive when dis/connections and uneasy translations, along with the frustrations of how discourses structure possible speech and actions, become part of our understanding of how social reality comes into being, and can be transformed.

SECTION II: POSTCOLONIAL MEMORY

While postcolonialism's "archive fever" may be well-known in the abstract, this section focuses specifically on postcolonial memory and evasion as manifested in contemporary neerlandophone texts, regions and spaces. Pamela Pattynama, Liesbeth Minnaard, Louise Viljoen and Sarah De Mul demonstrate how literature plays a role in the memorisation of the colonial past, focusing respectively on Indo-Dutch mixed race communities in the Netherlands, the German-Turkish Emine Sevgi Özdamar's "Bicycle on Ice," post-apartheid Afrikaans women's writing and Adam Hochschild's historical account of the Congo Free State under Leopold II.

In "(Un)happy Endings: Nostalgia in Postimperial and Postmemory Dutch Films," Pamela Pattynama scrutinizes the multivalency of postcolonial nostalgia with which Dutch culture is imbued. Although the East Indies doesn't exist any more as political entity, it inhabits a space on the cultural map of the Netherlands as a changing, evocative "memory site," even for people who have no first-hand knowledge of the ex-colony. Generations of Indies-Dutch migrants have produced literary texts and documentary films, emphatically claiming the Dutch East Indies as a collective identity marker. The essay looks closely at the relation between the re-creation of the Dutch East Indies as a "memory site" in postcolonial literature and the formation of Indies-Dutch identities and communities. It explores how far (post)colonial terms such as hybridity, mixed race and mnemonic community can be used in the postcolonial Dutch context so as to provide understanding of the complex ways in which the Dutch East Indies continues to provide identifications not only for a nostalgic late imperial elite, but for Indo-Dutch mixed race communities.

Liesbeth Minnaard's chapter "Transnational Contact-Narratives: Dutch Postcoloniality from a Turkish-German Viewpoint" considers the reconstruction of Dutch colonialism in "Fahrrad auf dem Eis" ["Bicycle on the Ice"] by the Turkish-German writer Emine Sevgi Özdamar. She critically juxtaposes Dutch and German multiculturality, and Dutch and German collective histories of violence against ethnic, cultural, colonial, religious Others. Exploring the resonances between these two, Özdamar directs the reader's attention to the blind spots and (in)sensitivities in the traumatic national memories of both Germany and the Netherlands. Her focus on *webs* of relation rather than on singular Self-Other relations enables an analysis of multiculturality and national identity that goes beyond binary pairs—colonizer vis-à-vis colonised, indigenous vis-à-vis migrant Dutch, the Dutch vis-à-vis the Germans, so acknowledging the fundamental complexity of contemporary Dutchness.

Louise Viljoen brings the question of postcolonial memory to bear on Afrikaans (women's) literature in the multicultural and multilingual context of post-apartheid South African society. Describing certain aspects of Afrikaans literature's postcoloniality after 1994, Viljoen focuses on writings by Antjie Krog, Marlene van Niekerk, Ingrid Winterbach and E.K.M. Dido. Images of South Africa as motherland and Afrikaans as mother tongue are explored, especially in narratives that trace family relationships (often with the mother). The question is addressed whether and how Afrikaans women's representations of the motherland and mother tongue reflect critically on current scenarios in South Africa.

In "The Holocaust as a Paradigm for the Congo Atrocities: Adam Hochschild's *King Leopold's Ghost*," Sarah De Mul explores the notion of the Congo atrocities as "a forgotten Holocaust" in Adam Hochschild's bestselling *King Leopold's Ghost*. Teasing out some of the similarities between Hochschild's *King Leopold's Ghost* and Edmund Dene Morel's *History of the Congo Reform Association*, De Mul argues that the Holocaust paradigm provides Hochschild with a new vocabulary for—and effectively prompts a resurgence of—nineteenth-century humanitarian discourse deployed by Morel, who is also the "hero" of Hochschild's historical narrative. Hence *King Leopold's Ghost* reconstructs the Congo atrocities through the framework of the Holocaust as a narrative with a clear-cut morality, even though it is now generally accepted that the Holocaust radically challenged the notion that a common set of premises exists for defining the good and the bad. This point was recently reiterated by Renzo Martens's documentary art film *Enjoy Poverty* (2008), which offers a compelling counterpoint to Hochschild's account by ruthlessly exposing the multiple complicities surrounding Western humanitarian action in the Democratic Republic of the Congo.

SECTION III: LITERATURE AND MULTICULTURALISM

In Western Europe generally as in the Low Countries in particular, the steady rise of extremist right-wing parties since 9/11 has been accompanied by fierce debates about religion, multiculturalism and immigration. This section looks at the Low Countries as migratory spaces and investigates the ways in which literature and cultural practices relate to such debates about multiculturalism and immigration. What do neerlandophone linguistic and cultural resources offer in the interpretation of a migrant or postcolonial world? In what ways is the experience of migration to the Low Countries substantially different from that in Britain or France and in what ways and through which techniques can neerlandophone literatures of migration be comparatively analysed?

In "Dutch Homonationalism and Intersectionality," Murat Aydemir explores how the qualified emancipation of lesbians and gays in the Netherlands has run side by side with the emergence of a new collective subject of discipline, "Moroccan boys." The relationship between Dutch gays and lesbians (because of *our* sexuality) and Moroccan young men (because of *their* culture, religion or race) is often perceived as antagonistic and mutually exclusive. Interrogating Puar's notion of "homonationalism," Aydemir argues that this alignment produces an uncanny "convergence" between the inclusion of homosexual citizens in the body politic and the increased exclusion of racial and class others. Aydemir discusses an exemplary case of Dutch homonationalism, revolving around an activist's protest at the hanging of gay men in Iran. The purpose is to inquire how the theory of intersectionality might help move beyond the deadlock of the "gay or Muslim" binary. Is it possible to recognize sex and race as located in the same place at the same time, or do they somehow invariably end up in disparate symbolic universes?

In "Becoming UnDutch: 'Wil je dat? Kun je dat?'" Mireille Rosello analyses the way in which the relationship between "water" and "the Netherlands" is articulated and made to perform political and ideological work in the recently developed immigration test for migrants who want to apply for a residence visa. The so-called unedited version of the test includes pictures of a topless woman and of two men kissing, passages that have become so controversial as to obscure what appears to Rosello as other important but less spectacular narratives. Comparing these stories to the ways in which creolization theory and Caribbean literature have politicized the sea and the ocean, Rosello analyses how the test successfully naturalizes its own politics. Focusing on what the documentary does to and with "water," the chapter tracks the way in which it is described as a simple and uncontroversial "natural" element, confined within the limits of a discipline and used to smuggle in a political argument that has everything to do with history, ideology and migration policies.

In "Unlike(ly) Homes: 'Self-orientalisation' and Irony in Moroccan Diasporic Literature," Ieme van der Poel explores the way in which Morocco continues to haunt literature by second- or third-generation migrant authors in Europe through an analysis of the Catalan *L'últim patriarca* by Najat el Hachmi and the neerlandophone *Paravion* by Hafid Bouazza. Taking her cues from Leslie Adelson, van der Poel examines the narrative modes in which Morocco is described as an imaginary geography incorporated into the host country. Old clichés about the "Orient" are recycled and disrupted and Morocco, consequently, becomes a home unlike home. Both in form and content, these novels, van der Poel argues, testify to the reconstitution of European cultural heritage alongside a notable modification of certain literary and stylistic practices inherited from the past, such as irony, orientalism, and the ethnographic novel.

In the final chapter, "Games of Deception," Henriette Louwerse discusses how post-migratory authors create upheaval and deregulation in the Dutch literary establishment. In a discussion of one of the most striking of Dutch post-migratory authors, Hafid Bouazza, she observes his rejection of categorisation, manipulation of reader expectations, and insistence on artistic freedom. Notions of home and identity, which are expected to be destabilised in the case of an outsider author, are redefined and redrawn. Her essay rounds off with an appropriately paradoxical turn in this kaleidoscopic and wide-ranging overview of how the relationship between postcolonial theory and the Low Countries might be fruitfully theorised and analysed.

NOTES

1. Chika Unigwe, *Fata Morgana* (Antwerp-Amsterdam: Meulenhoff-Manteau, 2007); *On Black Sisters' Street* (London: Jonathan Cape, 2009; New York: Random House, 2011).

2. Though the Dutch language novel *Fata Morgana* was published years before the English language edition *On Black Sisters' Street*, the former was based on an English language manuscript and as such cannot really be called the original source text in the traditional sense of the term.

3. Rebecca L. Walkowitz, "The Location of Literature: The Transnational Book and the Migrant Writer," *Contemporary Literature* 47, no. 4 (Winter 2006), 533.

4. Unigwe was nominated for the 2011 International IMPAC Dublin Literary Award. The acclaim of *On Black Sisters' Street* in the anglophone global literature market has been remarkably positive, with reviewers in the major UK- and US-based newspapers *The Independent* and *The New York Times* praising the book's literary merits. See Bernadine Evaristo, "*On Black Sisters' Street* by Chika Unigwe," *The Independent*, July 3, 2009; Fernanda Eberstadt, "Tales from the Global Sex Trade," *The New York Times*, Sunday Book Review, April 29, 2011. For a more extensive analysis of multilingualism in Unigwe's work, see Sarah De Mul & Thomas Ernst, "Multiculturalism and Multilingualism in Contemporary Prose in Flanders: The Writings by Chika Unigwe, Koen Peeters, and Benno Barnard." In W. Beschnitt, S. De Mul & L. Minnaard (eds.), *Literature, Language, and Multiculturalism in Scandinavia and the Low Countries* (Amsterdam/New York: Rodopi, 2012).

5. Moses Isegawa, *Abessijnse kronieken* (Amsterdam: De Bezige Bij, 1998); *Abyssinian Chronicles* (New York: Vintage International, 2001).

6. Abdelkader Benali, *Bruiloft aan zee* (Amsterdam, Vassallucci, 1996); Rachida Lamrabet, *Vrouwland* (Antwerpen/Amsterdam: Meulenhoff-Manteau, 2007).

7. The term "Dutch" conventionally denotes the languages spoken by populations in the metropolitan Netherlands, Flanders-Belgium and to a lesser extent Suriname. As this implies, a "pure" or "native" language of Dutch would be spoken by the inhabitants of these spaces, whereas "derivatory" or "acquired" variations of Dutch would be spoken elsewhere or by others, for example in formerly colonised parts

of the world or by immigrant citizens in the Netherlands or Flanders. However, this distinction is no longer valid if we consider the linguistic diversity, mixing and code-switching inherent in any real-life language situation. In this volume, we prefer to use the umbrella term "neerlandophone" to refer to the manifold Netherlands languages variations spoken by persons, groups or localities across the globe, including in the Netherlands, Flanders-Belgium, Suriname, the Caribbean island nations of Aruba, Curaçao, and Sint-Maarten, parts of France and Germany, Indonesia, South Africa, the United States, Canada, and Australia.

8. Isabel Hoving, "Review. The Postcolonial Turn in Dutch Literary Criticism," *Journal of Dutch Literature* 1, no. 1 (December 2010). http://journalofdutchliterature .org/jdl/vol01/nr01/art06

9. Michelle Keown, D. Murphy & J. Procter (eds.), *Comparing Postcolonial Diasporas* (London & New York: Palgrave Macmillan, 2009), 3.

10. B. Ashcroft, G. Griffiths, & H. Tiffin, *The Empire Writes Back: Theory and Practice in Post-Colonial Literatures* (London & New York: Routledge, 1989), 36.

11. Gayatri Chakravorty Spivak, *Death of a Discipline* (New York: Columbia University Press, 2003).

12. Charles Forsdick & David Murphy (eds.), *Francophone Postcolonial Studies: A Critical Introduction* (London, Arnold, 2003); Kamal Salhi (ed.), *Francophone Post-colonial Cultures: Critical Essays* (Lanham, Md.: Lexington Books, 2003); Anne Donadey and H. Adlai Murdoch (eds.), *Postcolonial Theory and Literature in a Francophone Frame* (Gainesville, University Press of Florida, 2004).

13. For an overview of discussion about the engagement of postcolonial theory in a German context, see Monika Albrecht, "Postcolonialism, Islam and Contemporary Germany," *Transit* 7, no. 1 (2011), 6–11. In an Italian context, see Graziella Parati, *Mediterranean Crossroads. Migration Literature in Italy* (Madison, N.J.: Fairleigh Dickinson University Press, 1999); Sandra Ponzanesi, *Paradoxes of Post-colonial Culture: Contemporary Women Writers of the Indian and Afro-Italian Diaspora* (Albany: State University of New York Press, 2004); Graziella Parati, *Migration Italy. The Art of Talking Back in a Destination Culture* (Toronto: University of Toronto Press, 2005); Jacqueline Andall & Derek Duncan (eds.), *Italian Colonialism: Legacy and Memory* (Oxford & Bern: Peter Lang AG, European Academic Publishers, 2005). In a Central and Eastern European context, see Ewa M. Thompson, *Imperial Knowledge. Russian Literature and Colonialism* (Westport, Conn.: Greenwood Press, 2000). For a comparative, intra-European approach, see P. Poddar, R. Patke, L. Jensen (eds.), *Historical Companion to Postcolonial Literatures—Continental Europe and Its Empires* (Edinburgh: Edinburgh University Press, 2008).

14. Stemming from the Greek roots *allos*/other, *authos*/same and *chtoon*/soil, the term "allochtoon" has nowadays replaced the term "migrant" to refer to the generations of citizens with non-native cultural backgrounds living in Flanders and the Netherlands. According to the Dutch governmental CBS (Centraal Bureau voor de Statistiek/Central Office for Statistics), an "allochtoon" is a person of whom at least one parent was born abroad. The CBS distinguishes between first-generation allochtoons who themselves were born abroad and second-generation allochtoons who were born in the Netherlands. In addition, the CBS makes a distinction between western

and non-western allochtoons on the basis of a (long) list of so-called non-western countries. See L. Minnaard, "Multiculturality in the Dutch Literary Field." In W. Beschnitt, S. De Mul & L. Minnaard (eds.), *Literature, Language, and Multiculturalism in Scandinavia and the Low Countries* (Amsterdam/New York: Rodopi, 2012). For critical analyses of the related terms "migrant"/"allochton" and authochony, see J. Blommaert & Jef Verscheuren, *Het Belgische migrantendebat: De pragmatiek van de abnormalizering* (Antwerpen: IPrA, 1992); Bambi Ceuppens, "Allochthons, Colonizers, and Scroungers: Exclusionary Populism in Belgium," *African Studies Review* 49, no. 2 (September 2006), 147–86; Peter Geschiere, *The Perils of Belonging: Autochthony, Citizenship, and Exclusion in Africa and Europe* (Chicago: University Press, 2009).

15. Ann Laura Stoler, *Carnal Power and Imperial Knowledge: Race and the Intimate in Colonial Rule* (Berkeley: University of California Press, 2002); *Along the Archival Grain: Epistemic Anxieties and Colonial Common Sense* (Princeton, N.J.: Princeton University Press, 2011).

16. Bambi Ceuppens, *Congo Made in Flanders? Koloniale Vlaamse visies op "blank" en "zwart" in Belgisch Congo* (Gent: Academia Press, 2004); Bambi Ceuppens & Sarah De Mul, "De vergeten Congolees: Kolonialisme, post-kolonialisme en multiculturalisme." In Karel Arnaut et al. *Een leeuw in een kooi: De grenzen van het multiculturele Vlaanderen* (Antwerpen-Amsterdam: Meulenhoff-Manteau, 2009).

17. "[. . .] de dwingende interpretatietraditie, die de neiging heeft zich oneindig voort te zetten [. . .]." In Ernst van Alphen & Maaike Meijer (eds.), *De canon onder vuur: Nederlandse literatuur tegendraads gelezen* (Amsterdam: Van Gennep, 1991), 105.

18. A piece of autobiographical evidence might be relevant here. One of the editors, Elleke Boehmer, a well-known postcolonial critic in Britain, though at the same time Dutch-speaking and of Dutch background, keen to find ways of linking British and Dutch postcolonial debates, has never been so routinely addressed as coming from elsewhere as when she appears as a postcolonialist in Dutch academic contexts.

19. Homi Bhabha, "Of Mimicry and Man: The Ambivalence of Colonial Discourse," in *The Location of Culture* (London: Routledge, 1995), 85–92.

20. Annejet van der Zijl, *Sonny Boy* (Amsterdam: Querido, 2004).

21. Isabel Hoving, "Niets dan het heden: Over Jamaica Kincaid, de postkoloniale literatuurstudie, en wat er van ons terecht moet komen." In M. van Kempen, P. Verkruijsse, A. Zuiderweg (eds.), *Wandelaar onder de palmen* (Leiden: KITLV Uitgeverij, 2004), 16.

22. Ibid., 17.

23. See T. D'haen (ed.), *Herinnering, herkomst, herschrijving: Koloniale en postkoloniale literaturen*, Semaian 4 (Leiden: Vakgroep Talen en Culturen van Zuid-Oost Azië en Oceanië, 1990); *Weer-Werk: Schrijven en terugschrijven in koloniale en postkoloniale literaturen*, Semaian 15 (Leiden: TCZOAO, 1996); T. D'haen & Gerard Termorshuizen, *De geest van Multatuli: Proteststemmen in vroegere Europese koloniën*, Semaian 17 (Leiden: Vakgroep Talen en Culturen van Zuid-Oost Azië en Oceanië, 1998); T. D'haen & Liebregts (eds.) *Tussen twee werelden: Het gevoel van ontheemding in de postkoloniale literatuur*, Semaian 21 (Leiden: Opleiding Talen en

Culturen van Zuidoost-Azië en Oceanië, 2001); T. D'haen (ed.), *Europa buitengaats: Koloniale en postkoloniale literaturen*, 2 vols. (Amsterdam: Bert Bakker, 2002).

24. This cursory outline pertains primarily to the Netherlands. In Flanders the situation is rather different. Generally Flemish-African literature is a relatively small corpus and to date a rather marginal object of study; existing literary histories and related critical paradigms often date back to the colonial period, for example Arthur Verthé and Bernard Henry, *Geschiedenis van de Vlaams-Afrikaanse letterkunde* (Leuven: Davidsfonds, 1961).

25. The politically inspired assassinations of the right-wing politician Pim Fortuyn in 2002, the anti-Islam film director Theo van Gogh in 2004 and death threats to the public figure of Ayaan Hirsi Ali shook the nation. In 2010 the Netherlands saw the stunning rise to political power of Geert Wilders' populist anti-Islam party PVV. These events support the assumption, increasingly reiterated nowadays, that the traditional idea of tolerance as a Dutch national virtue is nowadays replaced by the idea of tolerance as a naive form of blindness.

26. Hugo Brems, *Altijd weer vogels die nesten beginnen: Geschiedenis van de Nederlandse literatuur, 1945–2005* (Amsterdam: Prometheus, 2006), 177–85.

27. Small landmark events deserve, however, to be noted. In 2005, Ieme van der Poel and Elleke Boehmer organised an international expert meeting, "Transcolonialism: The Future of Postcolonial Studies from a Comparative Perspective," at the Netherlands Institute for Advanced Study in the Humanities and Social Sciences (NIAS) in The Hague. In 2008, the symposium "Postcolonial Theory and the Low Countries," organised by Sarah De Mul, was held at Leiden University.

28. During the last years, two postcolonial research platforms were inaugurated in the Netherlands and Flanders-Belgium by scholars working primarily on postcolonial literatures in English, French, Italian and Comparative Literature. The Platform for Postcolonial Readings, organised by scholars at the Free University of Brussels, Leuven and Leiden University, is an open network for scholars of postcolonial and globalisation studies in Belgium and the Netherlands. The Postcolonial Studies Initiative, coordinated by Utrecht University, is an international platform intended for research into postcolonial issues in Europe.

29. Ian Chambers, "The Mediterranean: A Postcolonial Sea," *Third Text* 18, no. 5 (2004), 426.

BIBLIOGRAPHY

Albrecht, Monika. "Postcolonialism, Islam and Contemporary Germany." *Transit* 7, no. 1 (2011), special issue "Cosmopolitical and Transnational Interventions in German Studies," edited by B. Venkat Mani and Elke Segelcke. http://german .berkeley.edu/transit/2011/articles/Albrecht.html, accessed November 25, 2011.

Andall, Jacqueline, and Derek Duncan, eds. *Italian Colonialism: Legacy and Memory*. Oxford & Bern: Peter Lang AG, European Academic Publishers, 2005.

Ashcroft, B., G. Griffiths, and H. Tiffin, eds. *The Empire Writes Back: Theory and Practice in Post-Colonial Literatures*. London and New York: Routledge, 1989.

Benali, Abdelkader. *Bruiloft aan zee.* Amsterdam: Vassallucci, 1996.

Bhabha, Homi. "Of Mimicry and Man: The Ambivalence of Colonial Discourse." In *The Location of Culture*, 85–92. London: Routledge, 1995.

Blommaert, J., and Jef Verscheuren. *Het Belgische migrantendebat: De pragmatiek van de abnormalizering.* Antwerpen: IPrA, 1992.

Brems, Hugo. *Altijd weer vogels die nesten beginnen: Geschiedenis van de Nederlandse literatuur, 1945–2005.* Amsterdam: Prometheus, 2006.

Ceuppens, Bambi. *Congo Made in Flanders? Koloniale Vlaamse visies op "blank" en "zwart" in Belgisch Congo.* Gent: Academia Press, 2004.

———. "Allochthons, Colonizers, and Scroungers: Exclusionary Populism in Belgium." *African Studies Review* 49, no. 2 (September 2006): 147–86.

——— and Sarah De Mul. "De vergeten Congolees: Kolonialisme, post-kolonialisme en multiculturalisme." In *Een leeuw in een kooi: De grenzen van het multiculturele Vlaanderen*, edited by K. Arnaut, S. Bracke, B. Ceuppens, S. De Mul, N. Fadil, and M. Kanmaz. Antwerpen-Amsterdam: Meulenhoff-Manteau, 2009.

Chambers, Ian. "The Mediterranean: A Postcolonial Sea." *Third Text* 18, no. 5 (2004): 423–33.

De Mul, Sarah, and Thomas Ernst. "Multiculturalism and Multilingualism in Contemporary Prose in Flanders: The Writings by Chika Unigwe, Koen Peeters and Benno Barnard." In *Literature, Language, and Multiculturalism in Scandinavia and the Low Countries*, edited by W. Beschnitt, S. De Mul, and L. Minnaard. Amsterdam/New York: Rodopi, 2012.

D'haen, T., ed. *Herinnering, herkomst, herschrijving: Koloniale en post-koloniale literaturen*, Semaian 4, Leiden: Vakgroep Talen en Culturen van Zuid-Oost Azië en Oceanië, 1990.

———, ed. *Weer-Werk: schrijven en terugschrijven in koloniale en postkoloniale literaturen*, Semaian 15, Leiden: Vakgroep Talen en Culturen van Zuid-Oost Azië en Oceanië, 1996.

——— and Gerard Termorshuizen, eds. *De geest van Multatuli: Proteststemmen in vroegere Europese koloniën*, Semaian 17, Leiden: Vakgroep Talen en Culturen van Zuid-Oost Azië en Oceanië, 1998.

——— and Liebregts, eds. *Tussen twee werelden: Het gevoel van ontheemding in de postkoloniale literatuur*, Semaian 21, Leiden: Opleiding Talen en Culturen van Zuidoost-Azië en Oceanië, 2001.

———, ed. *Europa buitengaats: koloniale en postkoloniale literaturen*, 2 Vols, Amsterdam: Bert Bakker, 2002.

Donadey, Anne, and H. Adlai Murdoch, eds. *Postcolonial Theory and Literature in a Francophone Frame.* Gainesville, University Press of Florida, 2004.

Eberstadt, Fernanda. "Tales from the Global Sex Trade," *The New York Times*, Sunday Book Review, April 29, 2011.

Evaristo, Bernadine. "*On Black Sisters' Street* by Chika Unigwe," *The Independent*, July 3, 2009.

Forsdick, Charles, and David Murphy, eds. *Francophone Postcolonial Studies: A Critical Introduction.* London, Arnold, 2003.

Geschiere, Peter. *The Perils of Belonging: Autochthony, Citizenship, and Exclusion in Africa and Europe.* Chicago: University Press, 2009.

Hoving, Isabel. "Niets dan het heden: Over Jamaica Kincaid, de postkoloniale literatuurstudie, en wat er van ons terecht moet komen." In *Wandelaar onder de palmen*, edited by M. van Kempen, P. Verkruijsse, A. Zuiderweg, 15–27. Leiden: KITLV Uitgeverij, 2004.

———. "Review. The Postcolonial Turn in Dutch Literary Criticism." *Journal of Dutch Literature* 1, no. 1 (December 2010). http://journalofdutchliterature.org/jdl/vol01/nr01/art06, accessed November 25, 2011.

Isegawa, Moses. *Abessijnse kronieken*. Amsterdam: De Bezige Bij, 1998.

———. *Abyssinian Chronicles*. New York: Vintage International, 2001.

Keown, M., D. Murphy, and J. Procter. eds. *Comparing Postcolonial Diasporas*. London & New York: Palgrave Macmillan, 2009.

Lamrabet, Rachida. *Vrouwland*. Antwerpen/Amsterdam: Meulenhoff-Manteau, 2007.

Minnaard, L. "Multiculturality in the Dutch Literary Field." In *Literature, Language, and Multiculturalism in Scandinavia and the Low Countries*, edited by W. Beschnitt, S. De Mul, and L. Minnaard. Amsterdam/New York: Rodopi, 2012.

Parati, Graziella. *Mediterranean Crossroads: Migration Literature in Italy*. Madison, N.J.: Fairleigh Dickinson University Press, 1999.

———. *Migration Italy. The Art of Talking Back in a Destination Culture*. Toronto: University of Toronto Press, 2005.

Poddar, P., R. Patke, and L. Jensen, eds. *Historical Companion to Postcolonial Literatures. Continental Europe and Its Empires*. Edinburgh: Edinburgh University Press, 2008.

Ponzanesi, Sandra. *Paradoxes of Post-colonial Culture: Contemporary Women Writers of the Indian and Afro-Italian Diaspora*. Albany: State University of New York Press, 2004.

Salhi, Kamal, ed. *Francophone Post-colonial Cultures: Critical Essays*. Lanham, Md.: Lexington Books, 2003.

Spivak, Gayatri Chakravorty. *Death of a Discipline*. New York: Columbia University Press, 2003.

Stoler, Laura Ann. *Carnal Power and Imperial Knowledge: Race and the Intimate in Colonial Rule*. Berkeley: University of California Press, 2002.

———. *Along the Archival Grain: Epistemic Anxieties and Colonial Common Sense*. Princeton, N.J.: Princeton University Press, 2011.

Thompson, Ewa M. *Imperial Knowledge: Russian Literature and Colonialism*. Westport, Conn.: Greenwood Press, 2000.

Unigwe, Chika. *Fata Morgana*. Antwerp-Amsterdam: Meulenhoff-Manteau, 2007.

———. *On Black Sisters' Street*. London: Jonathan Cape, 2009.

Van Alphen, Ernst, and Maaike Meijer, eds. *De canon onder vuur: Nederlandse literatuur tegendraads gelezen*. Amsterdam: Van Gennep, 1991.

Van der Zijl, Annejet. *Sonny Boy*. Amsterdam: Querido, 2004.

Verthé, Arthur, and Bernard Henry. *Geschiedenis van de Vlaams-Afrikaanse letterkunde*. Leuven: Davidsfonds, 1961.

Walkowitz, Rebecca L. "The Location of Literature: The Transnational Book and the Migrant Writer." *Contemporary Literature* 47, no. 4 (Winter 2006): 527–45.

Section I

TOWARDS A NEERLANDOPHONE
POSTCOLONIAL STUDIES

Chapter Two

Postcolonial Studies in the Context of the "Diasporic" Netherlands

Elleke Boehmer and Frances Gouda

In his recent and much-discussed bestseller *Het land van aankomst* [The Country of Arrival], the sociologist Paul Scheffer insists that in contemporary public discussions about the "multicultural drama" generated by the integration of new immigrants, the history of Dutch colonial governance in Southeast Asia and the Caribbean should play a constitutive role. He writes: "If we don't reconsider our image of the past and if we don't grant our colonial history a definite space in our collective memory, we violate the truth and distort the historical record."[1] The long-anticipated publication of *Het land van aankomst* generated an outpouring of critical review and debate in the printed media and television. However, none of the commentators seriously engaged with the irony of Scheffer's title, which alludes to a modernist classic in Dutch literature published in 1935, written by the Indo-Dutch Eduard du Perron, entitled *Het land van herkomst* [the country of origin]. As this suggests, the publication of Scheffer's book potentially might have—yet in the event did not—generated an exploration of the ways in which the Netherlands' history of colonization in South East Asia and the Caribbean is intertwined with the present day.

Scheffer's analysis of the Dutch situation in comparison to the treatment of and attitudes towards foreign immigrants in other European countries and the United States or Australia, touches throughout on the significance of the continuities between the colonial past and the postcolonial present.[2] In a context where such intertwinings are frequently avoided or denied, he formulates a subtle postcolonial and transnational perspective. No matter how remote the colonial period may now appear, he admonishes, Netherlanders should approach hotly contested political issues concerning ethnically "other" migrants in their society with a critical backwards look towards their past, an ongoing attention to colonial history. The Netherlands, he suggests, should not fail to acknowledge the etiolated yet indelible imprint of its colonial legacies—its history of participating in the trans-Atlantic slave trade; the astronomical profits earned in Java, which financed the infrastructural socio-economic modernity the country enjoyed during the second half of the 19th century and beyond; its nineteenth- and early twentieth-century colonial dealings with Islam.

In this essay, we want to address how and to what extent postcolonial perspectives inform contemporary political and academic discussion in the markedly "diasporic" Netherlands.[3] Our primary focus is on the academic analysis and pedagogy of literature. Therefore we want to emphasize from the outset our view that postcolonial practice in this context should be concerned to construct colonial histories not merely as a subsidiary national and trans-national backdrop to the study of literary texts. Rather, we suggest, a post-colonial perspective would see colonial history as formative in the making of imaginative literature, and to the construction of critical readings of that literature. Western cultural hegemonies over Asian or African worlds were woven into the very fabric of Europe's literary canons or, as Frantz Fanon powerfully put it, "the sweat and dead bodies of Negroes, Arabs, Indians and the yellow races have fueled the [literary] opulence of Europe."[4] It is true of course that even in the face of this stark reality, interpretations of the postco-lonial—whether as coming after the colonial period, or as a critical response present in the first act of colonization—are notoriously divergent. Here we settle for the working definition that in a context of cultural and physical op-pression, as described by Fanon, the postcolonial is that which interrogates the colonial master-servant (white/other) relationship, often in the language of the colonizer. The postcolonial embraces critical responses both insidi-ously oblique and starkly oppositional to the colonial experience.

In the British Isles, as is now widely accepted, the cultural lineages and community memory of the contemporary immigrant population are deeply imbricated in the history of the British Empire.[5] A different—possibly less obviously postcolonial—situation obtains in the Netherlands. Communi-ties designated as "problematic" in contemporary Netherlands multicultural society—whether Turkish or Moroccan, whether Croatian or Somali—have few to no cultural traditions or colonial antecedents providing them with historical points of connection, or constructed memories of and insights into Dutch culture, as we will show. The result is that the practice of postcolonial criticism, whether in the Netherlands political arena or in academic discourse, does not possess the relatively firm historical base it can in many ways draw upon in either Britain or France. Accordingly, as we will investigate, the criti-cal stance implied in postcolonial literary analysis elsewhere, reverberates differently or less loudly in Dutch academic writing and teaching. The lack of fit in terms of history between colonialism then and multicultural society now is taken to explain—and more importantly to justify—a hermeneutic disconnect between concepts drawn from (predominantly anglophone) colonial discourse theory and the analysis of contemporary diaspora cultures. At the same time, the hegemony of Anglo-American postcolonial and post-structuralist theory, which is sometimes cited as a factor contributing to the lack of fit between diaspora discourse and diaspora-in-practice, is allowed to go unchallenged. So the status of the Netherlands as an ex-colonial power remains unproblematized, and how the history of colonialism might link up with the formation of national and migrant identities today is left unexamined. Debates about, for example, race, racism and identity in university forums, are not seen to link up in a direct way with conditions in the country at large. Concomitantly, the Netherlands is widely said to lack a homegrown postcolonial critical discourse with which properly to address the experiences of its diasporic populations.

Written jointly by a postcolonial literary critic (Boehmer) and a historian of Dutch empire (Gouda), this essay explores the postcolonial pedagogic landscape at the tertiary level in the "diasporic" Netherlands, approaching this through a discussion of Netherlands' colonial legacies, and of how the postcolonial is interpreted in the Dutch present-day. We draw on long-standing teaching and research experience in these different, at times overlapping areas, on our critical perspectives on colonial and migrant discourses, and also on individual observations offered in a questionnaire format by academic colleagues involved in "postcolonial studies" (such as it is) in the Netherlands (see Appendix). (It is worth noting from the outset that those who chose to respond to our questionnaire came exclusively not from literary and historical studies, but from gender, media and cultural studies.) Throughout the essay, our contention will be that the critical literatures of the Netherlands' *uneven diasporas*—that is, diasporas lacking a straightforward, colonial relationship to the one-time "motherland'—represent at best a deeply belated writing, and in the main a still-virtual discourse awaiting its moment of articulation.[6]

DUTCH COLONIAL LEGACIES AND THE CONTEMPORARY "MULTICULTURAL DRAMA"

The Dutch East Indies embodied the prized colonial possession of the Netherlands. The colony was not only a "prolific Frisian cash cow," as one of several European commentators labeled it, but it also constituted a source of national pride and a model to other colonizing nations.[7] As the French expert on colonization Georges Henri Bousquet advised his compatriots as late as the 1930s: "I can't too strongly advise French colonists to go and study Dutch material accomplishments in the Indies on the spot . . . such investigations could only benefit the French empire."[8] Bousquet perceived what more recent commentators on the Netherlands multicultural arena have so far failed to acknowledge: the productive critical analogies that may be drawn between colonial (and also postcolonial) contexts. Without its enormous and lucrative empire in South-east Asia, the Dutch nation in the modern era would have been little more than an insignificant small European democracy "on a par with Denmark" (as the popular Dutch platitude has it). From the mid-nineteenth century, the experience and perceived success of the Netherlands in governing the Indies was tied to Dutch national identity. It provided the Dutch nation with its sense of being a *gidsland* (a guiding nation) displaying nothing but "superior energy and intelligence in the demanding work of empire."[9]

Of particular pertinence for the present-day was that this demanding work took place in a predominantly Muslim though multi-ethnic context. The ethnically and culturally diverse population of the former Dutch East Indies was ninety-percent Muslim: the Netherlands colonial regime had therefore ruled over more Muslims than any other European imperialist nation, as Bousquet indeed observed. In consequence, a reservoir of Orientalist scholarship and political expertise concerning Islamic religion, law and social practices informed Dutch colonial administration in the Indonesian archipelago until the transfer of sovereignty to the independent Indonesian nation took place in late 1949. Moreover—of further relevance to the present-day—the guiding principle of Netherlands colonial mastery had been cultural association or synthesis, a conscious policy designed to maintain the integrity and "authenticity" of ethnic cultures by adjusting Western norms and forms to local circumstances.[10] As this implies, colonial civil servants communicated not in Dutch but in Malay or other regional languages with the indigenous elites who were co-opted into the Dutch colonial administration. As late as 1961 A.D.A. de Kat Angelino, a theorist of efficacious colonial governance, hailed this allegedly unique system of cultural synthesis as flowing "naturally from the lifeblood of the Dutch nation." He noted: "only a people who had embraced in their daily lives a variety of autonomous institutions, languages, dialects, religions, sects, mores, habits and customs, dress and architecture, were capable of such an accomplishment."[11] Its embarrassing hyperbole aside, de Kat Angelino's celebration of the "Dutch" virtues of cultural synthesis and respect for the "autonomous circles" of distinct cultural and religious groups, has lingered on into the postcolonial era, and into contemporary popular understandings of Dutchness and Netherlands national identity.[12]

Since World War II, the Netherlands is said to have transformed itself from a monolithic colonial nation into a self-proclaimed multicultural society. Successive waves of ethnically diverse immigrants were greeted with the official reassurance, developed from that same laboratory of colonial rule in Southeast Asia and the Caribbean, that they might integrate into the body politic of the Netherlands on their own terms.[13] In other words, in the postcolonial era the so-called Dutch habit of cultivating respect for the unique cultural authenticity and religious traditions of former colonial subjects was formally encouraged and perpetuated, on home ground. This created a civil society in which Islamic schools and religious organizations, for example, were incorporated into the publicly financed network of socio-cultural "pillars" on a par with traditional Dutch institutions (a kind of separate-but-equal development). Until the late 1990s, Netherlands society continued to celebrate its policies of accommodation, association and cultural synthesis-instead-of-assimilation vis-à-vis Muslim and other non-Christian immigrants, thus underlining the ideological linkages between the colonial past and postcolonial present. However, at the beginning of the new millennium, and certainly since the killing of filmmaker Theo van Gogh, the ideological tenor began to alter.[14] The new era of what Paul Scheffer calls "the multicultural drama" was inaugurated, in which once-time-honored notions of respect for otherness were undermined by populist fears of Islamism and its apparent fifth-column presence in the Netherlands.

As in fellow EU countries such as Britain or France, the globalization of the world economy and the growing transnational mobility of peoples produced the effect in the Netherlands that a relatively large proportion of the population is of immigrant descent or is itself immigrant. In high-density areas like Amsterdam or Rotterdam close to 40% of people are resident migrants, whereas ethnic-minority children in elementary schools in the four major cities—Amsterdam, Rotterdam, The Hague and Utrecht—comprise more than 50% of the student population. In previous decades the Netherlands welfare state projected a well known if not always well-substantiated reputation for offering shelter and eventually a home to economic and political migrants from a range of countries. Certainly, between 1970 and 1995, the annual number of asylum seekers coming to the Netherlands grew at a steady pace. Even though this trend began to stabilize after 1995 and has even declined during the past five years, the Central Bureau for Statistics in the Dutch nation estimates that between 1972 and 2003 as many as three million foreign immigrants were added to the Dutch population.[15]

The prevailing situation of relatively tolerant accommodation was disrupted by a sharp shift to the right in the early twenty-first century following, first, an animal rights activist's murder in May 2002 of the populist political

candidate Pim Fortuyn. The shooting of maverick filmmaker Theo van Gogh
on 2 November 2004 by a Muslim extremist further aggravated public anxieties concerning the putative danger represented by "terrorists" in the Dutch
midst, a situation allegedly fueled by Dutch permissiveness. (Henceforth
right-wingers inaugurated the date of Van Gogh's death as the Netherlands'
equivalent to "9/11.") From that point onwards, the country began to chart a
contested but ineluctable retreat from its vaunted open-door policy. Among
the followers of the neo-conservative Partij van de Vrijheid (PVV/Freedom
Party, under the controversial leadership of Geert Wilders), these events
have given rise to what Australian political scientist Ghassan Hage describes
as white anxiety masking as aggressive self-assertion. Fantasies of "white
supremacy" are expressed in self-justificatory refrains of the nature of: "I-
am-white-and-therefore-I-worry-about-the-state-of-my-nation."[16] The retreat
from openness and tolerance has been expressed legally as well as politically.
It has led to the introduction of mandatory ID cards in 2005, and produced
a far more intensive screening of applications for immigration and asylum.
The "conservative turn" also inaugurated compulsory language and culture
classes for all newly arrived, non-Dutch-speaking immigrants.

Despite the fact that these concurrent practices of cultural accommodation and discrimination were self-evidently informed by the Netherlands
colonial project, it is striking that, as against conditions in Britain or France,
the new immigrants in this case were not former subjects of the (former)
empire. This represents the nub of why their experience is deemed resistant
to conventional postcolonial analysis. In the Netherlands, as in Germany and
the Scandinavian countries, immigration in large numbers began from the
1960s with the influx of unskilled workers from southern Europe and North
Africa. It is to their descendants that immigration problems now are seen to
relate—in particular they relate to second- and third-generation Turkish and
Moroccan immigrants, and, to a lesser extent, asylum-seekers from places
as diverse as Somalia, Ethiopia, Ghana, the former Yugoslavia and, more
recently, Iran, Iraq and Afghanistan. All of these newcomers have little or no
previous linguistic or cultural connection with their country of arrival. It is
therefore perceived to be complicated to acknowledge the inevitable role that
colonial histories play whether in the harmonious or the dissonant integration
of these people, and difficult to insert a postcolonial perspective drawn from
a different pedagogic tradition into the public debate. The hypothesis is that
Indians and Pakistanis in Britain, or Algerians and Moroccans in France, have
an easier time adjusting to their new homeland due to their long-standing
familiarity with the political style, social mores and language of their former
colonizers. Their funds of usable cultural capital are simply greater. Whereas
in France and Britain debates about colonial legacies engaged by migrant

spokespeople have entered the public domain and the academic arena, in the Netherlands, by contrast, questions concerning the "empire striking back" are not perceived to have a comparable critical purchase.

An important factor contributing to the Netherlands migrant disconnect is grounded in the manner in which the inflow of immigrants from Dutch colonial territories in the East and West Indies has been represented in public culture. Immigrants from the Dutch East Indies who arrived after independence was granted in 1949, and citizens of the Dutch colony Suriname which achieved independence in 1975, are regularly celebrated as successful immigrants, their initial problems with discrimination, social adjustment, and unemployment glossed over.[17] The relative success of "Indies" and Surinamese immigrants emerges especially prominently when their integration is compared and contrasted with Turkish and Moroccan newcomers who arrived in the Netherlands as guest workers during more or less the same period. The latter are earmarked as a problematic social group, whose Muslim identity—often defined in an imprecise way—is constructed as a hindrance to their productive adjustment to Dutch society.

It is symptomatic of the disconnect that we are attempting to describe, that what gets lost in the shuffle is the Netherlands political experience of having governed a vast Muslim region in South-east Asia for more than three centuries. When the Western press reports on modern Indonesia, the observation "more Muslims live in Indonesia than in the entire Middle East" will crop up as a kind of truism. In the early twentieth century, this demographic reality prompted Dutch administrators to develop a fund of sophisticated knowledge about Islamic religion, law, and social conventions, as we have observed, yet in the treatment of Moroccans and Turks in the present-day Netherlands none of this residual expertise is brought to bear. Netherlands government officials succumb to a wilful blind spot when it comes to Islam. Muslim immigrants are routinely represented as recalcitrant and ominous strangers incapable of accepting the core values of Dutch culture—values with which millions of Muslims in colonial times came into various forms of contact. Moreover, in populist and neo-conservative circles they are habitually represented as dangerous freeloaders, who abuse the generosity of the Netherlands welfare state by both their "idleness" and their (fundamentalist-related) "ungratefulness."

In sum, contemporary policy approaches Turkish, Moroccan, African and Middle Eastern immigrants within a recognizable colonialist matrix of segregation disguised as social accommodation ("pillarization"), alongside a promiscuous labelling of difference. Migrants are promised that their "un-Dutch" religious traditions and social conventions will be safeguarded, thereby recycling the motto of cultural synthesis that sustained colonial rule in Indonesia and in Suriname. Paradoxically, however, new immigrants are simultaneously urged to embrace the Dutch work ethic by integrating as productive, self-reliant citizens. Such representational practices self-evidently reify the cultural distance between "their/other" and "real" Dutch civic virtues. So, while Muslim immigrants are often depicted as fully-fledged citizens with equal rights and obligations, they are as frequently portrayed as "Others" congenitally incapable of mastering the basic lexicon of Dutch cultural norms and values. This contradictory vision—which is itself quintessentially colonialist—distorts a clear-sighted understanding of the continuities between the colonial past and the postcolonial present, and hence circumscribes any appreciation of the relevance for the Netherlands (academy and public sphere) of a postcolonial hermeneutic.

THE BELATEDNESS OF POSTCOLONIAL STUDIES AND THE BASTION OF *INDISCHE LETTEREN*

Based on statistics provided by the Central Bureau of Statistics, in 2004 the combined total of first- and second-generation immigrants from the Netherlands' former colonies in South-east Asia and the Caribbean was 860,000, comprising 5.3 percent of the Dutch population. In comparison, in 2004 the combination of first- and second-generation immigrants from other countries in Europe or the Middle East and Asia, Africa and Latin America, comprised a grand total of 2,228,000 people or almost 14 percent of the total population. These very rudimentary numbers indicate the extent to which a diverse immigrant population from elsewhere overtops the demographic presence of former colonized subjects in the Netherlands.

The Netherlands, in short, presents a situation of extremely heterogeneous diaspora. In comparison with a former colonial power like Britain, migrant conditions are anomalous and, relative to imported postcolonial paradigms, aberrant. There is little equivalent to that situation where the former colonial metropolis draws cultural influences and practitioners from around the world into a dominant yet broadly intelligible "europhone" hub. There is also little equivalent to the celebration of a hybridized English or a mongrelized Britishness. Especially given the fact that the British imperial experience is generally taken as definitive for postcolonialism, postcolonial paradigms such as borrowing, mimicry and translation do not attach in the same way. Moreover, even if these or related trends did in fact exist, they have not yet been isolated, defined, or theorized as such, *on their own terms*, within academic and critical institutions, as modes of adaptive exchange *particular to* the Netherlands' migrant situation, though also bearing comparison with ex-colonial contexts elsewhere. The situation of anomaly has arguably interrupted or frustrated the creation within the Dutch critical establishment and academe of a homegrown vocabulary through which postcolonial insights might be generated and developed. Postcolonial discussions there certainly are, as in the 2001 Book Week example cited below, but these are framed in borrowed, anglophone terms, and largely carried on *outside* literature departments, in the cultural pages of newspapers and the domains of cultural studies, under the heading of the investigation of the Other.

At a theoretical level, postcolonial concepts of mimicry and hybridity, as has been widely described, draw on the language-based approaches of poststructuralism. Therefore a crucial way of accounting for their lack of critical purchase in the Netherlands, must be with reference to the absence of linguistic continuities between the one-time colonies, their native élites, and the present-day ex-colonial power. As will be clear, disruptive slippages of meaning or resistant re-readings simply do not operate in the same way between distinct language groupings as they do between groups with differing yet convergent relations to a shared dominant language.

To expand with reference only to the largest former colony, the erstwhile Dutch East Indies, the Dutch language never displaced Malay as the primary lingua franca of the multi-ethnic, multi-lingual Indonesian archipelago at any point during the colonial period. A borrowed or "chutnified" Nederlands does not therefore form the medium of cultural expression of any social group in Indonesia today.[18] In the archipelago, the Malay language, originating in the coastal regions surrounding the Malaka Straits and eastern Sumatra, was long since the medium of inter-island trade and communication, binding together commercially and culturally regions colonized by the Dutch, one-time British territories in Malaysia and Burma, and the Philippines. As a mark of Malay's prominence, even the day-to-day administration of Dutch colonial power was conducted in Malay as well as other regional languages such as Javanese. The colonial state in fact encouraged popular literacy in Malay and regional languages rather than in Dutch, working through the *Balai Pustaka*—a government agency founded in the 1920s designed to increase the publication of Malay translations of classics in Dutch literature. As a result, Dutch as the language of colonial power and prestige was learned by only a small percentage of the native élite. In 1928 a strategic decision of the Indonesian nationalist movement was to proclaim that the lingua franca Malay rather than the demographically dominant Javanese would be the mother language of the independent nation of the future. And, during the twilight years of the Dutch East Indies, when a group of multi-ethnic, self-consciously modernist writers, the *Pujangga baru* (new writers), began to contemplate the nature of the new "Indonesian literature," they chose Malay as a medium in order to invoke a hoped-for, inter-ethnic solidarity.[19]

With respect to the Netherlands postcolonial context, therefore, we find no France *d'outre mer* or language hexagon. There is no equivalent to a Commonwealth of anglophone nations in which colonially educated élites are able to refer back to a repertoire in common of English school songs, nursery rhymes and well-known, canonical poems (Wordworth's "Daffodils" poem comes to mind). The greater part of the one-time empire does not write back as it has no linguistic overturning to accomplish, and postcolonial concepts of semantic recalcitrance or "sly civility" inevitably seem imposed and difficult to integrate. That the postcolonial vocabularies to analyze social and cultural processes like racial marginalization and discrimination by contrast *do* often relate closely to the Netherlands context, is something that is erased by the overriding appearance of disconnect and belatedness. The erasure is further upheld by a conservative, philological tendency in academic institutions—a tendency that finds no relevance in the seeming a-historicity of postcolonial critical thought, as will again be seen.

Netherlands belatedness is sharply focused by a debate that took place in 2001, on the occasion of the so-called Netherlands Book Week, as insightfully discussed in a study by the critic Sarah De Mul.[20] As De Mul describes, the Book Week each year takes a particular theme, which, as will be familiar from many contexts, shapes the nature of the readings and the other events organized. Each time, too, a single book published in that year is selected as promotional material, to be sent to sponsors, event convenors, participants, and so on. In 2001 the keynote theme was the impeccably postcolonial: "Het Land van Herkomst: Schrijven tussen twee culturen"/["Land of origin: Writing between two cultures"]. And the accompanying book was Salman Rushdie's *Fury*, translated into Dutch as *Woede* (which was in fact published before *Fury*).

Despite Rushdie's standing as a respected, widely read author in the Netherlands, the selection of his novel as a mascot book provoked heated protest and fierce debate—a debate which continued well beyond the bounds of Book Week. In a nutshell, the contention crystallized around the nature of that quintessential postcolonial concept of "in-betweenness" as it related to the Netherlands. The British-identified, New York resident Rushdie was rightly taken to typify the neither-nor of the diasporic borderline condition, yet the choice of his novel was at the same time perceived to signify an anglophone, postcolonial hegemony. That is, its nomination again implied—through no fault of Rushdie's of course—a belatedness to the Dutch postcolonial condition. Where was the Dutch instance of in-betweenness, of writing between cultures? commentators asked. Rushdie's novel had been set up as representing a mode of metropolitan yet postcolonial authority, a gold standard against which the diasporic expression of a smaller, once-colonial nation, conversant in a minority European language, was being forced to measure itself, and, inevitably, to appear as lacking by contrast. Netherlands writing of the in-between was, ironically, "not quite" right, not definitively borderline. As one critic put it, migrant writers in Dutch suffered from having to respond to the wrong sort of colonizers—less influential, less globally hegemonic. They were doubly disadvantaged, both by the marginality of the Netherlands colonial condition and by their marginality to postcolonial writing in English.

The Book Week debate raised interesting questions concerning the image of the Netherlands nation and nationality: how definitions of Dutchness or Netherlands identity (not necessarily the same thing) were impacted now by foreign, now by homegrown postcolonial work; how such identities were shaped by multicultural and migrant productions (in this case, novels). The discussion had recourse to a perceptibly nationalist concept of a homogeneous Netherlands culture and literary tradition, to which migrant writers in Dutch belonged, or belonged to a certain extent—or more self-evidently than did Rushdie. As the critic Danilo Verplancke put it:

> Was er now echt geen andere keuze te maken? Mischien één die dichter bij het Nederlandse klimaat staat? Desnoods een die eventueel niet in het Nederlands schrijft, maar er wel tenminste woont en bekend is met een beeld van ons land.

> Could no other choice have been made? Of a writer who at least stands a little closer to the Netherlands atmosphere or climate? If necessary one who does not perhaps write in Netherlands, but who is familiar with the image of our country.[21]

Would the selection of multicultural writing as a Book Week theme not have been an appropriate occasion, asked a third commentator, Roland Fragel, to champion a migrant writer working in the Netherlands language?[22] In this there was the interesting implicit admission that the Netherlands merited the appellation "postcolonial," at least at the level of embracing a sufficiency of "in-between" writers.

As this suggests, linguistically interrupted, historically anomalous, the "Netherlands postcolonial" represents a far from established terrain: it is in fact, we submit, something curiously defensive and undefined. Who are its authors? who its critics? It is not easy to tell from the course reading lists submitted by our questionnaire respondents. Names like Hafid Bouazza (a Moroccan-origin Dutch novelist), Ayaan Hirsi Ali (the Somali-origin activist), and Mieke Bal (the cultural critic), are cited but remain in the minority relative to the more usual anglophone suspects—Said, Spivak, Bhabha, Loomba, Huggan, McClintock, Hall. Among critics and teachers there would appear to be a shared preoccupation with migrant subjectivity, with what it is to be marginal and lack a recognized voice. Yet this exists side-by-side with a concern to escape from a condition of theoretical and writerly after-effect, or, within a differently postcolonial space, of offering little more than a reiteration of the already-known.

On one level, to be sure, as the very term belatedness suggests, the situation may be differently interpreted. The borrowed landscape of postcolonial criticism in Dutch and in the Netherlands adds a potentially interesting further level of translation to the epistemological frameworks through which the postcolonial is generally understood. Postcolonial writing is famously a liminal writing, composed of metaphors that have historically been "borne across," articulated through layers of cultural and linguistic translation. In the Netherlands context the multiply translated condition of postcolonial writing is arguably especially prominent, or unavoidable, in that postcolonial critical discourse is largely undertaken, and conceived of, through the medium first and foremost of the English language and must therefore be translated. What might seem from one point of view a restrictive commitment to an anglocentric focus, could equally be regarded as an invitation to examine the transmission and translatedness of critical discourse itself, and also to propagate the further adaptation of postcolonial terminologies. A further frame of transfer and translation is added on to the discussion of writing that is always-already seen as migrant, carried across and borrowed.

To date however this potential for the flexible adaptation of postcolonial terms has not been mobilized. Instead, postcolonialism's "translatedness" in the Netherlands context is allowed to get in the way of applying critical insights imported from academic debates elsewhere, to the country's untypical diasporic cultural materials. The situation is of a piece with the noticeable paucity in Dutch literary and cultural studies of an independent, homegrown critical discourse of otherness, *allochtoon* minority, and so on, as well as of a discourse of national identity, of what Dutchness comprises. With Mieke Bal and Isabel Hoving as clear exceptions, the frequently cited names are, as was seen, derived from Anglo-American and French cultural criticism. Obviously we are dealing here with an instance of the cultural cringe of a self-perceived small country. Yet perceptions of a derivative local postcolonial field have as an inevitable consequence the embedding of a certain academic parochialism, as reflected in the Book Week commentator's abject plea for a writer "who stands closer to the Netherlands atmosphere or climate." Under such conditions adaptive yet innovative postcolonial re-readings tend not to be quickened into being. Moreover, a license is given to those in the academy hostile to postcolonialism for its lack of empirical specificity or borrowed culturist paradigms, to dismiss its hermeneutic richness with regard to colonial representation, or its interventions in the study of migrant subjectivity.

In order to move on to what this institutional resistance in fact entails, we venture a provisional summary. The wholesale import of a postcolonial critical vocabulary into the Netherlands academy is, as has been intimated, circumscribed for several overlapping reasons. First, as suggested, postcolonialism based on the British imperial experience is seen to disregard the insights that Dutch diasporic and nominally postcolonial writing might offer, in that it is unable to respond to the historical and linguistic anomalies of the Netherlands ex-colonial context. Furthermore, as some of our questionnaire's respondents suggested, students and even academics in many tertiary institutions, are sufficiently convinced of the success of the multicultural experiment in the Netherlands, to fail to see how postcolonial concepts of cultural difference and otherness, say, might relate to their day-to-day reality. That is to say, their context is perceived to lack postcoloniality.

In departments of Dutch specifically, there remains a strong tendency to refuse to accept postcolonial perspectives on any terms. This tendency emerges in particular from scholars of Indies writing, a coterie identified with the journal *Indische Letteren*, whose intellectual antecedents lie in philology, and whose concerns with colonial *belletrie* are noticeably moved by a defensive nostalgia that expresses at times as anti-Foucauldian empiricism. Their remarkable point of view is that writing of the Netherlands colonial experience in Dutch, even that produced today, is strictly speaking a colonial writing (informed by the historical and linguistic hiatus described in this and the previous section). The colonial experience as articulated in Dutch represents a period frozen in time, a reality that does not recede. Especially for those who are more than merely baffled by postcolonial questions, there can no possibility of writing back or sly civility, by definition, as the idea of the non-colonial writer who deals in colonial experience is an impossibility.[23]

Then again, it must be conceded that in departments of Dutch in the Netherlands there is at least some consideration given to colonial representation. In departments of English literature, by contrast, outside Conrad criticism, postcolonial scholars and teachers are conspicuous by their absence. Yet this is in a country where most students are technically bilingual English-Nederlands, and therefore, potentially at least, sensitive to the issues of border-crossing that postcolonialism raises, and sufficiently confident of their proficiency in English, too, to explore beyond canonical boundaries. In the Netherlands, it is clear, literature is regarded as closely involved in unitary constructions of the nation (whether Britain, France, or the Netherlands)—constructions from which the colonial experience is evacuated. Against this backdrop it is significant that, to the knowledge of the writers, the Netherlands does not at this point in time have formal involvement as a participating country in the European Association of Commonwealth Literature and Language Studies

(EACLALS), which is part of worldwide ACLALS. ACLALS remains for all its old-fashioned entitling one of the primary forums within which post-colonial literary discussion is held within Europe and across the globe. When weighed against the active participation of Germany, France, Spain, Italy, Denmark, and Belgium, as well as Britain, Dutch non-membership is revealing of some form of institutional resistance. Also revealing is that most of the colleagues in literary studies in the Netherlands whom we approached with our short questionnaire, did not respond.

POSTCOLONIAL PEDAGOGY IN THE NETHERLANDS

In this section we move to relate our somewhat speculative and generalizing observations above, to specific findings raised by the questionnaire on postcolonial teaching we put to a number of Netherlands academics with experience of tertiary education in the humanities, specifically in literary, language and cultural studies. The questionnaire set out to discover, as the covering letter put it, whether postcolonial studies "remains poorly supported institutionally, and marginalized as a literary discipline." Of the twenty-five questionnaires sent out, there were nine respondents, of which one was a Dutch postcolonialist currently working outside the Netherlands, and one a freelance writer and critic. Their findings were combined with observations from a postdoctoral student of comparative literature, and anecdotal verbal remarks gleaned from an academic with a history of teaching in the Netherlands currently also working outside the country.

Our survey found that postcolonial critical discourses tended to be widely taught as part of gender and cultural studies, seemingly on the basis of the analogy that both gender and postcolonial perspectives are perspectives on forms of difference. Several colleagues had some background in comparative literary studies, but had moved away from this discipline in order, it seemed, to work more freely with critical theoretical approaches. The postdoctoral student described being introduced to postcolonial issues ("intersectionality," migrant writing) in eye-opening ways in a department of gender studies. Novels by, especially, women writers from other cultures (Mariama Ba, Jamaica Kincaid) were universally regarded by the respondents as sensitizing students to experiences of otherness, though, interestingly, such experiences were generally seen as taking place away from home, in other countries. Nearly all the respondents remarked on this in one or other form.

Although the pedagogic focus of the respondents tended to be on race, difference, and minority discourses, most commented that little more attention than a seminar or two was paid in the courses on which they taught to the Netherlands diaspora as such. For this they blamed institutional and course structures. Netherlands postcolonial topics generally featured in their curricula in a comparative frame, alongside examples drawn from other postcolonial areas: they tended not to be addressed in and for themselves. Equal prominence was given to film texts and life-writing as to literary texts as instances of key postcolonial issues. The situation that emerged corresponded to that schematized by Isabel Hoving in 2004 where she outlined two "postcolonial" approaches in the Netherlands academy. The first, as we have also noted, arose out of a traditional Orientalist philology, with its focal point in Leiden, which claimed intense faithfulness to the historical record and to indigenous cultural perspectives, to which it deemed itself uniquely privy through linguistic knowledge. The second was a more critical theoretical group that allied itself to cultural studies perspectives as developed within the Anglo-American academy.

Yet, from the evidence of the questionnaire, even this receptive second group had not taken significant steps to adapt their borrowed approaches in a sustained way to diasporic postcolonial conditions in the Netherlands itself—to look at representations of Islam past and present, for example, or examples of cultural in-betweenness. Their seminar discussions—arguably unlike that of the first group—were not informed by work on the ground. Relatedly, the postcolonial teaching of the second group, while it raised topics of multiculturalism and race, did not as often raise its critical accompaniment, that is, questions of the nation, national identity, and narratives of the colonial past. Where there was discussion of Dutchness it appeared that this was rarely tied to debates on the Netherlands' status as an ex-colonial power. As one respondent observed, in response to Mieke Bal's caustic theorization of the patronizing Zwarte Piet (Black Peter) tradition in Netherlands culture, students were resistant, "simply [refusing] to see this tradition as other than innocent play."[24]

Against this, the freelance respondent outside the academy wrote that a foremost aim in her work was to demonstrate that migrant writers were "part of the national history too." Concurring, another respondent sought in her classes, at least in principle, the "deconstruction of the Dutch canon as merely white and univocal Dutch." We are committed to "embedding" theories in the location and context of teaching, said yet another. These remarks illustrated something of Hoving's own bracing analysis of Dutchness, which she sees posited as an empty and excessive ideal of openness, cited by Dutch citizens as "an impassable obstacle to integration."[25] If this is taken as true, however, then the power of migrant writing must be that, like developer fluid in photography, it casts into relief the boundedness as opposed to the openness of Netherlands society. As this might suggest, it is from Dutch diaspora writing that new concepts of belonging, divided identity, resistant emotion, relationality and even Dutchness can be subversively drawn.

To close with a provocation, we suggest that it is in the Netherlands' heterogeneous diasporic writing—many-tongued, palimpsestic, only jaggedly connected to the former colonial project—that the deep belatedness of the Dutch postcolonial condition might prolifically and tumultuously generate new meanings. So newness enters the world: generated out of the anomalous, noisy and unlikely Netherlands of the multiply translated migrant condition.

APPENDIX

Questionnaire by Elleke Boehmer and Frances Gouda, 5 November 2007

[Our thanks to those who responded, several of whom preferred to remain nameless]

1. Please describe your academic discipline. (1–2 lines)
2. Within the remit of your discipline, which postcolonial approaches do you teach, and/or which theorists and writers?
3. In which language or languages do you teach postcolonial material? And under which subject headings (as defined by your institution)?
4. At which level (undergraduate, masters, postgraduate) do you tend to introduce postcolonial perspectives to students?
5. Do you teach neerlandophone counterparts (Bourassa, Buruma) alongside or as well as anglophone or francophone writers and theorists?
6. If so, which writers and theorists?
7. What kinds of resistance if any have you encountered whether in structures or in students to teaching postcolonial writers and approaches? Please describe fully. If your experience has been without resistance, please describe your situation fully also.
8. Would you say that the coverage of theories and approaches relating to race and racism, migration, identity and nationalism within your department or institution relates to or bears correspondence with conditions in the country at large?

NOTES

Acknowledgments. This chapter originally appeared in *Comparing Postcolonial Diasporas*, edited by Michelle Keown, David Murphy, and James Procter (London:

Palgrave Macmillan, 2009), pp 37–55. Reproduced with permission of Palgrave Macmillan.

1. P. Scheffer, *Het land van aankomst* (Amsterdam: De Bezige Bij, 2007), 183.

2. J. A. A. van Doorn, *Indische lessen: Nederland en de koloniale ervaring* (Amsterdam: Bert Bakker, 1995); Frances Gouda, "Gender en Etniciteit, gisteren en vandaag," in *Gemengde Gevoelens: Gender, Etniciteit en (Post)Kolonialisme. Jaarboek voor Vrouwengeschiedenis no. 27*, eds. Eva Geudekker, Frances Gouda (guest editor), Saskia Poldervaart, Kristine Steenbergh and Anna Tijsseling (Amsterdam: Aksant, 2007), 7–31.

3. Adriaan van Dis, "Vrijtaal," *Optima literair tijdschrift* 21, no. 4 (2006); Yvette Kopijn, "Duizend-en-één verhalen van een nacht. Representaties en interpetraties van Indische vrouwelijkheid," in *Gemengde Gevoelens: Gender, Etniciteit en (Post)Kolonialisme. Jaarboek voor Vrouwengeschiedenis no. 27,* eds. Eva Geudekker, Frances Gouda (guest editor), Saskia Poldervaart, Kristine Steenbergh and Anna Tijsseling (Amsterdam: Aksant, 2007), 7–31.

4. Frantz Fanon, *The Wretched of the Earth*, trans. Constance Farrington ([1961]; London: Penguin, 1986), 76–81.

5. To cite only three examples, Susheila Nasta, *Home Truths: Fictions of the South-Asian Diaspora in Britain* (London: Palgrave, 2002); John McLeod, *Postcolonial London: Re-writing the Metropolis* (London: Routledge, 2004); James Procter, *Writing Black Britain* (Manchester: Manchester University Press, 2000).

6. On belatedness, see Ali Behdad, *Belated Travellers: Orientalism in the Age of Colonial Dissolution* (Durham, NC: Duke University Press, 1996).

7. Pierre Leroy Beaulieu, *De la colonization chez les peoples modernes* (Paris: n.p., 1872), 293.

8. Georges Henri Bousquet, *A French View of the Netherlands Indies* (1939; trans. New York: Institute of Pacific Relations, 1940), 119.

9. J. C. van Eerde, *Koloniale volkenkunde: Eerste stuk: Omgang met inlanders* (Amsterdam: De Bussy, 1914), 54.

10. Frances Gouda, *Dutch Culture Overseas: Colonial Practice in the Netherlands Indies, 1900–1942* (Amsterdam: Amsterdam University Press, 1995); Ann Laura Stoler, *Carnal Knowledge and Imperial Power: Race and the Intimate in Colonial Rule* (Berkeley: University of California Press, 2002).

11. A. D. A. de Kat Angelino, "De ontwikkelingsgedachte in het Nederlands overzees bestuur," in *Balans van beleid: Terugblik op de laatste halve eeuw van Nederlands-Indië*, eds. H. Baudet and I. J. Brugmans (repr. 1984; Assen: Van Gorcum, 1961), 49.

12. Frances Gouda, *Dutch Culture Overseas: Colonial Practice in the Netherlands Indies, 1900–1942* (Amsterdam: Amsterdam University Press, 1995), 40–41.

13. Isabel Hoving, "Circumventing Openness: Creating New Senses of Dutchness," in *Transit* 1, no. 1 (2005), article 50909, http://repositories.cdlib.org/ucbgerman/transit/vol1/iss1/art50909.

14. See, for example, Marc de Leeuw and Sonja van Wichelen, "'Please, Go Wake Up!': Submission, Hirsi Ali and the 'War on Terror' in the Netherlands," *Feminist*

Media Studies 5, no. 3 (2005): 325–40; "Transformations of 'Dutchness': From Happy Multiculturalism to the Crisis of Dutch Liberalism," in *Identity, Belonging, and Migration*, eds. Gerard Delanty, Paul Jones and Ruth Wodak (Liverpool: Liverpool University Press, 2007), 261–78.

15. Andries de Jong, *Schatting aantal westerse en niet-westerse allochtonen in de afgelopen dertig jaar* (Centraal Bureau voor de statistiek, 2004), www.cbs.nl/nl.NL/menu/themas/bevolking/publicaties/artikelen/archief/2003.

16. Ghassan Hage, *White Nation: Fantasies of White Supremacy in a Multicultural Society* (Sydney: Pluto Press, 1998), passim.

17. Yvette Kopijn, "Duizend-en-één verhalen van een nacht: Representaties en interpetraties van Indische vrouwelijkheid," in *Gemengde Gevoelens: Gender, Etniciteit en (Post)Kolonialisme. Jaarboek voor Vrouwengeschiedenis no. 27*, eds. Eva Geudekker, Frances Gouda (guest editor), Saskia Poldervaart, Kristine Steenbergh and Anna Tijsseling (Amsterdam: Aksant, 2007), 7–31.

18. A situation more comparable to that of English in India operates in Suriname, in the positioning of Dutch, the one-time language of colonial administration, vis-à-vis Sranantongo, the Surinamese creole.

19. C. W. Watson. *Of Self and Nation: Autobiography and the Representation of Modern Indonesia* (Honolulu: University of Hawai'i Press, 2000), passim.

20. Sarah De Mul, "De Nomade ontwapend: De politiek van het nomadisme in *Woede* van Salman Rushdie en de pragmatiek van de institutionalisering in de Nederlandse Boekenweek 2001: 'Het land van herkomst: Schrijven tussen twee kulturen,'" unpublished MA thesis, University of Antwerp, 2001.

21. As quoted in Sarah De Mul, "De Nomade ontwapend: De politiek van het nomadisme in Woede van Salman Rushdie en de pragmatiek van de institutionalisering in de Nederlandse Boekenweek 2001: 'het land van herkomst: schrijven tussen twee kulturen'" (unpublished MA thesis, University of Antwerp, 2001), 42.

22. As quoted in Sarah De Mul, "De Nomade ontwapend: De politiek van het nomadisme in Woede van Salman Rushdie en de pragmatiek van de institutionalisering in de Nederlandse Boekenweek 2001: 'het land van herkomst: schrijven tussen twee kulturen'" (unpublished MA thesis, University of Antwerp, 2001), 43.

23. Theo D'haen, "Inleiding," in *Europa Buitengaats: Koloniale en postkoloniale literaturen in Europese talen*, ed. Theo d'Haen (Amsterdam: Bert Bakker, 2002), 7–29.

24. Mieke Bal, *Travelling Concepts in the Humanities* (Toronto: University of Toronto Press, 2002).

25. Isabel Hoving, "'Niets dan het heden': Over Jamaica Kincaid, de postkoloniale literatuurstudie, en wat er van ons terecht moet komen," in *Wandelaar onder de palmen: Opstellen over koloniale en postkoloniale literatuur en cultuur*, eds. Michiel van Kempen, Piet Verkruisse en Adrienne Zuiderweg (Leiden: KITLV, 2004), 15–28.

BIBLIOGRAPHY

Bal, Mieke. *Travelling Concepts in the Humanities.* Toronto: University of Toronto Press, 2002.

Beaulieu, Pierre Leroy. *De la colonization chez les peoples modernes.* Paris: n.p., 1872.

Behdad, Ali. *Belated Travellers: Orientalism in the Age of Colonial Dissolution.* Durham, NC: Duke University Press, 1996.

Boehmer, Elleke. *Colonial and Postcolonial Literature: Migrant Metaphors.* Oxford: Oxford University Press, 2005.

Bousquet, Georges Henri. *A French View of the Netherlands Indies.* 1939; trans. New York: Institute of Pacific Relations, 1940.

De Jong, Andries. *Schatting aantal westerse en niet-westerse allochtonen in de afgelopen dertig jaar.* Centraal Bureau voor de statistiek, 2004. http://www.cbs .nl/nl.NL/menu/themas/bevolking/publicaties/artikelen/archief/2003, accessed November 25, 2011.

De Mul, Sarah. "De Nomade ontwapend: De politiek van het nomadisme in *Woede* van Salman Rushdie en de pragmatiek van de institutionalisering in de Nederlandse Boekenweek 2001: 'Het land van herkomst: schrijven tussen twee kulturen,'" unpublished MA thesis, University of Antwerp, 2001.

D'haen, Theo. "Inleiding." In *Europa Buitengaats: Koloniale en postkoloniale literaturen in Europese talen*, edited by Theo D'haen, 7–29. Amsterdam: Bert Bakker, 2002.

Fanon, Frantz. *The Wretched of the Earth.* Trans. Constance Farrington (1961); London: Penguin, 1986.

Gouda, Frances. *Dutch Culture Overseas: Colonial Practice in the Netherlands Indies, 1900–1942.* Amsterdam: Amsterdam University Press, 1995.

———. "Gender en Etniciteit, gisteren en vandaag." In *Gemengde Gevoelens: Gender, Etniciteit en (Post)Kolonialisme. Jaarboek voor Vrouwengeschiedenis no. 27*, edited by Eva Geudekker, Frances Gouda (guest editor), Saskia Poldervaart, Kristine Steenbergh and Anna Tijsseling, 7–31. Amsterdam: Aksant, 2007.

Hage, Ghassan. *White Nation: Fantasies of White Supremacy in a Multicultural Society.* Sydney: Pluto Press, 1998.

Hart, Jonathan. *Comparing Empires: European Colonialism from Portuguese Expansion to the Spanish-American War.* Basingstoke: Palgrave MacMillan, 2003.

Hoving, Isabel. "Circumventing Openness: Creating New Senses of Dutchness." *Transit* 1, no. 1 (2005), article 50909, http://repositories.cdlib.org/ucbgerman/transit/vol1/iss1/art50909, accessed November 25, 2011.

———. "'Niets dan het heden': Over Jamaica Kincaid, de postkoloniale literatuurstudie, en wat er van ons terecht moet komen," in *Wandelaar onder de palmen: Opstellen over koloniale en postkoloniale literatuur en cultuur*, edited by Michiel van Kempen, Piet Verkruisse and Adrienne Zuiderweg, 15–28. Leiden: KITLV, 2004.

Kat Angelino, A. D. A. de. "De ontwikkelingsgedachte in het Nederlands overzees bestuur." In *Balans van beleid: Terugblik op de laatste halve eeuw van Nederlands-Indië*, edited by H. Baudet and I. J. Brugmans, 28–49. Repr. 1984; Assen: Van Gorcum, 1961.

Kopijn, Yvette. "Duizend-en-één verhalen van een nacht: Representaties en interpretaties van Indische vrouwelijkheid." In *Gemengde Gevoelens: Gender, Etniciteit en (Post)Kolonialisme. Jaarboek voor Vrouwengeschiedenis no. 27*, edited by Eva

Geudekker, Frances Gouda (guest editor), Saskia Poldervaart, Kristine Steenbergh and Anna Tijsseling, 7–31. Amsterdam: Aksant, 2007.

Leeuw, Marc de, and Sonja van Wichelen. "'Please, Go Wake Up!': Submission, Hirsi Ali and the 'War on Terror' in the Netherlands." *Feminist Media Studies* 5, no. 3 (2005): 325–40.

———. "Transformations of 'Dutchness': From Happy Multiculturalism to the Crisis of Dutch Liberalism." In *Identity, Belonging, and Migration*, edited by Gerard Delanty, Paul Jones and Ruth Wodak, 261–78. Liverpool: Liverpool University Press, 2007.

Maussen, Marcel. *Ruimte voor de Islam? Stedelijk beleid, voorzieningen, organisaties.* Apeldoorn/Antwerp: Het Spectrum, 2006.

McLeod, John. *Postcolonial London: Re-writing the Metropolis.* London: Routledge, 2004.

Nasta, Susheila. *Home Truths: Fictions of the South Asian Diaspora in Britain.* Basingstoke: Palgrave, 2002.

Procter, James. *Writing Black Britain.* Manchester: Manchester University Press, 2000.

Scheffer, Paul. *Het land van aankomst.* Amsterdam: De Bezige Bij, 2007.

Stoler, Ann Laura. *Carnal Knowledge and Imperial Power: Race and the Intimate in Colonial Rule.* Berkeley: University of California Press, 2002.

Symposium van de Stichting Koninklijk Paleis Amsterdam. *Nederlands buitengaats; een taalreünie.* Amsterdam: Stichting Koninklijk Paleis, 2006.

Van Dis, Adriaan. "Vrijtaal." *Optima literair tijdschrift* 21, no. 4 (2006).

Van Doorn, J. A. A. *Indische lessen: Nederland en de koloniale ervaring.* Amsterdam: Bert Bakker, 1995.

Van Eerde, J. C. *Koloniale volkenkunde: Eerste stuk: Omgang met inlanders.* Amsterdam: De Bussy, 1914.

Van Herten, Marieke, and Ferdy Otten, "Naar een nieuwe schatting van het aantal Islamieten in Nederland." Den Haag: Centraal Bureau voor Statistiek, 2007. http://www.cbs.nl/nl.NL/menu/themas/bevolking/publicaties/artikelen/archief/2007.

Chapter Three

Polderpoko

Why It Cannot Exist

Isabel Hoving

The title of this essay may sound a little desperate: it suggests that "polderpoko"—by which I mean the Dutch, or polder-, variety of postcolonial (Dutch spelling: postkoloniale) theory and criticism—might not exist; might even be unthinkable.[1] The statement is not just desperate, but seems obviously false, too. What about the long tradition of postcolonial studies in Leiden, for example, which, in the nineties, was energized by pioneers such as professor Theo D'haen? What about all those other dozens of pioneering colleagues in other Dutch and Belgian universities, from the enthusiastic PhD students to the professors who may be primarily or also interested in migration, postcoloniality, and globalization, of whom many are represented in this book? The facts prove that there *is* something like "polderpoko."

Nevertheless, this essay will argue that we should consider the existing practice of postcolonial criticism in the Low Countries with some productive *scepsis*. I will take a closer look at some of the vexed issues that seem specific for Dutch postcolonialism (at least in this particular form), to show that they cannot be addressed through the standard postcolonial approaches. A much more fundamental approach is in order. However, that fundamental approach also shows that in some senses, postcolonial theory simply comes *too late* to analyse some of the present-day problems in Dutch society, because that problem may already be part of a *post*-postcolonial social or political dynamics. In other senses, in the Netherlands, the time for a postcolonial analysis may not yet have come.

POSTCOLONIALITY IN THE NETHERLANDS:
NEO-REALISM AND ITS PARADOXES

My first question will be: what are the most productive academic approaches for the analysis of Dutch colonization and postcoloniality? This
question departs from a basic assumption: namely, that we "do" postcolonialism not just because it is an attractive academic subject, but because we
aim at participating in a larger project of cultural critique—say, the critique
of colonial discourse, and the tenacious discourses of race, identity, culture
upon which colonial discourse was built. This is Edward Said's postcolonial approach. If this form of postcolonial criticism wants to be effective
as a cultural critique in the Netherlands, it must begin by asking: what are
the peculiarities in the *Dutch* relation to key issues such as race, language
and identity?

Sportswriter Simon Kuper, who wrote an astonishing history about
football in the Netherlands during the Second World War, offers a thought
provoking case in point. I want to present this case to discuss one of the specific characteristics of the Dutch approach to race and language. Kuper first
confronts his readers with the well-known observation that the capital's
football team Ajax (every year the potential national champion) is considered to be a Jewish team. Non-Jewish Ajax supporters often call themselves
"Jews." During football matches, you will hear their opponents sing "We
are going on a Jew hunt," or "Hamas, hamas, Jews to the gas chambers."
Kuper explains that the references to World War Two became part of the
opponents' slogans in the 1980s; at the time, they were seen as inexcusably
provocative. By 2003, Kuper observes, the anti-Semitic slogans were often
defended as no more than football folklore.[2] A few years on, however,
football managers and the law began to adopt an active strategy of opposing them.[3]

In her excellent study on Dutch public discourse after Pim Fortuyn, philosopher Baukje Prins has argued that she would like to define the dominant
discourse in which issues of multiculturalization and migration are now being
addressed, as neo-realist. In other words, language is seen as the transparent
means to represent a clear-cut, unambiguous reality. Until the late nineties, it
is said, the truth of that reality could not be represented because of the ideological cowardice of the political left; now, the neo-realist politicians utter the
hidden truth. That truth would be that Muslim migrants are a threat to open,
tolerant Dutch society. According to this view, we should take the designation of Ajax as a team of Jews as the (presumably refreshing) description of a
racial or ethnic identity that had been prudishly masked by leftist hypocrisy.

In response, however, Kuper observes how different people who are closely associated to Ajax emphatically deny that Ajax has ever been a Jewish club.[4] This is a curious denial, says Kuper; Ajax clearly *was* immersed in a Jewish culture, like all Amsterdam institutions before the war, except the NSB (the Dutch national socialist party) and the churches.[5] Why then this resistance to an identification as Jewish? Kuper quotes one old Jewish supporter, who explains that he has never seen Ajax as a Jewish club either. "Ajax was a place where Jews and gentiles met [. . .] It was a melting pot, and that may have been one reason why [his, IH] father took his boys along. I think it was part of our education, that we were a part of the Dutch people."[6] This example suggests that Ajax's self-identification was much more complex and nuanced than the supporters' hostile identification—which can neither be dismissed, nor embraced.

What interests me here, is that the supporters who are responsible for these chants (among them those of the historical opponent, the Rotterdam football team Feyenoord) argue that the songs are *not meant seriously*. As Kuper has it, "the average Feyenoord fan is not talking about real Jews, none of whom they have ever met. To them the word 'Jew' simply connotes an Ajax fan."[7] This sharp observation demands a reconsideration of the realism that is at the heart of the neo-realism analyzed by Prins. It is apparently intertwined with its opposite: the *denial* of a connection between signifier and signified.

Anthropologist Daniel Miller helps to understand the racial context for the strategy of disconnection between stereotypes of the other on the one hand, and the historical group that is othered on the other.[8] He argues that primitivism, which is an important cultural strategy to stabilize the self through the racial imagination of the other, becomes problematic when the racial others whose images have been used to that effect, enter the everyday world inhabited by the self—and when that cultural other actually becomes a potential partner in discursive exchange. For the often European citizens who invested in these racial stereotypes, the stakes may be too high to just give up the strategy of stereotyping. Miller states that the primitivist imagination may then be placed at an even greater distance from everyday life; it may be expressed as exaggerated stereotype, in art, popular culture, or ritual, after which any relation between that codified imagination and real life will be vigorously denied. This is the more general frame within we can also understand the Dutch unwillingness to question the public effects of racial stereotypes. The heated present-day debates around that typically Dutch Blackface-tradition embodied by the figure of Zwarte Piet are a case in point.[9]

One of Kuper's friends, says Kuper, made an illuminating remark in this regard. After reading Kuper's account, which is more about the Second World War than about the present, she told him "she had found it ridiculously naive, as everyone already knew that the country had not been '*goed*' in the war. I had wasted my time restating a case made by many people before me."[10] Kuper comments that she had a point, but "the Dutch seemed to know they had been grey and cowardly, without wanting to think about it. There was a highbrow debate about the war full of breast-beating and remorse, and simultaneously a public sense that 'we' had been '*goed*' regardless."[11] This ambivalence seems characteristic for the Netherlands, where the Jewish community was not protected with the collective commitment found in many other European nations, but turned over to the Nazis in exceptionally large numbers (see for example Blom).

This strategy of simultaneous knowing and not-knowing again comes down to the anti-realism I discussed above: it dismisses the possibility that texts (including slogans and identifiers) relate to social reality. Again: signifier and signified are radically disconnected.

A remarkable conclusion announces itself. In neo-realist discourse, not unlike in the most innovative poststructuralist theories of language, language is seen as intensely *performative*. According to its adherents, language is not meaningful as a representation (as it only repeats the obvious) but it is a move in a power-invested play: it is an attack, or the smug advertising of one's superiority. This performativity, however, is not seen as trying to evoke response. It is understood as being a one-sided gesture, as mere autistic performance. The possibility of interaction is denied.

Edward Said's understanding of orientalism as a discourse, that is, less a representation than a strategy for defining and controlling the West's cultural other, is admirably suitable to Dutch actuality. One will wonder, however, about the effectiveness of his proposal to unmask the workings of this discourse in a public debate that already denies the representative function of any discourse (apart from the most conservative) in principle. The (fake) postmodernist neo-realist response would probably be: that is old news, *every* discourse has a political purpose—yours too—so what do you want? In this sense, for the purpose of addressing such cynicism, the poststructuralist-inspired postcolonial theory comes *too late*.

Or is it perhaps *too early*? Is it historically not yet possible to fully take it on board? If we agree that postcolonialism is a form of cultural critique, we could define postcolonialism as the project that aims at *working through* colonialism—the incessant, endless reflecting, analyzing, and deconstructing of colonialism, and its legacy (such as racism in all its varieties). This is Stuart Hall's definition of postcolonialism.[12] But if the loudest voices in this debate are the neo-realist voices described by Prins, and if the many anti-racist voices and initiatives, in education, in the neighbourhoods, are neglected, suppressed, ridiculed, and violently dismissed, rather than acknowledged, nothing can come of such an exercise. In his study *Postcolonial Melancholia*, social theorist Paul Gilroy discusses the importance of such a working-through, which implies a critique of the national colonial, racist, and anti-Semitic past that should have to be a fully integrated part of the public debate. The inability to engage in such a critique, he argues, results in the kind of violent white resentment that now dominates the talk shows and the internet, and that came to a chilling head in Norway in July 2011. In a 2006 essay on the reception of Edward Said's work in Israel, cultural theorist Ella Shohat implicitly supports this analysis. She points at the problematic position of postcolonial discourse in a national context that has not seriously engaged with *anti*-colonial discourse; it is "a 'post' without its past" (290).[13] We could use her insights (based on her analysis of the situation in Israel) to open a comparable reflection on the Dutch condition, inspired by Shohat's remarks on the United States, where postcolonial criticism was "prepared on the Left by a long series of struggles around civil rights, decolonisation, Third Worldism, Black Power and anti-imperialism."[14] In the late 1960s and 1970s, the Netherlands formed the scene of comparable protests, but on a much, much smaller scale. To what extent can we speak of a Dutch episode of anti-colonial resistance? In the absence of a successful, shared, and sustained national project of addressing the nation's involvement in colonialism, racism and anti-Semitism, we may indeed fear that postcolonial theory comes *too early*.

ON THE DUTCH UNEASE WITH HISTORY

Postcolonial theorist Homi Bhabha's understanding of postcoloniality as a specific temporality brings us to an even more fundamental level of postcolonial inquiry. Though his analysis is of course confined to anglophone cultural spaces, it enables us to get a better grasp of a second specificity of Dutch postcoloniality, and to understand why it is so hard to articulate a Dutch postcolonial cultural critique.

In *The Location of Culture*, Bhabha argues that in our postmodern, postcolonial times, the linearity of history is disturbed. He builds on Fredric Jameson's account of the postmodern as a disrupted historical narrative.[15] The "postmodern" seems to refer to a historical period (one stage in the "global transformations of capital"[16]) but this definition is then radically disturbed by that other, aesthetic or ideological definition of the postmodern, which emphasizes postmodern fragmentation. The split, schizoid subjectivity of the postmodern does not experience any continuity, but only an eternal present. Bhabha highlights the fact that this description characterizes the present-day epoch of globalization, postimperialism and transculturality. This allows him, and us, to move towards an understanding of the nature of postcoloniality as halted temporality too—as a provisional present.

The notion that history is halted makes sense for us, postcolonial critics: colonial historiography has indeed been fatally contested; notions of linearity and causality have come under attack because of the irretrievably split histories of those who were colonized or enslaved. For Bhabha, the postcolonial is a space of discontinuities. In those in-between spaces, a new kind of speaking emerges. He points out how postcolonial literature may no longer be representing a sense of continuity, but allows us to hear voices that "utter the present."[17]

I find this text strikingly illuminating for what is happening right now in the Netherlands. This perspective shows that we are really inhabiting the fragmented epoch of the postcolonial—but not in a critical sense. Complaints about the loss of an historical awareness can be heard all around us. It is suggested that we lost our historical sense because of the postmodern insistence to include the histories of minorities, including women, of the former colonies, of migrants, in our national history. As a result, it has been split, fragmented, and all but destroyed. The Dutch response has mainly been restorative.[18] It would be worthwhile to find out to what extent this conservatism should be understood in the same vein as the postimperial nostalgia analyzed by Paul Gilroy.

What is especially striking in the restorative view, is the opposition against the utterance itself. History has to be represented, it is said, but not by opening up a syncretic space of different voices, so that the minorities can be heard. The argument supporting this statement is didactic: people would not be able to relate to that plurality. As there is great need to be pragmatic and didactical, a new canon of Dutch history has been created, which now serves as the obligatory backbone of history education.[19]

I read this mistrust of dialogue and interaction as a strategy the Dutch have very often adopted to deal with otherness. In the most recurrent strategies of dealing with otherness in the Netherlands, that is, the passive forms of tolerance and the passive form of intolerance, evasion is the key attitude.[20] We might relate this attitude to the Dutch history of pillarization—that particular organization of society that situated and controlled otherness, and allowed one to evade any real interaction with one's social others.

Lately, I have encountered a few instances of the Dutch negotiation of otherness that made me aware of how the Dutch history of controlling otherness frustrates many efforts of engaging in interaction. I am talking about three very imaginative creative projects around trees and forests. The first I have discussed elsewhere: it concerns an environmental project entitled "The

Empty Spot," which consisted in the twining of an impenetrable thorny hedge around a small part of a forest, with the purpose of liberating a piece of Dutch landscape.[21] Though the event implied a thorough critique of the Dutch impulse to control and regulate, I criticized the artist's refusal to *think through* the complexities of what a non-destructive interaction between human beings and a partly natural, partly cultural landscape would look like. The artist aims at radical differentiation between man and nature, and is thus following the Dutch strategy of evasion. The second project happened a few years later, in 2008. "The Moving Forest," an event initiated by Droog Design, consisted in a series of trees that were planted in shopping carts, and left in a rather bare urban area in the North of Amsterdam. In this way, the public could create their own park wherever they went.[22]

The idea of an instant forest is appealing. However, one of the comments of the visitors was that the trees began to look frighteningly dried out after some time.[23] Apparently, there had been little thought given to the concrete need of trees: water, enough soil to root in. In spite of the project's title, that did grant agency to the trees, the project could only succeed by missing crucial interaction with the organisms that were involved.

The third project brings to the fore the shortcomings of the other two. Started in the mid-sixties, it is destined to be developed through a much longer span of time. Dutch artist, ecotect and philosopher Louis LeRoy created a green eco-cathedral in the North of the Netherlands (Mildam). With reference to chaos theory, he states that, to obtain diversity, one needs time. Lots of time. So he hopes to let his cathedral of trees, shrubs, and stones slowly, over the decades, develop into a highly diverse ecology, "through the collaboration between natural and creative human processes," as the website states. LeRoy sees humans as part of the global ecosystem, as landscape designer Jan Woudstra explains[24,] in contrast to the creator of the Empty Spot, his project does not aim to exclude people. This project of cultural critique makes me think that the Dutch impulse of evasion, to create absolute differentiations, is not merely an inability to interact, but also an inability to accept the social historicity, that is, the ever-changing, uncontrollable, dialogical nature of the world. LeRoy shows that history comprises nothing if not intense, inconclusive interaction, which then leads to increasing diversity. This approach has some affinity with Bhabha's postcolonial temporality, as it acknowledges the plurality of the present-day, and the uncontrollable productivity of interaction.

Postcolonial scholars, whether homegrown or from elsewhere, would accept the difficulty of teaching that irreducible complexity, but they would neither declare that complexity absolutely unteachable, nor want to reduce it. They would uphold people's ability to interact with complexity.[25] The tenacious, institutionalized Dutch tradition of evasion and exclusion is a serious obstacle to a postcolonial pedagogy that takes the necessity of interaction seriously. But as the examples of LeRoy, and the many other critical, oppositional voices in the public discourse on migration show, there are counter-discourses that do explore the possibilities of such complex interactions.

However, postcolonial theory is *too late* to address the Dutch reluctance to interact, and engage with the intertwining of ethnic, racial, sexual, religious, and other differences. Any political or social position that is inspired by a recognizably progressive tradition, for example by criticizing xenophobia or racism, is nowadays immediately dismissed as being stuck in what is seen as the repressive, disastrous leftist discourse of multiculturalism and political correctness. There are indeed very few platforms left that allow for anything other than a punishingly negative view of migration or multiculturalization. Notions of a shared humanity, equality, and tolerance of ethnic or religious otherness have lost their appeal, to give way to an obsession with oppositional identities. As the traditional humanist progressive voice is dismissed, I will now proceed to consider whether we can already identify a postcolonial *and posthumanist* approach in the Netherlands.

BEYOND THE POSTCOLONIAL?

Might not the paradoxical Dutch obsession with identity (as realistically transparent, as a non-realist stereotype) best be countered with the radical posthumanist refusal of identity as a productive concept? It makes good sense to see postcolonial theory as closely relating to posthumanism. As a critique of colonialism, postcolonial theory is also part of the broad project of the critique of Enlightenment. Its inquiries always lead back to a critical reconsideration of the fundamental concepts of modernity: identity, reason, humanity, the universal, etc. Postcolonial theory implies the difficult re-thinking of tenacious, still very influential affiliated discourses, such as universalism, humanism, individualism, colonialism. It therefore demands a constant critique of the basic terms through which we understand the world. Unfortunately, the popularity of the field has also, in many instances, led to its reduction to nothing more than just a method of reading with the help of certain isolated terms from the postcolonial toolbox (in-betweenness, orientalism, hybridity), and, as Bart Moore-Gilbert writes, to a routine treatment of race, gender, and class in the analysis of cultural texts.[26]

If postcoloniality should be understood in its specific sense, as partaking in the much broader critique of modernity, we might consider the Deleuzian and Italian neo-Marxist approaches as the most radically productive, and most appealing. In Edouard Glissant's work, for example, the Deleuzian emphasis on potentialities and becoming, rather than on identity, links up well with the present-day dissatisfaction with the more facile postcolonial politics of identity. In addition, the Deleuzian imagination of the world as an endless horizontal network of relations is paralleled by many actual artistic and virtual imaginations of globalization.

As we have now shifted into the age of globalization, the nature of power and repression has changed too, as philosophers Michael Hardt and Antonio Negri, authors of *Empire*, argue (3–41). The traditional Marxist framework of postcolonialism would therefore no longer be relevant. They have a point: if colonialism should be seen as a specific historical appearance of imperialism, situated in the centuries after the European age of discovery, and firmly intertwined with the need for expansion of Europe's booming capitalism, globalisation represents a new phase of imperialism. Therefore, a new conceptual framework would be needed. And again we can say, this time in a more global context, that postcolonial theory comes too late. One could argue that the postcolonial analysis of neo-colonial power, inspired by the Marxist tradition, would be too crude for the age of globalization.

But not everyone agrees with this point. The British philosopher Peter Hallward and American cultural theorist Timothy Brennan are among an energetic group of scholars who insist on the continuous need for a Marxist-inspired political analysis. Globalization may be a *new* phase of imperialism, but it is nevertheless a phase of *imperialism*, they suggest, a political and economical process that can only be studied through political and economical theories. For Hallward and Brennan, political and economical configurations must also be the starting point for a cultural analysis of this new epoch. In their eyes, the problem is that many theorists and writers fail to take the political and the economical into account. In his much-debated study *Absolutely Postcolonial*, Hallward points out that many postcolonial writers imagine globalization as governed by a singular force—that is, an autonomous force that is producing without being created itself (xi–xix, 1–19). Glissant's "Relation" would be a good example. But such a denial of agency in the dynamics of globalization, he objects, is problematic. There is a contradiction between these writers' explicit *aim* (to theorize the diversity of the world through an account of its irreducible specificity) and their actual *practice* (which denies specificity, as it imagines the world as the playing field of one singular force).[27] But without the analysis of the specific political and economical agencies in globalization, postcolonial theorizing loses its force as a cultural critique.

In the Netherlands, this debate has much less urgency than in the U.S. or the U.K. For many Dutch postcolonial scholars, who are working within the departments of languages and literature, Marxism has never been a popular

conceptual frame. Much postcolonial work in the Netherlands has been engaged with issues of language and identity, much less with the intertwining
of politics and economics with artistic and other discursive practices. As
many international scholars hold that the difference between postmodernism
and postcolonialism primarily lies in the specific postcolonial emphasis on
ethics and politics (see for example Appiah), we might suggest that there is
hardly an important body of postcolonial theorizing in the Dutch humanities
that answers to *this* definition of postcolonial theory—as an interdisciplinary
inquiry that relates cultural expressions to *particular* political and economical
developments, that acknowledges the (always *specific*) workings of (colonialist, imperialist, nationalist) power, and that partakes in the ongoing critique
of Enlightenment discourses.

The neglect of these distinctions in the Netherlands results in a certain
confusion about the nature of postcolonial theory, and its relevance. Hence, a
postmodern analysis of fragmented identities, or the study of migrant writing,
may be presented as being postcolonial theory without any further reflection.[28] There are important overlaps between the fields, but there are also crucial differences, as Gayatri Spivak argued, when objecting to the tendency to
take the (cosmopolitan) migrant as the paradigm for postcoloniality,[29] instead
of, for example, the forced labourer in India. But without this specific focus
on (neo)colonialism and imperialism, and the political and economical nature
of globalization, and without a sense of the varying forms and effects of economic deprivation, the force of postcolonial theory and criticism is reduced.

One of the outcomes of such an interdisciplinary approach might have
interesting implications for the study of postcoloniality in the Netherlands. *If*
we understand postcolonialism as a collective working-through of a colonial,
racist and anti-Semitic past, and *if* we redefine language and history as inter-
active, dialogical, and relational, and *if* we subscribe to the need to relate the
analysis of cultural expressions to the analysis of specific political and economical developments, then it follows that Dutch postcolonial scholars will
also want to focus on the specifically Dutch situation, and its public debates
and practices. It also means that they will address the actual workings of the
Dutch political field, and its effects on everyday life, popular culture, and art.

For some scholars, though, in the Netherlands and elsewhere, it is high
time to give up postcolonial theory altogether, push forward, and decide to
participate in the critique of modernity in an even more radical way. Leaving the questionable humanist accounts of identity that have been central to
postcolonial theories as well, this might open a space to explore the potentials
of posthumanism.[30] However, in spite of my observation that it is in these
new academic practices that we can find the innovative, liberating energies
that marked postcolonial theory twenty years ago, it might also be *too early*

for these new posthumanist approaches. For one thing, not just in the Netherlands, but all over Europe, we witness the re-emergence of right-wing, nationalist political parties, and their influence on a public debate, that, marked by the anxieties about globalization, is quickly absorbing the once contested statements about the threat posed by certain religious and ethnic minorities to national unity (Muslims, Roma). The academic inquiry into the posthumanist imagination seems far removed from the discourses that are needed to intervene in these urgent political developments. The actual political crisis suggests that the postcolonial insight into the interrelatedness of art, theory, and politics is more relevant than ever. Unfortunately, this same interrelatedness—that is, the fact that art and theory are also shaped by politics, including oppressive political developments—might also be one of the very causes of the relative failure of Dutch postcolonial criticism as an effective cultural critique for the twenty-first century. The publication of this book, however, represents one important initiative towards turning this situation around.

NOTES

1. For the sake of clarity, I will offer different definitions of postcolonialism as we go.
2. Simon Kuper, *Ajax, the Dutch, the War: Football in Europe During the Second World War* (London: Orion Books, 2003), 208–19.
3. In the autumn of 2011, BAN, a foundation against anti-Semitism demanded a summary procedure with the hope that the judge would oblige the major of Amsterdam and the board of the very popular Amsterdam football team, Ajax, to adopt a more active strategy against anti-Semitic slogans. The major's spokesperson responded by pointing to the major's earlier actions against the slogans, adding that it would take some time to completely ban them from the stadium (http://www.parool.nl/parool/nl/4048/AMSTERDAM-ZUIDOOST/article/detail/2912220/2011/09/16/Kort-geding-tegen-Ajax-en-Amsterdam-om-spreekkoren.dhtml; http://stichtingban.com/index.html).
4. Some (such as Evert Vermeer) hold that the misunderstanding that Ajax would be Jewish, comes from its topographical location. Before the war, supporters of other clubs, when they went to Ajax, arrived at the station "where there were a lot of Jewish street vendors. So they would say: "We're going to the Jews." (Kuper, *Ajax*, 18).
5. Kuper, *Ajax,* 18.
6. Kuper, *Ajax*, 23.
7. Kuper, *Ajax*, 216.
8. Daniel Miller, "Primitive Art and the Necessity of Primitivism to Art," in *The Myth of Primitivism: Perspectives on Art*, ed. Susan Hiller (London: Routledge, 1991), 35–54.
9. Zwarte Piet, or Black Peter/Black Pete, is the name for the helper of the very popular Saint Nicolas, the Dutch predecessor of, and counterpart to Santa Claus,

whose festivities are celebrated on December 5. The celebration—usually in the form primarily a children's party and takes place within the family, in schools and other communities—consists of the anonymous exchange of gifts that are accompanied by funny poems and practical jokes. The Saint's servant has not always been imagined as a black man dressed in a Moorish costume, but he came to be represented in this manner over the course of the nineteenth century. Originally presented as a threatening, disciplining figure, he nowadays chiefly acts as a dancing and joking buffoon. Up to this moment, the decades of critique of this racial imagery have generally met with hostility. For an analysis of the debates surrounding this event, see, for example, Bal, Brienen, Helsloot, Jordan, and Smith.

10. Kuper, *Ajax*, 12.

11. Kuper, *Ajax*, 12.

12. Stuart Hall, "When Was the 'Postcolonial'? Thinking at the Limit," in *The Postcolonial Question: Common Skies, Divided Horizons*, eds. Iain Chambers and Linda Curtis (London: Routledge, 1996), 242–60.

13. Ella Shohat, "Travelling 'Postcolonial': Allegories of Zion, Palestine and Exile," *Third Text* 20, nos. 3–4 (May/July 2006): 287–91.

14. Shohat, "Traveling," 291.

15. Homi Bhabha, *The Location of Culture* (London: Routledge, 1994), 214.

16. Bhabha, *Location*, 214.

17. Bhabha, *Location*, 215.

18. See, for example, Hans Wansink, November 8, 2008, De Volkskrant.

19. See M. Grever et al., *Controverses rond the canon* (Assen: Van Gorcum, 2006).

20. Dienke Hondius, *Gemengde huwelijken, gemengde gevoelens: Aanvaarding en ontwijking van etnisch en religieus verschil sinds 1945* (Den Haag: SdU Uitgevers, 1999). Hondius builds on the distinctions made by sociologist Peter Rose.

21. Thomas van Slobbe, *Dagboek van een lege plek* (Beek-Ubbergen, Uitgeverij wAarde, 2005); Isabel Hoving "Circumventing Openness: Creating New Senses of Dutchness," *Transit* 1, no. 1 (2005), http://german.berkeley.edu/transit/2005/TRAN SIT50909.pdf.

22. "'Moving Forest' is NL Architects' answer to the lack of green in contemporary urban environments. One might occasionally find a carefully designed patch of plants or shrubbery there, but nothing like the majestic parks and shady trees that can be found in historical city centers. So they designed a park on wheels, with trees in shopping carts. Around a small street bench, the public can rearrange their own little park and thus create a nice green view and a bit of shade." http://www.droog.com/presentationsevents/detail/boombench---moving-forest-by-nl-architects.

23. See artist Wildplukker's blog, including a picture of some of the trees, that, after three weeks, indeed look rather dried out. http://www.wildplukker.nl/?m=200810. Digital magazine *Environmental Graffiti* counters such a critique by stating: "And those worried about the plight of the trees used in Moving Forest will be happy to know they found good homes with local residents once the festival was over, just in time for Christmas." http://www.environmentalgraffiti.com/featured/amsterdams -moving-forest/4880. The reassurance is weakened by the thought that most Christmas trees do not long survive Christmas.

24. http://www.stichtingtijd.nl/pdf/Gaku2008-1-Woudstra.pdf.

25. Gayatri Chakravorty Spivak in particular insists on the importance of such a pedagogy. See *The Death of a Discipline*.

26. Bart Moore-Gilbert, *Postcolonial Theory: Contexts, Practices, Politics* (London: Verso, 1997).

27. Peter Hallward, *Absolutely Postcolonial Writing Between the Singular and the Specific* (Manchester: Manchester University Press, 2001).

28. Indeed, Dutch literary scholars may read postcolonial or migrant writing by addressing postmodern insights into the nature of identity and language, while claiming to practice postcolonialism. Though this in itself says nothing about the quality of their reading, the field of postcolonial theorizing is diminished by neglecting its specific history.

29. Gayatri Chakravorty Spivak, *Outside in the Teaching Machine* (New York: Routledge, 1993), 217.

30. For example, in Deleuzian-inspired approaches or in posthumanist approaches in the booming field of ecocriticism.

BIBLIOGRAPHY

Appiah, K. A. "Is the Post—in Postmodernism the Post—in Postcolonial?" *Critical Inquiry* 17 (1991): 336–57.

Bal, Mieke. "Zwarte Piet's bal masqué." In *Questions of Tradition*, edited by M. S. Phillips and G. Schochet, 110–51. Toronto: University of Toronto Press, 2004.

Bhabha, Homi. *The Location of Culture.* London: Routledge, 1994.

Blom, J. C. H. "The Persecution of the Jews in the Netherlands in a Comparative International Perspective." In *Dutch Jewish History II*, edited by Jozeph Michman, 273–89. Assen: Van Gorcum, 1989.

Brienen, R. P. "Types and Stereotypes: Zwarte Piet and His Early Modern Sources." In *Dutch Racism*, edited by P. Essed and I. Hoving. Amsterdam & New York: Rodopi, forthcoming.

Gilroy, Paul. *Postcolonial Melancholia.* New York: Columbia University Press, 2005.

Grever, M., E. Jonker, K. Ribbens, and P. Stuurman. *Controverses rond de canon.* Assen: Van Gorcum, 2006.

Hall, Stuart. "When Was the 'Postcolonial'? Thinking at the Limit." In *The Postcolonial Question: Common Skies, Divided Horizons*, edited by Iain Chambers and Linda Curtis, 242–60. London: Routledge, 1996.

Hallward, Peter. *Absolutely Postcolonial: Writing between the Singular and the Specific.* Manchester: Manchester University Press, 2001.

Hardt, Michael, and Negri, Antonio. *Empire.* Cambridge, Mass.: Harvard University Press, 2000.

Helsloot, John. "Het feest: De strijd om Zwarte Piet." In *Veranderingen van het alledaagse, 1950–2000*, edited by Isabel Hoving, Hester Dibbits and Marlou Schrover, 249–71. Den Haag: SdU Uitgevers, 2005.

Hondius, Dienke. *Gemengde huwelijken, gemengde gevoelens: Aanvaarding en ontwijking van etnisch en religieus verschil sinds 1945.* Den Haag: SdU Uitgevers, 1999.

Hoving, Isabel. "Circumventing Openness: Creating New Senses of Dutchness." *Transit* 1, no. 1 (2005), http://german.berkeley.edu/transit/2005/TRANSIT50909 .pdf, accessed November 25, 2011.

Jordan, Joseph. "The Enunciation of the Nation." In *Dutch Racism*, edited by P. Essed and I. Hoving. Amsterdam & New York: Rodopi, forthcoming.

Kuper, Simon. *Ajax, the Dutch, the War: Football in Europe During the Second World War.* London: Orion Books, 2003.

Miller, Daniel. "Primitive Art and the Necessity of Primitivism to Art." In *The Myth of Primitivism: Perspectives on Art*, edited by Susan Hiller, 35–54. London: Routledge, 1991.

Moore-Gilbert, Bart. *Postcolonial Theory: Contexts, Practices, Politics.* London: Verso, 1997.

Prins, Baukje. *Voorbij de onschuld: Het debat over de multiculturele samenleving.* Amsterdam: van Gennep, 2000.

Said, Edward W. *Orientalism.* New York: Pantheon Books, 1978.

Shohat, Ella. "Travelling 'Postcolonial': Allegories of Zion, Palestine and Exile." *Third Text* 20, nos. 3–4 (May/July 2006): 287–91.

Slobbe, Thomas van. *Dagboek van een lege plek.* Beek-Ubbergen: Uitgeverij wAarde, 2005.

Spivak, Gayatri Chakravorty. *The Death of a Discipline*, 2nd ed. New York: Columbia University Press, 2003.

Spivak, Gayatri Chakravorty. *Outside in the Teaching Machine.* New York: Routledge, 1993.

Woudstra, John. "The Eco-Cathedral: Lous Le Roy's Expression of a 'Free Landscape Architecture.'" *Die Gartenkunst* (May 2008): 185–202, http://www.stichting tijd.nl/pdf/Gaku2008-1-Woudstra.pdf, accessed October 7, 2010.

Chapter Four

The "Ends" of Postcolonialism

Theo D'haen

With the election of the Democrat Barack Obama as the President of the United States in 2008, it would seem that political emancipation in the United States has reached the point where it can no longer automatically assume the cloak of racism, as has been the case historically in that country. Still, the rise of the Tea Party as an important factor in American politics and the concomitant hardening of views of the Republican Party in the United States over the last few years have made it very difficult for Obama to pass into legislation many of the issues he had campaigned on during the 2008 election, with the result that many of the hopes his election raised have been much diminished. Moreover, the continuing, and even deepening, economic crisis since 2008 has negatively affected the material conditions of US minorities, along with the prosperity of the entire United States. What matters for my purposes here, however, is that in the cultural and educational arenas Obama's election signaled at one and the same time the ultimate triumph of multiculturalism and its end as a useful instrument with which to attack the hegemonic structures of an American society deemed inherently racially oppressive.

Although "multiculturalism" theoretically presupposed the equality of all cultures, at least as its practical goal within a particular state formation, in practice it served to challenge what was perceived as the majority culture, in opposition to which it profiled itself. This profiling required casting minority cultures collectively as eternal "underdogs" to a "naturally" discriminatory majority culture. Multiculturalism, then, sought to empower minority cultures by having them gain parity with the majority culture, either by redrawing that majority culture so as to allow for fair or equal representation of all constituent cultures of a particular nation or state, or, alternatively, by casting them as singular, separate, even essentialist traditions, next to, but equal with, a majority tradition decried as equally essentialist. By empowering himself as an individual Obama empowered not only the African American minority, but also its culture, of which he is usually seen as a representative. At least potentially he empowered all other US "minorities" too, thus effectively disempowering multiculturalism as oppositional strategy, and in effect rendering it superfluous in its original American context.

Of course, one could go on "practicing" multiculturalism as of old, but, using the terminology of the American anthropologist David Scott in a 2005 article, with the election of Obama multiculturalism passed from being "critique" to being "method."[1] Or, to put it another way, again in a formulation used by Scott, multiculturalism still had *meaning*, but it no longer had a *point* or, to use my own terminology from the title to the present article: by reaching its "end," or goal, it seemed to have also come to its "end," or demise. It is a paradigm that had served its purpose, but that was now superseded. At best, it would survive as an approach, or a method, allowing for the continual accumulation of ever further evidence to support its originally revolutionary or paradigm-shifting claims, but it would no longer be at the cutting edge of theoretical innovation in literary or cultural studies. Undoubtedly, analyses of multicultural works, by African Americans, Native Americans, Asian Americans, Latinos, and so on would continue to be produced in countless numbers, each and every one of them potentially interesting in itself, but they would merely add bulk to an already existing body, they would not fundamentally redraw its contours.

Although I have used his terminology to discuss multiculturalism, in the article I just referred to David Scott was not immediately concerned with multiculturalism, nor with things American, but rather with postcolonialism. For Scott there was a clear link between postcolonialism and multiculturalism, in that (writing from a conspicuously US vantage point) he situated the birth of both precisely in the wake of the emancipatory movements of the 1960s and '70s, and more specifically in the so-called culture wars resulting from them in the US. Putting things in a nutshell, Scott saw the founding texts of postcolonialism, most specifically Edward Said's *Orientalism*, but we might add to that the early work of Gayatri Spivak, as well as that of Sander Gilman, Homi Bhabha, Henry Louis Gates (and other contributors to the path-breaking *"Race," Writing, and Difference* volume originally published as a *Critical Inquiry* issue in 1992), as a spin-off, so to speak, of emerging multiculturalism American style.[2] These texts, he implied, again assuming a specific US vantage point, involved a transfer of multicultural thinking relative to the United States to the world outside. This transfer was aided by the so-called linguistic and cultural turns in the humanities, heavily influenced by French structuralist and poststructuralist thinking, and particularly that of Michel Foucault, Jacques Derrida and Jacques Lacan, whereby the emphasis came to lie on issues of representation, rather than on the analyses of actual policies. The cultural became political, so to speak. For Scott, this turn also marked the break between anticolonialism and postcolonialism. Anticolonialism (largely located outside the US) agitated for actual resistance to colonialism, the achievement of independence, and the act of nation-building immediately subsequent to independence. In other words, the anticolonial engaged with issues of real power. Postcolonialism was concerned with symbolic power, the power over the word, the image, a culture's "imaginary." Partially, Scott noted, this shift was the result also of disappointment with the lack of real achievements on the ground, be it on the level of the actual emancipation of minorities in the US, or be it with the relative failure of many, or most, newly independent states issuing from former colonies to make good on their initial promises.

In multiculturalism the cultural turn took the form of "deconstructing," using the particularly American form of French poststructuralist thinking introduced to, and largely shaped in, the US by the literary theoretician Paul de Man, the racial and ethnic prejudices at work in canonical American literature, and the promotion of the work of minority authors. In a parallel movement, postcolonialism, Scott has it, "drew its identity from the (largely Foucaultian) program of unmasking Eurocentric essentialisms at work in the West's representations of non-European ideas and behaviors."[3] In addition, it promoted the work of "postcolonial" authors, that is, of those non-European (and non-United States) authors that in their works were seen to subscribe to a similar process of unmasking. Most often, such creative unmasking took the form of re-writing those European classics that in a postcolonial reading were seen to strongly reveal the "Eurocentric essentialisms at work in the West's representations of non-European ideas and behaviors."[4] Favorite among these, at least in the anglophone world, which is also where the term and the practice of postcolonialism originated, were, and continue to be, Shakespeare's *The Tempest*, Daniel Defoe's *Robinson Crusoe*, Charlotte Bronte's *Jane Eyre*, and Joseph Conrad's *Heart of Darkness*. In its most lapidary and popular phrasing, this was "the empire writing back"—which is also, and not by coincidence, (almost) the title of a celebrated article by Salman Rushdie as well as of what I can only assume to have been the earliest "manual" of postcolonialism, by Bill Ashcroft, Gareth Griffiths and Helen Tiffin.[5] As the modeling of the phrase "the empire writes back" upon the popular expression "to talk back (to someone)" shows, this positioning of postcolonialism clearly implied an antagonistic move.

The title of Scott's article is "The Social Construction of Postcolonial Studies," and his whole point was that just as postcolonial studies, multiculturalism had been out to demonstrate the "social constructedness" of the

"Eurocentric essentialisms" alluded to earlier, so postcolonial studies, like multiculturalism, was itself a socially constructed discourse fitting a particular constellation of time and place, to wit the 1980s and '90s (and, we might add, in the United States). Partially, Scott was concerned with the very process of "social construction" itself, and what he had to say about the postcolonial was in fact only an instantiation of his more general quibble with this even more theoretical concept. Basically, what he argued was that the 1980s and '90s were precisely the moment where *all* theories and certainties hitherto valid were being challenged as being "constructed"—this implied, in fact, a translation into social science terms of what in literary and cultural studies used to be called postmodernism, and which likewise insisted on the ultimate "linguisticity" of all "realities." Drawing upon the work of Ian Hacking, and particularly upon the latter's *The Social Construction of What?*, Scott argued that once a particular paradigm has become commonly accepted, there is no "critical bite" to it anymore, because it has lost its "contrast effect" to the earlier paradigms it initially set out to attack, undermine, and replace. With regard to social constructionism, then, Scott remarked that "if we are all largely constructionists now, if we all subscribe more or less to the view that human action always takes place under a description and that such descriptions are historical (and therefore as located in social, institutional, and material circumstances) as the actions they describe, little critical point may obtain in staging a constructionist confrontation."[6] In other words, one might go on arguing and even proving the social constructedness of everything, but even though such exercises might have meaning, they no longer would have a point. As Scott saw "postcolonial studies (or discourse, or theory or criticism or whatever)" as a "subspecies of social and cultural constructionism," for him the moment had also come where postcolonialism had lost its critical bite.

Following Hacking, but also R.G. Collingwood and Quentin Skinner, Scott then went on to argue that what was at stake in all this was not so much the demonstrable truth or falsity of the particular views defended or attacked, but rather the positions they occupied in an ongoing question-and-answer dialogue. In other words, whatever the meaning such statements might have, it was the point they made in the ongoing dialogue that mattered. If social constructionism had been the answer to a particular question, or set of questions, relevant in the final quarter of the twentieth century, it might no longer be so to another, a changed set of questions relevant to a more immediate present. Scott indeed argued that with regard to postcolonial studies "the *demand* in the present had altered."[7] He summarized this as follows:

In the 1980s, when postcolonial studies was becoming established as a going scholarly domain in the North Atlantic academy (what I call the moment of postcolonialism), its project was to criticize (in the hermeneutical language of the day, to *deconstruct*) colonial knowledge and its assumptions. . . . Postcolonial social constructionism could claim a critical contrast effect with an older paradigm of discourse about colonialism (what I call the moment of anticolonialism) insofar as it enabled the recognition of a level of unproblematized assumptions governing it, teleological and essentialist assumptions largely, regarding history, politics, subjectivity, gender, race, and so on. As opposed to anticolonialism's description of the problem of colonialism in terms of the demand for political decolonization, postcolonialism commended its redescription as an epistemological problem, a problem about the politics of representation, about the relation between knowledge and power.

On this view, anticolonialism and postcolonialism are not progressively successive theoretical strategies, one providing better answers to questions addressed by the other. Contrary to the anti-essentialist dogma, postcolonialism's social constructionism is not better theory than anticolonialism's essentialism. Rather, to use Collingwood's terms, anticolonialism and postcolonialism should be understood as occupying different question-answer complexes; or as Skinner might put it, they are critical moves located in different arguments, interventions into different and differently constituted problem spaces. My concern, though, has been with whether the questions that have animated postcolonialism's genealogical critique of colonial knowledge continue to be questions worth having answers to. I wonder whether the historical context of problems that produced the postcolonial effect as a critical effect has not now altered such that the yield of these questions is no longer what it was. I wonder, in other words, whether postcolonialism has not lost its point, and become normalized as a strategy for the mere accumulation of meaning.[8]

His answer, not surprisingly I think, was that it had. To illustrate his point Scott referred to the research of Ann Stoler and Frederick Cooper, both Americans, the first an anthropologist, the second a historian. Jointly and together, these two scholars had been pleading, in their various publications, for extending the reach of postcolonial research to include, next to the colonies, also the "mother countries," seeing both as intimately tied by the bonds of colonialism, and as deeply changed, mutually so, by the colonial encounter and the colonial past. They did so starting from the critique that the dichotomizing of colony and mother country had been imposed by the colonizers, and hence was a "social construction" reflecting a "European essentialism."[9] Hence it was the all-comprising relation of "empire" that should be studied, Stoler and Cooper argued, rather than just the colony, or just the mother country. This plea, and the argument underlying it, had been very positively received, certainly so in the US, where it had been welcomed as a meaningful re-orientation of postcolonial studies. The reason I mention their work, and particularly that of Stoler, is that it is primarily concerned with the Dutch "empire," and particularly the relationship between the Netherlands and the

Dutch East Indies. Moreover, Stoler regularly and famously also draws on Dutch literary sources, such as for instance Multatuli and Couperus, for her analyses.[10]

Scott did not deny that there was "meaning" to Stoler's and Cooper's undertaking, in that it adduced more evidence to existing scholarship, and broadened the scope of postcolonialism beyond the anglophone world. He did deny, however, that it was a "fresh" departure for postcolonial studies in the sense of a radical paradigm shift. In particular, he critiqued Stoler and Cooper for not having considered the "point" of their enterprise. As Scott himself demonstrated, the rise of postcolonialism, with the work of Said, Spivak and Bhabha and others, in the 1980s answered a then present need born from changing political, economic and cultural circumstances. Stoler and Cooper failed to take into concern the more present need for what they were doing; theirs was a historical undertaking, not a critical one for their own present. For Scott,

> how colonialism ought to be understood for the present we live in has always to be a question we formulate and argue out, rather than something we generate abstractly on the basis of theoretical inclusiveness or ethnographic broadmind-edness. . . . It seems to me that unless we persistently ask what the point is of our investigations of colonialism for the postcolonial present, what the question is to which we are fashioning an answer, what the argument is in which we are making a move and staking a claim, unless we systematically make this part of our strategy of inquiry, we are only too likely to slide from criticism of the present to "normal" science.[11]

I encountered Scott's article at a particularly inconvenient moment. I had just been reading Stoler's *Carnal Knowledge and Imperial Power: Race and the Intimate in Colonial Rule*, a book that is primarily concerned with the former Dutch East Indies, present-day Indonesia, and which regularly refers to and cites Dutch colonial authors, amongst whom the great late nineteenth- and early twentieth-century writer Louis Couperus, with an eye to mounting a plea for a more comparative and more extensive, or if you want a more comprehensive and inclusive approach to postcolonialism, and this by way of a comparative postcolonial reading of two colonial classics published in 1900, Couperus' *De stille kracht* (The Hidden Force) and Joseph Conrad's *Lord Jim*, something which Pamela Pattynama, one of the contributors to his book, has also undertaken in her work.[12] My title would have been "unwritten empires," and I would have argued for nuancing existing theories of postco-lonialism by studying works from literatures hitherto relatively neglected, at least from an international "postcolonial" stance, alongside the already much studied English, and to a lesser extent French, colonial classics. However, after having, quite by coincidence, read Scott, I started to wonder what the "point" would have been of such an exercise, except adding to the already extensive body of postcolonial criticism. What would have been the purchase of the exercise on the then present, on our then present?

This was also where the parallelisms with multiculturalism struck me. If multiculturalism and postcolonialism constituted largely analogous answers to the same question, yet applied to different circumstances and localities, perhaps what stood out so glaringly for multiculturalism with the election of Obama also pertained for postcolonialism? Specifically, I started to wonder whether the "antagonistic" or oppositional stance implied by "the postcolonial" still had any validity for the more recent present. Now obviously I was not the only one to have explored this question. In fact, at least two then recent publications ventured onto the same terrain, and things had not stood still on the side of creative writing either.

The two publications I had in mind are two collective volumes weighing the state of postcolonial studies, especially in relation to then recent developments, at the beginning of the twenty-first century. The first of these appeared in 2005, and is also the volume in which featured the article by David Scott that I have been quoting so extensively. The volume's very title, *Postcolonial Studies and Beyond*, suggested a crisis in postcolonial studies that needed to be overcome, as well as the determination to do so. Indeed, after having briefly summarized the various contributions to the volume, by such well-known practitioners of postcolonialism as Peter Hulme, Vilashini Cooppan, Jean Comaroff, Timothy Brennan, Rob Nixon, Laura Chrisman, Robert Stam and Ella Shohat, Frederick Cooper, and Neil Lazarus, next to others, the editors concluded that:

> Taken together, the forceful critiques and inventive new applications of post-colonial methods on display in this volume suggest that the field has the resources and the momentum to reinvent itself and broaden its area of productive engagement. Indeed, stringent assessments of the limitations of the postcolonial paradigm prove essential to the work of assessing and creating its future directions. Our goal here has not been to defend the territory of postcolonialism, or the term, but to survey its usefulness in the past and meditate on its uses in the future, keeping a wary eye on narrow constructions of postcolonial studies too quick to paint it as passé, involuted, ethnocentric, or irrelevant.[13]

In what followed they raised, while at the same denying them any "galvaniz[ing]" influence on their own enterprise, the specters of "an intellectual crisis in the field" and "the challenge of globalization" as the causes for such "narrow constructions" of postcolonialism as they rejected. In response, they advocated a return to "a broad and ecumenical sense of the genealogy of the field" as the best guarantee for an "urgent, wide-ranging, and productive future for postcolonial studies."[14] Hence they also approvingly mentioned that "[their] contributors here expand the project of postcolonial studies because they extend similar insights to new objects (geographically, methodologically), but particularly because their essays recapture the original importance of postcolonial analysis as a complement to other kinds of engaged intellectual and political work."[15] Notwithstanding the paean to the "original importance of postcolonial analysis," all that was being advocated here was precisely the kind of postcolonial work that Scott, in his essay rather towards the end of the same volume, decried as "method" rather than "criticism." To be more specific, postcolonialism, in Scott's reading of it, had sprung into being as a strategy not so much for reading the past as for reading its own present. Through its interpretation of the colonial past, both history and representation, and of the contemporary works thought to be directly related to that past, it had served to position its practitioners in *their* present. In other words, it had been a strategic move towards a cultural/political end, and hence an instrument along Foucaultian lines to wrest the power of the word from those that had traditionally held it. "Postcolonial analysis" along these lines had had a point in its original context, but the world had moved on since then, and now, I suggest leading on from Scott, "the original importance of postcolonial analysis" had itself become the object of historical analysis from newer vantage points, relevant to our own present.[16]

The second volume that I briefly want to discuss is *The Postcolonial and the Global*, published in 2008, and edited by Revathi Krishnaswamy and John C. Hawley.[17] This book squarely posed the very question of the contemporary relevance of postcolonialism in the relationship raised in its title. In fact, "the global," or globalization, was precisely one of those newer vantage points that I hinted at just now. The rise of globalization reflected, next to many other things, the emergence of different constellations (economic, political, cultural), than those that had pertained at the time of the rise of the postcolonial. The world of the global was no longer marked by the binaries of colonizer/colonized, ex-colony/imperial center, Third World/First World, etc. Instead, it was a place where the relevant buzzwords were "sans-papiers," Wall Street or London City billionaire bonuses, diaspora and cosmopolitanism, where the dividing lines ran between those that had access to all forms of modern communication technology, that were extremely mobile, and that were part of a global financial, political and intellectual elite, and those that were excluded from all this. *The Postcolonial and the Global* tried to determine the usefulness of the postcolonial in an age of globalization. In its most optimistic formulation perhaps, Krishnaswamy in his introduction to the volume contended that "the two seem to have become one and the same so that to be global is first and foremost to be postcolonial and to be postcolonial is always already to be global."[18] The introduction then ran the gamut of the possible relationships between the postcolonial and the global as predicated by a number of prominent scholars. That these were mainly of the postcolonial bent is I think significant of the real relationship obtaining between the two phenomena discussed: for the "globals" postcolonialism was not a problem, as in a sense it floated below their horizon, whereas for the "postcolonials" globalization theory was a problem, as it threatened to displace them. In other words, the postcolonial paradigm was on the defensive against the global.

Krishnaswamy concluded his introduction by stating that in *The Postcolonial and the Global* he and his co-editor "had tried to make it possible for all those who believed in the possibility of a decolonized planetarity to clarify the connections, acknowledge the conflicts, and recognize the complicities between the postcolonial and the global."[19] With his final sentence he even tried to inscribe the postcolonial into a still more recent approach when he expressed the hope that "this exercise will help scholars as well as students chart new directions for producing knowledge about the fate of our fragile planet and its inhabitants."[20] Whether it was in relation then to the ecological, as in that very last phrase, or the global, as in the next to last, it was clear that postcolonialism here was no longer in the lead, but had come to be seen rather as ancillary. Postcolonialism no longer was the answer to a pressing question in the present, but rather had turned into a historical formation. The question "in question" no longer was how (former) colonial subjects relate with and to (former) imperial masters, but rather how in a world in which we are all "postcolonial" already, the newer formations can be accurately described.

My contention would be that at least one form such description took, was the advocacy of certain forms of local belonging. At first sight, this may have seemed rather ironical in an age of globalization, until we stop to think that what we are facing here is an instance of glocalization: the transformation into local varieties of what are world-wide phenomena. In an essay entitled "Nations and Literatures in the Age of Globalization," in *The Cultures of Globalization*, a 1998 volume edited by Fredric Jameson and Masao Miyoshi, Paik Nak-Chung pleaded from a theoretical point of view the necessity of a Korean national literature for that country's literary production to access the level of the global—a plea that reminded me somewhat of the Flemish author August Vermeylen's famous exhortation at the beginning of the twentieth century that in order to become European Flemings would first have to be Flemish![21] I knew too little (which is to say nothing!) of Korean literature to adequately judge the claims of Nak-Chung. I did however see some parallel developments in British, and perhaps also in Dutch and Flemish writing.

With regard to the British situation, I was thinking specifically of the emergence of what is now known as "Black British Writing," and of a novel such as Zadie Smith's *White Teeth* (2000).[22] Black British Writing was a term that first appeared in the early 1990s with reference to Afro-Caribbean and Indo-Caribbean writing, but that since then had come to be applied to all writing produced by "non-whites" in Britain, that is to say largely the descendants of non-white ex-colonized, regardless of their origin, so next to Caribbean also African and Asian, but even to descendants of ex-colonizers. Retrospectively, the term also had come to cover much of what in the past had been categorized as Commonwealth literature, literature in English, literatures in English, and, indeed, postcolonial literature. The distinctive factor was the "British," which locally grounded part of the earlier more extensive coinages that, in varying degrees, indicated precisely the remoteness from Britain of what they covered. James Procter and John McLeod rehearsed the history of "black" immigration from the Caribbean in *Writing Black Britain, 1948–1998* and *Postcolonial London: Rewriting the Metropolis*, respectively.[23] The South Asian presence was recounted in Susheila Nasta's *Home Truths: Fictions of the South Asian Diaspora in Britain*.[24] Sukhdev Sandhu covered both black and Asian writers in *London Calling*.[25]

Zadie Smith, herself the daughter of a Jamaican mother and a white English father, in *White Teeth* largely rehearsed the story of "black" immigration to Britain, and in what is arguably her main character, Irie Jones, created a distant double of herself. However, she also filled out another part of the "black" immigration story of Britain by introducing the Iqbal family, originally from Bangladesh, but like the Joneses settled in North London. If we add to this the Jewish Chalfen family, and the various other characters of Arab and other descent featured in Smith's novel, we got a fair idea of Britain's multicultural make-up. The interesting part in all this was that the novel reveled in the kind of Bhabhian hybridity that usually was being flaunted as postcolonial par excellence, but that in this particular instance went to underscore a very local sense of belonging: to a specific neighborhood, Neasden, and to a particularly British sense of identity. However, this was a British identity marked, precisely, by the impure and mixed rather than the pure. And this is also what Irie's daughter would be, fathered by any one of the Iqbal brothers, yet legally fatherless as Irie does not marry, with the Chalfen son as her mother's lover and therefore her substitute father, and bearing the "arch"-English name Jones, from her maternal grandfather not coincidentally named "Archie" Jones, a man without racial prejudice. In fact, in *White Teeth* there was no other "British" identity but this, which is also to say that Smith cast her characters, and certainly Irie, not as separate from the run of "normal" Britishers, but rather as one of them. In the same way her novel did not profile itself as particularly "Other" than any other British novel; instead, it deliberately inserted itself in the "national" body of British writing. This also seems to have been the overwhelming reaction from the literary critical community. Consider, for instance, the opening of Jan Lowe's 2001 article "No More Lonely Londoners," from *Small Axe*, a journal edited, interestingly, by the same David Scott that we met before: "*White Teeth* includes themes of Britain's imperial and colonial relationships with Africa, Asia and the Caribbean, and this gives it a stake in the literatures of those countries. . . . Enigmatically, it is also a deeply English novel."[26] Lowe spent the rest of the article demonstrating why *White Teeth* was so English, and concluded that

> the key to explaining the importance of the novel and why it has made such a huge impact in Britain, is found in decoding its semiotics, couched so deeply in popular language rendered in an extremely formal and sensitive literary style, of what it was for a new non-privileged generation (born in the mid 1970s) to grow up in London in the fissures of the Thatcher era when an older Britain was fragmenting or cracking up but its most nationalistic patriots were pretending the opposite by taking on the Falklands War.[27]

Anita Mathias claimed in *Commonweal* that "Zadie Smith, the daughter of a Jamaican immigrant to Britain, continues the enterprise of giving us the view from the margins, as she sweeps Jamaican and Bangladeshi immigrants into mainstream literature in English."[28] While both critics paid lip service to the colonial or postcolonial antecedents of Smith, they both finally came down on the side of her novel's "Englishness."

Following in the wake of Salman Rushdie, Hanif Kureishi, Beryl Gilroy and others, Smith's *White Teeth* seemed to me to have helped achieve for British literature what Obama's election did for the United States: the transcendence of the antagonistic *raison d'être* of postcolonialism and multiculturalism, and the healing of a thitherto torn national body. This healing, however, did not imply a simple falling back into the old pieties of the nation-as-was. Instead, it signalled the advent of a nation transformed, local, glocal, global.

I think it would bear looking into whether in Dutch-language writing, both in the Netherlands and in Belgium, as well as in writing about Dutch-language literature, there are signs of a re-alignment such as I tried to sketch with respect to British writing. Of course, we can go on practicing "postcolonialism" in its more predictable format here too, accumulating ever further material on the Dutch and Belgian colonial pasts as represented in these literatures, and obviously this has its merits, but the question, to return to Scott's line of reasoning again, is whether this is really still addressing the "real questions" of our present times. Perhaps instead we should be asking how our literatures, and our ways of studying them, fit, or answer, issues of national and international belonging, including belonging to newly emerging trans- or postnational cultural entities such as "Europe." If not necessarily the "end" of postcolonialism altogether, as many of the issues and concerns raised by Smith are eminently postcolonial ones, I think this means at least the end of a certain kind of postcolonialism that risks keeping us locked up in what seem to be at heart bygone discussions.[29]

NOTES

1. David Scott, "The Social Construction of Postcolonial Studies," in *Postcolonial Studies and Beyond*, ed. Ania Loomba et al. (Durham, NC: Duke University Press, 2005), 385–400.

2. Henry Louis Gates Jr. and Kwame Anthony Appiah, eds., *"Race," Writing, and Difference* (Chicago: The University of Chicago Press, 1992).

3. Scott, "Social Construction," 389.

4. Scott, "Social Construction," 389.

5. Bill Ashcroft, Gareth Griffiths, and Helen Tiffin, *The Empire Writes Back: Theory and Practice in Post-Colonial Literatures* (London: Routledge, 1989).

6. Scott, "Social Construction," 388.

7. Scott, "Social Construction," 391.

8. Scott, "Social Construction," 391–92.

9. Scott pursues a similar argument in his *Conscripts of Modernity: The Tragedy of Colonial Enlightenment* (Durham, NC: Duke University Press, 2004).

10. Ann Laura Stoler, *Carnal Knowledge and Imperial Power: Race and the Intimate in Colonial Rule* (Berkeley: University of California Press, 2002).

11. Scott, "Social Construction," 399.

12. Pamela Pattynama, "Secrets and Danger: Interracial Sexuality in Louis Couperus's *The Hidden Force* and Dutch Colonial Culture around 1900," in *Domesticating the Empire: Race, Gender, and Family Life in French and Dutch Colonialism*, ed. Julia Clancy-Smith and Frances Gouda, (Charlottesville: University Press of Virginia), 84–107.

13. Ania Loomba et al., eds. *Postcolonial Studies and Beyond* (Durham, NC: Duke University Press, 2005), 35.

14. Loomba et al., *Postcolonial Studies and Beyond*, 35.

15. Loomba et al., *Postcolonial Studies and Beyond*, 34.

16. *Postcolonial Studies and Beyond* has also been discussed, far more critically than I do here, by Elleke Boehmer and Rosinka Chaudhuri in their introduction to *The Indian Postcolonial* (London: Routledge, 2010), published after the present article was completed. Boehmer and Chaudhuri also speak of announcements of the demise of the postcolonial as a constitutive condition of the postcolonial. In other words, Boehmer and Chaudhuri insist that the postcolonial has always already anticipated its imminent sell-by date.

17. Revathi Krishnaswamy and John C. Hawley, eds., *The Postcolonial and the Global* (Minneapolis: University of Minnesota Press, 2008).

18. Krishnaswamy and Hawley, *Postcolonial and Global*, 3.

19. Krishnaswamy and Hawley, *Postcolonial and Global*, 16.

20. Krishnaswamy and Hawley, *Postcolonial and Global*, 16.

21. Paik Nan-Chung, "Nations and Literature in the Age of Globalization," in *The Cultures of Globalization*, ed. Fredric Jameson and Masao Miyoshi (Durham, NC: Duke University Press, 1998).

22. Zadie Smith, *White Teeth* (London: Penguin, 2000).

23. James Procter, *Writing Black Britain, 1948–1998* (Manchester: Manchester University Press, 2000); John McLeod, *Postcolonial London: Rewriting the Metropolis* (London: Routledge, 2004).

24. Susheila Nasta, *Home Truths: Fictions of the South Asian Diaspora in Britain* (London: Palgrave Macmillan, 2002).

25. Sukhdev Sandhu, *London Calling: How Black and Asian Writers Imagined a City* (London: HarperCollins, 2003).

26. Jan Lowe, "No More Lonely Londoners," *Small Axe* 9 (March 2001): 166.

27. Lowe, "No More Lonely Londoners," 179–80.

28. Anita Mathias, "View from the Margins," *Commonweal* (August 11, 2000), 27.

29. The present essay was written in the immediate wake of Obama's election and long before the ethnically inspired riots that wracked London and a number of other British cities in the summer of 2011. I may have been overly optimistic in my assumptions and conclusions, however, as I think my readers will realize, these were also inspired by hope.

BIBLIOGRAPHY

Ashcroft, Bill, Gareth Griffiths, and Helen Tiffin. *The Empire Writes Back: Theory and Practice in Post-Colonial Literatures.* London: Routledge, 1989.

Boehmer, Elleke, and Rosinka Chaudhuri, eds. *The Indian Postcolonial.* London: Routledge, 2010.

Gates, Henry Louis, Jr., and Kwame Anthony Appiah, eds. *"Race," Writing, and Difference.* Chicago: The University of Chicago Press, 1992.

Krishnaswamy, Revathi, and John C. Hawley, eds. *The Postcolonial and the Global.* Minneapolis: University of Minnesota Press, 2008.

Loomba, Ania, Suvir Kaul, Matti Bunzl, Antoinette Burton, and Jed Esty, eds. *Postcolonial Studies and Beyond.* Durham, NC: Duke University Press, 2005.

Lowe, Jan. "No More Lonely Londoners." *Small Axe* 9 (March 2001): 166–80.

Mathias, Anita. "View from the Margins." *Commonweal* (August 11, 2000): 27.

McLeod, John. *Postcolonial London: Rewriting the Metropolis.* London: Routledge, 2004.

Nan-Chung, Paik. "Nations and Literature in the Age of Globalization." In *The Cultures of Globalization*, edited by Fredric Jameson, and Masao Miyoshi, 218–29. Durham, NC: Duke University Press, 1998.

Nasta, Susheila. *Home Truths: Fictions of the South Asian Diaspora in Britain.* London: Palgrave Macmillan, 2002.

Pattynama, Pamela. "Secrets and Danger: Interracial Sexuality in Louis Couperus's *The Hidden Force* and Dutch Colonial Culture around 1900." In *Domesticating the Empire: Race, Gender, and Family Life in French and Dutch Colonialism*, edited by Julia Clancy-Smith and Frances Gouda, 84–107. Charlottesville: University Press of Virginia.

Procter, James. *Writing Black Britain, 1948–1998.* Manchester: Manchester University Press, 2000.

Sandhu, Sukhdev. *London Calling: How Black and Asian Writers Imagined a City.* London: HarperCollins, 2003.

Scott, David. "The Social Construction of Postcolonial Studies." In *Postcolonial Studies and Beyond*, edited by Ania Loomba, Suvir Kaul, Matti Bunzl, Antoinette Burton, and Jed Esty, 385–400. Durham, NC: Duke University Press, 2005.

Smith, Zadie. *White Teeth.* London: Penguin, 2000.

Stoler, Ann Laura. *Carnal Knowledge and Imperial Power: Race and the Intimate in Colonial Rule.* Berkeley: University of California Press, 2002.

Chapter Five

"Is the Headscarf Oppressive or Emancipatory?"

Field Notes on the Gendrification of the "Multicultural Debate"

Sarah Bracke and Nadia Fadil

Since the end of the 1980s, Western Europe has witnessed the eruption of public debates weaving together a myriad of topics such as migration, integration, cultural identity, Islam and secularism. In the UK, the publication of Salman Rushdie's *Satanic Verses* in 1988, and the intense discussions and demonstrations in its wake, is usually believed to have inaugurated these debates. In France, this honour befell the first "affaire du foulard," which flared up when in 1989 three pupils in Creil were suspended for refusing to remove their headscarves in class. In the Dutch context, Frits Bolkestein declares the failure of Dutch "integration policies" and the incompatibility between Islam and Western liberal values in his famous Luzern speech at the Liberal International in 1991. These public discussions have presented themselves as ways of "debating diversity,"[1] and in many cases they became known as "the multicultural debates."

From the very outset of these public debates "the multicultural society" was problematized—as the use of expressions like "the multicultural drama" (by the Dutch essayist Paul Scheffer) testify—yet not only by those who sought to criticize it. In fact, also the defense of multiculturalism often unfolded on shaky and conditional grounds, which served to problematize certain understandings and affirmations of identity and culture. Furthermore, more recently various voices within the European political elite have been heard firmly declaring "the end of multiculturalism."[2] "Multicultural debates," in other words, is hardly a descriptive term. Rather, it is a discourse which structures debates on identity and culture in particular ways, and needs to be carefully situated and contextualized.

This essay seeks to examine more closely the vicious circles in which certain conversations within the "multicultural debate" get caught, as questions and topics are set up in certain ways that already structure how the conversation will proceed and what the range of answers can be. More specifically, we are looking at conversations at the intersection of multiculturalism and gender, where many of the discussions are structured around the question whether "multiculturalism is bad for women"—to paraphrase Susan Miller Okin's well-known interrogation.[3] The significance of this intersection points at how questions and understandings of gender structure the ways in which the multicultural debate is conceived, that is, the way in which "multicultural society" is imagined and discussed. It signals, in other words, that gender operates as a critical terrain in the processes of constituting cultural differences and constructing the national self and its others. A central figure in this intersection between gender and multiculturalism, and in debates about multiculturalism *tout court*, is the headscarf. While many protagonists in these debates have declared veiling to be a sign of women's oppression, others have embarked on understanding the various meanings of veiling, and serious scholarship has sought to demonstrate the "active agency" of veiled women.[4]

We consider discussions about the headscarf through a case-study of a recurrent question which became an important reference point throughout twenty years of multicultural debate across Europe, namely the question *Is the headscarf oppressive or emancipatory?* As we trace what occurs in the posing of this question, we reflect on our participation in debates structured by the question whether the headscarf is an oppressive practice, or whether on the contrary it might emancipate women. In the past decade, we have both been invited on various occasions to take part in such debates—mostly in Belgium—and we have become fluent in speaking the language these conversations require.[5] In this essay we reflect on the performative effect of the question: what does it reproduce, what kinds of discussion does it enable and what kinds of imaginary, speech and action does it render impossible.

The position from which we write is one of engaged intellectuals who are regularly invited to take part in the discussions and conversations that "the multicultural debate" consists of. While in our scholarly work we have commented on and critiqued "multicultural debates,"[6] we also participate in political mobilizations, social movements and actions that relate to questions of multiculturalism. The frames of the multicultural debates, in other words, are frames in which we have regularly operated, frames we have appropriated and learn to navigate in order to find ways to articulate our critiques which were often precisely aimed at the frames themselves. This kind of positioning, oscillating between scholarly critique and de-construction on the one hand, and political participation and action on the other, is all but comfortable. Yet it is potentially productive when dis/connections and uneasy translations, along with the frustrations of how discourses structure possible speech and actions, can become part of our understanding of how social reality comes into being, and can be transformed.

The essay is structured as follows. In the first part, we briefly sketch our theoretical outlook on "multiculturalism," as the larger frame in which our case-study is embedded, discerning three analytical distinct but related (and often overlapping) theoretical (and simultaneously methodological) approaches. This section details what we have in mind when we subscribe to the view that multiculturalism is all but a descriptive term. In a second part we briefly rehearse the significance of gender to the multicultural debate, in order to substantiate the argument that gender effectively structures the multicultural debate. These brief discussions provide the analytical grounds for our subsequent analysis of what happens in public and scholarly debate structured by the recurring question "Is the headscarf oppressive or emancipatory for women?". Our analysis particularly considers the operations of hegemonic notions of agency and rights, and relies on the seminal work of Saba Mahmood.[7]

APPROACHING MULTICULTURALISM CRITICALLY

We understand multiculturalism not as a descriptive term, which supposedly characterizes a certain kind of society, or points at an increased degree of "diversity" within existing societies, but rather as a site of critical inquiry. Multiculturalism, as David Theo Goldberg puts it, cannot simply be reduced to a political doctrine nor an intellectual paradigm, a pedagogical framework or an academic rhetoric, an institutionalized orthodoxy or a radical critique.[8] Its meaning cannot be fixed in a way that does justice to the various symbolic and material realities (concerns and considerations, principles and practices, concepts and categories, in Goldberg's words) it might refer to. A critical inquiry of multiculturalism, moreover, takes the historical context and geo-political location of "multicultural debates" into account; and hence we understand contemporary discussions of multiculturalism in Europe, as they occur in the context of a postcolonial world shaped simultaneously by neo-colonial dynamics and the decentering of the West, increasing globalization and its effects on the nation-state, and new flows of postcolonial migration, as debates about *transformations of national identity* in and of Europe. In other words, we recognize multiculturalism as a correlate of nationalism, and believe that discussions about "cultural difference" and "the other" ought to be considered in tandem with discussions about "the national self." In this vein, we can conceive of multiculturalism as an epistemological field that is structured according to distinct exclusionary mechanisms and which fulfills a functional role in the constitution of the idea of a "nation." In methodological terms, this means taking up the question of "multiculturalism" as a *dispositif* that creates distinctive fields of problematization (i.e. the question of "integration" turns into a new object of study), identifies a particular set of actors (i.e. "the immigrants" or "Muslims") and is accompanied by an institutional apparatus that seeks to transform the non-integrated "other" in order to include it into the social body.[9] Thus multiculturalism cannot be reduced to merely another social topic, but rather can be approached as a power field constructing and shaping its own object of debate and regulating individuals according to those very categories it creates (i.e. the integrated vs. the non-integrated). We thereby draw on three distinct, albeit connected, modalities of analyzing these operations of power. While these three ways of critically analyzing multicultural debates rely on related (poststructuralist and postcolonial) understandings of how power operates, and these approaches effectively overlap in the work of many scholars on the matter, the distinction does draw attention to different dimensions of how power operates through these debates.

Firstly, there is a general question of *framing*, and the way these debates are framed and how such frames regulate notions of cultural and religious difference. Frames, as Judith Butler points out, are operations of power that occur on an ontological, epistemological and ethical level. They regulate the affective and ethical dispositions through which phenomena are not only understood but also constituted. Frames matter in terms of what is problematized and how, and interventions into hegemonic frames from minority positions are notably difficult, as such questions, topics and concerns get reframed in a framework that sustains dominant power relations. They also matter on the level of who and what gets recognized as a life. The question of the recognition of life, upon which Butler elaborates, begs the question of norms and normativity: which norms operate in producing certain subjects as "recognizable" persons and make others more difficult to recognize.[10]

The multicultural debates offer plenty of opportunities and an abundance of material to carefully investigate the ways in which subjects have been framed. An essential argument about frames in the context of multiculturalism is formulated by Blommaert and Verschueren, in their sharp discourse analysis of the official multicultural discourse in Belgium.[11] These debates about "cultural diversity," their argument goes, in fact set up cultural difference as a problem to begin with. The debates on multiculturalism indeed presuppose the idea of a homogeneous society (which they describe as the ideology of *homogeneism*) which is defined according to a particular (and fictive) understanding of the "norms and values" that hold such a society together, and which the question of "diversity" comes to challenge. Framing the presence of ethnic minorities in terms of the "diversity challenge" becomes, hence, not only a way to constitute them as "other" (and thus exclude them from the national imaginary) but also to construct and enact a particular understanding of the national self.

This brings us to the second (and related) dimension of a critical investigation of the multicultural debate: a focus on the intertwined constructions of "*self*" and "*other*." Debates about "the other" indeed reveal much about the concerns and construction of the "self." Hence analyzing discourses of multiculturalism provides a way to map out crises and transformations of the national self, through tracing how "self" and "other" get constructed through the debates, and which mechanisms of representation sustain such constructions. An investigation of official multiculturalist discourse along these lines can be found in the work of Ghassan Hage. Looking at multiculturalist discourse in Australia, Hage dissects how otherness functions in the presentation of the national self, and elaborates this functionality of "the other" to the self in the following way. Multiculturalism, he argues, figures as a central societal debate because it acts as the solution to a problem of dominant (white) society. Thus multiculturalism is imagined as an object performing a function for the national body, Hage argues, as a technology of the (national) body. The relation of exteriority between self and other, however, needs to be carefully examined in its complexity. On the one hand multiculturalism is perceived to have an *external* relationship to the body—as "the other" outside of the national self—while at the same time it is an *extension* of that body, in analogy with the way clothes relate to a human body. This implies that multiculturalism operates as a tool in (and for) the presentation of the self, while it is simultaneously part of the presented self.[12]

Thirdly, we can look at the multicultural debates as a form of governmentality understood in the Foucaultian sense, that is, as "the conduct of conduct" or the ways in which governments try to produce "the citizen" and all the organized practices and techniques through which subjects are governed. In this perspective the multicultural debates can be analyzed in terms of the practices, mentalities, rationalities and techniques through which "proper" citizens of a multicultural society are produced, and hence how cultural and religious difference should be organized appropriately in a liberal modern capitalist democracy. The latter are then fortified, especially in countries such as Belgium, the Netherlands or Denmark, by an institutional apparatus (i.e. *inburgeringstest*) that "teaches" those citizens considered as "other" how to become a "proper" citizen, that is, how to integrate into the social body.

THE "WOMEN'S QUESTION": FROM BAD TO VICIOUS

If the previous section has highlighted some of the ways in which multiculturalism can be understood in terms of the regulation of "self" and "other" within the realm of cultural identities, we subscribe to the view that the problem of diversity cannot simply be posed in "cultural terms" but is from the start mediated by a set of transversal regulatory structures, among which is that of gender. As many commentators have pointed out, gender matters to the ways in which the multicultural debates are set up.[13] On a concrete level, we can observe that a substantial part of "the multicultural debates" directly bear on women, questions of femininity and masculinity, and sexuality. Debates about women's oppression immediately come to mind, most often cast through discussions about religious practices and attire (and notably the headscarf) as well as through discussions about violence (violence against women, criminality and unsafe streets, etc.).

The most well-known account bringing gender to bear on multiculturalism is arguably Susan Moller Okin's essay "Is Multiculturalism Bad for Women?," which asserts that gender equality often clashes with a respect for minority cultures. The essay was not only influential in a scholarly context (provoking a lively debate in the *Boston Review* in 1997, in which a number of well-known scholars responded to Okin's argument), but also in circles of feminist and women's groups, where the essay circulated widely and was often used as a way to discuss questions of multiculturalism within the women's movement.[14] Okin frames the relationship between feminist and multicultural concerns, and subsequently the debate about the tensions between them, through the following question: "what should be done when the claims of minority cultures or religions clash with the norm of gender equality that is at least formally endorsed by liberal states?" The question needs to be understood as a feminist intervention within the field of political theory: Okin's argument is a critique on the concept of group rights, and for this purpose she turns to the social relations of gender. Advocates of group rights, she argues, commonly treat cultural groups as monolithic, and they pay little attention to the private sphere. This renders them blind to the fact that the sphere of the personal, sexual and reproductive life functions is the central focus of most cultures, and that most cultures aim at control by men over women. In other words, theories of group rights remain blind for the fact that the organisation of gender relations lies at the very heart of what a culture is about. Okin's argument is further framed by the following two assertions: while all of the world's cultures have patriarchal pasts, some, that is, mostly Western liberal cultures, have departed further from them than others, and many cultural minorities claiming group rights are more patriarchal than the surrounding "majority" cultures. Hence, Okin concludes, feminism is opposed to "the cultural relativism of group rights multiculturalism."

Okin's argument has been widely discussed and critiqued, notably in the responses accompanying the publication of the original essay,[15] and the critiques, which we will not rehearse at length here, often revolve around, firstly, the problematic notions of culture and more specifically the ironic way in which Okin's argument supports a monolithic and unifying notion of culture,[16] and secondly, the way in which in Okin's argument culture tends to be "the stuff that sticks" to minority groups while cultural and national formations within majority cultures simply remain invisible.[17] As a product of the way Okin's argument is set up, minority groups get "cultured" in disproportionate ways, leaving "culture" to signify the difference from an invisible norm.

A central element that emerges however throughout Okin's essay as well as the different critiques it provoked, is the need for a broader understanding of how gender relations pertain to questions of culture and indeed community and nation; an understanding in which the constitutive dimension of gender relations within various kinds of social, political and cultural formations is rendered visible. The challenge becomes then to understand how particular cultural, political and economic regimes are couched on distinctive gender relations, and how a "gendered/sexual division of labor" is integral to both liberal and non-liberal cultural and structural modes of organization, including capitalist modes of production. Indeed, Okin's line of reasoning, focusing on gender relations in "other" cultures, fails to account for a number of things. Firstly, the way in which gender relations are central to the constitution of national and cultural identities, and to *any* form of national boundary making, *tout court*, and secondly, how a concern with "the position of Muslim women" is functional to the constitution of Western-European national identities.

The work of Nira Yuval-Davis engages some of these challenges, and has begun to elaborate the ways in which gender matters to the nation, and by extension to an understanding of "culture" or a cultural community we would add, more systematically. *Gender and Nation* was written as a critical intervention in relation to classical theories about nations and nationalism where gender appears irrelevant. Instead, Yuval-Davis argues, gender relations are located at the heart of (the reproduction of) the nation—which is commonly conceptualized as an extension of family and kinship relations, most often understood as based on the "natural" sexual division of labour. Yuval-Davis proposes us to trace this centrality of gender on the level of biological, cultural and symbolical reproduction.[18] In biological terms, the demographic reproduction of the nation takes place through women bearing children, which is couched in a context of bio-politics that seek to encourage or discourage, with various degrees of pressure, (certain groups of) women to bear children.[19] In terms of cultural reproduction, in the "mythical unity" of the imagined community, the divide between "us" and "them" is maintained and reproduced by social constructions of manhood and womanhood, and sexuality, deemed "appropriate" to the nation. In this sense, women structurally fulfill a "border guard" function as they come to structurally embody the collectivity, which results in specific expectations, notably cultural codes, of style of dress and behaviour. This theoretical framework allows us, in other words, to understand how gender relations matter to the formation of all national and cultural entities: how gender comes into being in relation to national and cultural formations, and vice versa.

And this might give us a first indication of how the focus on Muslim women (and the headscarf) in the current multicultural debates can be understood. Gender relations, or the ascription of specific gender patterns, operate as a demarcation line that is functional in the process of "othering" of the concerned group, which, moreover, is consolidated as a "group" precisely through this process of othering. By addressing the issue of the headscarf, by "problematizing" it as Foucault would have it, the gendered character of the nation is not only highlighted (along the lines of what are appropriate vs. inappropriate ways of presenting female bodies in the public sphere), but the primary way in addressing and constructing the other occurs similarly through the same gendered register.[20] More than providing an account of Muslim women, the gendered dimension in the multicultural debate figures as a reenactment of the gendered and sexual boundaries of the nation.

IS THE HEADSCARF EMANCIPATORY OR OPPRESSIVE?

The headscarf debate—as it has come to be known—figures as one of the central points of discussion around which our interventions in "the multicultural debates" have been organized. Not unlike what happened in several other West-European countries, also in Belgium the religious practice of hijab has become one of the chief symbols of what is perceived as a growing visibility of Islam in the public sphere. The debate in Belgium closely follows the rhythms of that of its southern neighbour France. While the first episode of the French headscarf debate, between 1989 and 1992, mostly affected the Francophone audience in Belgium, at the turn to the twenty-first century this debate reached a broader and national scope implicating both Francophone and Flemish protagonists.[21] These different episodes have been structured according to two broad interrogations: firstly, the question of women's emancipation and hijab as a potential site of oppression and secondly, hijab's compatibility with the neutrality of the public sphere. The first question has been critical to how the issue of hijab in schools has been addressed and to justifying bans comparable to the ones implemented in France. While Belgium has not adopted a general (national) regulation with regard to hijab, an overwhelmingly majority of public and private schools do prohibit this practice[22]—often justifying this measure in relation to the social pressure (to veil) endured by young Muslim women or cases of forced veiling.[23] Another important argument that recurs throughout this discussion is that of the neutrality of the public sphere. While this argument has not consistently been used in relation to students, it has figured as a ground to justify the prohibition of headscarves in the case of public officials and teachers.

At several occasions we have been invited, or have invited ourselves, to intervene in this polemic setting. The positions we have upheld in these contexts were often defensive. To the allegations that veiled women were "victims of social coercion (or tradition)" or suffered forms of "false consciousness" (in thinking they "choose" to veil),[24] we would retort that their agency is complex, and would point at several stories of strong, emancipated women who consciously chose to wear the veil. And to depictions of veiled Muslim women as "fundamentalist" or "culprits" we would, both in our scholarly and public interventions, point to the ways these women were often at the source of new forms of feminism wherein Islam and feminist commitments converge, and account for new forms of subjectivity.[25] Yet after almost a decade of debating "on the headscarf" and "veiled women" we have come to a point of intellectual and political exhaustion. This is the kind of exhaustion that not only comes from repeating the same arguments over and again in a context in which hegemonic notions about woman and Islam continue to be shaped by racism, but also from our increasing awareness of the paradoxical role we play as scholars, by attempting to defend the "voices" of the women who are too often singled out as a problem, in sustaining the very conditions and terms through which such an interpellation of "veiled women" occurs.

A first problem lies in the way our interventions willingly or unwillingly contribute to the problematization of the headscarf and veiled women. By using this term we refer to the Foucaultian approach of examining how, in a specific moment of history, certain practices are turned into a matter of concern and debate. Rather than pointing at the existence of a particular problem, problematization announces the establishment of a set of discourses (scientific and non-scientific) and institutional practices that seek to regulate a distinctive conduct that is singled out as an object of concern.[26] This also means that, according to this perspective, the eruption of societal controversies is not considered to be a result of the mere manifestation of specific social phenomena or practices. Rather, social controversies are the very process through which certain practices are turned into "social problems" and become, thus, subjected to a set of biopolitical regulations.[27] Thus for Foucault, this construction of a specific phenomenon into a "social problem" is not a neutral enterprise, but closely tied with the establishment of specific regulatory ideals or a regime of truth. Applied to our case, this means that the question no longer revolves around the issue whether the headscarf does or does not obstruct the principle of neutrality or that of women's emancipation. According to this perspective, the hijab in itself is void of social meaning, and veiling only becomes constituted into a meaningful act by a distinctive discursive apparatus. Thus the question becomes: how to account for the very notion of neutrality and emancipation that is constructed by singling out veiled women and turning them into an object of debate? The critical task that awaits us, in other words, consists of understanding how the headscarf debate is functional to the constitution of (a specific idea of) "neutrality" on the one hand, and that of an "emancipated gender identity" on the other hand, and the extent in which both are seen to implicate each other. Several analyses have shown how addressing the question of hijab redefines the contours of the nation and emancipation in exclusionary terms.[28] Hence the mere act of addressing the headscarf, either in its affirmation or negation, contributes to the way this sartorial practice becomes singled out from other practices, to be attributed a status of *exceptionality*.[29] Within this kind of discursive regime, non-veiled women's bodies are attributed a status of ontological neutrality, as Fadil argues elsewhere, while veiling is seen to obstruct the homogeneity—both in terms of forging a "neutral" public space as well as in terms of what counts as an emancipated female body—of that space.[30]

A second problem lies in the "framing" of this practice. While advocates of the headscarf ban have often done so on the grounds that hijab acts as a (religious or political) "symbol" that breaches the principle of neutrality, opponents of the ban—like us—have tended to question these claims by underlining the religious character of this practice and thus claiming its constitutional guarantee. Our reliance upon the juridical language of fundamental rights—including that of religious freedom—reflects the epistemic weight that is attributed to this discourse in not only advocating certain claims, but also in rendering them intelligible. The idea that all individuals are "free" to choose and practice their religiosity is often viewed as an essential corner stone of liberal democracy, enabling the articulation of a distinctive set of claims that are seen to fall under its auspices. By taking a case against what we present as "forced unveiling," the same liberal taxonomy is therefore used to defend veiled women. Yet this primary reliance on the liberal language of rights confronts us with a number of dilemmas linked to the performative effects of framing the headscarf primarily as a religious right.[31]

Firstly, throughout these debates, the practice of veiling is fixed in its meaning—either as a symbol or as a religious practice—thus obscuring the variety of significations it may carry. Various studies have indeed shown that the headscarf can mean a variety of things. While it does figure as part of an economy of pious conduct,[32] it can also simultaneously be part of a stronger affirmation of one's Muslim identity or a sartorial practice that enables the expression of a modern Muslim identity.[33] Moreover, in addressing the head-scarf primarily as a religious practice that is considered to be crucial for Muslim identity, we unwillingly participate to the fundamental attribution of this practice to Muslim identity—a move that authorizes claims of "authenticity." There is a long legacy, both within social sciences as well as within women's movements and feminism, of critically considering the colonial legacies of the ways in which the hijab (or other practices) has been constructed into an essential attribute of Muslim identity, and investigating how the colonial marking of Muslims as "religious other" has been pivotal in this process.[34] Addressing the hijab in terms of a religious practice that is primarily tied with Muslim identity risks fixing its signification and contributes to how this colonial framing of Islam, and the ways in which it is structured by gender, has been continued throughout the "multicultural debates."

Defending the hijab as a "religious right" or "religious freedom," further-more, not only frames the hijab in a specific vocabulary, but these very terms also imply a particular understanding of agency which fails to fully capture the ethical and political locations of the women concerned. A central argu-ment in many of our interventions has been to undo the often posited claim that veiled women do not willingly or consciously subject themselves to this sartorial practice. Such a claim usually relies on either a notion of "coercion" (forced veiling) or of "false consciousness," both pointing to the power re-lations in which veiling is embedded and which are too often denied by its apologists or by the women themselves.[35] While these argumentations turn out to be problematic for how questions of power and regulation only seem to be implicated in the case of veiling (and subsequently are considered to be absent in the cases of not-veiling or unveiling, which are taken to be the re-flection of an immanent and autonomous will), they often do confront us with a discursive terrain wherein little else is left to say than arguing and empiri-cally demonstrating that Muslim women who veil are "active agents" of their destiny. It is this latter position that we wish to critically address, both in the ways it reiterates a naturalized (humanist) understanding of the agent or "au-tonomous will" that exists outside of any power structure, as well as through the ways such a position participates in maintaining those other voices, that do not sit comfortably with the liberal and secular grammar undergirding our prevailing conception of agency, unintelligible.

By arguing that Muslim women are donning the veil as a result of their own will, we in fact reproduce the very same agency model upon which problematic allegations of "false consciousness" or "coercion" draw, that is, one which opposes the question of individual choices to that of power structures.[36] Such an understanding of agency has seriously been challenged with the elaboration of more complex, post-Althusserian understandings of the relationship of the subject to ideology and power.[37] In this perspective any relationship to the self is conceived as mediated by norms and power structure.[38] This means that *all* "choices" or bodily practices are considered as the emanation of prevailing normative ideals or regulative structures. Furthermore, by emphasizing the "autonomous will" of the women involved, we very much rely on a liberal normative framework that takes a number of concepts (such as the emancipation of women, separation of church and state, freedom of speech) as a central kernel of what counts as "modern" or "European" (i.e. as integrated). At the same time, it also takes for granted that the meaning of these concepts is already known, and hence arrests their on-going unfolding and puts a definite claim on their signification. The challenge becomes then to put veiled women and the headscarf to the test of that very specific liberal framework in order to deliberate upon their integration in the space of citizens. While the defenders of the headscarf ban adopt a position which views the hijab as intrinsically incompatible with this liberal apparatus, advocates of the "right to veil" will go at length to show why veiled women in fact fit with these liberal requirements and can perfectly integrate into the public space which is defined according to these liberal terms.

At the heart of the matter, however, lies a critical question about whether other trajectories, which do not necessarily fit the hegemonic liberal grammar, can be rendered intelligible. While we have repeatedly made strong arguments against the position that equals the headscarf to women's oppression, we have both felt uncomfortable adopting a liberal vocabulary compelling us to argue that the headscarf is emancipatory. Firstly, and almost evidently, even if the near self-evidence of this point repeatedly gets lost in the so-called headscarf debate, we subscribe to the argument that a piece of clothing cannot in and of itself be oppressive or emancipatory.[39] The significance of the headscarf is always a matter of context, and the context consists of interpretative frameworks, including the frameworks of the agent herself, as well as material conditions and their complex interplay. A more important contention, however, lies, in the ways this dominant framework does not enable us to address nor render intelligible the various voices and trajectories that do not fit in similar liberal registers. For many of the women we have encountered throughout our studies, wearing the hijab was not simply a matter of choice but in many cases also framed as a "duty" that was part of the set of virtuous disposition they cultivated in order to "please God."[40] The question at stake is how to account for these voices in ways that do not disavow the narratives of "subjection" as merely an authorizing discourse masking the presence of "real agency,"[41] or that take them as evidence for an absence of agency. We are confronted, in other words, with the question of how to render those voices intelligible according to their specific terms.

The seminal work of Saba Mahmood has offered a powerful critique to how commonsensical understandings of agency suffer from the teleology of liberal understandings of emancipation, as it seeks to locate the political and moral autonomy of the subject in the face of power.[42] Despite the important insights it has enabled, Mahmood argues, this model of agency also limits our ability to understand the lives of certain subjects, and notably women whose subjectivity has been shaped by nonliberal traditions. The conceptual problem more precisely lies in the articulation of agency with understandings of "resistance to power." In other words, if women's decisions to wear the hijab are to be seen as the exercise of their agency, the evocation of women's agency in its feminist use would in the same breath suggest such decisions are to be seen as "resistance to power" and "emancipation." The "oppressive or emancipatory" question would then be settled on the side of emancipation. Yet it is precisely this chain of associations that is problematic, and urges us to rethink the notion of agency. Mahmood's work takes up this theoretical challenge, and reconceptualizes agency in terms of a capacity for action that historically specific relations of subordination enable and create. Agency understood in this way puts in relief the capacities and skills required to undertake particular kinds of acts (including, but not restricted to resistance) as well as the recognition that these are bound up with the historically and culturally specific disciplines through which a subject is formed.[43] Hence, the question "is the headscarf oppressive or emancipatory?" relies on a problematic notion of agency: the question itself seems to suggest that, if she is oppressed, she lacks agency; if her agency is recognized, however, it situates her on the side of emancipation. The question already excludes the possibility of recognizing her agency yet acknowledging that emancipation is a significantly different matter from agency. Yet with shunning or questioning this liberal conception of "emancipation," comes the pull of "oppression," which already reflects the hegemonic position on the matter—indeed, the suggested symmetry of the question does not reflect a real symmetry in prevalent opinions—and once more denies the agency of covered Muslim women. However, defending the headscarf as emancipatory as a tactic of countering the prevalence of the oppression arguments, ultimately fails, precisely because of the tensions played out in the notion of agency: the notion of agency which informs this concept of emancipation is in fact already premised on an understanding that the subject needs to shed her "particular" (cultural, religious, . . .) attachments.

CONCLUSION

This essay has sought to examine the gendered contours of the multicultural debate through an analysis of a specific case which has turned into one of the main objects of contentions in various Western-European countries, that is, the headscarf. The purpose of this investigation has not been to analyze the different arguments mobilized in these various debates, but rather to offer a critical account of the frames through which these debates are set up, and their epistemic effects upon our understanding of the hijab as well as our role as scholars and public intellectuals. We have examined how these debates on the headscarf contribute to the delineation and articulation of a secular understanding of the public space, whereby the question of secularism becomes redefined according to very distinctive and exclusionary terms.[44] The headscarf controversies do, thus, not simply figure as a way to account for the lived realities of veiled Muslim women, nor do they simply address the practical concerns that may arise from this practice—but they are discursive moments throughout which the national imaginary is constructed, in exclusion of this specific sartorial practice (and its carriers). Secondly, our investigation has also brought us to question the dominant frames through which the voices of veiled Muslim women can be rendered intelligible, and especially the central position of the language of rights. Whilst not disputing the agency such frames enable, we have questioned its limiting capacities both in the semiotic fixation of the hijab as well as the particular model of agency undergirding this language of rights.[45] The work of Mahmood convincingly shows the problematic ways in which an understanding of resistance, and by extension emancipation, informs the prevalent concept of agency, and notably the usage of it in feminist scholarship. Yet precisely this reference to a notion of emancipation undermines the argument of the headscarf as emancipatory from the very outset, given that the prevalent notion of emancipation is premised on an understanding that the subject needs to shed her "particular" (cultural, religious, . . .) attachments, to which donning a headscarf, until further notice, stands in sharp contrast.

These observations, consequently, lead us to Spivak's interrogation on the subaltern's capacity to speak—or more precisely: to make its voice heard. In considering the hegemonic structure of the liberal grammar, the question remains how we may render those voices intelligible within a discursive structure that not only defines what counts as emancipation in liberal terms, but equally conceptualizes the very idea of a "willful subject" through those terms. More than giving a set of definite answers to this weighty interrogation, we rather wish to conclude by a number of rhetorical questions that make us reflect upon the various elements this interrogation implies. A first one concerns the process of "translation" that seeks to render those voices intelligible. What occurs throughout this process? What gets lost and how are specific practices resignified? Which voices are being observed and why? How can we situate the liberal grammar in its specificity (as well as in its potentiality) and the ways in which it becomes mobilized in exclusionary terms, yet without ignoring the ways in which all forms of life are marked by it? How can we avoid the essentializing trap of addressing and relating to those non-recognized voices in idealized terms? Finally, what is the role of critique, and how can we articulate a critique refusing the trap of new essentialisms or identity discourses, yet that provides a powerful tool in the interrogation of the hegemonic structures of the liberal-secular grammar?

The premise of these questions, and indeed of this essay, is that framing matters to how social reality comes into being. Our participation in public debates has taught us time and time again that this is not a popular line of argumentation—it does most often not easily fit into an appropriate sound bite nor is the point readily understood. Yet in the light of the ever more nationalist, racist and exclusionary dynamics throughout the European societies we are familiar with, we are increasingly convinced it is one of the crucial critical tasks that awaits us. And to those who then ask for the alternatives—what questions should we be discussing if not whether headscarfs are oppressive or emancipatory?—we answer that this must be a matter of collective conversation in which excluded and marginalized perspectives are central. Such a point of departure of course raises many other questions—such as, how are such conversations already structured by power relations in the way they are set up and the notions of speech they rely upon—yet these are precisely the conversations we believe are important to have.

NOTES

Acknowledgments. This chapter originally appeared as "'Is the Headscarf Oppressive or Emancipatory?' Field Notes on the Gendrification of the 'Multicultural' Debate," *Religion and Gender* 2, no. 1 (2012): 36–56.

1. Jan Blommaert and Jef Verscheuren, *Debating Diversity: Analysing the Discourse of Tolerance* (London: Routledge, 1998).

2. Alana Lentin and Gavan Titley, *The Crises of Multiculturalism: Racism in a Neoliberal Age* (London: Zedbooks, 2011).

3. Joshua Cohen, Matthew Howard, and Marta C. Nussbaum, eds., *Is Multiculturalism Bad for Women? Susan Moller Okin with Respondents* (Princeton, NJ: Princeton University Press, 1999).

4. For good examples of studies seeking to underscore the "active agency" of veiled Muslim women, see Farhad Khosrokhavar, *L'Islam des jeunes* (Paris: éd. Flammarion, 1997) or Sara Silvestri, *Europe's Muslim Women: Potential, Aspirations and Challenges* (Brussels: King Baudouin Foundation, 2008).

5. In fact, merely in the process of thinking and writing this article, we were invited twice to take place in a discussion (one in the Belgian parliament, another one in an academic environment) organised under the auspices of this question.

6. Karel Arnaut et al., *Een leeuw in een kooi: De grenzen van het multiculturele Vlaanderen* (Amsterdam: Meulenhoff/Manteau, 2009).

7. And most notably Saba Mahmood, *Politics of Piety: The Reform of the Feminist Subject* (Princeton, NJ: Princeton University Press, 2005).

8. David Theo Goldberg, ed., *Multiculturalism: A Critical Reader* (Cambridge, MA: Basil Blackwell, 1994).

9. Willem Schinkel, *Denken in een tijd van Sociale Hypochondrie: Aanzet tot een theorie voorbij de maatschappij* (Kampen: Uitgeverij Klement, 2008).

10. Judith Butler, *Frames of War: When Is Life Grievable?* (London: Verso, 2009), 6.

11. Jan Blommaert and Jef Verscheuren, *Debating Diversity: Analysing the Discourse of Tolerance* (London: Routledge, 1998).

12. Ghassan Hage, *White Nation: Fantasies of White Supremacy in Multicultural Society* (London: Routledge, 2000), 148–51.

13. For a brief selection of literature addressing the precise intersection of the question of gender and multiculturalism, see Gloria Wekker and Rosi Braidotti, *Praten in het donker: Multicuturalisme en anti-racisme in feministisch perspectief* (Amsterdam: Kok Agora, 1996); Joshua Cohen, Matthew Howard, and Marta C. Nussbaum, eds., *Is Multiculturalism Bad for Women? Susan Moller Okin with Respondents* (Princeton, NJ: Princeton University Press, 1999); Maayke Botman, Nancy Jouwe, and Gloria Wekker, *Caleidoscopische visies: De zwarte, migranten, en vluchtelingenvrouwen beweging in Nederland* (Amsterdam: KIT Publishers, 2001); Gily Coene and Chia Longman, *Eigen emancipatie eerst?: Over de rechten en representatie van vrouwen in een multiculturele samenleving* (Gent: Academia Press, 2005); Sarah Bracke and Sarah De Mul, "In naam van het feminisme: Beschaving, multiculturaliteit en vrouwenemancipatie," in *Een leeuw in een kooi: De grenzen van het multiculturele Vlaanderen*, ed. Karel Arnaut et al. (Amsterdam: Meulenhof/Manteau, 2009); Eva Midden, *Feminism in Multicultural Societies: An Analysis of Dutch Multicultural and Postsecular Developments and Their Implications for Feminist Debates* (unpublished PhD dissertation, University of Central Lancashire, 2010).

14. For example, see Gily Coene and Chia Longman, *Eigen emancipatie eerst?: Over de rechten en representatie van vrouwen in een multiculturele samenleving* (Gent: Academia Press, 2005).

15. Joshua Cohen, Matthew Howard, and Marta C. Nussbaum, eds., *Is Multiculturalism Bad for Women? Susan Moller Okin with Respondents* (Princeton, NJ: Princeton University Press, 1999).

16. For example, see Bhabha in Cohen, Howard, and Nussbaum, *Is Multiculturalism Bad for Women?*

17. For example, see Honig and Al-Hibri in Cohen, Howard, and Nussbaum, *Is Multiculturalism Bad for Women?*

18. Nira Yuval-Davis, *Gender and Nation* (London: Sage, 1997).

19. For just one example of how "the demographic argument" figures in discussions about culture, multiculturalism and civilization, see Huntington's (in)famous "clash of civilization" thesis.

20. Joan W. Scott, *The Politics of the Veil* (Princeton, NJ: Princeton University Press, 2007).

21. For an overview of the Belgian headscarf debate see Chia Longman, "Over Our Heads? Muslim Women as Symbols and Agents in the Headscarf Debate in Flanders, Belgium," *Social Justice: Anthropology, Peace, and Human Right* 4, nos. 3–4 (2003): 300–332; Nadia Fadil, "Het hoofddoekendebat: Meer dan een debat over een stukje stof?" *Ethische Perspective/Ethical Perspectives* 14, no. 4 (2004): 373–86.

22. 40% of schools in Belgium are directly organised and funded by public authorities while 60% are initiated by local communities (mostly Catholic churches and organizations) and publicly funded.

23. This argument has been central to the decision of the board of education of the Flemish public schools to adopt a general ban after a similarly adopted ban by the Atheneum of Antwerp (the Royal Atheneum) in June 2009 had been largely contested. For an account of the headscarf ban of the Flemish public school, see Nadia Fadil, "On Not-Unveiling as an Ethical Practice," *Feminist Review* 98 (2011): 83–109.

24. For an illustration of this type of argumentation, see Geert Van Istendael, "Het masker van de dwang," *De Standaard*, August 23, 2008.

25. Sarah Bracke, "Feminisme en islam: Intersecties," in *Vrouw(on)vriendelijk? Islam feministisch bekeken*, ed. I. Arteel, H. Müller, M. De Metsenaere, S. Bossaert (Brussels: VUB-Press, 2007), 13–38; Sarah Bracke, "Subjects of Debate: Secular and Sexual Exceptionalism, and Muslim Women in the Netherlands," *Feminist Review* 98 (2011): 28–46; Nadia Fadil, "Witte Mannen tegen de hoofddoek," *De Morgen*, September 9, 2008.

26. Michel Foucault, *The History of Sexuality 1: The Will to Knowledge*, trans. Robert Hurley (London: Penguin, 1998), 13.

27. Although Foucault does not necessarily link the issue of problematization with "biopolitical regulations," a term he restricts to a very specific form of power which he locates historically in the 18th century, we adopt a position here which links both questions.

28. See, for instance, J. W. Scott, *The Politics of the Veil* (Princeton, NJ: Princeton University Press, 2007); A. Moors, "The Dutch and the Face-veil: The Politics of Discomfort," *Social Anthropology* 17, no. 4 (2009): 393–408.

29. For an understanding of exceptionality we borrow from Mayanti Fernando; see M. L. Fernando, "Exceptional Citizens: Secular Muslim Women and the Politics of Difference in France," *Social Anthropology* 17, no. 4 (2009): 379–92.

30. N. Fadil, "On Not/Unveiling as an Ethical Practice," *Feminist Review* 98 (2011): 83–109.

31. We draw here on the work of scholars who have pointed at the way human rights discourse not only enables individual agency but equally functions as the vehi-

cle through which state power operates, see, for instance, W. Brown, "'The Most We Can Hope For . . .': Human Rights and the Politics of Fatalism," *The South Atlantic Quarterly* 103, nos. 2/3 (2004): 451–63.

32. See, for instance, the work of S. Amir-Moazami, *Politisierte Religion: Der Kopftuchstreit in Deutschland und Frankreich* (Bielefeld: transcript, 2007); V. Amiraux, "Discours Voilés Sur Les Musulmanes En Europe: Comment Les Musulmans Sont-ils Devenus Des Musulmanes?" *Social Compass* 50, no. 1 (2003): 85–96; J. S. Jouili and S. Amir-Moazami, "Knowledge, Empowerment, and Religious Authority among Pious Muslim Women in France and Germany," *Muslim World* 96 (October 2006): 617–42.

33. See, for instance, the work of Y. Navaro-Yashin, "The Market for Identities: Secularism, Islamism, Commodities" in *Fragments of Culture: The Everyday of Modern Turkey*, ed. Kandiyoti and Saktanber (New Brunswick, NJ: Rutgers University Press, 2002), 1–53, or the work of Emma Tarlo, "Islamic Cosmopolitanism: The Sartorial Biographies of Three Muslim Women in London" *Fashion Theory: The Journal of Dress, Body, and Culture* 11, nos. 2–3 (2007): 143–72.

34. See in these cases Leila Ahmed's seminal historical account of the way the hijab has been constructed as a religious practice that is essentially tied to the Muslim identity throughout modernising and colonial discourses, Leila Ahmed, *Women and Gender in Islam: Historical Roots of a Modern Debate* (New Haven, CT: Yale University Press, 1991). For a similar process albeit with a different case (i.e., that of Sati—widow burning—in India), see Lata Mani, *Contentious Tradition: The Debate on Sati in Colonial India* (Berkeley: University of California Press, 1998).

35. A recent example of such a critique can be found in M. Lazreg, *Questioning the Veil: Open Letters to Muslim Women* (Princeton, NJ: Princeton University Press, 2009).

36. Saba Mahmood, *Politics of Piety: The Reform of the Feminist Subject* (Princeton, NJ: Princeton University Press, 2005); Sarah Bracke, "Conjugating the Modern/ Religious, Conceptualizing Female Religious Agency: Contours of a 'Post-secular' Conjuncture," *Theory, Culture, and Society* 25, no. 6 (2008): 51–67.

37. See notably the reflection of Foucault on the question of ideology and his critique on the way this concept presupposes a pre-existing imminent substance or conscious subject who remains unaffected by normative structures. Michel Foucault, *Power/Knowledge: Selected Interviews and Other Writings, 1972–1977* (New York: Pantheon Books, 1980).

38. Judith Butler, *Gender Trouble: Feminism and the Subversion of Identity* (New York: Routledge, 1990).

39. Talal Asad, "Trying to Understand French Secularism," in *Political Theologies*, ed. Hent de Vries (New York: Fordham University Press, 2006).

40. Nadia Fadil, *Submitting to God, Submitting to the Self: Secular and Religious Trajectories of Second-Generation Maghrebi in Belgium* (unpublished dissertation, K.U. Leuven, 2008); Sarah Bracke, "Conjugating the Modern/Religious, Conceptualizing Female Religious Agency: Contours of a 'Post-secular' Conjuncture," *Theory, Culture, and Society* 25, no. 6 (2008): 51–67.

41. Amy Hollywood, "Gender, Agency, and the Divine in Religious Historiography," *The Journal of Religion* 84, no. 4 (2004): 514–28.

42. Saba Mahmood, *Politics of Piety: The Islamic Revival and the Feminist Subject* (Princeton, NJ: Princeton University Press, 2005).

43. Saba Mahmood, "Feminist Theory, Embodiment, and the Docile Agent: Some Reflections on the Egyptian Islamic Revival," *Cultural Anthropology* 6, no. 2 (2001): 202–36.

44. See also in this context, Sarah Bracke and Nadia Fadil, "Tussen dogma en realiteit: Secularisme, multiculturalisme en nationalisme in Vlaanderen" in *Een leeuw in een kooi: De grenzen van het multiculturele Vlaanderen*, ed. Karel Arnaut et al. (Amsterdam: Meulenhoff/Manteau, 2009), 93–110.

45. This observation parallels Saba Mahmood's analysis of the performative effects of the usage of the juridical language of anti-discrimination in the mobilisation of Muslims against offending images during the Danish Cartoon riots in 2005. For a fuller account see, Saba Mahmood, "Religious Reason and Secular Affect: An Incommensurable Divide?" *Critical Inquiry* 35(Summer 2009): 836–62.

BIBLIOGRAPHY

Ahmed, Leila. *Women and Gender in Islam: Historical Roots of a Modern Debate.* New Haven, CT: Yale University Press, 1991.

Amiraux, V. "Discours Voilés Sur Les Musulmanes En Europe: Comment Les Musulmans Sont-ils Devenus Des Musulmanes?" *Social Compass* 50, no. 1 (2003): 85–96.

Amir-Moazami, S. *Politisierte Religion: Der Kopftuchstreit in Deutschland und Frankreich.* Bielefeld: transcript, 2007.

Arnaut, Karel, Sarah Bracke, Bambi Ceuppens, Sarah De Mul, Nadia Fadil, and Meryem Kanmaz. *Een leeuw in een kooi: De grenzen van het multiculturele Vlaanderen.* Amsterdam: Meulenhoff/Manteau, 2009.

Asad, Talal. "Trying to Understand French Secularism." In *Political Theologies*, edited by Hent de Vries. New York: Fordham University Press, 2006.

Blommaert, Jan, and Jef Verscheuren. *Debating Diversity: Analysing the Discourse of Tolerance.* London: Routledge, 1998.

Botman, Maayke, Nancy Jouwe, and Gloria Wekker. *Caleidoscopische visies: De zwarte, migranten, en vluchtelingenvrouwen beweging in Nederland.* Amsterdam: KIT Publishers, 2001.

Bracke, Sarah. "Feminisme en Islam: Intersecties." In *Vrouw(on)vriendelijk? Islam feministisch bekeken*, edited by I. Arteel, H. Müller, M.De Metsenaere, S. Bossaert, 13–38. Brussels: VUB-Press, 2007.

———. "Conjugating the Modern/Religious, Conceptualizing Female Religious Agency: Contours of a 'Post-secular' Conjuncture." *Theory, Culture, and Society* 25, no. 6 (2008): 51–67.

——— and Sarah De Mul, "In naam van het feminisme. Beschaving, multiculturaliteit en vrouwenemancipatie." In *Een leeuw in een kooi: De grenzen van het multiculturele Vlaanderen*, edited by Karel Arnaut, Sarah Bracke, Bambi Ceuppens, Sarah De Mul, Nadia Fadil and Meryem Kanmaz. Amsterdam: Meulenhof/Manteau, 2009.

—— and Nadia Fadil. "Tussen Dogma en Realiteit: Secularisme, multiculturalisme en nationalisme in Vlaanderen." In *Een leeuw in een kooi: De grenzen van het multiculturele Vlaanderen*, edited by Karel Arnaut, Sarah Bracke, Bambi Ceuppens, Sarah De Mul, Nadia Fadil and Meryem Kanmaz, 93–110. Amsterdam: Meulenhof/Manteau, 2009.

——. "Subjects of Debate: Secular and Sexual Exceptionalism, and Muslim Women in the Netherlands." *Feminist Review* 98 (2011): 28–46.

Brown, W. "'The most we can hope for . . .': Human Rights and the Politics of Fatalism." *The South Atlantic Quarterly* 103, nos. 2/3 (2004): 451–63.

Butler, Judith. *Gender Trouble: Feminism and the Subversion of Identity*. New York: Routledge, 1990.

——. *Frames of War: When Is Life Grievable?* London: Verso, 2009.

Coene, Gily, and Chia Longman. *Eigen emancipatie eerst?: Over de rechten en representatie van vrouwen in een multiculturele samenleving.* Gent: Academia Press, 2005.

Cohen, Joshua, Matthew Howard, and Marta C. Nussbaum, eds. *Is Multiculturalism Bad for Women? Susan Moller Okin with Respondents*. Princeton, NJ: Princeton University Press, 1999.

Fadil, Nadia. "Het hoofddoekendebat: Meer dan een debat over een stukje stof?" *Ethische Perspectieve/Ethical Perspectives* 14, no. 4 (2004): 373–86.

——. "Witte Mannen tegen de hoofddoek." *De Morgen*, September 9, 2008.

——. *Submitting to God, Submitting to the Self. Secular and Religious Trajectories of Second-Generation Maghrebi in Belgium.* Unpublished Dissertation, K.U. Leuven, 2008.

——. "On Not-Unveiling as an Ethical Practice." *Feminist Review* 98 (2011): 83–109.

Fernando, M. L. "Exceptional Citizens: Secular Muslim Women and the Politics of Difference in France." *Social Anthropology* 17, no. 4 (2009): 379–92.

Foucault, Michel. *The History of Sexuality 1: The Will to Knowledge*. Translated by Robert Hurley. London: Penguin Books, 1998.

——. *Power/Knowledge: Selected Interviews and Other Writings, 1972–1977.* New York: Pantheon Books, 1980.

Goldberg, David Theo, ed. *Multiculturalism: A Critical Reader*. Cambridge, MA: Basil Blackwell, 1994.

Hage, Ghassan. *White Nation: Fantasies of White Supremacy in Multicultural Society*. London: Routledge, 2000.

Hollywood, Amy. "Gender, Agency, and the Divine in Religious Historiography." *The Journal of Religion* 84, no. 4 (2004): 514–28.

Jouili, J. S., and S. Amir-Moazami. "Knowledge, Empowerment and Religious Authority Among Pious Muslim Women in France and Germany." *Muslim World* 96 (October 2006): 617–42.

Khosrokhavar, Farhad. *L'Islam des jeunes*. Paris: éd. Flammarion, 1997.

Lazreg, M. *Questioning the Veil: Open Letters to Muslim Women.* Princeton, NJ: Princeton University Press, 2009.

Lentin, Alana, and Gavan Titley. *The Crises of Multiculturalism: Racism in a Neoliberal Age.* London: Zedbooks, 2011.

Longman, Chia. "Over Our Heads? Muslim Women as Symbols and Agents in the Headscarf Debate in Flanders, Belgium." *Social Justice: Anthropology, Peace, and Human Rights* 4, nos. 3–4 (2003): 300–332.

Mahmood, Saba. *Politics of Piety: The Reform of the Feminist Subject.* Princeton, NJ: Princeton University Press, 2005.

———. "Feminist Theory, Embodiment, and the Docile Agent: Some Reflections on the Egyptian Islamic Revival." *Cultural Anthropology* 6, no. 2 (2001): 202–36.

Mani, Lata. *Contentious Tradition: The Debate on Sati in Colonial India.* Berkeley: University of California Press, 1998.

Midden, Eva. *Feminism in Multicultural Societies: An Analysis of Dutch Multicultural and Postsecular Developments and Their Implications for Feminist Debates.* University of Central Lancashire, unpublished PhD dissertation, 2010.

Moors, A. "The Dutch and the Face-veil: The Politics of Discomfort." *Social Anthropology* 17, no. 4 (2009): 393–408.

———. "Religious Reason and Secular Affect: An Incommensurable Divide?" *Critical Inquiry* 35 (Summer 2009): 836–62.

Navaro-Yashin, Y. "The Market for Identities: Secularism, Islamism, Commodities." In *Fragments of Culture: The Everyday of Modern Turkey*, edited by Kandiyoti and Saktanber, 1–53. New Brunswick, NJ: Rutgers University Press, 2002.

Schinkel, Willem. *Denken in een tijd van Sociale Hypochondrie: Aanzet tot een theorie voorbij de maatschappij.* Kampen: Uitgeverij Klement, 2008.

Scott, Joan W. *The Politics of the Veil.* Princeton, NJ: Princeton University Press, 2007.

Silvestri, Sara. *Europe's Muslim Women: Potential, Aspirations, and Challenges.* Brussels: King Baudouin Foundation, 2008.

Tarlo, Emma. "Islamic Cosmopolitanism: The Sartorial Biographies of Three Muslim Women in London." *Fashion Theory: The Journal of Dress, Body, and Culture* 11, nos. 2–3 (2007): 143–72.

Van Istendael, Geert. "Het masker van de dwang." *De Standaard*, August 23, 2008.

Wekker, Gloria, and Rosi Braidotti. *Praten in het donker: Multicuturalisme en antiracisme in feministisch perspectief.* Amsterdam: Kok Agora, 1996.

Yuval-Davis, Nira. *Gender and Nation.* London: Sage, 1997.

Section II

POSTCOLONIAL MEMORY

Chapter Six

(Un)happy Endings

Nostalgia in Postimperial and Postmemory Dutch Films

Pamela Pattynama

Longingly, Dutch publicist Rudy Kousbroek (1929–2010) looks at an old photograph of his father as a young man. Dressed in a white *jas toetoep* (the usual attire for colonial men) his young father leans nonchalantly against the fragile railing of a narrow bamboo bridge above an Indonesian kali (stream):

> Ach, laat mij toch voor één keer schaamteloos terug verlangen naar het land zoals ik het heb gekend: vredig, lieflijk en schoon . . . !

> Oh, could I just for once shamelessly yearn for the country the way I knew it: peaceful, lovely and clean . . . ![1]

In the Netherlands, Kousbroek is widely recognised as a keen writer of penetrating essays, but his biting pen also made him notorious in certain communities of Indies migrants.[2] Born in the Dutch East-Indies Kousbroek spent his youth in the former colony and was never tired of pointing out the mythical and to his mind false and romanticised representations of the Dutch colonial past which continue to circulate in both national memory and memories of Indies migrants. However, in spite of his never-ending exposure of false myth-making in others, he himself time and again could not resist the temptation of presenting idyllic images of his youth in the East-Indies.[3]

In memory texts about the Dutch East-Indies, a "youth in the Indies" is irrevocably described as heaven on earth. In Dutch-Indies literature, a happy child romping about on sun dappled lawns under huge palm trees is a familiar trope. This idyllic representation of a paradise lost has become a metaphor for the colonial past as a whole and often crops up both in private family histories which are passed on from generation to generation, and in public histories such as academic oral history projects. In Indies literature, nostalgic tales persist in spite of studies and representations that tell opposite stories.[4]

The work of Indo-Dutch author Paula Gomes for example contains many suggestions of fear and domestic violence in her descriptions of growing up in the East-Indies: she rather wishes to forget than to remember her youth:

> Het liefst wil ik de huizen vergeten waar we gewoond hebben en waar mijn broer werd geslagen. Waar ik altijd bang was. 's Nachts hoorde ik deurknoppen naar beneden drukken, maar gelukkig, de deuren gingen niet open, ze zaten op slot. Ik zag schaduwen die groter en groter werden, wanstaltig, gedrochten. Als ik naar een bepaalde hoek keek, zou daar een gedaante oplichten, erger dan een mòmòh.

> I would much rather forget the houses where we lived and where my brother was often beaten. Where I was always scared. At night I heard door knobs turning, but thank heavens the doors never opened because they were locked. I saw shadows looming larger and larger, ominously shaped, monstrosities. When I looked at a certain corner, an apparition would appear, worse than a mòmòh (ghost).[5]

Whilst the memory of the colonial past is drastically reshaped due to the fact that memories of the East-Indies are becoming increasingly nuanced, holy cows are being attacked and stereotypes broken down, the nostalgic projection of the East-Indies as a tropical paradise lost remains and continues to be passed on. How and why does this happen?

AESTHETICS OF NOSTALGIA

The aesthetics of nostalgia has become an alluring and fascinating subject in the postimperial "memorial culture" of contemporary western societies.[6] Triggered by the effects of globalization, nostalgia presents us with an escapist longing for a past place and time, which is highly idealized. In spite of its alluring effect or precisely because of it, nostalgia has been sharply criticized by many social critics. Since its appearance in the last decades of the twentieth century words such as "reactionary," "escapist," "inauthentic" and "unreflexive" are used to condemn the emergence of nostalgic memories. In critical essays, written mainly in the UK, the US and Germany, a variety of media texts, including movies, literary texts, coffee table picture books, and TV series are blamed for feeding us with marketable if distorted memories. In Britain where nostalgic memory has been viewed as an inauthentic tool of the British heritage industry, Salman Rushdie blamed the rise of conservative ideologies for the nostalgic comeback of a "false Orient" on television and in the cinema. In the US Christopher Lasch termed nostalgia "a betrayal of history," whereas film critic Lutz Koepnick has observed that in Germany, the visual presentation of the Holocaust as dramatic spectacle by converting "bad history into a good story" is seen as "distorted."[7] These views, based on the opposition between true history and false memories regard nostalgia as a simplification if not falsification of history which would obscure viewers' understanding of the underlying political forces.

Recently, and in contrast with such studies, the specific social functioning of nostalgia and its varied consequences have become the object of analysis. Students of memory have begun to approach nostalgia as a particular kind of feeling and thought, even calling it an indispensable part of human life. Pointing out nostalgia's "critical potential," they furthermore recognize the great variety of ways in which nostalgic thinking may become a force that "complicates" rather than simplifies.[8]

In this essay I will follow the latter line of thought in exploring the kind of nostalgia rooted in a longing for former colonies or a former empire. My concern is motivated by the postcolonial legacies in the Dutch cultural imagination, particularly pertaining to the relationship between the present-day Netherlands and its former colony, the Dutch East-Indies, nowadays Indonesia. The beloved colony has always been imagined as the exotic mysterious Other, a female space awaiting Dutch male enterprise, adventure and sexuality.[9] From the first contacts between local populations and European newcomers, fictional narratives, including travel journals, memoirs, letters, songs, and literary works carried across knowledge, fantasized or not, about the far exotic region to the motherland. Intertextually connected, such memory texts were immensely popular: they related to national pride and provided the Calvinistic motherland with an erotic space filled with "piquancies," and adulterous characters.[10]

Decolonization did not bring this flow of intertextual imaginations to a halt. Since Indonesian nationalists proclaimed the autonomy of their country in 1945 and the Dutch subsequently conceded to the formal loss of their profitable colony in 1949, the continuing (post-)colonial relationship between the Netherlands and the East-Indies/Indonesia has generated a wide and on-going range of intricate and conflicting memories. As political entity, the East-Indies doesn't exist any more, but as *lieu de mémoire* it inhabits an eternal space on the cultural map of the Netherlands. After decolonization the nostalgic image of the Indies as "sunken continent" became wide-spread. From the immediate post-World War II period up to the present day, it has become one of the most popular motives in modern Dutch literature.[11] Almost monthly, new narratives about the Indies are published of which many soon gain high positions on best-seller charts (e.g. Hella Haasse, Reggie Baay, Eveline Stoel). For the most part, the popularity of these Indies memory texts can be derived from the fact that they are both diachronically and synchronically linked up: familiar themes, stylistic elements and standard images emerge time and again, consolidating and embedding the constant presence of the beloved colony in the Dutch cultural imagination. In fact, the East-Indies returns repeatedly through what Paul Connerton has called "acts of transfer," and Ann Rigney "memorial dynamics," in postcolonial media as diverse as literary works, *Pasar Malams* (typical Indo-Dutch combinations of market and cultural festivals held in cities and towns across the country), music, movies, TV series, historiography, monuments, documentaries, comics, family histories, and commemorative events. Such memory texts mediate and transform an endless interaction of intertextually connected postcolonial memories.[12]

A case in point is writer Maria Dermoût's first publication *Only yesterday (Nog pas gisteren,* 1959), which contains all the images usually associated with the former East-Indies: exotic nature featuring an exuberant plant life and animal world, a paradise-like youth, the usual crowd of servants, the motherly *baboe* (nanny) sleeping on a mat nearby. Other aspects are also well-known: the novel's realism, its supernatural phenomena and the indecent sexual practices dramatized. From the first sentence on, the novel focuses on pastness and distance, while at the same time recalling a deeply hidden, safe "home":

> Op Java, ergens op Midden-Java, tussen de Bergen Lawoe en Wilis in, maar dichter naar de kant van de Lawoe toe, lag diep in een ommuurde tuin onder donkere groene bomen een huis.

> On Java, somewhere in Middle Java, between the mountains Lawoe and Wilis, but closer to Lawoe, there was a house, situated in the depths of a walled garden, under dark green trees.[13]

The ending of *Only Yesterday* speaks of loss and farewell, which, from a postcolonial perspective, foreshadows the national loss of the Indies. Interestingly, its enigmatic title *Only Yesterday* adds to this visionary image. It refers to past-ness, but rather than a time forever gone, it suggests proximity or even more, the *presence* of the past: only yesterday something existed that keeps lingering on.[14] Dermoût is known as a nostalgic Indies writer. I would like to suggest, however, that if her imagery influenced the nostalgic metaphors by which the Dutch represent their colonial past, her narrative techniques inspired the generation of Indo-Dutch writers succeeding her. In fact, the second generation of Indo writers and filmmakers carried on Dermoût's Indo-Dutch practice of intertextual fusion and mixing. Below, I will come back to their use of intertextual nostalgia in order to imagine a common past and collective identity.

However, rather than simply dismissing nostalgia as reactionary kitsch, I would like, as anticipated, to suggest an alternative reading, one that moves beyond the opposition of true history or false nostalgia, and argue for the recognition of the mutual dependence between history, memory, identifications and colonial nostalgia. Rather than privileging so-called proper history, I will argue for the agency of distinct audiences as well as for the function of nostalgic images for processes of identification in Dutch memorial culture.[14]

MEMORIAL DYNAMICS

To underline the cultural dimension of nostalgia it is important to foreground the concept of collective or cultural memory here. Many recent studies on memory share the starting point that remembering is never an individual act because it is always already connected to the present dynamics of social memory. Introduced by French philosopher and sociologist Maurice Halbwachs in 1925 and extended by Jan and Aleida Assmann, this idea defines collective memory in terms of individual participation in communities. Individuals participating in communities adopt the group's social frames, which implies the sharing of a collective past. While memory is the central medium through which identities are constituted, these processes of mediation and identification shape the way we develop and retain a sense of the past and a narrative about ourselves.[15] Drawing on Halbwachs' assertion that memories are always to be mediated through current social frames in order to be remembered, nostalgia can be regarded as less an affair of the past than of the present. Many memory critics approach the phenomenon as a complex mediated projection of current fears, obsessions and hopes, that invokes both an imagined past and self image. In fact, recent discussions on the transference of memory through public artefacts, popular culture and collective rituals emphasize the significance of, on the one hand, the flows and re-mediation of memory and, on the other, processes of identification among members of distinct "mnemonic" communities. Mnemonic or remembering communities are groups (families, friends, generations, migrants, nations) in which individuals participate and which also socialize them to what should be remembered and forgotten.[16] The notion is a continuation of Maurice Halbwachs' assertion that through a constant process of adaptation, re-creation and change, every community develops a memory or memories of its own past that highlights its unique identity. Through such processes of shared remembering and forgetting, distinct though sometimes overlapping groups in the Netherlands create a sense of togetherness and articulate often conflicting recollections of the East-Indies and the colonial past.

These processes of memorial dynamics are the point of departure in my exploration of the connections between cultural memory, nostalgia, and identity. Starting from the assumption that nostalgia may take on many dimensions, I will explore the use of nostalgia and the varying effects that it may

have on viewers participating in mnemonic communities. As examples of
such dialogues I will explore two movies and "read" them within the context
of Dutch memorial culture. Both *Girdle of Emerald* (*Gordel van Smaragd*
directed by Orlow Seunke, 1997) and *Far from Family* (*Ver van Familie*
directed by Marion Bloem, 2009) are present acts of memory that construct
an imagined colonial past and in this way play a significant role in the reconstruction and continuity of postcolonial individual and collective self images.
Fredric Jameson once argued: "a history lesson is the best cure for nostalgic
pathos."[17] We shall therefore first have a short detour and look at the Dutch
memorial culture through which the two films have been produced.

INTRICATE MIXTURE OF NOSTALGIA AND AMNESIA

After Indonesia's independence in 1945 and after World War II, more than
three hundred thousand migrants came to the Netherlands from the former
colony. Most of them were of mixed race. Colonialism was not only a war
machine; it was also a "desiring machine" that produced its own "darkest
fantasy," to use Robert Young's terms, that fuelled such interracial unions,
and was then bequeathed to their offspring.[18] Since the seventeenth century,
Dutch racial and sexual politics in the East-Indies had involved the condoning
and even encouragement of interracial concubinage and miscegenation. In
stark contrast to British or French colonialism, and mainly for economic reasons, the Dutch saw advantages in unions between European men and Asian
women.[19] Whereas the political authority of the Netherlands remained remote, and white-European women were scarce, the mixing of European men
and Asian women evolved into a *mestizo* society in which local and European
habits, rituals, traditions, morals and behaviour were constantly blended. By
the twentieth century most Dutch citizens in the late-colonial settlements
were, in fact, of mixed race.[20] When they migrated to the Netherlands, Indo-
Dutch migrants lost their homeland because they were, due to their mixed
origin, considered outsiders and traitors by Indonesian nationalists. Their
experiences during the violent Indonesian war of independence which took
place from 1945 to 1949, were often even worse than their experiences inside
as well as outside Japanese camps during World War II in the Pacific.[21] Upon
arriving in the Netherlands, supposedly their "motherland," they found themselves both a problem to a nation recovering from the German Occupation,
and an unwelcome reminder of a colonial past the Dutch were eager to wish
away. For the Dutch nation, Indonesia's independence marked not only the
loss of its profitable and beloved colony, but also the collapse of the Dutch
Empire. During the postwar reconstruction of the Netherlands, memories of
the German Occupation left little room for commemoration of the war in the

Pacific. The colonial past seemed closed, like a finished and forgotten book. The Dutch East-Indies disappeared from the public eye and became a well-kept "family secret," the blind spot on the national retina.[22] The Indo-Dutch soon realized that their traumatic recollections were incompatible with the prevailing postwar rhetoric on national reconstruction and unity. Effectively silenced they were compelled to forget their past and subjected to a rapid process of assimilation. For years their stories were withdrawn from the public eye and banished to the private domain. All of this, the prevailing amnesia in the public domain, the silencing of personal memories and the marginalizing of postcolonial critique, perpetuated existing myths of an idyllic era, a source of national pride. The exclamation: "daar is wat groots verricht!" (those were our glory days!) is heard to this day.[23]

Public debate only made its faltering entrance during the rebellious late 1960's. Prompted by international critical movements such as the Civil and Gay Rights movements, feminism and the protests against the Vietnam war, the "forgotten" colonial past was first formally remembered in 1969 during an interview on national television with J.E. Hueting, a military veteran who was completely unknown up until then. He appealed to the public that research be done into war crimes committed by Dutch forces during the Indonesian war of Independence in an effort to regain power in the Indies. His revelation of war crimes via the forceful medium of TV is burned in national memory because of the incredible outrage it evoked. It forced the nation's self-image to shift from one of a victim under Nazi Occupation to one revealing the Dutch to be perpetrators of war crimes in the lost colony. This reactivation of memories marked a dramatic change in national thinking about the colonial past. In the postcolonial public mind, the cherished Dutch East-Indies suddenly emerged as a source of shame and guilt about racism, exploitation and war crimes. These shame and guilt discourses invariably upset deeply anchored myths of an idyllic, proud era. From that moment on the national amnesia around the colonial past began to lift, and, although nostalgic memories continued to appear, the East-Indies equally became a source of shame and guilt about racism, exploitation and war crimes.[24] Hueting's public appeal for research into war crimes became a key moment that not only generated a dramatic transformation of discourses about the colonial past, but also shifted the location of Indo-Dutch memories after they were moved from the private to the public domain and became part of a broader cultural memory. Furthermore, Hueting's key intervention initiated a new visual focus on the memory of the East-Indies in the media.

The way in which Hella Haasse's well-known novel *Oeroeg* (1948) was visualized and adapted for the movie *Oeroeg* (1993) is a case in point. Narrated by a young white man, son of a wealthy Dutch plantation owner in the East-Indies, Haasse's novel concentrates on his friendship with Oeroeg, son of one of his father's Javanese underlings. The film takes up the ending of the source novel through a second time-line that is situated in the *Bersiap* (as the beginning of the war of independence is called), and uses flashbacks that present the gist of the novel. While the first narrative line foregrounds racial hostility, its images of crisis and war dissolve repeatedly into flashbacks, which visualise Johan's fond memories of a privileged boyhood and precious interracial friendship. We thus see the two boys pictured in an unspoiled landscape swearing for better or for worse to be blood brothers forever; we also witness the demise of their bond when Oeroeg becomes involved with Indonesian nationalism, turns against the Dutch colonisers and rejects his white friend, who leaves for Holland. The contrast between the images of war and loss and idyllic youth, evokes a deep sense of nostalgic longing for a lost era. Interestingly, the film also represents the change in discourse through noticeably transnational imagery. Forty-five years after the publication of the book, the film embodied altered memories with roots in international activist politics of the late 1960s. We see for example an impressive sequence of a burnt-down Indonesian native village in the jungle, which inevitably reminds the viewer of the My Lai atrocities often displayed in American anti-Vietnam movies. As it passed from one medium to another, the narrative as represented in the film operated on the shame-and-guilt discourses that had entered Dutch memorial culture. In combination with Hueting's notorious appeal on TV, the reference of the My Lai atrocities by association foregrounded long-silenced Dutch war crimes—something which was never part of the novel. At the same time, it re-shaped the colonial discourse that permeated its literary source. Through the use of flashbacks, the film contrasted postcolonial discourses with the novel's projection of the East-Indies as a lost paradise which offered happy children an "innocent" space for interracial friendship and, simultaneously, introduced a new kind of nostalgia.[25]

The current, continuous range of often contradictory memories testify to the ambivalent fascination the East-Indies exercises in the cultural landscape of postcolonial Holland. Especially since the 1970s the voices of Indo-Dutch migrants, however internally divided, have complemented and complicated the existing, already inconsistent national memories. The "other" memories of the past that they brought into circulation have clashed, interacted with and have become entangled with national, so-called postimperial memories.[26] In the context of a dynamic national memory-making process, the colony has come to stand for an ongoing range of partly overlapping, partly conflicting "textured" memories, which engage different modes of nostalgic and shame-bearing discourses.[27] The dynamic interaction of such diverse memories over time has continuously changed the meaning of the East-Indies as a memory site, and simultaneously has shaped and reshaped national and migrant mnemonic communities.

Released amidst the contradictions of Dutch memorial culture, *Girdle of Emerald* and *Far from Family* belong to an archive of Dutch cinema. Between the recurring tensions raised by on the one hand popular Hollywood films and on the other elite art-house films, Dutch cinema over time has become a regional mass medium, which engages a broad local audience.[28] Rather than through pure entertainment or art, it operates through national identification. As films are, however, always open for more than one interpretation, viewers can negotiate the messages produced in mass communication. In fact audiences may appropriate, reconfigure and oppose the intended meanings of the film texts they watch.[29] Films offer us, as British film critic Pam Cook argues, "imaginative encounters" that rely on empathy and identification and, in varying ways, invite viewers to negotiate interpretations and memories.[30] Though such memories may not be based on first-hand experiences, they nevertheless have a powerful emotional affect. In that sense viewers are not simply passive recipients of the intended nostalgic codes that public narratives pass on. In order to (re)-invent and reconfigure their memories and self images viewers may appropriate, borrow and change the meaning of encountered cultural texts, images or sounds. As part of the Dutch memorial culture both *Girdle of Emerald* and *Far from Family* engage divers audiences in the Low Countries who may identify with, negotiate, or oppose and reconfigure the intended meanings of the nostalgia they experience.

Below I will explore the two films as postimperial acts of memory that are performed and re-performed in the present. By attempting to appropriate a missing past, these "historicist" films both feed on the available flows of nostalgia produced in the Netherlands over time, albeit in divergent ways.[31] In *Girdle of Emerald* I will focus on the production of national or postimperial memory and explore the theme of interracial contacts as a privileged metaphor. In the analysis of *Far from Family* my focus is on the deliberate use of nostalgia in order to shape and transform Indo mnemonic communities.

GIRDLE OF EMERALD

The widely known term *gordel van smaragd* (girdle of emerald) which indicates the Indonesian Archipelago, first appeared in the ending to Multatuli's famous novel *Max Havelaar* (1860), which constitutes an appeal to King William II about the moral duty of the Dutch with regard to its splendid colonial possession. Evolving across time, the term nowadays is widely used and recalls, as I have already demonstrated, a far-away exotic archipelago, forever lost in time. In Orlow Seunke's film the title points to the nostalgia that is evoked throughout. Conscientiously selected "authentic" clothes, music, objects and architecture capture the viewer's imagination as signifying the "real" East Indies, while striking exotic landscapes, bathed in mellow golden light, equally turn the viewers' eyes to the idyllic colony which once was "ours." The aura of past-ness that is conveyed by the soundtrack, the objects and costumes, is underlined by the historical "truth" that is highlighted in the way the film is structured. Brief pieces of original newsreel in black and white footage divide the otherwise full Technicolor film in ten parts, each encompassing a year between 1939 and 1949. These ten turbulent years were decisive for Indonesia's independence and for the collapse of the Dutch empire, though the subsequent process of decolonization also determined the fate of all groups involved. This background of historical events provides highly dramatic cinematic material, which informs the fictional setting of the film. The use of documentary material at the beginning of each part allows, in other words, "real" history with its truth-claim to act upon cinematic representation. This claim is however complicated by the alternating voices of the film's hero and heroine which accompany the newsreels. Framed in historical documentary style, their voices turn *Girdle of Emerald* into a memory film that looks back from a postimperial Dutch perspective to the colonial past.

As is well known, *Girdle of Emerald* is focused on an interracial romance in the colony. Discussing the postcolonial relationship between imperial France and Indo-China, Panivong Norindr has argued that the "passionate romance or stormy love affair" remains to this day the most pervasively used metaphor for describing the conquest, colonization and subsequent loss of the colony in recognizable cinematic figures.[32] His observation finds resonance in the Dutch context. Indeed, *Girdle of Emerald* belongs to the international heritage film industry criticised by Renato Rosaldo for fabricating imperialist nostalgic images of interracial contacts in an idealized paradise. Striking a pose of "innocent yearning" such images capture people's imaginations and, at the same time, conceal their complicity with "brutal domination."[33]

Director Orlow Seunke, who, as far as I know has no personal connections to the ex-colony, claimed that he "wanted to tell the historical truth."[34] However, most of his film is devoted to the impossibility of the interracial romance along the lines of the familiar Romeo-and-Juliet literary motif of a forbidden love. European newcomer Theo, newly arrived from the Netherlands, falls in love with Ems, a married woman of mixed race, born and bred in the Indies. The romance runs parallel to the historical events and follows the conventional depiction of love in times of disaster. At first it is staged against an idyllic background of lush, green rice fields and colonial society life. When Japan invades the colony, Ems' husband is killed and Theo ends up in a camp. He is tortured, but Ems saves her lover's life by offering sexual services to a high ranking Japanese officer. During the Bersiap—the chaotic early years of the Indonesian war of independence—the couple marries, but both Theo and Ems are traumatized by their different war experiences. Alienation grows when Ems distributes medicine to the Indonesian guerilla fighters who destroy Theo's plantation. Soon afterwards they decide to migrate to the Netherlands, but at the very last minute Ems jumps off the train to stay in the country of her birth.

Girdle of Emerald is an ambitious film in its mediation of conflicting images and memories of the colonial past. However, the troubling portrayal of female mixed race and interracial contacts has made the movie an easy target of feminist and postcolonial critique.[35] Ems is portrayed as the illegitimate child of an unknown white father and poor Indonesian mother and as such she is made to act out some of the tensions and sensibilities that surrounded interracial sexuality in the late colonial Indies. Given the fact that in Dutch public memory the experiences of the Indo-Dutch have long been invisible, the representation of a mixed race woman speaking "from below" is a welcome historical turn. Unfortunately, however, Ems' performance is largely discredited by sexualised and racialized stereotypes where clichés of the exoticized "oriental woman" join with old myths pertaining to the unreliability of the "tragic half-blood." Not only is she the seductive girl saved from native backwardness by a rich, white father-figure, she is also framed within the notorious inferiority complex assigned to people of mixed race. In reality, this pathological complex resulted from a version of colonial discourse produced as part of the ever prevailing sense of white (masculine) superiority. Mixed-race Ems, a *kampoeng* (native village) girl, turns out to be the source of all the problems that arise in her relationship with her romantic Dutch man. While these orientalist views confirm once more the dominance of white masculinity in colonial affairs, the troubling representation of mixed-race and interracial romance in *Girdle of Emerald* also re-inscribes colonial stereotypes, perpetuating thereby nostalgic discourses of the colony as the Netherlands' lost paradise.

Girdle of Emerald is framed by a larger postimperial memory industry that has proliferated in Holland since the late 1970s.[36] Even as cinema and TV documentaries began to focus more on groups that had always been excluded from the dominant images of history, such as women and people of mixed race, many of the films about the colonial past fell back on stereotypes. All open with all-too-familiar idyllic settings of ricefields and indigenous *kampoengs*, which are then disrupted by shots of the attack on Pearl Harbor after which the agony for the colony begins.[37] In accordance with this line of visual aesthetics, *Girdle of Emerald* presents the past, predictably, as a site of splendid landscapes, alluring objects, exotic sex, and fascinating stories, all brought to an end by the Japanese Occupation. As such, like the film *Oeroeg*, it partakes in the visual imagery of decolonization that continues to represent the East-Indies as a national loss.

NATIONAL ENGAGEMENT

Benedict Anderson's well-known argument that novels provide the technical means for "imagining" the nation can be extended to include movies.[38] In modern societies the technology of mass media is extremely influential in shaping and reshaping collective relations to history. Alison Landsberg argues, for instance, that the emergence of the mass medium of film has created a new form of public memory. Film immerses viewers in impressions and experiences they may not have actually experienced. Through this process a viewer does not simply apprehend a historical narrative but takes on a "more personal, deeply felt memory of a past event through which he or she did not live."[39] Landsberg's argument that such "prosthetic memory" has the ability to shape a viewer's subjectivity and politics, helps to explain *Girdle of Emerald*'s role in reshaping postimperial memory concerning the colonial past.

Overall *Girdle of Emerald* operates within that romantic nostalgia that Pavelong Norindr has coined "colonial blues."[40] By using the Dutch language and touching on national sentiments evoked by World War II and the colonial past, *Girdle of Emerald* participates in the search for a shared past and the reconstruction of national identity while, at the same time, making colonial memory part of Dutch viewers' personal archive of experience, without having experienced the colony themselves. By engaging its audience through its display of familiar idyllic and nostalgic images, *Girdle of Emerald* participates in, but also powerfully shapes, the never-ending process of negotiation and contestation that organises public memory concerning the colonial past. It shows the difficulty of remembering and representing a past permeated by pride, guilt and nostalgia. Refraining from closure or a happy ending, it foregrounds loss and incompleteness in negotiating national relationships to the past. This articulates, in particular, the incapacity and failure of the Dutch nation to engage effectively with its colonial past. More than anything else, the unhappy ending suggests that for the Dutch nation the colonial past continues to be a memory fraught with anxiety as well as desire.

NEW SENSE OF SELF

In contrast to this at once national and postimperial nostalgia, second generation Indo-Dutch writers and filmmakers have negotiated nostalgia in a different manner.[41] They re-write Indo-Dutchness through what might be termed a transnational sense of self, straddling home and abroad. Born within Dutch culture, in the colonial mother country, they grew up with a confusing sense of the past. Their parents either told bitter stories about racial inequality and Dutch ignorance, or passed on nostalgic tales about a country that no longer existed to visit. Silence about the past, however, dominated the intergenerational transference, both in public and in migrant living rooms. Framed by emotionally charged silences and events that took place before they were born, the "postmemories" produced by the second generation were mediations of this heritage.[42] While they were busy growing up, due to the newly emerging processes of displacement, multiculturalism and globalism, new groups of migrants and refugees began to "perform" their ethnic identities in the multicultural Netherlands. Second-generation Indo-Dutch began to resist the silent adaptation of the older generation to Dutch cultural standards and their denial of their colonial Indonesian "roots." Indo-Dutch filmmakers, artists, writers and musicians such as Claire Pijman, Peter van Dongen, Merapi Obermayer, Joyce Bloem and Wouter Müller self-consciously employed the contested past and emphasized their mixed-race identity by turning back to and reinterpreting that past. Through divers acts of remembrance, for example landscape art, websites, comics, installations, documentaries, art photography and literature, they claimed the East-Indies as a collective identity marker. Over time, the East-Indies turned into a changing and evocative memory site for those who had no first-hand knowledge of the ex-colony—second-generation postcolonial migrants and their children alike.

Among the second-generation Indo-Dutch authors and filmmakers multi-talented Marion Bloem takes a leading position. She is best known as author of the much-acclaimed, best-selling novel *No Ordinary Indo Girl* (*Geen gewoon Indisch meisje*, 1983). Released in the same year, her documentary *My Parents' Country* (*Het land van mijn ouders*) enjoyed both critical and commercial success. Much of Bloem's postmemory work evolves around an artistic exploration of Indo identity and culture, which puts her in the tradition of the legendary Indo spokesman Tjalie Robinson. Like Robinson, who explored and benchmarked his Indo-Dutch identity from a global perspective, Bloem puts her search for gendered Indo identity in the broader perspective of international immigration.[43] In her many books, the author develops this theme from what at first sight appears to be an autobiographical matter into a generational issue, and beyond that into the fate of the so-called homeless Indo generation, in search for a "home" of its own in an uprooted world. Rather than in-between figures, as often is asserted, Bloem's protagonists are transnational subjects who invent a home and shape identities through the creative re-writing of stories and myths about being mixed race. Her first long feature film *Far from Family* continues this sustained quest. Based on her book of the same name, Bloem wrote the screenplay and directed several Indo icons, including popular Indo singers.[44]

INDO IDENTIFICATIONS

Far from Family tells the story of the Königs, an extended Indo family who migrated to the Netherlands after the independence of Indonesia. The main story line is situated during the mid-1980s when the adult second-generation Indo-Dutch had begun to perform and express their mixed-race identity. In *Far from Family* new identity claims come to the fore in the stories of various family members, all of which shed a different light on a multifaceted family history. In this web of narratives, one of the granddaughters of "Oma" (grandma) Em, named Barbie, makes a dramatic entrance into the family circle. As a young child, Barbie was taken to the United States by her father and stepmother where her father then disappeared. After her stepmother passed away, and following a devastating love affair, Barbie finds herself on her own and travels back to the Netherlands longing to meet the heart of the family in the form of her Oma Em. The unexpected presence of the young woman among the Königs opens up a past of hushed-up secret family stories about adultery, queer sexuality and the mysterious death of Barbie's mother. The main story-line of the film concerns Barbie's arrival, her search for her Oma Em and the family's efforts to keep her out of sight of her old grandmother who is very ill. The Königs fear that contact with Barbie will be detrimental to the old woman's health. This main line is continuously interrupted by stories of family members representing various generations. The most prominent interruption is the voice-over of Oma Em who half-consciously looks back at her life in the East-Indies. Coming and going in rhythmic waves, her flashback interventions narrate the concealed colonial past, forever present although buried in families with an Indies heritage.

The film works intertextually on several levels through its links to well-known tropes and images from the "Indies mobile archive" of narratives. Similar to what happens in many other Indo stories, the "family" plays a large part. Likewise, Bloem's film echoes the secrets and desires which obsessed family members in many older Indies narratives, amongst which Louis Couperus' *Of Old People, the Things that Pass* (*Van oude mensen, de dingen die voorbij gaan*, 1906) is a well-known example. The film also reminds us of the intriguing plots in another family saga connected to earlier Indo narratives: Rob Nieuwenhuys' *Faded Portraits from an Indies Family Album* (*Vergeelde portretten uit een Indisch familie album*, 1954). The main intertext, however, is Bloem's own literary work. Her ambitious novel *Fathers of Importance* (*Vaders van betekenis,* 1989), for instance, offers us a reconstruction of a family chronicle which centres around a "Buddy." Buddy epitomises the elusive male Indo in Bloem's work, an immortal character who persists in narratives through the centuries. In *Far from Family* this Buddy turns up again as Barbie's mysterious father who continues to affect the stories of the Königs long after his death.

INDO NOSTALGIA

As in *Girdle of Emerald*, nostalgia works in *Far from Family* both visually and through the narrative structure. Selected "authentic" memory objects and visualised fragments of Indo history or "typical" Indo habits and values are designed to awaken our nostalgic imagination. The protective space of the Indo family to which each and every member supposedly wishes to belong and never do without, is foregrounded. Furthermore, inserted sepia-coloured photographs of the Indies evoke sentiments about so-called *tempo doeloe* past times, while cluttered Indo living rooms "typical" for Indo migrants call up the notorious seventies when in the public domain young people challenged old traditions and the second Indo generation grew up with a silenced past and an urgent need to re-shape Indo-Dutch identities. Indo nostalgia is also implied in the apron "Uncle Lex" wears when making Indo titbits, in the abundance of Indo food carried along in plastic buckets, in the family members gathered in rows at Oma Em's deathbed, the noisy family gatherings where young and old intermingle, chat, nibble and partake in the Indonesian martial-arts dance *pentjak silat*. Indo nostalgia is equally expressed in the references to the legendary beauty of Indo women and their excellent cooking skills, as well as in the hints at whispered stories, secrets and scandals. In contrast to *Girdle of Emerald*, where nostalgia relates in the first place to national memory, the display of nostalgia in *Far from Family* addresses Indo audiences and works to disrupt the idea of a closed Indo family or of fixed traditions.

In the film the tradition of Indo hospitality is destabilized when no one has time to fetch Barbie from the airport and nobody welcomes her into the heart of the family. Until the (un)happy ending of the film, viewers are kept in uncertainty whether anything remotely resembling family unity will come to pass. The *koempoelan* or family gathering which is organised for Barbie is a stingy affair instead of a generous occasion. Rather than a joyful welcoming party it is a smokescreen to prevent her from seeing her grandmother. Significant is the disrupted tradition of the highly reputed *rijsttafel*, which has always functioned as an identity marker for Indo-Dutchness. "Aunt Joyce" has made this abundant array of dishes in full knowledge of the fact that the guest of honour abhors this kind of food. The scenes in which everyone sits down to eat together remind us of the traditional cohesion and continuity of Indo families, but in fact lay bare various mechanisms of exclusion, foreclosure and suffocation.

Another working out of Indo nostalgia happens in the persistent scenes showing cluttered Indo living rooms. Bloem's film visualizes such "migrant aesthetics in the home" through a clashing overlap and blending of distinct collections of things in the living room.[45] These decorative reminders of a long-lost past in the East-Indies are conventionally intended to dissipate the feeling of strangeness in the Netherlands. Next to those decorative ornaments all sorts of cheap handy utensils are also on display. Acquired in Holland after migration, they can be recognized as the silent witnesses of the new life being built up in this new space. Many second-generation migrants will have memories of growing up in such rooms, regardless of whether they actually experienced this or not. The cluttered domestic interiors of Indo migrants shown in *Far from Family* emphasise in these ways the complex layered meanings reflecting personal, social, cultural and historical dynamics within the everyday practices of migrants.

Oma Em personifies another nostalgic memory. As the matriarchal pillar and oldest member of the family she is loved and respected by everyone. She therefore on the one hand represents typical grandmother nostalgia which is often evoked in Dutch advertisements for national dishes such as pea soup with smoked sausage from "grandma's kitchen." On the other hand she represents the Indo family as Indo home and most intimate place of belonging. Barbie's quest for her roots is therefore consciously focused on her. The function of Oma Em can also be explained in terms of a lineage of female stereotypes within the family. In *Far from Family* Oma Em is defined via the flashbacks through which her everyday life in the Indies as a mother and wife is imagined. In this way, she undermines the embedded images through which Indonesian or Indo women, mainly in Indies-Dutch literature, are immortalized either as sexualized danger zones (for white men) or as powerless victims.

In the East-Indies, local women, so-called *nyais*, as we have already seen, were the sexual partners of European men within unequal domestic arrangements. As unpaid housekeeper and concubine the *nyai* had no legal rights in respect to herself or the children she bore. Over time, however, interracial concubinages became the equivalent of Christian marriages and the most common domestic arrangement between European men and local women. Yet, from the 1870s onwards numerous fictional and autobiographical accounts by European women and men alike portrayed the *nyai* as a contentious figure, either idolized for being the loving nanny ("better" than white mothers), or portrayed as the threatening embodiment of exotic sexuality, representing the complications occasioned by the encounter between European and indigenous worlds. To this day the nostalgic figure of the *nyai* lingers on in "innocent" images of interracial contacts in the East-Indies.[46] In contrast to these mediations of imperialist nostalgia, Oma Em's disruptive flashbacks in *Far from Family* refer to the lived experience of Indo women.

A last instance of the workings of nostalgia in the film is represented by the making of a family tree. "I want to recall our history," the artist Astrid König states in *Far from Family*. Embodied by a large, fragile and mobile tree, her own family is the centre piece of the exhibition she puts together. Extensive detail concerning each family member, the in-laws, children and grandchildren, are portrayed by way of objects and photographs which are hung on the tree. In this way it illustrates all the different times and places embodied by Indo memories, whilst family stories—the familiar ones as well as those kept secret—hover over the same tree. In itself this representation of the family seems an overworked cliché evoking nostalgic feelings of belonging, continuity and a secure home. However, framed by its fragility, mobility and the well-intentioned efforts of an over-excited Indo artist, the making of the family tree is turned into an "ironical experiment" referring to the presence of the past within the present.[47] Interestingly, the tree serves the *mise-en-abîme* effect of the film, which occurs via a reduplication of images and concepts referring to the film as a whole.[48] In *Far from Family*, the family tree represents the film as a whole which in its turn represents the Indo mnemonic community as a whole. By visualizing the making of the family tree in an ironic mode, *Far from Family* defines the making of Indo mnemonic communities as a fragile, unfixing experiment. Rather than showing a closed community sharing fixed stories, *Far from Family* represents the Indo mnemonic community as a dynamic archive of transmitted stories shaping a variety of identifications. The use of nostalgia is one of the means by which this process of (re)-invention and reconfiguration of memories and self images takes place.

Far from Family's layered scenario as well as its complex narrative are not easy to get a hold on, while its length has been the subject of complaint. Bloem's production, however, mixes the codes of conventional filmmaking that traditionally demand a central narrative and clear goal-oriented main characters. Its so-called mosaic style of intertexual play, flashback, different time zones, multiple main characters, and interwoven story lines is an appropriate vehicle through which to engage with the complex imagined past, migratory mobility and continual re-shaping of Indo-Dutch identities.[49]

As many other displaced people, migrants from the East-Indies tend to articulate a strong, if ambivalent, longing for a place in which to belong. Their public texts, mainly autobiographical literature and documentaries, often feed on a deep sense of nostalgia, to the extent that immensely popular *tempo doeloe* texts, such as those discussed, have often been rejected as conservative acts of colonialism. First-generation migrant texts indeed include problematic yearnings for an idealized homeland in which unequal power relations are obscured. Nonetheless, as part of the dynamics of Dutch memorial culture, they have worked in important ways to create and recreate mnemonic communities for displaced Indies migrants. Whereas the first generation often used nostalgic literature to imagine a community and a place of belonging, the second generation tended to use nostalgic images of the East-Indies in what Avtar Brah calls a "homing desire": the positioning of a home between a "mythic place of desire" and "the lived experience of a locality."[50] Second-generation authors and filmmakers thus tap into the warehouse of nostalgia offered by the large archive of intertextual connected narratives and memories already assembled. Through the creative revision and re-mediation of such nostalgia they make sense of their lives both in relation to a narrated past and their current position in the Netherlands. *Far from Family* is another example of such a constantly re-imagined past and identity.

CONCLUSION

Focusing on the literary writings of first-generation migrants, Sarah De Mul has convincingly argued that there is a "plethora of different voices, generations and ethnicities in the paradigm of *tempo doeloe* and that the mode of nostalgia they foster and construct serves different aesthetic and even political objectives in different texts."[51] In focusing on feature films which alchemize nostalgia in different though related ways, I have argued that colonial nostalgia in Dutch popular media and Indo-Dutch migrant memories should not glibly be rejected as conservative and inauthentic. If we instead perceive audiences as active recipients and producers of media, then nostalgia may, in different ways, emerge as a dynamic, meaningful tool of identification for remembering communities. Svetlana Boym's distinction between reflective and restorative nostalgia may be helpful here. Boym understands nostalgia as employed in *Far from Family* as "reflective nostalgia" which would dwell on the "ambivalences of human longing and belonging, calling the truth in doubt."[52] Her concept of restorative nostalgia as an "attempt to construct a lost home through truth claims" is also useful to explain the deployment of nostalgia in *Girdle of Emerald.*

In my discussion of Dutch postimperial cinema I have argued that the recurring images of nostalgia in *Girdle of Emerald* reveal the many ongoing postimperial negotiations and elaborations involved in the makeup of the current Dutch nation. Rather than showing the closed *pastness* of the colonial past, the film exposes the dynamic *presence* of postimperial legacies in the Dutch imagination. Similar to *Girdle of Emerald, Far from Family* plays on a longing for a past long gone by. Contrary to *Girdle of Emerald* where nostalgia calls up a longing for the past and an incomplete present, the display of nostalgia in *Far from Family* specifically addresses Indo audiences by providing a means of identification through recognition. As a postmemory film it negotiates the lived experiences of Indo-Dutch migrants in the present day. As a particular mode of feeling and thought, nostalgia involves a wide variety of ways in which it may become a complicating rather than a simplifying force, both in postimperial memory and in migrants' memories.

NOTES

1. Rudy Kousbroek, *Het raadsel der herkenning. Fotosynthese 3* (Amsterdam: Augustus, 2007), 124.

2. There is no consensus about the terminology referring to the Dutch East-Indies and its inhabitants. Here I will use "Indies" (*Indisch*) for any Dutch citizen who was or is connected to the East-Indies by birth, family ties, or a self-defining stay, independent of ethnic origin or skin colour. "Indo" or "Indo-Dutch" is my term for people of mixed race. "Indies" or "Indies-Dutch" literature/texts refers to all narratives and images that have influenced the representation of the Dutch East-Indies or the Dutch colonial past.

3. See, e.g., Rudy Kousbroek and Paula Gomes, *Verloren goeling* (Amsterdam: Meulenhoff, 1998), 52. Also read between the lines of Kousbroek's *Het Oostindisch kampsyndroom* (Amsterdam: Meulenhoff, 1992).

4. Some of the work that has been done in this area are: Jan Breman, *Taming the Coolie Beast: Plantation Society and the Colonial Order in Southeast Asia* (Oxford: Oxford University Press, 1989); Rudy Kousbroek, *Het Oostindisch kampsyndroom* (Amsterdam: Meulenhoff, 1992); Pamela Pattynama, "Memories of Interracial Contacts and Mixed Race in Dutch Cinema," *Journal of Intercultural Studies* 28, no. 1 (2007, Special Issue: Pigments of the Imagination: Theorising, Performing, and Historicising Mixed Race): 69–82; Ewald Vanvugt, *Zwartboek van Nederland overzee: Wat iedere Nederlander moet weten* (Soesterberg: Aspect BV, 2002).

5. Kousbroek and Gomes, *Verloren goeling*, 93.

6. For the concept of "memorial culture," see Andreas Huyssen, *Twilight Memories: Marking Time in a Culture of Amnesia* (New York: Routledge, 1995).

7. Salman Rushdie, *Imaginary Homelands: Essays and Criticism, 1981–1991* (London: Granta/Penguin, 1992), 92; Christopher Lasch, "The Politics of Nostalgia" *Harper's* (November 1984): 65–70; Lutz Koepnick, "Reframing the Past: Heritage Cinema and Holocaust in the 1990s," *New German Critique* 87 (Autumn 2002, Special Issue on Postwall Cinema): 72.

8. Nadia Atia and Jeremy Davies, "Nostalgia and the Shapes of History: Editorial," *Memory Studies* 3, no. 4 (July 2010): 181. For an extensive discussion of *"tempo doeloe"* as a culturally and historically specific manifestation of nostalgia for the East-Indies in postcolonial literature, see Sarah De Mul, "Nostalgia for Empire:

'Tempo Doeloe' in Contemporary Dutch literature," *Memory Studies* 3, no. 4 (October 2010): 413–28.

9. See Pattynama, "Memories of Interracial Contacts."

10. For a discussion of specific Indo-Dutch intertextuality, see my essay "26 februari 1948. Oeroeg van Hella Haasse verschijnt als boekenweekgeschenk. Herinneringsliteratuur en 'post'herinneringen bij eerste en tweede generatie Indische schrijvers," in *Cultuur en Migratie in Nederland: Kunsten in beweging, 1900–1980*, ed. Rosemarie Buikema and Maaike Meijer (Den Haag: Sdu, 2003), 207–21. For the reception of Indies literature in fin de siècle Netherlands, see Jacqueline Bel, "Indische romans," in *Nederlandse literatuur in het fin de siècle: Een receptie-historisch overzicht van het proza tussen 1885 en 1900* (Amsterdam: Amsterdam University Press, 1993), 304–13.

11. In his *Met vreemde ogen: Tempo doeloe—een verzonken wereld. Fotografische documenten uit het oude Indië, 1870–1920* (Amsterdam: Querido, 1988), Rob Nieuwenhuys has coined the well-known postcolonial term "verzonken continent" (sunken continent) in relation to the Dutch East-Indies.

12. For artefacts as "acts of transference," see Paul Connerton, *How Societies Remember* (New York: Cambridge University Press, 1989). For an explanation of "memorial dynamics," see Ann Rigney, "Portable Monuments: Literature, Cultural Memory, and the Case of Jeanie Deans," *Poetics Today* 25, no. 2 (2004): 368. For a discussion of "memorial interaction," read my: *". . . de baai . . . de binnenbaai . . .": Indië herinnerd* (Amsterdam: Vossiuspers, 2007).

13. Maria Dermoût, *Nog pas gisteren* (Amsterdam: Querido, 1959), 7. See also chapter 5 of Sarah deMul, *Colonial Memory: Contemporary Women's Travel Writing in Britain and the Netherlands* (Amsterdam: Amsterdam University Press, 2011) for a discussion of Aya Zikken's *Terug naar de atlasvlinder* (*Back to the Atlas Butterfly*, 1981) in terms of nostalgic memory. In this chapter De Mul refers to Dermoût's title *Nog pas gisteren* (*Only Yesterday*).

14. In arguing in favour of the agency of audiences, I follow the insights of film critic Pam Cook in her *Screening the Past: Memory and Nostalgia in Cinema* (London: Routledge, 2005).

15. Maurice Halbwachs, *Les cadres sociaux de la mémoire* (Paris: Librairie Félix Alcan, 1925). Aleida Assmann, "Four Formats of Memory—From Individual to Collective Forms of Constructing the Past," paper presented at the International Conference Theatres of Memory, Amsterdam, 2004, 1–27; Jan Assmann and John Czaplicka, "Collective Memory and Cultural Identity," *New German Critique* 65 Cultural History/Cultural Studies (Spring-Summer 1995): 125–33.

16. Recently many memory critics focus their attention on the complex ways in which images of the past are communicated, mediated, and shared. For discussions of mnemonic communities, see Iwona Irwin-Zarecka, *Frames of Remembrance* (New Brunswick, NJ: Transaction Books, 1994). See also Eviatar Zerubavel, *Social Mindscape: An Invitation to Cognitive Sociology* (Cambridge, MA: Harvard University Press, 1997).

17. Fredric Jameson, *Postmodernism, or, the Cultural Logic of Late Capitalism* (Durham, NC: Duke University Press, 1991), 156.

18. Robert J.C. Young, *Colonial Desire. Hybridity in Theory, Culture and Race* (London and New York: Routledge, 1995), 98.

19. For an analysis of the colonial society in Asia from the perspective of Dutch social relations with local populations and the influence of Asian-born women on the colonial ruling elite, see Jean Gelman Taylor, *The Social World of Batavia: European and Eurasian in Dutch Asia* (Madison: The University of Wisconsin Press, 1983).

20. Ulbe Bosma and Remco Raben, *De oude Indische wereld, 1500–1920* (Amsterdam: Bert Bakker, 2003).

21. H. Th. Bussemaker, *Bersiap! Opstand in het paradijs. De Bersiap-periode op Java en Sumatra, 1945–1946* (Zutphen: Walburg Pers, 2005).

22. Elsbeth Locher-Scholten, "Verwerking en koloniaal trauma—Balans van begrippen," *Bzzlletin* 25, no. 228 (1995): 3–9.

23. See this continuation exemplified in a recent theatrical performance about the maker's European ancestors in the Dutch East-Indies, (ironically) entitled, *Daar Werd Wat Groots Verricht!* (http://www.diederikvanvleuten.nl). For a discussion of the lack of postcolonial debate in the Netherlands, see Elleke Boehmer and Frances Gouda, "Postcolonial Studies in the Context of the 'Diasporic' Netherlands," in *Comparing Postcolonial Diasporas*, ed. Michelle Keown, David Murphy, and James Procter (Houndsmill, Basingstoke: Palgrave Macmillan, 2009), 37–55. See also chapter 2 of this volume.

24. See, for example, Breman, *Taming the Beast.*

25. See Renato Rosaldo's argument on "innocence" in "Imperialist Nostalgia," *Representations* 26 (Spring 1989): 107–22.

26. Pattynama, *". . . de baai,"* 7. I follow here Ann Rigney's suggestion to approach literary texts as "portable." Rigney, "Portable Monuments," 2004.

27. James E. Young, *The Texture of Memory: Holocaust Memorials and Meaning* (New Haven, CT: Yale University Press, 1993).

28. Bart Hofstede, *Nederlandse cinema wereldwijd: De internationale positie van de Nederlandse film* (Amsterdam: Boekmanstudies, 2000).

29. Stuart Hall, "Encoding/Decoding," in *Media Studies: A Reader*, ed. Paul Marris and Sue Thornham (Edinburgh: Edinburgh University Press, 2000), 51–61.

30. Cook, *Screening the Past*, 2.

31. For an explanation of "historicist films," see Jameson, *Postmodernism*, xvii.

32. In contrast to the rather critical dealings with the colonial subjugation of the Maghreb and Africa, French contemporary cinema displays what Panivong Norindr calls "the erotic and libidinal" dimensions of the "French romance for Indochina" in recognizable cinematic figures, "Filmic Memorials and Colonial Blues: Indochine in Contemporary French Cinema," in *Phantasmatic Indochina: French Colonial Ideology in Architecture, Film, and Literature* (Durham, NC: Duke University Press, 1996), 131–54.

33. Rosaldo, "Imperialist Nostalgia," 108.

34. See Mark Duursma, "Indië zoals het werkelijk was" *De Filmkrant* 182 (1997).

35. For a feminist, postcolonial critique, see Pamela Pattynama, "Innerlijk verscheurde speelfilm: Gordel van Smaragd van Orlow Seunke," *Pasarkrant* (November 1997): 5.

36. For an analysis of the widespread nostalgia for the East-Indies in the Dutch contemporary culture, see Lizzy van Leeuwen, *Ons Indisch erfgoed. Zestig jaar strijd om cultuur en identiteit* (Amsterdam: Bert Bakker, 2008).

37. Frank van Vree, "'Our Tortured Bride': The Japanese Occupation of the Dutch East Indies in Dutch Films and Documentaries" in *Representing the Japanese Occupation of Indonesia: Personal Testimonies and Public Images in Indonesia, Japan, and The Netherlands*, ed. Remco Raben (Zwolle: Amsterdam: Waanders Publishers & Netherlands Institute for War Documentation, 1999), 212.

38. Benedict Anderson, *Imagined Communities: Reflections of the Origins and Spread of Nationalism* (London: Verso, 1991).

39. Alison Landsberg, *Prosthetic Memory: The Transformation of American Remembrance in the Age of Mass Culture* (New York: Columbia University Press, 2004), 2.

40. Norindr, "Filmic Memorials."

41. In the Netherlands, the children of Indies migrants who migrated to the mother country due to the processes of decolonization are defined as "second generation." After their parents embarked for an often unknown country this generation was born and raised in the Netherlands. The "Indo-Dutch" among them are of mixed race (see note 2).

42. According to Marianne Hirsch, postmemory is distinguished from memory by generational distance and from history by deep personal connection: it is a "powerful and very particular form of memory precisely because its connection to its object or source is mediated, not through recollection but through an imaginative investment and creation. . . . Postmemory characterises the experience of those who grow up dominated by narratives that preceded their birth, whose own belated stories are evacuated by the stories of the previous generation shaped by traumatic events that can be neither understood nor recreated." Marianne Hirsch, *Family Frames: Photography, Narrative and Postmemory* (Cambridge: Cambridge University Press, 1997), 22.

43. For a discussion of Bloem's *No Ordinary Girl*, see my "Herinneringsliteratuur en 'post'herinneringen," 317–18. For Robinson's transnational aspirations, see Wim Willems, *Tjalie Robinson: Biografie van een Indo-schrijver* (Amsterdam: Bert Bakker, 2008). In 2004 Marion Bloem extended her activities to include the fate of modern-day asylum seekers in the Netherlands. She started a foundation named A Generous Gesture. This very successful internet action generated much support for the 26,000 asylum seekers who have been living in the Netherlands for four years and longer without a residence permit http://www.nlpvf.nl/basic/auteur1.php?Author_ID=307 (accessed September 21, 2010).

44. Including singers Anneke Grönloh and Riem de Wolff (The Blue Diamonds). Second-generation Indo migrant singers such as Gronlöh and De Wolff were immensely popular in the sixties, after in the fifties the so-called Indo-rock (Rock & Roll music played by Indo bands) changed the sound of Dutch youth music forever.

45. For an illustration of migrant living rooms, see Michael McMillan, *The Front Room: Migrant Aesthetics in the Home* (London: Black Dog Publishing, 2009).

46. For the intertextual figuration of the nyai-figure, see Jean Gelman Taylor, "Nyai Desima: Portrait of a Mistress in Literature and Film," in *Fantasizing the*

Feminine, ed. Laurie J. Sears (Durham, NC: Duke University Press, 1996), 225–48. For a history of interracial concubinage, see Reggie Baay, *De njai—Het concubinaat in Nederlands-Indië* (Amsterdam: Atheneum-Polak & van Gennep, 2008) and for an overview of the representation of the njai-figure in Dutch imaginations, see Pamela Pattynama, "De revival van de njai-figuur," *Indische Letteren* 26, no. 3 (2011): 128–43.

47. Drawing on Linda Hutcheon's theory of the postmodern, I approach *Far from Family* here as a postmodern experiment, which is always a critical and ironic reworking of the past and "never a nostalgic return." For Hutcheon, the contradictory phenomenon of postmodernism is an "ironic rethinking of history" through parodic references. Linda Hutcheon, "Theorizing the Postmodern: Toward a Poetics," in *A Poetics of Postmodernism: History, Theory, Fiction* (London: Routledge, 1988), 4–5.

48. See for an explanation of mise-en-abîme as part of the process of deconstruction: Susan Hayward, "Mise-en-Abîme," in *Cinema Studies: The Key Concepts* (London: Routledge, 2006), 222.

49. According to film critic Patricia Pisters, the pervasive "aesthetics of the mosaic" is related to migratory movements and contemporary globalized media culture: Patricia Pisters, "The Mosaic Film—An Affair of Everyone: Becoming Minoritarian in Transnational Media Culture," http://home.medewerker.uva.nl/m.g.bal/bestanden/Pisters%20Patricia%20Encuentro%20Migratory%20Politics%20READER%20OPMAAK.pdf (accessed August 20, 2010).

50. Avtar Brah, *Cartographies of Diaspora: Contesting Identities* (London: Routledge, 1996), 192.

51. De Mul, "Nostalgia for Empire," 425.

52. Svetlana Boym, *The Future of Nostalgia* (New York: Basic Books, 2001), xviii.

BIBLIOGRAPHY

Anderson, Benedict. *Imagined Communities: Reflections of the Origins and Spread of Nationalism*. London: Verso, 1991.

Assmann, Aleida. "Four Formats of Memory—From Individual to Collective Forms of Constructing the Past." Paper presented at the International Conference Theatres of Memory, Amsterdam, 2004, 1–27.

Assmann, Jan, and John Czaplicka. "Collective Memory and Cultural Identity." *New German Critique* 65. Cultural History/Cultural Studies (Spring-Summer 1995): 125–33.

Atia, Nadia, and Jeremy Davies. "Nostalgia and the Shapes of History: Editorial." *Memory Studies* 3, no. 4 (July 2010): 181–86.

Baay, Reggie. *De njai—het concubinaat in Nederlands-Indië*. Amsterdam: Athenaeum-Polak & Van Gennep, 2008.

Bel, Jacqueline. "Indische romans." In *Nederlandse literatuur in het fin de siècle: Een receptie-historisch overzicht van het proza tussen 1885 en 1900*, 304–13. Amsterdam: Amsterdam University Press, 1993.

Boehmer, Elleke, and Frances Gouda. "Postcolonial Studies in the Context of the 'Diasporic' Netherlands." In *Comparing Postcolonial Diasporas*, edited by Michelle Keown, David Murphy, and James Procter, 37–55. Houndsmill, Basingstoke: Palgrave Macmillan, 2009. See also chapter 2 of this volume.

Bosma, Ulbe, and Remco Raben. *De oude Indische wereld, 1500-1920*. Amsterdam: Bert Bakker, 2003.

Boym, Svetlana. *The Future of Nostalgia*. New York: Basic Books, 2001.

Brah, Avtar. *Cartographies of Diaspora: Contesting Identities*. London: Routledge, 1996.

Breman, Jan. *Taming the Coolie Beast: Plantation Society and the Colonial Order in Southeast Asia*. Oxford: Oxford University Press, 1989.

Bussemaker, H. Th. *Bersiap! Opstand in het paradijs. De Bersiap-periode op Java en Sumatra, 1945-1946*. Zutphen: Walburg Pers, 2005.

Connerton, Paul. *How Societies Remember*. New York: Cambridge University Press, 1989.

Cook, Pam. *Screening the Past: Memory and Nostalgia in Cinema*. London: Routledge, 2005.

De Mul, Sarah. "Nostalgia for Empire: 'Tempo doeloe' in Contemporary Dutch Literature." *Memory Studies* 3, no. 4 (2010): 413–28.

———. *Colonial Memory: Contemporary Women's Travel Writing in Britain and the Netherlands*. Amsterdam: Amsterdam University Press, 2011.

Dermoût, Maria. *Nog pas gisteren*. Amsterdam: Querido, 1959.

Halbwachs, Maurice. *Les cadres sociaux de la mémoire*. Paris: Librairie Félix Alcan, 1925.

Hall, Stuart. "Encoding/Decoding." In *Media Studies: A Reader*, edited by Paul Marris and Sue Thornham, 51–61. Edinburgh: Edinburgh University Press, 2000.

Hayward, Susan. *Cinema Studies: The Key Concepts*. London: Routledge, 2006.

Hirsch, Marianne. *Family Frames: Photography, Narrative and Postmemory*. Cambridge: Cambridge University Press, 1997.

Hofstede, Bart. *Nederlandse cinema wereldwijd: De internationale positie van de Nederlandse film*. Amsterdam: Boekmanstudies, 2000.

Hutcheon, Linda. "Theorizing the Postmodern: Toward a Poetics." In *A Poetics of Postmodernism: History, Theory, Fiction*, 3–21. London Routledge, 1988.

Huyssen, Andreas. *Twilight Memories*. New York: Routledge, 1995.

Irwin-Zarecka, Iwona. *Frames of Remembrance*. New Brunswick, NJ: Transaction Books, 1994.

Jameson, Fredric. "Nostalgia for the Present." *The South Atlantic Quarterly* 88, no. 2 (1989): 527–37.

———. *Postmodernism, or, the Cultural Logic of Late Capitalism*. Durham, NC: Duke University Press, 1991.

Koepnick, Lutz. "Reframing the Past: Heritage Cinema and Holocaust in the 1990s." *New German Critique* 87 (Autumn 2002, Special Issue on Postwall Cinema): 47–82.

Kousbroek, Rudy. *Het Oostindisch kampsyndroom*. Amsterdam: Meulenhoff, 1992.

———. *Het raadsel der herkenning. Fotosynthese 3*. Amsterdam: Augustus, 2007.

Kousbroek, Rudy, and Paula Gomes. *Verloren goeling*. Amsterdam: Meulenhoff, 1998.

Landsberg, Alison. *Prosthetic Memory: The Transformation of American Remembrance in the Age of Mass Culture*. New York: Columbia University Press, 2004.

Lasch, Christopher. "The Politics of Nostalgia." *Harper's* (1984): 65–70.

Leeuwen, Lizzy van. *Ons Indisch erfgoed: Zestig jaar strijd om cultuur en identiteit*. Amsterdam: Bert Bakker, 2008.

McMillan, Michael. *The Front Room: Migrant Aesthetics in the Home*. London: Black Dog Publishing, 2009.

Nieuwenhuys, Rob. *Met vreemde ogen: Tempo doeloe—een verzonken wereld. Fotografische documenten uit het oude Indië, 1870–1920*. Amsterdam: Querido, 1988.

Norindr, Panivong. "Filmic Memorials and Colonial Blues: Indochine in Contemporary French Cinema." In *Phantasmatic Indochina: French Colonial Ideology in Architecture, Film, and Literature*, 131–54. Durham, NC: Duke University Press, 1996.

Pattynama, Pamela. "Innerlijk verscheurde speelfilm. Gordel van Smaragd van Orlow Seunke." *Pasarkrant* (November 1997): 5.

———. "26 februari 1948. Oeroeg van Hella Haasse verschijnt als boekenweekgeschenk. Herinneringsliteratuur en 'post'herinneringen bij eerste en tweede generatie Indische schrijvers." In *Cultuur en Migratie in Nederland: Kunsten in beweging, 1900–1980*, edited by Rosemarie Buikema and Maaike Meijer, 207–21. Den Haag: Sdu, 2003

———. ". . . de baai . . de binnenbaai . . .": Indië herinnerd* Rede uitgesproken bij de aanvaarding van het ambt van bijzonder hoogleraar Koloniale en postkoloniale literatuur- en cultuurgeschiedenis aan de Universiteit van Amsterdam vanwege de Stichting Het Indisch Huis op donderdag 16 december 2005 ed. Amsterdam: Vossiuspers, 2007.

———. "Memories of Interracial Contacts and Mixed Race in Dutch Cinema." *Journal of Intercultural Studies* 28, no. 1 (2007, Special Issue: Pigments of the Imagination: Theorising, Performing and Historicising Mixed Race): 69–82.

———. "De revival van de njai-figuur." *Indische Letteren* 26, no. 3 (2011): 128–43.

Pisters, Patricia. "The Mosaic Film—An Affair of Everyone: Becoming-Minoritarian in Transnational Media Culture." 2004. http://home.medewerker.uva.nl/m.g.bal/bestanden/Pisters%20Patricia%20Encuentro%20Migratory%20Politics%20READER%20OPMAAK.pdf (accessed August 20, 2010).

Rigney, Ann. "Portable Monuments: Literature, Cultural Memory, and the Case of Jeanie Deans." *Poetics Today* 25, no. 2 (2004): 361–96.

Rosaldo, Renato. "Imperialist Nostalgia." *Representations* 26 (Spring 1989): 107–22.

Rushdie, Salman. *Imaginary Homelands: Essays and Criticism, 1981-1991*. London: Granta/Penguin, 1992.

Taylor, Jean Gelman. *The Social World of Batavia: European and Eurasian in Dutch Asia*. Madison: The University of Wisconsin Press, 1983.

———. "Nyai Desima: Portrait of a Mistress in Literature and Film." In *Fantasizing the Feminine*, edited by Laurie J. Sears, 225–48. Durham, NC: Duke University Press, 1996.

Young, James, E. *The Texture of Memory: Holocaust Memorials and Meaning.* New Haven, CT: Yale University Press, 1993.

Young, Robert J. C. *Colonial Desire: Hybridity in Theory, Culture and Race.* London: Routledge, 1995.

Vanvugt, Ewald. *Zwartboek van Nederland overzee. Wat iedere Nederlander moet weten.* Soesterberg: Aspect BV, 2002.

Vree, Frank van. "'Our Tortured Bride': The Japanese Occupation of the Dutch East Indies in Dutch Films and Documentaries." In *Representing the Japanese Occupation of Indonesia: Personal Testimonies and Public Images in Indonesia, Japan, and The Netherlands,* edited by Remco Raben, 202–17. Zwolle: Waanders Publishers & Netherlands Institute for War Documentation, 1999.

Willems, Wim. *Tjalie Robinson: Biografie van een Indo-schrijver.* Amsterdam: Bert Bakker. 2008.

Zerubavel, Eviatar. *Social Mindscape: An Invitation to Cognitive Sociology.* Cambridge, MA: Harvard University Press, 1997.

Chapter Seven

Transnational Contact-Narratives

Dutch Postcoloniality from a Turkish-German Viewpoint

Liesbeth Minnaard

This chapter offers a slightly different take on postcolonial studies in the Low Countries than the other chapter in this volume. It crosses the borders of Dutch literature towards the east and discusses a representation of Dutch postcoloniality as imagined in a work of German literature: the story "Fahrrad auf dem Eis" ["Bicycle on the Ice"] by the Turkish-German writer Emine Sevgi Özdamar.[1] I will explore critical questions about the Dutch (and German) postcolonial ethnoscape(s) that Özdamar's story triggers, and will demonstrate how this story, in which a Turkish-German woman strolls through Amsterdam as a contemporary female flaneur, offers a reflection on issues of national identity, ethnic diversity, and (Dutch and German) national histories of violence. Özdamar's story does so from an innovative perspective, mixing the standpoint of the tourist with the perspective of migration. The Turkish-German protagonist of "Fahrrad auf dem Eis" perceives postcolonial Dutch society in a very particular way: she mixes impressions of her various encounters with inhabitants of the Dutch metropolis with imaginative juxtapositions of labour migration, fascism and colonialism. These histories—or meta-narratives—resonate meaning as so-called contact-narratives in the story's contemporary Dutch and German worlds. I will argue that the narrated scenes of encounter between the Turkish-German protagonist and her Dutch interlocutors can be considered as moments of critical insight into such multiple, transnational webs of relation. They lay bare the overlap and interplay between (German and Dutch) collective memories that are not often thought in relation to each other. This becomes clear in close-readings that focus on *webs* of relation and on interference and intertwinement rather than on singular Self-Other relations. These readings move beyond the still predominant mode of thought in binary pairs—colonizer vis-à-vis colonised, indigenous vis-à-vis migrant Dutch, the Dutch vis-à-vis the Germans. In this way they demonstrate how Özdamar's "Fahrrad auf dem Eis" prompts its reader to acknowledge as well as explore the fundamental complexity of national—postcolonial and postfascist—identities.

CONCEPTS OF INTERRELATION

When it comes to the international (largely anglophone) field of postcolonial studies, Germany generally remains rather invisible, even more so than the Low Countries. This is regrettable, since a lot of interesting research that can be of inspiration for postcolonial studies in general is done in the field of German Studies and German literature. This research not only investigates the short-lived but impactful German colonial Empire, but it also addresses so-called colonial fantasies and imperial desires that date back to long before the actual coming into being of the German Empire.[2] It is worthwhile to take this scholarly work and its critical insights into account when studying the postcolonial Low Countries, as it can contribute to the process of acknowledging, mapping and investigating the *trans*-national, global character of the imperialist project and of postimperial responses to it.

A particular point of interest within the field of German studies is the discursive intersection of apparently separate or distant German histories, memories, and narratives. Several scholars in the field address possible intersections between, for instance, the Holocaust, colonialism and labour migration. In an article on the trialogue between Turks, Germans and Jews in literature Leslie Adelson proposes the concept of "touching tales" and in his study *Twilight Memories. Marking Time in a Culture of Amnesia* Andreas Huyssen uses the term triangulation.[3] Most recently Michael Rothberg coined the term "multidirectional memory" to indicate the acknowledgement of the proximity and multiple overlappings of histories of violence that are mostly seen as separate from one another.[4] The works of these theorists resonate with one another in their pleas for a mode of investigation that aims to do justice to the ways that so-called meta-narratives of the Holocaust, (de)colonisation and labour migration co-constitute and mutually influence each other—in literature as well as in other discourses.

Adelson, for instance, presents her concept of "touching tales" as an analytic tool to investigate "literary narratives that commingle cultural developments and historical references generally not thought to belong together in any proper sense."[5] In her path-breaking study on *The Turkish Turn in German literature*, she elaborates on this idea and further conceptualizes "touching tales" as contact narratives with strong affective dimensions that are rarely thought of in relation to one another.[6] She rejects the search for analogies between these narratives, but instead makes a plea for acknowledging their complex, and often disorientating intersections. The concept of "touching tales" encourages us to reframe our understanding of *either* (post) colonialism *or* migration history by investigating how they resonate meaning in relation to one another.

Huyssen's concept of "triangulation" also directs the attention to the complex intersections and interactions of various forms of difference that constitute as well as complicate new narratives and figurations of history and identity.[7] The concept of triangulation looks beyond binary structures that are normally used to determine and interpret the world and, instead, takes multiple webs of relation into account. As a model of thought that can also be used to study Low Countries contexts, triangulation prompts a more differentiated mode of reflection that challenges discourses of (one) Self and (one) Other in a productive way.[8]

Rothberg's concept of "multidirectional memory," finally, sets out to counter the dominant logic of *competing* collective memories that keeps these memories neatly apart and puts them even in concurrence to each other.[9] He proposes to acknowledge and study memories which "emerge in the interplay between different pasts and a heterogeneous presence."[10] He calls this "the multi-directionality of memory: the interference, overlap, and mutual constitution of seemingly distinct collective memories that define the postwar era and the workings of memory more generally."[11]

In the following I will argue that Özdamar's story "Fahrrad auf dem Eis" invites us to think jointly about "touching tales," "triangulation" and "multidirectional memory"—in a transnational way. The story juxtaposes Dutch and German worlds, in particular, Dutch and German multiculturality, and Dutch and German collective histories of violence against various—ethnic, cultural, colonial, religious—Others. It directs the reader's attention to the blind spots and (in)sensitivities in the traumatic national memories of both Germany and the Netherlands by exploring the resonances between the two. By juxtaposing these tales and memories "Fahrrad auf dem Eis" prompts a search for webs of relation across national boundaries.[12] Özdamar's story points at rhizomatic identity structures that do not halt at national borders and brings to the fore what people have in common: what "we" share, what connects "us."

IMAGINING NEW CONSTELLATIONS

Almost all of Özdamar's work features a first-person narrator named Sevgi, a Turkish-German woman who tells, mostly in retrospect and in a quasi-naïve mode,[13] about her migrant or even nomadic life: in Turkey, in Germany and, in this particular story, in the Netherlands. In "Fahrrad auf dem Eis" Sevgi travels to Amsterdam to spend some time as a writer in residence. The story opens with a flashback to the protagonist's first visit to Amsterdam 20 years earlier. She brings up a memory-image connected to this first visit, an image of a bicycle lying on a frozen canal. In the context of the story this image, which is also captured in the title, opens up several levels of interpretation—and it does so in a productive way. Firstly, it combines three stereotypical Dutch national symbols—a bicycle, the canals, and the ice on the canals—and becomes emblematic for the Dutch world that the protagonist presents to the reader. That the chosen combination of these things seen as typically Dutch is, because of its dependence on very cold winter weather, quite uncommon and of a temporary nature, turns the emblematic image into an ephemeral one: an image at the edge of transformation. When read for this emblematic quality the temporality of the image invokes Dutch society as a transitional society where traditional symbols appear in new and innovative constellations.

On a second level, the image of the bicycle holds a certain guiding quality for the protagonist Sevgi as an orientation marker during her second visit to the Dutch capital. She tags the depicted situation on her "personal city map" as a significant place to which to return.[14] The obviously disappeared bicycle—this is a memory image—gives Sevgi's new wandering through the city a particular motivation. The possibility that this specific bicycle might turn up again and the hope for this moment of recognition and reunion remain present throughout the story.

The guiding quality of the bicycle image recurs on a third level, where it functions as an incentive for the process of imagination. In the remembered situation of actually seeing the unusual constellation, the image fascinates the protagonist and sets her wondering about the bicycle's story: why did the bicycle lie there, to whom did it belong, what has now happened to it? She suggests several different possibilities by way of propositional narrative constructions without favouring or dismissing any of them.[15] This nonhierarchical mode of making up possible stories prompts the reader to wonder and wander along with the protagonist. The image unites narrator and reader in a situation of not-knowing and in a shared deliberation of possibilities where one is as good as the other.

Uniting these three levels of meaning—an image of Dutchness, a personal orientation marker, and a trigger for the imagination—the bicycle image becomes of central symbolic significance for the story. The bicycle functions both as a station on the protagonist's wandering way and at the same time, in the form of a memory image, as a metaphoric vehicle for the imaginary transportation of both protagonist and reader. The image of the bicycle contains a promise of movement that in its given situation on the ice is rather improbable, but that in its capacity as metaphor is actualised in the imagination. In this way stasis and movement, past and future come together in one and the same image.

After presenting this bicycle image as an explorative opening figure of thought, the story proceeds its wandering exploration of the Dutch capital. Amsterdam appears as a friendly open city, an intercultural contact-zone. Several people spontaneously approach the protagonist and ask her where she is from. The repeated question about her origin reminds Sevgi of her visit to another metropolitan port-city, New York, and she quotes the writer Thomas Brasch, who commented: "In New York ist jeder fremd"—"In New York everyone is a stranger."[16] She adds: "Seaports. New foreign people always came down the stairs of these ships. Can a city become addicted to foreign people?"[17] The question is followed by a description of the colonial toys and household goods that Dutch children grow up with, suggesting the abundant availability of traces of the foreign in the Dutch everyday.[18] Both the historical store houses and the toys and attributes that the protagonist mentions, are historical traces of the Dutch "Golden Age"—a highly disputable term—that was of course so violently entwined with, not to say part and parcel of, the colonial past. The rhetoric of the question in combination with the reference to this everydayness suggests that Amsterdam is indeed "addicted to the foreign."

Within the story the suggestion of such an addiction to the foreign points to the ethnic diversity of the Amsterdam population and works to explain the recurring question about Sevgi's origins: "Where are you from?"[19] In the protagonist's perspective—and in the story's narrative linkage of German and Dutch multiculturalism—the question predominantly carries positive connotations. She reads the question as a sign for an open interest in non-native others and an acknowledgement of their presence. The welcoming and non-judgemental responses to her answers to this question add to this positive impression. However, the unmistakable colonial overtones of aspects of Dutch diversity—colonialism being the main explanation for the presence of several minority groups—complicates a solely positive interpretation, as does the use of the term addiction in this context. The reference to an "addiction to the foreign" in relation to Dutch colonialism also gives out negative connotations: a connection to material obsessions, greed and violence. It is an addiction, in other words, that can have destructive consequences. In the postcolonial Dutch context the term conveys a semantic dimension of violent coercion that Özdamar's text certainly does not try to cover up. The predominantly positive marking of the "where are you from?"-question in the story-world also contrasts with the actual extra-diegetic Dutch context where this same question is subject to fierce critique. The Dutch *zmv*-women's movement, a collaboration of women activists of various backgrounds, has taken great pains to disqualify the question about origins which it considers to be prejudiced and exclusionary.[20] Esther Captain and Halleh Ghorashi argue that this kind of self-positioning is only demanded from persons who are (visually or verbally) perceived of as not belonging.[21]

It is striking that Sevgi never answers the question as regards her origin. Her use of the German language indirectly functions to identify her as being German. Her Dutch interlocutors all smoothly continue the conversation in German or in any other West European language as soon as they find out that she does not speak Dutch. For instance, when she visits a book presentation and a Jewish friend introduces the protagonist to her uncle, "He could speak German, but we talked in French. The famous football player Cruyff was also there. 'Sorry, I can't speak Dutch.' Cruyff said: 'Let's talk German.'"[22]

It is also the German language, however—the protagonist's second language—that *confronts* the protagonist with her German identity in an uncomfortable way. As well as the incident involving the Jewish uncle, the story offers other instances where people solicit the protagonist to speak a language other than German: "do you only speak German, can't you speak French?"; "I don't want to talk in German. Can't you speak Dutch?"[23] In both cases, the characters who request that the conversation continues in another language have explicitly introduced themselves as being Jewish. In Sevgi's conversations with these Jewish-Dutch characters German appears as a taboo language, scarred by the history of the Holocaust. For the migrant-Sevgi these experiences, new experiences of "being German abroad," constitute important moments of realising the multiple dimensions of what it means to identify *and* to be identified as German.

Whereas German national history is *implicitly* presented as problematic and even stained, Dutch national history is *explicitly* addressed as problematic by almost all the Dutch characters in the story. One after the other mentions the atrocities perpetrated by the Dutch during their dominion as a colonial power. All comment on the violent Dutch past in ethical terms and in a self-blaming mode.[24] This preoccupation with the Netherlands' role as a colonial perpetrator amazes the protagonist to the extent that she addresses the topic in a conversation with one of her self-critical Dutch interlocutors: "Christany, you know, you are already the third person in Amsterdam today who tells me about the colonial time. Sometimes this also happens in Germany. There I sometimes also hear my friends say 'bloody Nazis' three times a day."[25] In this comment the protagonist links the in-her-eyes-salient Dutch pose of self-blame in respect to the colonial past to the repeated instances of angry and outspoken conviction of German fascism by her friends in Germany. Dutch colonialism and German fascism feature as historical contact-narratives in this passage. The "touching tales" both revolve around the question of guilt. In the encounter with the Turkish-German woman, the repetitive behaviour of both the Dutch and the German characters testifies to what might be called an obsession with historical guilt. The triangular constellation, linking the German and the Dutch to the Turkish-German protagonist in their expressions of affect, is interesting here. Her particular presence seems to function as a silent encouragement to address these national traumas in a self-blaming manner.[26]

The strikingly eloquent instances of Dutch self-blame in respect to colonialism seems to outdo the angry and upset but verbally rather dissatisfactory German reflections on the Nazi past. The contrite Dutch attitude adds up to the strikingly positive image of Dutchness, and of Netherlands men in particular, that the protagonist creates on the basis of her experiences in Amsterdam. She maintains this image despite the critical differentiations that the Dutch characters themselves provide. On several occasions she romanticises these Dutch men as gentle "children of the water" ["Kinder vom Wasser"][27], and naïvely wonders whether they have addressed girls in foreign countries overseas in a similarly kind tone. Her conversational partners, however, keep emphasising the extremely problematic aspects of Dutch history. One of them, Christany's father who refers to himself and other Dutch as "we" "old colonialists" ["alte Kolonialisten"][28], replies to her inquiry about Dutch men's apparent gentleness as follows: "When you think of our ancestors, they are not [gentle]. In the seventeenth century Dutch men bled dry whole colonies. I hope that now everything in Holland will intermingle."[29] With the previous juxtaposition of German and Dutch self-blame in mind, a discrepancy in modes of self-blame between the two becomes clear. In contemporary Germany it is unthinkable that Germans would appellate themselves as "we old Nazis." This discrepancy, however, is brought to the fore through juxtaposition without measurement or judgement. The Holocaust and colonialism circulate in the text as historical references that trigger distinctive, nationally specific, affective dimensions.

Another German-Dutch juxtaposition appears in a dialogue between the protagonist and the German Rudi, one of her new friends:

"Die Holländer haben ihre Sprache vor langer Zeit in die Kolonien gebracht, deswegen sprechen viele Ausländer so selbstverständlich Holländisch."
"Und in Deutschland mußte die deutsche Sprache, die von Ausländern gesprochen wird, einen langen Weg machen, sich biegen, gebrochen werden und wieder geradestehen. Was war dein erstes Gefühl, Rudi, als du herkamst?"
"Kälte."[30]

"The Dutch took their language to the colonies ages ago, that's why many foreigners speak Dutch so naturally."

"And in Germany the German language spoken by foreigners had to go a long
way, to bend, to be broken and then to stand straight again. Rudi, what was your
first feeling when you came here?"

"Cold."

Again, several transnational connections come together in this passage. The
sudden transition from the statement on German language acquisition by
"foreigners" to the personal question addressed to Rudi is striking, as there
is no apparent logic connecting them.[31] The dialogue on the Dutch and German language spoken by "foreigners" ends in indeterminacy, juxtaposing the
two statements without further comment. The indeterminacy prompts readers
to reflect on the stated historical difference between the two neighbouring
countries themselves.

Rudi's answer as regards his first impression of the Netherlands is meaningful in this respect, as it seems to hint at a particular aspect of German-
Dutch relations. The one-word phrase—"Cold"—opens up a realm of ambivalence, as semantically it can refer either to the weather or to the interpersonal
climate that Rudi encountered in the Netherlands. The first meteorological
possibility is not very probable—although not impossible. A more plausible
interpretation reads Rudi's answer as an experiential reference to the negative
and condescending attitude that many Dutch tend to adopt in regard to their
German neighbours.[32] The vital memory of the German occupation during the
Second World War, as well as the—slowly diminishing—public perception
in the Netherlands of Germany as xenophobic, continues to feed Dutch feelings of superiority toward the Germans.[33]

This dialogue, or, better expressed, exchange of statements, both connects to
and complicates this last idea. It again refers to the long and painful process of
acquiring, "bending and breaking" a new language.[34] Germany's "foreigners"
(still) have to go through this process that is described in strikingly forceful,
almost violent terms. Rudi's contention that Dutch "foreigners"—those from
the former colonies—speak Dutch "self-evidently" is, however, problematic.
Taking the first part of the sentence into account, the apparently innocent term
"self-evidently" acquires a signalling as well as a cynical function. It simultaneously obscures and highlights the violent process of "colonial education"
that sustains this fluency in the Dutch language. Certainly the implementation
of Dutch did not occur in the Dutch "crown colony," the Dutch East Indies.
Once again two historical dealings with Otherness—Dutch colonialism and
German labour migration—are juxtaposed and connected in their joint impli-
cation in language coercion. In this juxtaposition the Dutch situation appears
further advanced. The ostensibly self-evident fluency of the Dutch "foreign-

ers" sets the exemplary standard for the not-yet-so fluent German "foreigners." The structures of colonial force that undergird this fluency remain implicit in the dialogue, but nevertheless resonate meaning in the larger text, as a result of the repeated gestures of self-blame by the Dutch characters.

All in all, the nomadic protagonist experiences the Netherlands as a successful multicultural society. She sketches a harmonious ethnoscape of befriended citizens, mellow and open in accordance with the Dutch landscape. A Dutch idyll of tolerance: the native Dutch father has words of praise for the Turkish girlfriend of his lesbian daughter, whose best friend is Jewish, whose partner is of Moroccan origin.[35] The self-critical statements of these very diverse Dutch characters, however, work in the opposite direction and modify this perhaps too-rosy image. One after the other points to the important process of coming to terms with the traumatic aspects of the past. All insist on the enduring necessity of working through national "misbehaviour" in respect to the ethnic Other. It is in this aspect that the repeated juxtapositions of the German and the Dutch situation resonate meaning: both of the neighbouring nation-states have difficulties with integrating histories of violence against Others in the national memory. The Holocaust, colonialism and labour migration feature in Özdamar's story, not as comparable histories, but as histories that complicate both German and Dutch identity constructions in comparable ways.

Özdamar's Sevgi is the narrative figure or medium that brings these histories together. She enables both their juxtaposition and the subsequent mutual reflection of Self and Other within a transnational frame even though at times her quasi-naïve narration seems to trivialise these historical moments of great complexity. To give a final example:

> Mir kommen die [niederländische] Männer so weich vor. Sie haben am Meer gestanden und haben gesehen, daß die Welt groß ist. Und Deutschland ist ein Wald. Bis sie den Weg raus gefunden hatten, war die Kolonialzeit vorbei. Man sagt, deswegen haben die Deutschen die Kolonien im Land selber geschaffen, die Gastarbeiter.[36]

> [Dutch] men seemed so soft to me. They stood by the sea and saw that the world was large. And Germany is a forest. The colonial time had come to an end by the time they had found the way out. People say that for that reason the Germans have created colonies in their own country, the guest workers.

The protagonist's trivialising parallelisation lends this passage a certain humoristic effect, representing Germans as incapable scouts who did not manage to find their way out of their forest "in time." The Dutch on the contrary, determined by their proximity to the wide horizon of the sea, had a broader vision of the world with consequences that here are only vaguely gestured at. The juxtaposition connects kind and open-minded Dutch men to a history of colonialism to German forest people who—presumedly—came too late to have a share in colonialism's pie. Yet another narrative juxtaposition follows when guest workers are described as being colonised within the German borders.

Let me emphasise again that Sevgi sits in judgement on these juxtapositions; she only brings the historical references together in a suggestive and thought-provoking way. Her trivialising combinations trigger critical reflection on both the mentioned histories and their transnational connections. The quasi-naïve tone of narration re-calibrates the traumatic purport of these histories and makes them thinkable in alternative ways. Sevgi's positive representation of Dutch society and its open-to-the-world attitude functions as an encouragement to the reader to imagine alternative forms of diverse, multi-ethnic community. The larger text, including self-reflective Dutch objections to any idealisation of Dutch history, prompts reflection on the possibilities that exist to work through the affective dimensions of traumatic national histories in the present.[37]

CONCLUSION

"Fahrrad auf dem Eis" ends with the following enigmatic play on words: "Tut sins."[38] Although neither a Dutch expression, nor a German, its meaning can be retrieved with a little knowledge of both languages: in particular, Dutch vocabulary and German phonetics. Via this detour, the pidgin phrase is retraceable to the Dutch expression for goodbye: "*Tot ziens*" or "See you"/"Till we see each other again," in English. These final words conclude the text—and simultaneously open up the future and hint at a repetition of the encounter. While in the final scene within the world of the story Özdamar's protagonist says "see you again" to the city of Amsterdam, when we consider the expression as poised on the boundary between the story and the actual world, it involves the reader in the possibility of a reunion after the goodbye. In other words, the hybrid expression "Tut sins" functions as an emblematic expression for the story's fundamental idea of relation and continuity. Like the title-image of the bicycle on the ice, it connects stasis and movement, past and future, Germany and the Netherlands, in an evocative way.

NOTES

1. The story "Fahrrad auf dem Eis" was published in Emine Sevgi Özdamar's story collection *Der Hof im Spiegel: Erzählungen* [The CourtYard in the Mirror: Narrations] (Köln: Kiepenheuer & Witsch, 2001).

2. The German colonial empire possessed overseas territories between the 1880s (in 1884 Bismarck proclaimed German "imperial protection" in southwest Africa) and the end of the First World War. Susanna Zantop's fascinating study, *Colonial Fantasies: Conquest, Family and Nation in Precolonial Germany, 1770–1870. Post-Contemporary Interventions* (1997) demonstrates, however, that German colonialism cannot be restricted to this short period of actual imperial expansion.

3. Leslie A. Adelson, *The Turkish Turn in Contemporary Literature: Toward a New Critical Grammar of Migration* (New York: Palgrave Macmillan, 2005); Andreas Huyssen, *Twilight Memories: Marking Time in a Culture of Amnesia* (New York: Routledge, 1995).

4. Michael Rothberg, "Between Auschwitz and Algeria: Multidirectional Memory and the Counterpublic Witness," *Critical Inquiry* 33 (Autumn 2006): 158–84, and idem, *Multidirectional Memory: Remembering the Holocaust in the Age of Decolonization, Cultural Memory in the Present* (Palo Alto, CA: Stanford University Press, 2009).

5. Adelson, *Turkish Turn*, 20.

6. Adelson discusses several examples from Turkish-German literature in which narratives of Turkish migration, the Holocaust, the Cold War, or the Armenian genocide appear as "touching tales."

7. In *Twilight Memories* Huyssen uses the concept of triangulation to reflect on the eruption of xenophobic violence shortly after German-German reunification. He writes: "Only this triangulation of foreigners, East Germans and West Germans fully explains the intensity of the escalation in xenophobia since unification." Huyssen, *Twilight Memories*, 80–81.

8. An example of triangulation in the current debate on the multicultural society in the Netherlands is that between indigenous Dutch, Jews and Muslims. The influential populist-right party PVV of politician Geert Wilders combines an outspoken pro-Israel standpoint with a strong anti-Islam rhetoric. It supports this positioning by claiming that the violent anti-Israel stance of a small group of Moroccan-Dutch youngsters is representative of the fundamental anti-democratic orientation of all Dutch Muslims.

9. Rothberg focuses on the ways in which memories of the traumatic histories of the Holocaust and colonialism interfere with and constitute one another, for instance in France of the late 1960s. His analysis of Charlotte Delbo's *Les Belles Lettres* aims to contribute to "a new understanding of the emergence of Holocaust memory and the unfolding of decolonization as overlapping and not separate processes." Rothberg, "Between Auschwitz and Algeria," 159–160.

10. Rothberg, "Between Auschwitz and Algeria," 162.

11. Rothberg, "Between Auschwitz and Algeria," 162.

12. The idea of (webs of) Relation is conceptualised by Glissant in his work, *Poetics of Relation*. Here Glissant defines Relation as a process of changing mentalities and transforming communities, a process that is propelled forward by the imagination. Referring to Deleuze and Guattari's theory of the rhizome, he writes: "Rhizomatic thought is the principle behind what I call the Poetics of Relation, in which each and every identity is extended through a relationship with the Other." Édouard Glissant, *Poetics of Relation* (Ann Arbor: University of Michigan Press, 1997), 11.

13. This quasi-naïve mode of writing can be considered as a typical strategy in Özdamar's writing. See my discussion of this strategy in Liesbeth Minnaard, *New Germans, New Dutch: Literary Interventions* (Amsterdam: Amsterdam University Press, 2008), 71–73.

14. Özdamar, *Der Hof*, 85.

15. Özdamar uses a lot of propositional constructions in her writing, often signalling both possibility and doubt. They are characteristic of the wondering attitude of the protagonist and underscore the idea of interpretive openness and possibility.

16. Özdamar, *Der Hof*, 84.

17. "Hafenstädte. Immer sind von den Treppen der Schiffe neue fremde Menschen heruntergestiegen. Kann eine Stadt süchtig werden nach den Fremden?" Özdamar, *Der Hof*, 84.

18. This aspect of Amsterdam's history as a prosperous port city is foregrounded when the protagonist metaphorically imagines its city plan as a spider-web. A Dutch character alters the "natural" image into a violent manmade one by stating that half of the web was "knitted" ["gestrickt"] over the heads of foreign countries during colonial dominion. Özdamar, *Der Hof*, 86.

19. Özdamar, *Der Hof*, 84.

20. The term "zmv-women's movement" is a self-identificatory term with the "zmv" standing for "zwart, migranten- en vluchtelingen": "black, migrant, and refugee." As is explained in the introduction to the volume *Caleidoscopische visies: De zwarte, migranten- en vluchtelingenvrouwenbeweging in Nederland* [*Kaleidoscopic Visions. The Black, Migrant, and Refugee Women's Movement in the Netherlands*], the term tries to take the diversity of backgrounds of various ethnic minority groups in the Netherlands into account. In respect to Özdamar's story it is important to distinguish between the protagonist who is asked where she is from as a tourist, and nonnative Dutch citizens who often experience the question as an exclusionary gesture. Maayke Botman, Nancy Jouwe, and Gloria Wekker, eds., *Caleidoscopische visies: De zwarte, migranten- en vluchtelingenvrouwenbeweging in Nederland* (Amsterdam: Koninklijk Instituut voor de Tropen, 2001).

21. Esther Captain and Halleh Ghorashi, "'Tot behoud van mijn identiteit': Identiteitsvorming binnen de zmv-vrouwenbeweging," in *Caleidoscopische visies: De zwarte, migranten- en vluchtelingenvrouwenbewegingin Nederland*, eds. Maayke Botman, Nancy Jouwe, and Gloria Wekker (Amsterdam: KIT Publishers, 2001), 153–85.

22. "Er konnte Deutsch, wir sprachen aber Französisch. Der berühmte Fußballer Cruyff war auch da. 'Entschuldigung, ich kann kein Holländisch.' Cruyff sagte: 'Reden wir doch Deutsch.'" Özdamar, *Der Hof*, 92.

23. "Sprichst du nur Deutsch, kannst du nicht Französisch?" Özdamar, *Der Hof*, 88. "Ich will nicht Deutsch reden. Kannst du nicht Holländisch?" Özdamar, *Der Hof*, 106.

24. This counts, for instance, for the very first person that the protagonist meets: Isis. Isis responds to the question whether she likes her city: "The city is pretty, but our history is not pretty. And young people don't know anything about our colonial time. Young people believe that our prosperity has always been there" ["Die Stadt

ist schön, aber unsere Geschichte ist nicht schön. Und die Jugend weiß nichts von unserer kolonialistischen Zeit. Die Jugend glaubt, dass unser Reichtum immer da war"]. Özdamar, *Der Hof*, 84.

25. "Christany, weißt du, du bist heute schon der dritte Mensch in Amsterdam, der mir von der Kolonialzeit erzählt. Manchmal passiert das in Deutschland auch. Ich höre dort auch manchmal dreimal an einem Tag von meinen Freunden 'Scheiß Nazis.'" Özdamar, *Der Hof*, 89.

26. In his article "Diaspora and Nation: Migration into Other Pasts," Huyssen discusses the contemporary significance of (the memory of) the Holocaust for the Turkish-German population. He argues that "the public memory discourse in Germany remains fundamentally and persistently national, focused on German perpetrators and Jewish victims. [. . .] Turkish immigrants and their German descendants remain largely absent from Germany's memorial culture." Andreas Huyssen, "Diaspora and Nation: Migration into Other Pasts," *New German Critique* 88 (Winter 2003): 164.

27. Özdamar, *Der Hof*, 82.

28. Özdamar, *Der Hof*, 86.

29. "Wenn man an unsere Vorfahren denkt, sind sie es nicht. Holländische Männer haben im 17. Jahrhundert in den Kolonien alles ausgesaugt. Ich hoffe, daß sich jetzt alles in Holland vermischen wird." Özdamar, *Der Hof*, 87.

30. Özdamar, *Der Hof*, 95.

31. Whereas the German term "Ausländer" is a common (albeit also criticised) designation for people of non-German ethnic origin—irrespective of whether these people hold German citizenship or not—the equivalent term "buitenlander" in the Dutch language holds strongly pejorative connotations. In the Dutch language context the term cannot be used in the relatively neutral meaning in which it is used in the citation. For that reason I continue to use the term in quotation marks when referring to the Dutch situation.

32. In this second possibility, his answer resonates the word that many first-generation guest workers associated with Germany—also in its double semantics of meteorological and interpersonal climate.

33. This last attitude reached a peak in 1993 when a racist attack on "foreigners" (in fact German citizens) in the small town of Solingen shocked Germany as well as its neighbours. A Dutch broadcast company responded with a (successful) campaign in which it encouraged its listeners to send a postcard to the German government with the simple text: "I am angry." For a long time the German *communis opinio* seemed to foster the idea of a Dutch superiority in respect to issues of multiculturality. However, since the Islamist-fundamentalist murder of the Dutch film director Theo van Gogh and the outcries of violence and polarisation following his death, this assumption of Dutch superiority has clearly lost ground.

34. Multiple dimensions of the acquisition of a foreign language appear in Özdamar's early writings, for instance in her debut *Mutterzunge*.

35. In Özdamar's story-world, Amsterdam is as open to homosexuality as it is to ethnic diversity. "Fahrrad auf dem Eis" confirms Amsterdam's acclaimed symbolic status as the gay capital of Europe at that time.

36. Özdamar, *Der Hof*, 95. This passage echoes the line of reasoning—linking "successful" colonialism to "successful" multiculturality—that Özdamar developed earlier in an interview with Horrocks and Kolinsky: "It is true that the older colonial powers have managed the business of immigration more successfully. The Germans came by their colonies relatively late in the day, and they have ended up creating new colonies on their home territory." David Horrocks and Eva Kolinsky, eds., *Turkish Culture in German Society Today* (Providence, RI: Berghahn Books, 1996), 52–53. Simultaneously the passage echoes the myth of German colonial innocence that Susanne Zantop discusses in her study *Colonial Fantasies*. Susanne Zantop. *Colonial Fantasies: Conquest, Family and Nation in Precolonial Germany, 1770–1870* (Durham, NC: Duke University Press, 1997).

37. The distinction between the protagonist's and the text's perspective is important, as the one modifies the other. The protagonist's narration seems to foreground a positive valuation of the idea that the Dutch managed to acquire more colonies than the Germans did. It suggests that either the Dutch had no guest workers or, if they had, that these—other than the guest workers who appear as the new colonised within German society—have been fully integrated into Dutch society. The rhetoric of the larger text, however, undermines these assumptions.

38. Özdamar, *Der Hof*, 112.

BIBLIOGRAPHY

Adelson, Leslie A. *The Turkish Turn in Contemporary Literature: Toward a New Critical Grammar of Migration.* New York: Palgrave Macmillan, 2005.

Botman, Maayke, Nancy Jouwe, and Gloria Wekker, eds. *Caleidoscopische visies: De zwarte, migranten- en vluchtelingenvrouwenbeweging in Nederland.* Amsterdam: Koninklijk Instituut voor de Tropen, 2001.

Captain, Esther, and Halleh Ghorashi, "'Tot behoud van mijn identiteit': Identiteitsvorming binnen de zmv-vrouwenbeweging." In *Caleidoscopische visies: De zwarte, migranten- en vluchtelingenvrouwenbewegingin Nederland,* edited by Maayke Botman, Nancy Jouwe, and Gloria Wekker, 153–185. Amsterdam: KIT Publishers, 2001.

Glissant, Édouard. *Poetics of Relation,* trans. Betsy Wing. Ann Arbor: University of Michigan Press, 1997.

Horrocks, David, and Eva Kolinsky, eds. *Turkish Culture in German Society Today.* Providence, RI: Berghahn Books, 1996.

Huyssen, Andreas. *Twilight Memories: Marking Time in a Culture of Amnesia.* New York; London: Routledge, 1995.

———. Diaspora and Nation: Migration into Other Pasts. *New German Critique* 88 (Winter 2003): 147–64.

Minnaard, Liesbeth. *New Germans, New Dutch: Literary Interventions.* Amsterdam: Amsterdam University Press, 2008.

Özdamar, Emine Sevgi. *Der Hof Im Spiegel. Erzählungen.* Köln: Kiepenheuer & Witsch, 2001.

Rothberg, Michael. "Between Auschwitz and Algeria: Multidirectional Memory and the Counterpublic Witness." *Critical Inquiry* 33 (Autumn 2006): 158–84.

———. *Multidirectional Memory: Remembering the Holocaust in the Age of Decolonization, Cultural Memory in the Present.* Palo Alto, CA: Stanford University Press, 2009.

Zantop, Susanne. *Colonial Fantasies: Conquest, Family and Nation in Precolonial Germany, 1770–1870.* Durham, NC: Duke University Press, 1997.

Chapter Eight

Representing Post-Apartheid South Africa

Mothers, Motherlands and Mother Tongues in the Work of Selected Afrikaans Women Writers

Louise Viljoen

AFRIKAANS WOMEN WRITERS AND THE TRANSITION

Afrikaans women's writing was one of the marginal discourses in Afrikaans literature that however, for all its marginality, played an important part in interrogating the structures of power in South Africa during the apartheid era. As such, Afrikaans women's writing formed part of Afrikaans literature's history of resistance and dissidence which grew especially strong after 1960, as political repression, too, grew stronger.[1] Using broad and over-simplified strokes, one can paint early Afrikaans literature as largely nationalist. On the one hand it could be seen as a postcolonial literature, resisting colonial oppression by the British; on the other hand it could be regarded as a colonial literature, co-opted culturally to reinforce an Afrikaner nationalism which itself continued the colonial oppression of the past.

From the 1960s onwards Afrikaans literature came to show strong strains of resistance against the political dominance of Afrikaner nationalism. In the early sixties writers like André Brink and Breyten Breytenbach took up the dissidence voiced by earlier writers like Uys Krige, Jan Rabie and Peter Blum. From then onwards Afrikaans literature gradually became one in which resistance to different kinds of oppression became a prominent feature. The resistance manifested itself in various distinct bodies of writing such as: the overtly political writing of Breytenbach, Brink, John Miles, Elsa Joubert and others who protested against the injustices of Apartheid in their literary texts; the sub-genre of "border literature" in which young male writers who had experienced military conscription, criticized the South African government's war against insurgents on the Namibian border with Angola; gay and lesbian writing which questioned the principles and values of the patriarchal, (hetero)sexist and racist society in which they lived; and women's writing which became increasingly gender conscious and politicised after the Soweto riots in 1976.

After playing a relatively minor role in Afrikaans literature up till about 1970, Afrikaans women writers became more prominent during the seventies and eighties after the debut of a series of important women poets in 1970 (Sheila Cussons, Wilma Stockenström and Antjie Krog).[2] Apart from those writers who focused on broadly existential rather than political questions (Elisabeth Eybers, Sheila Cussons, Ina Rousseau, Lina Spies), this period also saw unfold in incremental fashion: the publication of major political works by established writers (Elsa Joubert, Antjie Krog), the introduction of several lesbian voices that challenged patriarchal conceptions of sexuality (Jeanne Goosen, Joan Hambidge, Welma Odendaal, Emma Huismans), the emergence of new modes of writing which interrogated conventional narrative strategies (Jeanne Goosen, Wilma Stockenström, Lettie Viljoen), and the rise of a less high-brow variety of fiction that was highly popular (Dalene Matthee, Marita van der Vyver). Some of these works openly challenged the existing political order whereas others questioned oppression on the basis of gender, race, class and sexuality.

After South Africa's transition to democracy in 1994 Afrikaans women writers continued to deal with political and social developments in the country. Shortly before and after the transition several studies commented on their willingness and ability to engage with the emerging new order.[3] It was indeed the case that Afrikaans women writers added their own gendered perspectives to the trends that became prominent in Afrikaans literature after the transition. Several writers responded to the challenges of the new order by re-visiting South African and Afrikaner history (Elsa Joubert, Lettie Viljoen/ Ingrid Winterbach, Marlene van Niekerk, Engela van Rooyen). Others were engaged in the reconstruction of identity in reaction to a rapidly transforming society (Antjie Krog, Wilma Stockenström, Petra Müller, Rachelle Greeff, Riana Scheepers). The transition also brought the introduction of new voices to Afrikaans literature, in particular Coloured writers of whom E.K.M. Dido was the first Coloured Afrikaans woman to publish a novel in that language and Ronelda Kamfer the first Coloured woman to publish a volume of poetry in Afrikaans.[4] In addition to this the post-Mandela years also saw the publication of texts in which Afrikaans women took part in a more general trend of critically reflecting on the social, political and ecological problems of postcolonial South Africa within the larger global context.[5] This inquiry will focus on yet another facet of post-apartheid writing by Afrikaans women, namely their response to the challenges of conceptualising postcolonial South Africa by interrogating the notion of South Africa as their motherland and reflecting on the position of their mother tongue Afrikaans.

Although the use of gendered parental metaphors with regard to the nation, country and language is not limited to the figure of the mother, it is well-known that the symbolic discourses of nationalism often make use of the mother to envisage the state or the nation. Elleke Boehmer spells it out in her work on gender and narrative in the postcolonial nation when she writes: "The image of the mother invites connotations of origins—birth, hearth, home, roots, the umbilical cord—and rests upon the frequent, and some might say 'natural' identification of the mother with the beloved earth, the national territory and the first-spoken language, the national tongue."[6] Colonial and postcolonial South Africa do not deviate from the norm in this regard. The discourse of early Afrikaner nationalism made frequent use of the figure of the *volksmoeder,* the mother of the white Afrikaner nation, symbolically elevating Afrikaner women while at the same time keeping them politically subservient and implicating them in the racial oppression of apartheid.[7] The image of the woman as mother was also deployed in the struggle against apartheid in which black women were also invoked as mothers of the nation.[8] In their comparative analysis of the role that nation, race and motherhood played in Afrikaner Nationalism and the African National Congress, Deborah Gaitskell and Elaine Unterhalter do however argue that motherhood is a "very fluid and manipulable notion, especially in the context of a divided society where class and race divisions overlap."[9] The search for women who could serve as symbolic mothers of the newly integrated postcolonial nation emerging from a history of oppression and struggle, focused on figures like Krotoa/Eva, Sarah Baartman and Nongqawuse who were referred to in political speeches and literary texts alike.[10] Although some Afrikaans women writers evoke these symbolic mothers (for instance, Dalene Matthee's novel *Pieternella van die Kaap* focuses on Eva/Krotoa's daughter born from her marriage to Pieter van Meerhof,[11] and Diana Ferrus on Sarah Baartman[12]), others interrogate the notion of the motherland and the mother tongue in texts which feature complex and ambivalent mother figures.

These texts are also marked by complex reactions to the mother tongue, more specifically the language Afrikaans in which these writers express themselves. These women have different affiliations to Afrikaans, the South African language which was formed by the interaction of the Dutch spoken by the first white colonizers of South Africa with the Malay spoken by slaves from the Dutch East Indies, the Creole-Portuguese used by sailors and slaves, the indigenous language Khoi of the local hunter-gatherer peoples, the German and French of early settlers at the Cape, and also Arabic, African languages and English.[13] Although Afrikaans became associated with the political oppression of the apartheid regime, it was also used in the oppressed's struggle against apartheid (more than half of all Afrikaans mother tongue speakers to this day are Coloured people who were excluded from Afrikaner nationalism on the basis of race).[14] The language's history as well as questions about its sustainability in a post-apartheid South Africa increasingly dominated by English as *lingua franca*, also impacts on the way in which Afrikaans writers write in and about their mother tongue. The idea that the term mother tongue "denotes not only one's first language but some kind of more primal, essential or original language" and that speaking "one's mother tongue is thus also figured as a recovery of an essential maternal connection, establishing lineage, a process often talked about as a homecoming in language,"[15] is considerably complicated by the history and current situation of Afrikaans. The literary texts by the Afrikaans women writers I intend to discuss question the essentialist notions and easy naturalizations which the metaphor of the mother in the terms motherland and mother tongue lends itself to.

In what follows I will contend that the literary and semi-literary texts I focus on reveal the subtle gradations, unexpected slippages and grainy textures not visible in the theoretical abstractions often favoured in postcolonial studies.[16] Analyses of these kinds of texts focus attention on the "messy seams between the past and the transitional present" and reveal the "contradictory and conflicting experiences of women" which are obscured by the symbolic discourses of nationalism and its originary narratives.[17] The texts I have selected for discussion are E.K.M. Dido's novel *'n Stringetjie blou krale [A string of blue beads]* (2000), Marlene van Niekerk's novel *Agaat* (2004, translated into English in 2006), and Antjie Krog's autobiographical fiction *Begging to be black* (2009).

BETRAYING THE MOTHER (TONGUE): E.K.M. DIDO'S *'N STRINGETJIE BLOU KRALE*

E.K.M. Dido was the first woman to establish herself as a novelist in the canon of black Afrikaans writing. Although most of the writers referred to as black Afrikaans writers are of mixed racial descent, many of them made the ideological choice to refer to themselves as black, rather than Coloured, during the struggle against apartheid, in order to place themselves and their writing explicitly in the political arena.[18] Although strong feelings of resistance to the use of the term Coloured as a reference to the socio-political groupings constructed under colonialism and apartheid persist, it has resurfaced in discussions around the question of Coloured identities and its relationship to black identities since 1994, amongst others in the work of Zoë Wicomb and Zimitri Erasmus.[19] I will therefore follow Dido in her use of the term Coloured, as distinct from black, in public forums as well as in the novel under discussion. Asked about her childhood in an interview, Dido stated that she grew up as the child of Coloured parents in the village of Tsomo in the Transkei where she learnt to speak both Afrikaans and Xhosa, often not knowing which one of the two was her first language.[20]

Dido's first novel *Die storie van Monica Peters* [*The story of Monica Peters*] was published in 1996 and told the story of an interracial couple's participation in the struggle against apartheid, their exile in Britain, and their joyful return to South Africa in 1990. Her subsequent novels all dealt with social issues such as alcoholism, violence against women, racism, the post-traumatic stress suffered by policemen, crime and homelessness. *'n Stringetjie blou krale [A string of blue beads]* is her third and most accomplished novel so far, and also the one she herself speaks of as cherishing the most.[21]

The way in which the novel represents the mother and the use of the mother tongue has a direct bearing on the way in which it comments on the politics of identity in postcolonial South Africa. The novel's narrator is Nancy, an Afrikaans-speaking Coloured woman living in post-apartheid Cape Town with her husband and two children. Even though she has acquired all the trappings of a successful middle-class life, she is tormented by nightmares. Because of her husband's unsympathetic reaction she seeks advice from her parents who ask MaRhadebe, a Xhosa sangoma (traditional healer), to help her. She guides Nancy to discover the source of her psychological distress in a manner reminiscent of the "talking cure" practiced by Western psychoanalysis. In the resulting narrative Nancy gradually remembers the past she repressed, revealing that she is actually Nomsa Hlabathi, born in 1949 to Xhosa parents in the settlement eZibeleni near the town of Tsomo in Transkei and adopted by her Coloured parents when she was about six years old. She tells MaRhadebe that she had two mothers as a Xhosa child in a polygamous culture: her biological mother and her father's second wife, known as Mama Omncinci (literally the mother who is small, referring to the second or junior wife), and her father's first wife known as Mam'omkhulu (the mother who is big, referring to the first or senior wife). According to the narrative this did not represent a problem to the child because she was loved, nurtured and disciplined by both of them (82).[22] When her father died in a mining accident in Johannesburg and the family then experienced financial problems, her mothers took her from the rural school she attended and placed her in foster care with a childless Coloured couple, Jan and Siena Hendrikse, those she thinks of as her real parents, in the nearby town of Tsomo so that she could continue her schooling there.

This move signals the start of radical changes in the six-year-old child's relationship to her mothers, her mother tongue and eventually her motherland. Siena Hendrikse does not send her to the Mission School with the other black children as she promised Nomsa's mothers she would do, but teaches

her Afrikaans so that she can go to school with the other Coloured children
in Tsomo. She changes Nomsa's name to Nancy and takes her to the Roman
Catholic Church where she is eventually christened and confirmed. Siena
also starts changing her appearance by dressing her in Western-style clothes
and straightening her hair. Nomsa/Nancy starts to feel ashamed of her Xhosa
mothers' tribal dress and manners when they come to visit her and starts deliberately avoiding them even though Mam'omkhulu warns her not to forget
that she is a Xhosa (95). Thus Nomsa's acceptance of her new identity is
partly based on her feelings of shame for her mothers and the culture they
represent. This eventually leads to the drastic repression of her past which
results in her psychological crisis.

Her new identity is also built on Siena's betrayal of the trust that Nomsa's
mothers have put in her to act as foster parent. She formally adopts Nomsa
without asking her mothers or even telling them about it. She tells the relevant
authorities that the light-coloured Nomsa is a Coloured child abandoned by
her parents, so that she is registered as a Coloured in the population register
(89–90). However brutal this process may have been, Jan and Siena become
Nancy's parents to whom she remains loyal and loving. In telling MaRhadebe
the story of her life, Nancy compares her Xhosa mothers' undemonstrative
love with her Coloured mother Siena's warm and affectionate nature, saying
that Siena's expressions of love made her feel "wonderfully safe" ["wonder-
lik veilig"] (83). She is also grateful to her Coloured father Jan for teaching
her to stand up for herself and to express her emotions rather than to be sub-
missive and stoic as she was taught by her Xhosa mothers.

Breaking the bond with her two Xhosa mothers also means breaking the
bond with her mother tongue, Xhosa. The betrayal is reproduced throughout
her adult life. Especially after she marries the Coloured man Bennie Karelse
who is fiercely prejudiced against black people, she is hesitant to reveal the
fact that she can speak the language fluently. Throughout the novel Xhosa
phrases and words slip into Nancy's speech (as well as into the Afrikaans in
which the novel is written), similar to the way in which Freudian slips of the
tongue signal the "return of the repressed" and the speech of the colonised
other sometimes infiltrates that of the colonising other. Although the Coloured woman Siena is herself a victim of apartheid and eventually experiences the same kind of poverty that drove Nomsa's mothers to place her in
foster care, she has internalized certain aspects of the racial hierarchy which
valued coloured people higher than black people. This also happens to Nancy
who initially rejects her second child Jean when he is born with a much darker
skin colour than either of his parents. It is her Coloured father Jan who admonishes her to "stop her nonsense" and gets her to accept the baby (124).

The second part of the novel deals with Nancy's life after MaRhadebe has
helped her to confront the past she has repressed. The revelation that she is in

fact of Xhosa descent leads her husband with his entrenched racial prejudices to reject and eventually divorce her, taking their children with him. Her adoptive parents urge her to return to the Transkei and visit her Xhosa mothers in order to make amends and to gain peace. On her return she finds that they both died a few years earlier. With the help of her brother she undergoes certain ceremonies in which she is able to show her remorse for betraying them and to ask for forgiveness at their graves. After her return to Cape Town from the Transkei Nancy gradually wins back the love of her children, estranged from her by her ex-husband. She also goes through the slow process of gaining financial and emotional independence from him. Seen from the perspective of postcolonial identity politics the most important step in this process is her decision formally to take back her Xhosa name Nomsa and use it together with the name Nancy given by her adopted parents, thus acknowledging her Xhosa mothers and her mother tongue without rejecting her adopted parents and language.

Tracing the emotional line of the novel, it is possible to say that Nancy's betrayal of her Xhosa identity leads to the psychological anguish that has to be resolved by a confrontation with the past, confession, remorse and penance. It is not difficult to see certain similarities with the hearings of the 1996 Truth and Reconciliation Commission that worked through similar processes of confrontation, confession and remorse. In Nancy's case the process leads to the reconciliation of her black identity with her Coloured identity. The novel seems to opt for a fluid and pragmatic integration of identities rather than for an exchange of the one for the other. Nancy/Nomsa's Coloured identity (the strong attachment to her adoptive parents Jan and Siena, her immersion in their way of life, her identification with Afrikaans) has to be integrated with her Xhosa identity (her early childhood in a Transkei settlement, her mothers, her mother tongue Xhosa). Apart from this the novel's depiction of Bennie's fate implies disapproval of his openly racist attitude towards black people: he is shot and paralysed during the hijacking of his car, blaming Nancy and "her people" (the blacks who hijacked his car) for his predicament. Although the novel implies that a betrayal of the origins identified with the biological mother and mother tongue can lead to severe psychological distress, it is also open to the possibility of new identities emerging under the pressure of changing circumstances.

FLEEING THE MOTHER(LAND): MARLENE VAN NIEKERK'S *AGAAT* (2004)

The complexity of Marlene van Niekerk's *Agaat,* published in Afrikaans in 2004 and translated into English by Michiel Heyns as *Agaat* in 2006, allows for a variety of different readings. Within the frame provided by a prologue and an epilogue, the novel tells the story of the intertwined lives of the white Afrikaner woman Milla Redelinghuys and the coloured woman Agaat on the farm Grootmoedersdrift in the Southern Cape district of South Africa. Milla takes Agaat from her abusive family when she is about five years old and raises her as her own child, but moves her into an outside room and the position of maidservant shortly before the birth of Milla's only child Jakkie seven years later. Milla is the narrator in the central part of the novel which roughly spans the years during which the Afrikaner National Party was dominant in South Africa: it starts with Milla's marriage to Jak de Wet in 1948, moves on to her informal adoption of Agaat in 1953, the birth of her son Jakkie in 1960, his desertion from the army and flight from South Africa to seek asylum in Canada in 1985, her husband Jak's death in 1985, and her death from motor neuron disease while being nursed by Agaat in 1996.

Within the context of this inquiry, my reading of the novel will focus on the way in which it comments on the notions of the mother, the motherland and the mother tongue in the aftermath of apartheid and the beginnings of a new dispensation in South Africa. At the heart of the novel lies a concern with mother-child relationships. The position of Milla's mother in the family is of a domineering and manipulative matriarch whom Milla experiences as cold, critical and unforgiving. This dysfunctional relationship is perpetuated in the problematic mother-child relationships and perverse mother figures presented in the novel. Although Milla finds the love, tenderness and intimacy lacking in her own relationship with her mother, in the bond with the child Agaat, she exposes her to brutal forms of discipline and eventually also rejection when she relegates her to the position of maidservant. Agaat's revenge is to use her position as nursemaid to take possession of Milla's child Jakkie from the moment that he is born and to alienate him emotionally from his biological parents by becoming his second "mother." Although she feels the greatest of tenderness and love for Jakkie, Agaat has been too well trained by Milla to avoid falling into the pattern of capable but domineering women set by Milla and her mother. When Jakkie leaves South Africa it is not only to escape from his parents and his motherland's politics, but also from the hold that his devoted "second mother" Agaat has over him.

The concept of a motherland is problematized by the novel's complex rendering of Milla's relationship with the farm Grootmoedersdrift. It is not a coincidence that the narrated time of the novel covers the time of the National Party's dominance; Marlene van Niekerk herself has suggested that the family in this novel can be read as allegorical of the Afrikaner nation.[23] Although the context of the novel is one in which Afrikaner patriarchy rules, Milla becomes part of a line of women landowners when she inherits the farm

Grootmoedersdrift (a name meaning "Grandmother's Ford") from her mother who in turn inherited it from her mother's side of the family (30).[24] The farm is thus quite literally Milla's "motherland." The way in which Milla's mother and later Milla handle the maps of the farm shows that the sense of ownership, entitlement and domination is intertwined with emotional attachment, a feeling of responsibility and reverence. The relationship with the (mother) land is given concrete form in the way that Milla farms the land in contrast with the way that her husband Jak does it. She aims at improving the land, preserving the ecological balance and using sustainable farming methods whereas Jak simply farms for profit. Despite this Milla does not hesitate to establish herself as the undisputed authority figure on the farm. She ruthlessly displaces the Okkenels who live on the farm as sharecroppers and exploits the farm labourers who live in primitive conditions despite the farm's financial success. When Jakkie makes over the farm to Agaat after his mother's death (708), Afrikaner land is given to someone from a previously dispossessed group. There are however also signs that the matriarchy established by Milla and her ancestors will be perpetuated in Agaat who has already shown signs of being as hard and unforgiving a landowner as her predecessors. Although the "promised land" is now hers, Jakkie feels that she will not be able to escape the influence of her creator Milla who will keep "remote control" from "six feet under" (682). His comment on Agaat's relationship with her land and her mother tongue is bitterly ironical: "She knows the soil. She knows the language. She knows her place" (682).This implies that Agaat has internalized Milla's (Afrikaner) conceptions of the farm as motherland, of her mother tongue in more than one sense of the word, and, most of all, that she knows her place, namely that her standing socially and psychologically will always be that of servant relegated to the outside room.

When Milla takes Agaat from her family the child has already mastered the rudiments of her mother tongue Afrikaans. Milla is however the one who becomes fully identified with the mother tongue: she is the one who coaxes the bewildered child into speech by teaching her to breathe and articulate properly before gradually extending her linguistic range through teaching her nursery rhymes and songs. She then extends her education by initiating her into a range of knowledges through a series of texts symbolising the master narratives of Afrikanerdom: the Bible (Christianity), a handbook for farmers (landownership), an Afrikaans songbook (culture), and a book on embroidery (womanly crafts). The novel shows however that the gift of speech, language and knowledge is not an unambivalent gift. To a certain extent one can argue that Milla quite literally becomes Agaat's mother tongue; through her charity project she becomes Agaat's mother and provides her with the tongue that will determine the way in which she will speak to and deal with the world.

Milla's behaviour as creator shows that this process includes the utmost extremes of tenderness and brutality. One can also argue that the Afrikaans Agaat is taught by Milla is a cultured and sophisticated language (the extraordinary command of Afrikaans of the narrative voice bears testimony to this), but also the language in which Agaat is taught about exclusion, racism, brutality and authoritarianism. These are patterns which she will later replicate in her own relationships with Milla, with Jakkie and the farm labourers. Jakkie is the one who understands to what extent Agaat is the product of his mother's making when he refers to her as an "Apartheid Cyborg. Assembled from loose components plus audiotape" (677).

The framing of the novel by a pro- and epilogue is important from the perspective of narrative technique and meaning. The prologue quite literally sets the scene for Milla's narrative which the reader is about to experience, whereas the epilogue ruptures the reader's intense emotional identification with both Milla and Agaat following the reading of Milla's narrative. The narrator in both pro- and epilogue is Milla's son Jakkie, who leaves South Africa in the 1980s to seek political asylum in Canada after deserting from the army, exchanging his career as pilot and engineer for one as ethnomusicologist.

The prologue in which Jakkie describes his journey from Canada to his mother's deathbed in South Africa introduces the reader to the two main characters in the novel as well as the setting in which the events take place. The prologue's introduction to his two mothers is cursory: Jakkie describes Milla as "(m)elancholy" and "oversensitive" (2), remembering her "airs" (3) and mocking her dream of him becoming a world-famous *lieder* singer; Agaat he paints as the one with whom he has a strong emotional bond as his confidante and prime nurturer. The prime focus of the prologue is however his memories of the motherland he is returning to. It is clear that he experiences his motherland (a term which encapsulates a geographical as well as a politico-cultural space) as a troubling memory and that he finds it very difficult to reconcile its beauty with its cruelty: "Took me years to fashion my own rhymes to bind the sweetness, the cruelty in a single memory" (4). On the one hand he exalts that "sweetness" in a lyrical description of the country's mountains, rivers, woods and the names they have been given. On the other hand he constantly checks this exaltation to remember that his motherland harbours a people and a history that he can no longer identify with, quoting a line from Buffy Sainte-Marie's protest song: *"My country 'tis of thy people you're dying"* (5). He is critical of himself for being overwhelmed by the physical appeal it makes on his senses, his memory and his unconscious. Attachment is therefore constantly checked by detachment, identification by alienation. The prologue also refers to the connection between his ambivalent feelings about his mothers, his motherland and his mother tongue. His mother Milla was the first to tell him about the different names for the Breede River, including the earliest name derived from a word in the indigenous language Nama (4–5). The fact that his motherland's sweetness and its cruelty is thus inscribed in the Afrikaans language carries his ambivalent feelings about his motherland over to his mother tongue. This is emphasised through the untranslatability of the various Afrikaans names for the rivers (5), for the farm Grootmoedersdrift ("Translate Grootmoedersdrift. Try it. Granny's Ford. Granny's Passion?" 6) and for certain features of its architecture and landscape.[25]

When Jakkie describes himself in the prologue as a "(n)omad without a flock," a "listener outside the tent," and asks himself whether anyone can "play the ethnographer at his mother's deathbed" (7), it raises an expectation that the epilogue will respond to these statements and questions. In the epilogue Jakkie tells the story of his stay in South Africa on his way back to Canada. His mother died before his arrival in South Africa so that he could only attend her funeral. The confrontation with his two mothers, Milla and Agaat, comes when he surreptitiously enters the bedroom in which his mother died. He senses that the room is "the murky realm of the mothers" (679) from which he is shut out. At this stage of the novel the reader knows more than Jakkie because he/she has just experienced Milla's narrative and knows the meaning and history of the objects in this room which Jakkie suspects to be "samples of some weird mnemonic" (679). The confrontation with the death-room leads to a final break with his mother Milla rather than a postmortem reconciliation with her memory. He enters the room prepared to acknowledge his love for her and to commemorate her in his own way, but his mind is changed when he reads the pious and self-congratulatory dedication of her diary that Agaat pinned to the reading frame above her bed. "I loved her, in my way. But that I should not have read," he says (681). He coldly describes her as my "sentimental, hypochondriac mother with her head full of romantic German melodies […] force-fed with the insanity of this country" (681). The prologue also brings his relationship with Agaat to some kind of closure. He acknowledges that his relationship with Agaat was a much closer and sustaining one than that with his biological mother. He also shares with the reader Agaat's story of how she came to be first Milla's child and then her servant, a tale which she often told him when he was a child. The story tells how Milla turned a "thing" into a human being, but also gives insight into the way in which Agaat replicated certain aspects of the process when she appropriated Jakkie to be her child, calling him, in an echo of Biblical speech, "You-are-mine" (690–1). Both mother-figures are compared to god-like creators, almost patriarchal in their power over the children they create (in both cases children they have not given birth to). It thus seems inevitable that Jakkie

should break his bond with his two mothers by leaving his motherland and
his mother tongue behind him.

The epilogue also replaces the prologue's romantic effusions about the
motherland with feelings of distance, even disgust. Jakkie's overriding perception of South Africa when he returns in 1996 is one of "(d)iscrepancy,"
of privilege and abundance in the midst of drought, neglect and poverty. He
refers to his motherland South Africa as "a world that is at the same time
both heaven and hell" (676), saying emphatically that he doesn't belong there
(677). Although he realises that his sense of self is unavoidably determined
by the farm Grootmoedersdrift, which can be read as symbol of his motherland, he feels: "the meaning of my existence is elsewhere, always and in
principle elsewhere, even if I were to stay here, in a realm of thought where
the thoughts assess themselves, the region where you always listen at a distance" (682). Thus it becomes clear that it is indeed possible for him to be
an "ethnographer at his mother's deathbed," as the prologue envisaged. He
chooses for distanced observation and reflection rather than identification,
stating that his motherland is "not a country for [him] to live in. To study,
yes" (682). The only mode of identification available to him is that of mourning that which he cannot abide: "That is what I must do then. Must learn to
do. Mourn my mother, my mothers, the white one and the brown one. Mourn
my country" (683).

Jakkie has been considered a pivotal figure in more than one reading of
the novel's implications. I will cite only two. Johann Rossouw reads the
novel as a plea for the self-eradication of the Afrikaner, interpreting Jakkie's departure from South Africa and his giving of the farm to Agaat, as an
indication that the Afrikaner has no future in South Africa and in Africa.[26]
Marlene van Niekerk's own reading of Jakkie is placed within the context
of a lecture about the similarities between the character Lambert Benade in
her novel *Triomf* and the character Agaat. If one reads both Lambert and
Agaat as symbolic of the romantic and shamanistic artist in the backroom
of the national(ist) family, she contends, one can read Jakkie's position as
an indication of yet another position the artist can take in the twenty-first
century. Instead of being a "navelstaarderige benepen romantische sjamaan"
["navelgazing small-minded romantical shaman"], she argues, Jakkie is an
international philosophical anthropologist who often has reservations about
his own enterprise, wondering whether he should not join forces with humanitarian efforts rather than engage in ethnomusicological research.[27] Van
Niekerk makes it clear that she shares certain of Jakkie's convictions when
she declares: "Zelfbegoocheldende her-betovering van so 'n wereld vanuit
een familiegebonden/volksgebonden of naëve humanistische optiek lijkt mij
geen optie meer" ["Self-deluding re-enchantment of such a world from the

perspective of a family-/nation-bound or naïve humanistic perspective does not seem to be an option to me anymore"].[28] My own reading veers in the direction of seeing Jakkie as a complicit outsider, someone who acknowledges that he was profoundly influenced by his mothers, his motherland and his mother tongue, but who knows that he cannot take refuge in the comfort of the mother figure (whether it is in the guise of the biological or emotional mother, as motherland or as mother tongue) because that would be to deny the messiness and ambiguity attending this figure. To complete successfully the Oedipal passage as person, as artist and as political subject he has to move away from the influences of his past to work out a new and ethical way of dealing with the world. His position serves as a warning to subjects of the postcolonial South African state as regards a renewed investment in romantic notions of the nation, especially when based on the figure of the woman as mother. Jakkie takes the option of becoming transnational, inscribing himself into a larger global space, in a way reminiscent of how Van Niekerk's novel written in her mother tongue Afrikaans has inserted itself into an international arena by means of translation.

ENGAGING WITH THE MOTHER: ANTJIE KROG'S *BEGGING TO BE BLACK* (2009)

The third writer I want to discuss is Antjie Krog who has made significant contributions to the debates on transformation in postcolonial South Africa. She recently published the third book in a trilogy consisting of *Country of My Skull* (1998), *A Change of Tongue* (2003) and *Begging to Be Black* (2009). In contrast with the fictional texts by Dido and Van Niekerk, Krog's trilogy combines autobiographical fact with elements of fiction, making use of a range of generic devices and styles. Certain passages in the third volume of the trilogy suggest that Krog wants to abandon fiction and the imaginative in favour of non-fiction. "Whatever novelistic elements I may use in my non-fiction work, the strangeness is not invented. The strangeness is real, and the fact that I cannot ever really enter the psyche of somebody else, somebody black. The terror and loneliness of that inability is what I don't want to give up on. […] I want to suggest that at this stage imagination for me is over-rated," she tells one of her conversational partners in *Begging to Be Black* (267–268).[29]

One of the ways in which Krog deals with her motherland and mother tongue is through the figure of her biological mother. Krog herself stated that she tries to answer to the influence of her mother in each of her books: "In elke boek wat ek skryf, is daar 'n poging om verantwoording te doen van haar invloed op my. In *'n Ander tongval* was dit byna 'n derde van die boek self, in die laaste *Begging to be Black*, is dit 'n stel briewe." ["In each book that I write, there is an attempt to give an account of her influence on me. In *A Change of Tongue* it was almost a third of the book, in the last *Begging to Be Black*, it was a set of letters."].[30] Although my primary focus will be on *Begging to Be Black*, I will make a few comments on the highly relevant narrative "A Town" in *A Change of Tongue*. This section of the book gives a detailed account of the important role that Krog's mother, Dot Serfontein, played in her daughter's development as a writer. It shows how Serfontein, who was a journalist and later made a name for herself as a writer of essays and popular fiction, introduced her daughter to literature and taught her the rudiments of writing, giving her insight into the relationship between fact and fiction and making her aware of the tension between managing a family and maintaining a creative life. It also tells of the way in which she tried to protect her daughter against unfriendly publicity and what she felt to be cynical exploitation by certain political players, when a media storm erupted after poems published in a school yearbook by Krog were deemed sexually precocious and politically unacceptable. The end of the narrative makes it clear that the political paths of mother and daughter would diverge and suggests that Krog's career would play out the complex patterns of association and disassociation common to the relationship between (literary) mothers and daughters.[31] The years since the publication of Krog's first volume of poetry in 1970 have indeed shown that mother and daughter occupy opposite positions on the political spectrum in South Africa, with Krog getting involved in the struggle for liberation and Serfontein remaining true to the Afrikaner nationalist values of her youth. The latter values form the ideological undercurrent of Serfontein's own memoirs, *Vrypas* [*Free Pass*], published in 2009. This autobiography gives the mother's version of the events around the publication of Krog's first poems and acts as counterpoint to Krog's (auto)biographical rendering of the events. Although Serfontein only hints at the emotional impact her daughter's political career had on her as mother (276), she concludes that her daughter should tell her own life story "met die nodige digterlike vryheid" ["with the necessary poetic freedom"] (275). There is also an interesting example of the reversal of literary "patronage" between daughter and mother, when she speculates whether her later works were published on merit or because she was the mother of "ons-weet-almal-wie" ["we-all-know-who"] (275).[32]

Begging to Be Black embeds the story of Krog's relationship with her mother and, through her, with the motherland and the mother tongue in the midst of several other stories. In a manner similar to the first two texts in the trilogy, this text weaves together seemingly disparate fragments in an attempt to identify a common framework by which South Africans can live interconnected and morally responsible lives. The first fragment of this interwoven whole tells of a murder in which Krog was unwittingly implicated because certain pieces of evidence were hidden on her property; the second is an exploration of the life and ideas of the Basotho king Moshoeshoe in whom Krog sees a precursor of leaders like Nelson Mandela and Desmond Tutu; the third is a report of her stay as research fellow in Berlin and includes diary entries, letters to her mother and conversations; the fourth tells of a visit to Lesotho during which she does research on Moshoeshoe, meets with a Sotho student Bonnini and visits historical sites. Although each of these segments unfolds over a considerable stretch of narrated time and they are mediated in a variety of styles and discourses, it is clear that they centre on the question of how Krog can re-imagine her own identity as a white person in post-post-apartheid South Africa. Krog's relationship with her mother as well as the related concepts of a motherland and mother tongue feature mostly in the letters that she writes to her mother from Berlin. Although this part of the text has been criticized for not being integrated into the whole,[33] I read them as an important part of the text because they introduce issues that have a direct bearing on Krog's project to find common ground with other South Africans. These issues are her own history as white Afrikaner, her literary and cultural background, and the bond with her mother tongue. In order to make my point I will highlight three moments in these letters.

The first of these moments has to do with the author's sense of coherence and incoherence. One of the things that Krog shares with her mother in these letters is her feeling of familiarity with Germany and Berlin, partly due to the fact that she studied German at school and is familiar with German literature, music and art. She marvels at the sophistication of the journalism and the language in which the public discourse is conducted. She also conveys her astonishment, sometimes even dismay, about the differences between Germany and South Africa. She is amazed by the luxury of her position at the research institute, by the trust put in German citizens not to take what is not theirs, by the safety of the public spaces in the city, and by the elaborate systems of social support. It is not by chance that these subjects surface in her letters to her mother, whom she has identified as the one from whom she inherited her political instinct, even though they hold opposing ideological positions.[34] Krog is conscious of the fact that her admiration for all things German may have a political subtext that has to do with her history as an Afrikaner. She writes in her diary that she suspects that her feeling of being in a familiar and supportive environment is

> not *only* the product of the exceptional, generous support systems provided by the *Wissenschaftskolleg,* or the safety and comfort of the surroundings, or my

self-disciplined solitude, but because this place forms part of a larger German
coherency to which I as an Afrikaner have access—being from a post-Anglo-
Boer War community which modelled itself on the only anti-English nation-
building group in Europe. (123)

The "coherency" she refers to has to do with her sense that all Germans share
the same language, the same range of cultural references and the same history. This coherency does not exist in South Africa "where we all live in inco-
herency" and look back on a history of which no part "is without its exclusion
and destruction of some part of the population" (125). Referring to her own
background as a Free State Afrikaner, she explains that she herself grew up in
a "completely closed coherent world" in which she could function entirely in
Afrikaans without having to resort to any other language (126). The postcolonial dynamic in South Africa has however destroyed that sense of coherence.
Whereas some Afrikaners are "deeply resentful about the incoherence of their
lives" (126), Krog is inspired to go in search of a way of thinking herself out
of the "heart of whiteness" (154) and into "becoming-black" (a reference to
Deleuze and Guattari's concept of becoming-other), something that will finally underpin the interconnectedness she is longing for. That Krog's mother,
to whom she is deeply attached, represents the old coherency becomes clear
when she writes to her mother about the feelings she experienced when she
received her mother's first letter in Berlin. She is overcome with emotion
when she sees her mother's handwriting, because it evokes the whole of
her history with her mother (which includes moments of motherly support
as well as fierce opposition to her daughter's political views). The envelope
of this letter is one on which their old farm address was stamped: *W Krog
Middenspruit Kroonstad.* This makes her think: "We needed no post-box, no
postal code, no gender—only four words to say exactly who and where we
were. How invincibly contextualized we felt ourselves once upon a time!"
(128). Krog's text demonstrates that letting go of the coherency embodied in
the beloved and intractable mother is an arduous and difficult process. Dot
Serfontein's response in an interview captures something of the difficulty
of this severing of the past. When asked about the correspondence between
her and Krog while the latter was in Berlin, she states that she experienced
Krog's letters as "dieselfde noodkreet van vanmelewe as sy my nodig het"
["the same cry of help as before when she needed me"].[35]

In another significant moment in the letters the mother is linked to the
mother tongue via Krog's observations about German language and literature. She comments indirectly on the history of her own mother tongue Afrikaans when she writes to her mother about their shared admiration for the
German language ("God's language, as you used to say," Krog writes to her
mother, 129), as well as German culture and literature. In one of her letters
she reminds her mother of the German painter who was supposed to paint the

portraits of Afrikaner leaders freed from British rule by a victorious Germany after the Second World War (156). Before he was interned by the South African government during the war, this man hid on the farm of her mother's parents in the Free State and developed a bond with her mother. She asks her mother how she reconciled the presence of this man with that of the German-Jewish record dealer in their town from whom she bought her recordings of German music. Krog writes about the latter: "What did he make of this seventeen-year-old Afrikaner girl who was his only client listening to and buying German *Lieder?* This we do not talk about, nor about the language in which the longings of both these men, one in hope, one in despair, were lodged thousands of kilometers away from Germany." (157). Krog's question about the German language and culture that were able to house the aspirations of the German Nazi as well as the German Jew, can be read as an oblique comment on her mother tongue Afrikaans that also voiced the aspirations of white nationalists (like Serfontein) as well those resisting them (like Krog). Taking German classes in Berlin, Krog is reminded of the time when she was a pupil in her mother's German class at school. She writes to her mother that she remembers the sound of her voice when she read Goethe's poem "Nur wer die Sehnsucht kennt" ["Only one who knows this yearning"]. She writes: "something else, something *unbestimmt* entered your voice, something that made my body, as young as I was, turn cold, a sound that I never heard from you ever again, but maybe am spending a lifetime now finding its source for you" (99). As in *A Change of Tongue* the narrative registers moments in which the mother's firm convictions about the happiness of her own life and the rightness of her own convictions are put into doubt. Here the daughter senses something *unbestimmt [uncertain],* yearning and unfulfilled in her mother. This constitutes a slippage, a small crack in the mother's resolve into which her daughter can enter to justify her own longing and her own search for something outside the known parameters and coherencies of her life.

A third moment that I want to touch on is Krog's letter to her mother about the *Stolpersteine* she sees all over Berlin. One of Krog's diary entries describes the New Year's Eve party after which she had a disturbing vision of the weighted histories and piles of dead bodies underpinning the security of Germany (153–155). Shortly after this she writes to her mother about the way in which the Germans are dealing with their guilt about the past and tells her about the *Stolpersteine* (stumbling stones) to be found all over Berlin. These copper plaques mark the places from which Jews disappeared during the Nazi reign. Writing to her mother about the possibility of similar projects in South Africa, she comments that one would not need plaques or memorials in South Africa because the reminders of the past are walking around everywhere, also because "shame belongs to a colour—the colour is the reminder" (159). This remark, almost guaranteed to provoke the mother, is linked to the text's project of finding an interconnectedness on which a future in South Africa can be based. It also demonstrates the complex negotiations necessary between her relationship with her mother and her hopes for her motherland. The text ends with Krog's departure from the *Wissenschaftskolleg* in Berlin. When she lays the key on the table and closes the door of her flat behind her, an arduous process of researching, thinking, conversing, talking, discussing and enquiring comes to an end. Amongst the people she talked with during this period, her mother occupies an important place as a touchstone, perhaps also a *Stolperstein*, a constant reminder of a past coherence which is no more. Her own longing to find the space of interconnectedness that will enable her to live an ethically responsible life in her motherland seems to be lodged at precisely those points where she senses an uncertainty and longing in her mother and mother tongue.

CIRCUMVENTING ESSENTIALISM

The way in which the motherland and the mother tongue feature in these texts by Afrikaans women demonstrates that literature does indeed have the ability to reveal the messy details that complicate simplistic notions about the transition to a new South African society. Each of the three writers I have discussed engage with the motherland and the Afrikaans mother tongue via the figure of the mother in a way that circumvents the essentialism potentially present in the use of the mother metaphor. E.K.M. Dido's novel shows a subject who has to negotiate deep feelings of guilt and remorse before she can integrate seemingly opposing elements in her identity. Van Niekerk's novel suggests that an oedipal break with the mother, the motherland and the mother tongue, rather than identification, is necessary to ensure a clear view of the past and the future. Krog's text about imagining a meaningful first premise for an interconnected South African future needs the figure of the mother as a constant reminder of the past that has (in)formed her and has to be negotiated in order to reach her goal. These three texts show that Afrikaans women writers are grappling with what it means to be a South African and a writer in Afrikaans after the transition: their texts lay bare the subtle gradations, slippages, inconsistencies and human emotions involved, in a way that overarching theories rarely do.

NOTES

1. The history of Afrikaans literature is charted from a variety of perspectives in the following publications: Ampie Coetzee, *Letterkunde en krisis: 'n honderd jaar*

Afrikaanse letterkunde en Afrikanernasionalisme (Johannesburg: Taurus, 1990); J. C. Kannemeyer, *Die Afrikaanse literatuur, 1652–2004* (Cape Town: Human & Rousseau, 2005); H. P. van Coller, ed., *Perspektief en profiel. Deel 1–3* (Pretoria: Van Schaik, 1998, 1999, 2006).

2. For an overview of Afrikaans women's writing, see Annemarie van Niekerk, "Die Afrikaanse vroueskrywer—van egotekste tot postmodernisme (18e eeu— 1996)," in *Perspektief en profiel. Deel 2,* ed. H. P. van Coller (Pretoria: Van Schaik, 1999), 305–443. See Henriette Roos, "Die Afrikaanse prosa 1997 tot 2002," in *Perspektief en profiel. Deel 3,* ed. H. P. van Coller (Pretoria: Van Schaik, 2006), 60–62.

3. For further discussions of Afrikaans women writers' response to the transition, see Christell Stander and Hein Willemse, "Winding through Nationalism, Patriarchy, Privilege and Concern: A Selected Overview of Afrikaans Women Writers," *Research in African Literatures* 23, no. 3 (Autumn 1992): 5–24; Kenneth Parker, "In the 'New South Africa': W(h)ither Literature?" *Wasafiri* 19 (Summer 1994): 3–7; Louise Viljoen, "Postcolonialism and Recent Women's Writing in Afrikaans," *World Literature Today* 70, no. 1 (Winter 1996): 63–72.

4. See E. K. M.Dido, *Die storie van Monica Peters* (Cape Town, Kwela Boeke, 1996); Ronelda Kamfer, *Noudat slapende honde* (Cape Town, Kwela Boeke, 2008).

5. See Henriette Roos, "Die Afrikaanse prosa 1997 tot 2002," 99.

6. Elleke Boehmer, *Stories of Women: Gender and Narrative in the Postcolonial Nation* (Manchester: Manchester University Press, 2005), 27. See also Anne McClintock, *Imperial Leather: Race, Gender and Sexuality in the Colonial Contest* (New York: Routledge, 1995), 354–55.

7. For detailed discussions of the concept of the *volksmoeder* within the context of Afrikaner Nationalism, see Elsabé Brink, "Man-made Women: Gender, Class and the Ideology of the *Volksmoeder*," in *Women and Gender in Southern Africa to 1945,* ed. Cheryl Walker (Cape Town: David Philip, 1990), 273–92; Elsabé Brink, "Die volksmoeder: beeld van 'n vrou," in *Van Volksmoeder tot Fokofpolisiekar: Kritiese opstelle oor Afrikaanse herinneringsplekke,* ed. Albert M. Grundlingh and Siegfried Huigen (Stellenbosch: Sun Press, 2008), 7–16; Anne McClintock, *Imperial Leather,* 368–79.

8. See McClintock, *Imperial Leather,* 379–89.

9. Deborah Gaitskell and Elaine Unterhalter, "Mothers of the Nation: A Comparative Analysis of Nation, Race and Motherhood in Afrikaner Nationalism and the African National Congress," in *Women-State-Nation,* ed. Nira Yuval-Davis and Flora Anthias (Hampshire: MacMillan, 1989), 75.

10. Meg Samuelson, *Remembering the Nation, Dismembering Women? Stories of the South African Transition* (Scottsville: University of KwaZulu-Natal Press, 2007), 11, has shown that there exists a wide rift between the reverence for these symbolic mothers and the real situation of South African women who are still subjected to "physical, psychic and discursive violence" despite the adoption of a woman-friendly constitution after the transition.

11. Dalene Matthee, *Pieternella van die Kaap* (Cape Town: Tafelberg, 2000).

12. Ferrus's poem "Vir Sara Baartman" played a part in the return of Sara Baartman's remains to South Africa when it was quoted in the French parliament. It was

subsequently included in Diana Ferrus's volume of poetry *Ons komvandaan* (Cape Town: Diana Ferrus Publishers, 2006).

13. See the following sources for information about the history of Afrikaans: Hans den Besten, "Double Negation and the Genesis of Afrikaans," in *Substrata versus Universals in Creole Languages, Papers from the Amsterdam Creole Workshop April 1985*, ed. Pieter Muysken and Norval Smith (Amsterdam: Benjamins, 1986), 185–230; Fritz Ponelis, *The Development of Afrikaans* (Frankfurt am Main: Peter Lang, 1993), 99–120; Paul T. Roberge, "The Formation of Afrikaans," in *Language and Social History. Studies in South African Sociolonguistics*, ed. Rajend Meshtrie (Claremont: David Philip, 1995), 68–88; Paul T. Roberge, "Afrikaans," in *Germanic Standardizations*, ed. Ana Deumert and Wim Vandenbussche (Amsterdam: Benjamins, 2003), 15–40. See also Isabel Hofmeyr, "Building a Nation from Words: Afrikaans Language, Literature and Ethnic Identity, 1902–1924," in *The Politics of Race, Class and Nationalism in Twentieth Century South Africa*, ed. Shula Marks and Stanley Trapido (London: Longmans, 1987), 95–123, for a discussion of the Afrikaans "language movement" in the early twentieth century.

14. See Hein Willemse, "The Black Afrikaans Writer: A Continuing Dichotomy," *Triquarterly* 69 (Spring/Summer 1987): 237–47.

15. Mara Scanlon, "Mother Land, Mother Tongue: Reconfiguring Relationship in Suleri's *Meatless Days*," *LIT* 12 (2001): 411–25.

16. See Graham Huggan, *Interdisciplinary Measures. Literature and the Future of Postcolonial Studies*. (Liverpool: Liverpool University Press, 2008), 10–14; Michael Chapman, "Postcolonialism: A Literary Turn," in *Postcolonialism: South/African Perspectives*, ed. Michael Chapman (Newcastle: Cambridge Scholars Publishing, 2008), 8–12.

17. See Meg Samuelson, *Re-membering the Nation*, 232.

18. See Ampie Coetzee, "Swart Afrikaanse Skrywers: 'n diskursiewe praktyk van die verlede," *Stilet* 14, no. 1 (2002): 149–66; Hein Willemse, *Aan die ander kant: Swart Afrikaanse skrywers in die Afrikaanse letterkunde* (Menlopark: Protea Boekhuis, 2008).

19. Zoë Wicomb, "Shame and Identity: The Case of the Coloured in South Africa," in *Writing South Africa: Literature, Apartheid, Democracy, 1970–1995*, ed. Derek Attridge and Rosemary Jolly (Cambridge: Cambridge University Press, 1998), 91–107; Zimitri Erasmus, "Re-imagining Coloured Identities in Post-Apartheid South Africa," in *Coloured by History, Shaped by Place. New Perspectives on Coloured Identities in Cape Town*, ed. Zimitri Erasmus (Cape Town: Kwela Books/Maroelana, 2002): 13–28.

20. Dido uses the Afrikaans word "bruin" (brown) to refer to her race in an interview with Stephanie Nieuwoudt, "'As mense maar net mekaar wil verstaan'," *Beeld*, November 29, 2000, 8, in which she also discusses her ability to speak both Afrikaans and Xhosa fluently.

21. See interview with Maryke Roberts, "Land en sand met E. K. M. Dido," *Die Burger* 14 (November 2006): 10.

22. Page numbers refer to E. K. M. Dido, *'n Stringetjie blou krale* (Cape Town: Kwela Books, 2000).

23. Marlene van Niekerk, "Het 'Scheppingsverhaal' van *Agaat*" (paper read at meeting of Stichting Literaire Activiteiten Amsterdam, February 22, 2008), 2.

24. Page numbers refer to the South African edition of Michiel Heyns' translation of the novel, see Marlene van Niekerk, *Agaat* (Johannesburg: Jonathan Ball, 2006). The UK edition of this translation is titled *The Way of the Women* (London: Little, Brown, 2007).

25. See the translator of the novel on his strategies for coping with this aspect of the novel, Michiel Heyns, "Irreparable Loss and Exorbitant Gain: On translating *Agaat*," *Journal of Literary Studies* 25, no. 3 (2009): 124–35.

26. Johann Rossouw, "O moenie huil nie, o moenie treur nie, die jollie bobbejaan kom weer: Oor Marlene van Niekerk se *Agaat*," *Die Vrye Afrikaan* 2005, http://vryea frikaan.co.za/lees.php?id=105 (accessed October 7, 2010). For critical responses to this reading see Anton van Niekerk, "Oor die wegbly van die jollie bobbejaan: Wie is dit wat regtig treur?" *LitNet Seminaarkamer* January 26 , 2005, http://www.oulitnet .co.za/seminaar/agaat_vniekerk/asp (accessed October 7, 2010); Andries Visagie, "*Agaat* as kultuurdokumentasie vir die toekoms: 'n reaksie op Johann Rossouw se politieke lesing van Marlene van Niekerk se *Agaat* in *Die Vrye Afrikaan*," *LitNet Seminaarkamer* 4 February 2005, http://www.oulitnet.co.za/seminaar/agaat_visague/ asp (accessed October 7, 2010).

27. Marlene van Niekerk, "Het kind in de achterkamer: Lambert Benade en Agaat Lourier, sjamenen van de familie? (vuurmakers onder het volk?)" (Faculty Lecture on Own Work, University of Utrecht, February 21, 2008), 17.

28. Marlene Van Niekerk, "Het kind in de achterkamer," 17.

29. Page numbers refer to Antjie Krog, *Begging to Be Black* (Cape Town: Random House Struik, 2009).

30. Quoted by Willem de Vries, "Dot Serfontein: Vreeslose Vrystater se stem nie stil," *Volksblad*, May 4, 2010, 7.

31. For a discussion of the mother-daughter relationship in *A Change of Tongue*, see Louise Viljoen, *Ons ongehoorde soort. Beskouings van die werk van Antjie Krog* (Stellenbosch: Sun Press, 2009), 167–87.

32. Page numbers refer to Dot Serfontein, *Vrypas* (Pretoria: Protea Boekhuis, 2009).

33. This is the view of Rustum Kozain voiced in a joint article by Hans Pienaar and Rustum Kozain, "Hoe swart kan wit dan word?" *Rapport*, December 26, 2009, 2.

34. Krog said in an interview: "Ons is al twee gróót politieke diere, so as ons klaar familienuus uitgeruil het dan praat ek en sy politiek. Dit is eintlik verskriklik. Maar sy is oud nou; jy weet, 'n mens baklei of stry nie eintlik meer nie. Jy neem maar met genade waar, soort van." ["We are both big political animals, so when we have finished exchanging family news, then we talk politics. It is actually terrible. But she is old now, one doesn't really fight or argue anymore. You only observe with mercy, kind of."], see Murray la Vita, "Verlig oor elke omstrede bundel," *Beeld*, March 14, 2009, 9.

35. Dot Serfontein, "'n Skrywer, 'n joernalis en 'n akademikus klop aan," *Rapport*, June 4, 2006, 4.

BIBLIOGRAPHY

Boehmer, Elleke. *Stories of Women: Gender and Narrative in the Postcolonial Nation.* Manchester: Manchester University Press, 2005.

Brink, Elsabé. "Man-made Women: Gender, Class and the Ideology of the *Volksmoeder.*" In *Women and Gender in Southern Africa to 1945*, edited by Cherryl Walker, 273–92. Cape Town: David Philip, 1990.

———. "Die volksmoeder: beeld van 'n vrou." In *Van Volksmoeder tot Fokofpolisiekar: Kritiese opstelle oor Afrikaanse herinneringsplekke*, edited by Albert M. Grundlingh and Siegfried Huigen, 7–16. Stellenbosch: Sun Press, 2008.

Chapman, Michael. "Postcolonialism: A Literary Turn." In *Postcolonialism: South/ African Perspectives*, edited by Michael Chapman, 1–15. Newcastle: Cambridge Scholars Publishing, 2008.

Coetzee, Ampie. *Letterkunde en krisis: 'n honderd jaar Afrikaanse letterkunde en Afrikanernasionalisme.* Johannesburg: Taurus, 1990.

Den Besten, Hans. "Double Negation and the Genesis of Afrikaans." In *Substrata versus Universals in Creole Languages, Papers from the Amsterdam Creole Workshop April 1985*, edited by Pieter Muysken and Norval Smith, 185–230. Amsterdam: Benjamins, 1986.

De Vries, Willem. "Dot Serfontein: Vreeslose Vrystater se stem nie stil." *Volksblad* May 4, 2010.

Dido, E. K. M. *Die storie van Monica Peters.* Cape Town: Kwela Boeke, 1996.

———. *n Stringetjie blou krale.* Cape Town: Kwela Boeke, 2000.

Gaitskell, Deborah, and Elaine Unterhalter, "Mothers of the Nation: A Comparative Analysis of Nation, Race and Motherhood in Afrikaner Nationalism and the African National Congress." In *Women-State-Nation*, edited by Nira Yuval-Davis and Flora Anthias, 58–78. Hampshire: MacMillan, 1989.

Heyns, Michiel. "Irreparable Loss and Exorbitant Gain: On translating *Agaat.*" *Journal of Literary Studies* 25, no. 3 (2009): 124–35.

Hofmeyr, Isabel. "Building a Nation from Words: Afrikaans Language, Literature and Ethnic Identity, 1902–1924." In *The Politics of Race, Class and Nationalism in Twentieth Century South Africa*, edited by Shula Marks and Stanley Trapido, 95–123. London: Longmans, 1987.

Huggan, Graham. *Interdisciplinary Measures: Literature and the Future of Postcolonial Studies.* Liverpool: Liverpool University Press, 2008.

Kamfer, Ronelda. *Noudat slapende honde.* Cape Town, Kwela Boeke, 2008.

Kannemeyer, J. C. *Die Afrikaanse literatuur, 1652–2004.* Cape Town: Human & Rousseau, 2005.

Krog, Antjie. *A Change of Tongue.* Johannesburg: Random House, 2003.

———. *Begging to Be Black.* Cape Town: Random House Struik, 2009.

La Vita, Murray. "Verlig oor elke omstrede bundel." *Beeld*, March 14, 2009.

McClintock, Anne. *Imperial Leather: Race, Gender and Sexuality in the Colonial Conquest.* New York: Routledge, 1995.

Nieuwoudt, Stephanie. "'As mense maar net mekaar wil verstaan.'" *Beeld*, November 29, 2000.

Parker, Kenneth. "In the 'New South Africa': W(h)ither Literature?" *Wasafiri* 19 (Summer 1994): 3–7.

Pienaar, Hans, and Rustum Kozain. "Hoe swart kan wit dan word?" *Rapport*, December 26, 2009.

Ponelis, Fritz. *The Development of Afrikaans.* Frankfurt am Main: Peter Lang, 1993.

Roberge, Paul T. "The Formation of Afrikaans." In *Language and Social History: Studies in South African Sociolinguistics*, edited by Rajend Meshtrie, 68–88. Claremont: David Philip, 1995.

———. "Afrikaans." *Germanic Standardizations*, edited by Ana Deumert and Wim Vandenbussche, 15–40. Amsterdam: Benjamins, 2003.

Roberts, Maryke. "Land en sand met E. K. M. Dido." *Die Burger*, November 14, 2006.

Roos, Henriette. "Die Afrikaanse prosa 1997 tot 2002." In *Perspektief en profiel. Deel 3*, edited by H. P. van Coller, 43–104. Pretoria: Van Schaik, 2006.

Rossouw, Johan. "O moenie huil nie, o moenie treur nie, die jollie bobbejaan kom weer: Oor Marlene van Niekerk se *Agaat*." *Die Vrye Afrikaan.* 2005. http://vryea frikaan.co.za/lees.php?id=105 (accessed October 7, 2010).

Samuelson, Meg. *Remembering the Nation, Dismembering Women? Stories of the South African Transition.* Scottsville: University of KwaZulu-Natal Press, 2007.

Scanlon, Mara. "Mother Land, Mother Tongue: Reconfiguring Relationship in Suleri's *Meatless Days.*" *LIT* Volume 12 (2001): 411–25.

Serfontein, Dot. *Vrypas.* Pretoria: Protea Boekhuis, 2009.

———. "'n Skrywer, 'n joernalis en 'n akademikus klop aan." *Rapport*, June 4, 2009.

Stander, Christell, and Hein Willemse. "Winding through Nationalism, Patriarchy, Privilege and Concern: A Selected Overview of Afrikaans Women Writers." *Research in African Literatures* 23, no. 3 (Autumn 1992): 5–24.

Van Niekerk, Annemarie. "Die Afrikaanse vroueskrywer—van egotekste tot postmodernisme (18e eeu—1996)." In *Perspektief en profiel. Deel 2*, edited by H. P. van Coller,305–443. Pretoria: Van Schaik, 1999.

Van Niekerk, Anton. "Oor die wegbly van die jollie bobbejaan: Wie is dit wat regtig treur?" *LitNet Seminaarkamer.* January 26, 2005. http://www.oulitnet.co.za/semi naar/agaat_vniekerk/asp (accessed October 7, 2010).

Van Niekerk, Marlene. *Agaat*, trans. Michiel Heyns. Johannesburg: Jonathan Ball, 2006.

———. "Het kind in de achterkamer: Lambert Benade en Agaat Lourier, sjamenen van de familie? (vuurmakers onder het volk?)." Faculty Lecture on Own Work, University of Utrecht, February 21, 2008.

———. "Het 'Scheppingsverhaal' van *Agaat*" Paper read at meeting of Stichting Literaire Activiteiten, Amsterdam, February 22, 2008.

Viljoen, Louise. "Postcolonialism and Recent Women's Writing in Afrikaans." *World Literature Today* 70, no. 1 (Winter 1996): 63–72.

———. *Ons ongehoorde soort: Beskouings oor die werk van van Antjie Krog.* Stellenbosch: Sun Press, 2009.

Visagie, Andries. "*Agaat* as kultuurdokumentasie vir die toekoms: 'n reaksie op Johann Rossouw se politieke lesing van Marlene van Niekerk se *Agaat* in *Die Vrye*

Afrikaan," *LitNet Seminaarkamer.* February 4, 2005. http://www.oulitnet.co.za/seminaar/agaat_visague/asp (accessed October 7, 2010).

Willemse, Hein. "The Black Afrikaans Writer: A Continuing Dichotomy." *Triquarterly* 69 (1987): 237–47.

———. *Aan die ander kant. Swart Afrikaanse skrywers in die Afrikaanse letterkunde.* Menlopark: Protea Boekhuis, 2008.

Chapter Nine

The Holocaust as a Paradigm for the Congo Atrocities

Adam Hochschild's King Leopold's Ghost

Sarah De Mul

As is now generally accepted, memory affects our moral criticisms, political analyses, and affective responsiveness to the past in the present. Yet, although few people in this post-Holocaust age would doubt the moral obligation to remember past catastrophes, there seems to be far less agreement on how precisely they should be remembered. Eclectic as they are in ideological and philosophical terms, postcolonial theories on the one hand and trauma theory and Holocaust studies on the other are among the fields of knowledge that put questions of remembrance, forgetting, and particularly the representational modes these could take on the table. Although both fields have paid particular attention to the ways in which literature could offer particular modes of understanding and responding to catastrophic events and histories, they have often done so in parallel and disparate ways. For instance, narrative acts and discourses of witnessing have formed an important topic of both postcolonial and Holocaust discussions, yet these discussions have developed in strikingly dissimilar ways, with visible variations in emphasis and differences in theoretical concepts of violence, victimhood, and agency. Recently, a number of fruitful attempts have been made to build bridges between theoretical discourses of postcolonialism and the Holocaust in mutually productive ways, as well as to theorize the interconnectedness of distinct forms of violence. In his recent study *Multidirectional Memory* Michael Rothberg examines how memories of the Holocaust and postcolonial historical reconstructions interconnect, overlap, and influence one another, for instance in the work of authors such as Caryl Phillips, Aimé Césaire, or Charlotte Delbo.[1] In what follows, I will build on these newer theoretical discourses by analyzing negotiations of Holocaust memory in Adam Hochschild's *King Leopold's Ghost* (1998), a historical non-fiction book about colonial violence and torture in the Congo Free State under Leopold II's rule.[2]

Although various people—from Hannah Arendt to Nadine Gordimer—have brought the atrocities that happened in the Congo Free State into connection with the Jewish Holocaust, it was not until 1998, when Adam Hochschild's bestselling *King Leopold's Ghost* was first published, that the notion of a "forgotten Holocaust" gained the currency it currently has. In this essay, I will examine the Holocaust paradigm in Hochschild's historical account as a strategy of commitment to exposing the humanitarian disaster in the Congo Free State and assess the ethico-political repercussions of this portrayal of colonial history in contemporary commemorations of the colonial past and debates on its legacy in the Belgian context. Focusing in particular on analogies and comparisons between the Congo atrocities and the Jewish Holocaust and the deployment of tropes of forgetting, I will show how *King Leopold's Ghost*'s negotiation of Holocaust memory strategically serves to commemorate and celebrate the actions and commitments of the late-nineteenth-century humanitarians who mounted resistance against Leopold's colonial regime. In effect, the Holocaust paradigm provides Hochschild with a new vocabulary for—and effectively prompts a resurgence of—the nineteenth-century humanitarian discourse deployed by the British liberal humanitarian Edmund Dene Morel, who is also the "hero" of Hochschild's historical narrative. In so doing, however, *King Leopold's Ghost* harbors the following rhetorical paradox: it relies on Holocaust metaphors and imagery while simultaneously appealing to a pre-Holocaust moral tradition of liberal humanitarianism that the Holocaust has rendered anachronistic—a point recently reiterated by Renzo Martens's documentary art film *Enjoy Poverty* (2008), which, in ruthlessly exposing the multiple complicities surrounding Western humanitarian action in the Democratic Republic of the Congo, offers a compelling counterpoint to Hochschild's account. Against this background I will explore a number of tensions and contradictions in Belgian postcolonial memory discourse in the wake of Hochschild's book, in which the Holocaust plays a prominent role.

THE CONGO ATROCITIES AS A FORGOTTEN HOLOCAUST

Published in 1998, the historical non-fiction book *King Leopold's Ghost* by the American journalist Adam Hochschild was immediately translated into various languages and reached bestseller lists in four countries.[3] One was Belgium, where the book sparked off considerable controversy, particularly surrounding the deployment of the Holocaust term in the discussion of the humanitarian disaster in the Congo Free State under Leopold II's rule. Although it was certainly not the first book to reference the Holocaust in this context—Hannah Arendt brought together the Holocaust and the Congo atrocities in

The Origins of Totalitarianism already in 1951—*King Leopold's Ghost* has probably enjoyed the widest acclaim among the general public.

The French translation includes the term "Holocaust" in the subtitle, *Les fantomes du roi Leopold. Un holocauste oublié.* Furthermore, Hochschild writes in the introduction: "The Congo of a century ago had [...] seen a death toll of Holocaust dimensions" (4). The subsequent historical narrative is a densely patterned surface of comparisons and analogies that direct us, beyond Hochschild's observations and reconstructions of the late-nineteenth-century colonial atrocities in the Congo, to the memory of the more recent Jewish Holocaust. Similarity and correspondence manifest themselves, for instance, in instances where personal characteristics of Hitler are invoked in depictions of Leopold II's psychology, when Nazism and the Belgian colonial regime are weighed against each other and considered identical in terms of their systematically destructive nature, or when the personal words of well-known Holocaust witnesses such as Primo Levi or Nazi officers testifying at the Nuremberg trials are referenced to bring home to the reader the nature and scope of terror and torture in the Congo Free State.

King Leopold's Ghost is not only informed by the paradigm of the Jewish Holocaust through literal analogies and comparisons, but Hochschild's insistent deployment of tropes of forgetting also requires attention in this respect. Hochschild indeed refers to the colonial atrocities in the Congo Free State as a "forgotten Holocaust." While comparisons, juxtapositions, and analogies emphasize that the two catastrophes are somehow alike, they are, to Hochschild's mind, perceived and treated in dissimilar ways in the present: while the Jewish Holocaust is remembered, the colonial genocide in the Congo is forgotten. The ethical significance of the adjective "forgotten" depends on the public memory of the Jewish Holocaust, if we consider that the broadening debates about the Jewish Holocaust in Europe and the United States since the 1980s have energized and promoted the sense that there exists such a thing as an ethical imperative to remember ("never again"). Commemorating catastrophes such as the Holocaust and its victims is considered to be a fundamentally ethical practice. We are "obliged by memory"; our incessant awareness or memory of the devastation left in the wake of Nazism forecloses the possibility of its re-occurrence in the future.[4] From this perspective, Hochschild renders his account of the Congo atrocities with a particular ethical urgency. The metaphor of a forgotten Holocaust appeals to our ethical codes twice: first, by emphasizing that the colonial violence in the Congo Free State amounted to a catastrophe with the magnitude of a Holocaust, and second, by summoning readers to remember.

Despite the wide resonance of *King Leopold's Ghost*, or precisely because of the controversy it triggered, Hochschild clarified his reasons for adopting the Holocaust analogy in a number of writings and newspaper articles published in the years after the publication of *King Leopold's Ghost*, for instance as follows:

> If, [. . .], as both Belgian officials at the time and various modern scholars have estimated, the loss may have been in the neighborhood of 50 percent, what do we call this? Does it not constitute reckless destruction of life? That phrase is from one of the definitions, in the *Random House Unabridged Dictionary*, for "holocaust," with a small "h." Long before the Nazis, the word came down to us from the ancient Greeks, and it is surely reasonable to apply it to the vast human toll taken in Central Africa.[5]

As is clear from this fragment, estimations of the casualties led Hochschild (and others) to comparisons with the Holocaust—with a capital H—as well as to the use of the term "holocaust," meaning massive destruction, but automatically alluding to the mass destruction of Jews in Europe during World War II.[6]

If, in the words of Judith Butler, "the story and the image of the Holocaust lays claim to the most unimaginable suffering," what does it mean to use this story and image to tell another story of suffering which we have nowadays, as Hochschild says, forgotten?[7] The deployment of this kind of comparative memory discourse for a "forgotten" historical event can only be effective if a story and image of the Jewish Holocaust as the most unimaginable suffering is already presumed to be known to the readers. Hochschild's narration of the Congo atrocities indeed hinges to a great extent upon the story and image of the Jewish Holocaust as the most unimaginable suffering for its effect.[8] Only then could the narrative tropes and themes conventionally associated with the narrative about the Jewish Holocaust provide readers of *King Leopold's Ghost* with a retrospective reading grid for the lesser-known tragedy in the Congo Free State.

Although these two political catastrophes are set in different moments in history and dissimilar geographical locations, *King Leopold's Ghost* brings them together and, in so doing, separates them to a considerable extent from their historically specific circumstances. Relations of likeness are drawn insofar as the Congo atrocities involved a degree of violence, torture, and suffering that reminds one of the Jewish Holocaust, while at the same time these notions of violence, torture, and suffering are stripped of their historical particularities. The latter explains why references to the human loss under the Stalinist regime also occur frequently in *King Leopold's Ghost,* although it has been particularly the comparison with the Jewish Holocaust that has resonated among the general public. It is precisely the level of ahistoricism involved in the act of comparison which has attracted most criticism; as one

Belgian historiographer, Jean-Luc Vellut, put it: "To compare it [the violent history of Leopold's Congo] with the Holocaust or Auschwitz is an insult to the truth. We need to put our history in perspective and be cautious."[9] If we leave the question of empirical history and historical accuracy aside, however, the practice of oscillating between the generic and specific meaning of the term 'h/Holocaust' allows Hochschild to make use of the known image of the Jewish Holocaust as the most unimaginable suffering, while at the same time assigning this particular story a universal resonance.[10]

Consider, for instance, the following description of colonial officers in the Congo Free State as perpetrators of torture who accept their assignments without asking questions:

> The white men who passed through the territory [...] generally accepted the use of the *chicotte* as unthinkingly as hundreds of thousands of other men in uniform would accept their assignments, a half-century later, to staff the Nazi and Soviet concentration camps. "Monsters exist," wrote Primo Levi of his experience at Auschwitz. "But they are too few in number to be truly dangerous. More dangerous are . . . the functionaries ready to believe and to act without asking questions." (121)

The latter portrayal largely depends on the comparison with the Holocaust in its double sense. The depiction of compliant and subservient Nazi and Soviet soldiers is invoked to convey that, in a similar vein, colonial officers in the Congo unthinkingly accepted their task to commit torture practices—symbolized by the tool of the *chicotte* (which is arguably a mythical symbol drawn from the popular imagination of Leopold's Congo). Next, a reference to Primo Levi is inserted as a powerful claim about those colonial officers who acted violently without thinking. Neither empirical research nor historical expertise on the Congo Free State, but, rather, Levi's authority as a first-hand witness of the Jewish Holocaust is called upon to support the trustworthiness of this claim. In so doing, the idiosyncrasy of the historical context of the Congo Free State is bracketed, while Levi's words serve as an interpretive lens for the reader to gain more insight into this context.

Deploying the Holocaust as a paradigm of political violence and human loss, Hochschild suggests to his readers of the postwar era a frame of reference for understanding the Congo atrocities of the pre-war world he is about to describe. In presupposing this frame of reference, moreover, *King Leopold's Ghost* reveals its Eurocentric perspective. It speaks by and large to a Western readership that is already convinced of the significance of the Jewish Holocaust to twentieth-century history (in Europe). It is worthwhile noting in this respect that African perspectives are absent from *King Leopold's Ghost*, as Hochschild himself acknowledges (5).

The Belgian debates in the wake of Hochschild's book confirm Andreas Huyssen's observation of a "globalization of traumatic memory discourses in which the tropes and rhetoric of the Holocaust play an increasingly prominent role in different national and political contexts."[11] Among Belgian historians, Hochschild's assertions have been widely discussed and have attracted defenders as well as opponents, which suggests that the notion of the Holocaust has significantly contributed to defining the contours and limits of the debate. On the occasion of the controversial exhibition "The Memory of Congo: The Colonial Era" in the Royal Museum for Central Africa in Tervuren, by token, the Belgian historiographer Jean-Luc Vellut said that "this enterprise had to work in the face of polemics where, partly thanks to Hochschild's exertions, the concept of holocaust loomed large."[12] Although it would nowadays be hard to find full-blown revisionist voices disputing that massive Congolese deaths took place under Leopold's rule, to a considerable extent discussions have been dominated by disagreement on issues such as the exact number of deaths, the validity of the words "genocide" or "Holocaust," the degree of personal responsibility of Leopold II, and the deliberate intent of the perpetrators. The result has been described as an unproductive situation of antagonistic positions, which has led historiographer Geert Castryck to the rather bleak conclusion that the contemporary Belgian debate on Leopold's Congo has evolved into an "impasse,"[13] a "debate between believers and disbelievers."[14] In what follows, I will problematize the nineteenth-century moral discourse revitalized by *King Leopold's Ghost*, which has become an important dimension of the ideological framework in which contemporary postcolonial discussions in Belgium have unfolded in the wake of the book's publication.

KING LEOPOLD'S GHOST'S RESURGENCE OF LATE-NINETEENTH-CENTURY HUMANITARIAN DISCOURSE

As the cover of *King Leopold's Ghost* announces, "This is an enthralling story, full of fascinating characters, intense drama, high adventure, deceitful manipulations, courageous truth telling, and splendid moral fervor." Informed by cross-references to Adolf Hitler and Nazi officers committing the Jewish Holocaust, the deeds and actions of Leopold II and the colonial officers committing the Congolese genocide are framed primarily in a narrative with a clear moral ethos, its portrayal of Leopold's Congo a moral landscape populated by heroes, villains, and deplorable victims. *King Leopold's Ghost*'s subtitle—*A Story of Greed, Terror and Heroism*—alludes to virtues and vices, and chapter 8—"Where There Are No Ten Commandments"—refers to the well-known list of religious and moral imperatives according to the Judeo-Christian tradition.

It is paradoxical that *King Leopold's Ghost* reconstructs the Congo atrocities through the frame of the Holocaust and simultaneously adheres so strictly to religiously grounded moral values. It has often been noted that the events of the Jewish Holocaust have radically challenged the notion that a common set of premises exist for defining the good and the bad; that the Holocaust did not happen because people are evil; rather, the Holocaust was possible because "a significant critical mass of people did not find it to be an evil from which they should abstain."[15] The Holocaust exposed the crisis not of individual moral agency but rather of the ethical codes and standards against which individual moral behavior had been measured. "After Auschwitz, the simple reaffirmation of pre-Holocaust ethics will not do anymore," John Roth contends in *Ethics after the Holocaust*, "because the Western religious, philosophical, and ethical traditions have shown themselves to be problematic. Far from preventing the Holocaust, they may have been seriously implicated in that catastrophe."[16] *King Leopold's Ghost,* by contrast, repeats a pre-Auschwitz ethical discourse and its clear-cut moral categories, while simultaneously invoking the Holocaust paradigm to summon readers of the postcolonial, postwar era to remember the colonial brutalities in the Congo.

Hochschild has a particular agenda for reaffirming a pre-Holocaust ethical discourse, which is visible from the very first to the last page of his book. "A young man's flash of moral recognition," Hochschild says, is the "central incandescent moment" (1) of his narrative. This particular young man is introduced as Edmund Dene Morel, the British liberal humanitarian critic and founder of the Congo Reform Movement. During the late nineteenth and early twentieth centuries, this international movement disseminated testimonies and eyewitness accounts exposing the Congo atrocities to European metropolitan audiences and played a crucial role in the political events which would eventually lead to the transfer of Leopold's Congo Free State to the Belgian government in 1908. Hochschild writes:

> Brought face to face with evil, Morel does not turn away. [...] Seldom has one human being—impassioned, eloquent, blessed with brilliant organizing skills and nearly superhuman energy—managed almost single-handedly to put one subject on the world's front pages for more than a decade. (2)

Containing such celebratory portrayals of Morel, *King Leopold's Ghost* could be considered not only a historical excavation of a neglected human tragedy but also, in the terms of Robert Burroughs, "a somewhat hagiographic history of the Congo reform movement and its founders."[17] These two objectives are inherently interrelated in *King Leopold's Ghost*'s binary moral scheme. The torturing practices under Leopold II's colonial regime provide the negative pole for the humanitarians who mounted resistance against them. It is necessary to remember the former in order to flesh out the actions and commitments of the latter.

If memory is an act of "cultural recall in the present" modifying and re-describing the past through a selective filter, then Hochschild draws attention to his predilection in the final paragraphs of *King Leopold's Ghost*.[18] Contemporary human-rights organizations—Amnesty International and Médecins Sans Frontières—are praised for continuing the humanitarian tradition in which the Congo Reform Movement played a vital role: "Dating back to the French Revolution and beyond," this tradition "draws on the example of men and women who fought against enormous odds for their freedom [...] the Congo reform movement was a vital link in that chain, and there is no tradition more honourable." (306) One of *King Leopold's Ghost*'s main ambitions, then, is to reconstruct Leopold's Congo in order to recover a humanitarian tradition leading towards contemporary human-rights organizations in a teleological fashion.

Generally referred to as an ethics of benevolence and sympathy in the face of human suffering or abuse, humanitarian ideology took on a multi-faceted, dynamic, and historically contingent form in the late nineteenth century. It was central to the ideological and cultural framework of the political protest and debate over European imperial labor policies between the 1880s and the 1920s, and played a crucial role in the history of European imperialism in Africa and the new slaveries. In *A Civilised Savagery*, historian Kevin Grant distinguishes between three branches of humanitarian ideology, which were operative in late-nineteenth-century British discourse on the new slaveries in Africa: advocates of trusteeship, evangelical philanthropists, and proponents of human rights.[19] Their visions conflicted as well as mutually constituted each other, and they all shared a commitment to capitalist development and racial hierarchy: "Each group declared its principles to be universal, but these principles were similarly circumscribed in practice by capitalism and racism."[20] In other words, when humanitarian critics perceived the condition of slavery in imperial labor systems in territories such as the Congo Free State, they saw this as a violation of humanitarian concerns but also of the liberal principles of commerce and free trade supported by the Berlin conference.

The latter point indicates how humanitarian discourse and its miscellaneous manifestations lay claim to a notion of universality, which often is at odds with the spectrum of political strategies, personal interests, and complicities with empire which humanitarian ideology and campaigns have served in the concrete historical context of late-nineteenth-century imperial Europe. In *Travel Writing and Atrocities*, Robert Burroughs charts how testimonies and eyewitness accounts distributed by the Congo Reform Movement brought home to the readers in Europe the colonial brutalities in the Congo Free State, yet in so doing also implicated Britons and British industries in the continuing existence of slave labor in regions formally ruled by other nations.[21] The antislavery discourse of the Congo Reform Movement, Burroughs shows, was inseparable from the ambition to bring an end to the trading monopolies in the Congo Free State. Moreover, as Clarence Lusane noted in *Hitler's Black Victims*, Edmund Dene Morel's humanitarian activism did not at all seem incompatible with xenophobic discourse and his leading role in another international campaign, one against the presence of black French troops stationed in Germany as a consequence of the 1919 Treaty of Versailles.[22] These are just a few concrete examples that reveal some of the limits and contradictions of humanitarianism.

Such tensions and contradictions are, however, suppressed in *King Leopold's Ghost*'s epic-heroic portrayal of Morel and the Congo Reform Movement. Instead, Hochschild duplicates in various ways the moral discourse of the late-nineteenth-century humanitarian critics of the Congo Free State: *King Leopold's Ghost* rhetorically rehearses the moral discourse of the very humanitarian tradition it thematizes. Indicative is Hochschild's reference to the fight for freedom in his description of humanitarian ideology; it resonates with the epigraph of Edmund Dene Morel's renowned posthumously published *History of the Congo Reform Movement:* "In remembrance of a struggle successfully waged on behalf of human liberties."[23] The latter resonance is but one among many echoes, repetitions, and reverberations of Morel's *History of the Congo Reform Movement* in *King Leopold's Ghost*.[24]

In both books, the charges against Leopold II are supported by an estimate of the human costs and by calculations of the revenues gained by the Belgian king. These facts, figures, and mathematical considerations are juxtaposed with, and indeed intensified by, a metaphorical discourse of obscurity, mystery, and secrecy that recalls Conrad's *Heart of Darkness*. Morel considered Conrad's novella as "the most powerful thing ever written on the subject."[25] Although Conrad did not actively participate in the Congo Reform Movement, he was acquainted with Morel and did support the movement's cause.[26] Hochschild writes that "Conrad fully recognized Leopold's rape of the Congo for what it was: 'the Horror, the Horror!'" (146) and also provides photographs of the colonial officers Léon Rom and Guillaume Van Kerckhoven with the description: "prototypes for Kurtz" (n.p.). Many of these photographs, moreover, are reprints of photo material that was circulated by the Congo Reform Movement during the late nineteenth century.

In addition to the reference to *Heart of Darkness* as an authoritative factual discourse on the slaveries in the Congo Free State, *History of the Congo*

Reform Movement and *King Leopold's Ghost* are also rhetorically indebted to Conradian discourse presenting the Congo as a heart of darkness. For example, Morel rewrites the fog over the Congo River and its concomitant qualifiers of impenetrable mystery in *Heart of Darkness* as a fog enveloping the Congo atrocities: "Over the Congo itself there hung a dense fog of mystery. Now and again a corner of it would lift. When that happened, scenes of apparently purposeless carnage and delirious chaos were sometimes [. . .] visible. [. . .] then the fog would settle down again as impenetrable as ever."[27] Hochschild uses the aforementioned trope of the forgotten Holocaust, which allows him to "discover" the Congo atrocities personally, and in so doing, to re-enact the exploratory role of Morel, who wanted to lift "the elaborate veil of secrecy with which the high officials of the Congo Free State in Brussels conducted their master's business."[28]

Suggesting that the Congo atrocities are hidden, both Hochschild and Morel introduce their discoveries through an account of their autobiographical journeys into growing awareness. *History of the Congo Reform Movement* recounts a chronological sequence of Morel's personal anecdotes, involving his memory of his uncle's death in the Congo Free State and his employment by Liverpudlian ship owners as a clerk responsible for the service of steamers between Antwerp and the Congo. In *King Leopold's Ghost*, Hochschild's trajectory of memories gradually takes him back in time, in analogy with Holocaust memory providing a re-visitation of the Congo atrocities that happened earlier in time. Reading about Mark Twain's involvement in the Congo Reform Movement instigated Hochschild to reinterpret and correct older memories of the Congo, for instance of his journey to the Congo after independence and of reading *Heart of Darkness*, which he "had mentally filed away under fiction, not fact" (3).

Similarities and parallels such as the ones described here are significant, particularly considering that Morel's *History of the Congo Reform Movement* and Hochschild's *King Leopold's Ghost* describe the same events but do so from a considerably different moment in time. One way in which Hochschild's postwar perspective manifests itself is in the deployment of the Jewish Holocaust paradigm. The Holocaust paradigm indeed provides Hochschild with a frame through which Morel's nineteenth-century humanitarian account of the Congo atrocities can be resurrected. But if it is true that *King Leopold's Ghost* remembers an earlier humanitarian *recollection* of the tragedy, this assumption sheds a new light on one of *King Leopold's Ghost*'s pivotal rhetorical strategies, which is precisely based on the assumption that the tragedy has been *forgotten*. Hochschild's tropes of forgetting will be explored below.

THE FORGOTTEN HOLOCAUST, A REPEATED DISCOVERY

"The great forgetting"—which is the title of *King Leopold's Ghost*'s final chapter—is seen to pervade the material and imaginary landscape of Belgium in particular: "There is no hint of the deaths anywhere in Brussels" (293). Only nineteenth-century colonial buildings and monuments, such as the Royal Palace in Brussels or the "larger-than-life" statue of Leopold II, stand as physical reminders of "the blood spilled in the Congo, the stolen land, the severed hands, the shattered families and orphaned children [that] underlie much that meets the eye" (293). Hochschild relates the politics of forgetting to a range of actors and factors. First, to Leopold II, who ordered the destruction of the Congo archives. Second, to Belgium's collective memory of victimhood, which he relates to the experience of German invasion and the killings of a large number of Belgian civilians during the First World War, and which relegated the memory of the Congo atrocities to a dark corner of national history (295–296). Finally, to the contemporary situation in Belgium, described as a "country uneasily divided between its two language groups and urgently in need of unifying myths."[29]

Although in its current federal state-structure Belgium has increasingly been characterized by linguistic and cultural divisions, Hochschild's assumption that this situation automatically leads to an "urgent" quest for unifying myths needs to be challenged. The incoherent and inherently diversified nature of Belgian postcolonial cultures of remembrance, rather, could be an important reason why *King Leopold's Ghost*'s resurgence of a nineteenth-century moral vision of empire could so readily strike a chord with the public. Although providing an in-depth analysis of the complex question of Belgian postcolonial cultures of remembrance is beyond the scope of this essay, it is worthwhile to address a number of issues to illustrate the assumption that what is at stake is a general absence of a collective postimperial memory discourse.[30] Put in general terms, reconstructions of empire in postcolonial Belgium are affected by the process of working through the radical transformations of socio-political circumstances provoked by decolonization, labor immigration, and federalization in the postwar era.

It is often said that the Belgian colonization of the Congo was the last national project to transcend the linguistic and ideological differences among Belgian citizens, and that, when the Congo was decolonized in 1960, the loss of this national project stimulated Belgium's political reforms towards federalization, which started at approximately the same time. As soon as Congolese independence was realized, the Belgians lost their interest in their former colony without shifting their attention to the other "foreigners" or "guest workers" (as contract labor migrants were called at the time), with whom they were confronted in the 1960s. Instead, debates on Belgian society have since then almost entirely been devoted to communitarian issues and tensions between the Francophone and Dutchophone regions and language communities, which are accompanied by discourses emphasizing their cultural difference. One of the consequences is that for a long time, Belgians could maintain an image of themselves as a bicultural rather than a multicultural nation. When debates on multiculturalism finally started emerging at the end of the 1980s (in the wake of the electoral success of the Flemish far-right party *Vlaams Blok*), these focused primarily on the presence of Moroccan and Turkish labor immigrants in Belgium and were, hence, historically disconnected from the experience and memory of colonialism in the Congo. Communitarian tensions and linguistic divisions have continued to play a significant role in debates on the colonial past, not only because Belgium in its current constellation lacks a national media space or bilingual forum where a collective debate on the colonial past could be held, but also because the colonial past is often interpreted in light of the contemporary relations between the two language groups. From this perspective, debates about the national project of colonialism, determined as they are by communitarian sensitivities and perspectives, more often than not pertain to the future of federal Belgium rather than to the past. At stake, then, is a general absence of a collective postcolonial memory discourse or series of memory discourses in Belgium, which creates the conditions for specific, repetitive memory patterns of empire to thrive, without the colonial past being structurally remembered.

In light of this, it is worthwhile to consider the position of Jean-Luc Vellut, who does not deny that there is a strong wish to ignore and forget, but says that "regarding the Congo, the accusation has become a cliché."[31] Regardless of whether there exists a culture of amnesia initiated by Leopold II in the nineteenth century, as Hochschild contends, it is striking that the Congo atrocities under Leopold's rule have been discovered anew approximately every ten years since then. "The Congo Question" first became a topic of fierce discussion around 1890; that is, almost immediately after Leopold II started ruling the Congo Free State.[32] The British writer and humanitarian campaigner Henry Fox Bourne, for instance, observed in his *The Other Side of the Emin Pasha Relief Expedition* in 1891 that the charge of "wanton murdering and village-burning" in the Congo had become routine for European audiences.[33] Although the humanitarian criticism of the Congo atrocities dates back to this period, successive generations have forgotten the Congo atrocities so that these could be brought to attention again. Time and again, the remembered events are condemned or denied; subsequently they are buried again, rediscovered, condemned, and denied, and so on. What is striking is, furthermore, that with each new rediscovery the impression is created that the facts are revealed for the first time.

While Hochschild's *King Leopold's Ghost* stirred controversy in 1998, the book is largely based on publications written by two authors who had provoked a similar commotion during the preceding decades: a four-volume history by Jules Marchal and Daniël Vangroenweghe's *Rood rubber* (1985; *Du sang sur les lianes*, 1986).[34] And to name but a few earlier examples: the Flemish television series *Als een wereld zo groot waar uw vlag staat geplant* (*As a World so Large Where Your Flag is Planted*, 1986) devoted particular attention to the Congo atrocities, the Flemish author Hugo Claus wrote the theater play *The Life and Works of Leopold II* in 1970–1971, and Omer De Munck rejected the criticism of Leopold II in an article suggestively entitled "Congo Atrocities?" published in 1957 in the Flemish colonial journal *Band* and written in response to the highly critical *Inside Africa* (1955) by the American journalist John Gunther.[35]

This series of texts illustrates that the Congo atrocities have never really been forgotten, but, rather, that the memory has relentlessly been unearthed. While a certain degree of forgetfulness is undoubtedly involved, the afore-mentioned sequence of texts suggests a highly specific form or pattern of remembering the Congo atrocities. These texts can perhaps be better un-derstood as "cloistered memories" in Richard L. Derderian's sense of the term; that is, as narrow and fragmentary forms of memory which consist of idealistic versions of a truth that are most suited to the goals and history of the group doing the remembering.[36] Analyzing French postcolonial memory of the Algerian war, Derderian observes that the Algerian war similarly pres-ents itself as an ongoing site of re-discovery in France. Each work discover-ing the Algerian war sees itself as standing alone in representing the truth in the face of the absence of a cohesive memory or collection of memories. In cases where different groups struggle to see their own version of the truth put forward, society as a whole cannot fully grasp the complexities of what pre-cisely happened in the past and evaluate the troubling implications this holds for the present. In a similar vein, the public memory of the Congo Free State in Belgium has long been dominated by a narrow and mythologizing form of "cloistered memory" endorsed by ex-colonials who promote celebratory im-ages of Leopold II and his colonial project. Because of the relatively general lack of a coherent colonial memory or collection of colonial memories of the Congo Free State, however, various groups promote their own version of what happened and dispute each other's versions.

In the Belgian context, then, Hochschild's notion of a forgotten Holocaust is framed within a specific memory pattern consisting of contradictory discov-eries of the truth about the Congo atrocities and varying moral appreciations of colonialism and colonial violence. Various interlocutors seem indeed primarily concerned with formulating ethical judgments about colonialism as a system or with assessing the moral qualities of related figures, Edmund Dene Morel and Leopold II, who are often staged as caricatured personifications of good and evil and subsequently celebrated or held personally responsible. For instance, the portrayal of Leopold II as founder of Belgian colonial history, the visionary genius who "gave" Belgium its colony, is the direct opposite of Hochschild's description of Leopold II. More than anything, the moral terms of the debate in general and *King Leopold's Ghost* in particular suggest that the Congo atrocities have found a language that functions in an economy of guilt, blame, and culpability.

From this perspective, it is no coincidence that, together with the publication of Ludo De Witte's *De moord op Lumumba* (*The Assassination of Lumumba,* 2001), *King Leopold's Ghost* led to a parliamentary inquiry into Belgium's responsibility for the assassination of Patrice Lumumba in 1961. The kind of moral discourse it deploys seems to fit well within the conventional legal frame, as did late-nineteenth-century humanitarian critics who urged the British House of Commons to pass a critical resolution on the Congo and to instruct the British consul Roger Casement to investigate the matter in more detail. Published in 1904, Casement's report confirmed Morel's accusations and had a considerable impact on public opinion. The Belgian government pressured Leopold II to set up an independent commission of inquiry, which largely confirmed Casement's findings. This directly led to the arrest and punishment of officials who had been responsible for murders during a rubber-collection expedition in 1903. Such legal inquiries are of course necessary and useful, but it is, however, also worthwhile underscoring the pitfalls of reducing examinations into colonial violence to a legal and moral frame focused on questions of guilt and responsibility.

In her essay on the American framing of 9/11 and the war against terror, Judith Butler calls for more attention to the frames we use for understanding violence, since "the frame works both to preclude certain kinds of questions, certain kinds of historical inquiries, and to function as a moral justification for retaliation."[37] Hochschild's indictment of the atrocities manifests itself as a discovery of a horrible memory, the depiction of the wrongdoings of the colonial perpetrators in terms of individual pathology and responsibility, and, finally, the renewal of a liberal humanitarian discourse. This view, however, discharges us from coming up with broader, structural explanations for the event and from examining, for instance, what kind of historical conditions gave rise to such acts of violence, what the relationship is between these conditions and individual acts of violence, and how these conditions affect and implicate all of us in the postcolonial, postwar world. Instead, moral visions of the Congo atrocities such as *King Leopold's Ghost* assure liberal humanitarians that they are not accountable. They can know who they are and what their future will be, since their predecessors were good while the perpetrators of violence were irredeemably evil.

Considering that the memory of the Congo atrocities has continuously been buried and rediscovered, then, *King Leopold's Ghost* lays claim, not to the unearthing of a forgotten catastrophe, but, rather, to an intertextual tradition of humanitarian narratives that Hochschild appropriates, extends, transvalues, and reformulates for the contemporary historical moment. This implies the recovery of a moral discourse which has come to define the contours of contemporary Belgian debates on the Congo Free State, one which hardly differs from late nineteenth-century humanitarian discourse, even though, or precisely because, it is narrated in a present-day vocabulary in which the Jewish Holocaust takes centre stage.

COMMITMENT AND COMPLICITY IN THE CONGOLESE CATASTROPHE: *ENJOY POVERTY*

Building on some of the recent theoretical discourses on the interconnectedness of distinct forms of violence, I have analyzed how *King Leopold's Ghost* negotiates Holocaust memory for the purpose of relating the Congo atrocities under King Leopold's rule from a humanitarian perspective. The Holocaust paradigm enabled Hochschild to re-enact and repeat Edmund Dene Morel's humanitarian account of the atrocities through a new frame, an enterprise which is, however, not without internal contradictions. *King Leopold's Ghost* reconstructs the Congo atrocities through the framework of the Holocaust as a narrative with a clear-cut morality, which is paradoxical considering that it is now generally accepted that the Holocaust radically challenged the notion that a common set of premises exists for defining the good and the bad.

The latter point has recently been reiterated in a mounting body of critical studies of humanitarianism, such as David Rieff's *A Bed for the Night. Humanitarianism in Crisis,* Doug Mayhew's *The Dark Sides of Virtue,* and Ashby and Brown's *Humanitarianism and Suffering: The Mobilization of Empathy.*[38] These studies have questioned humanitarian ideology and practice, including its normative foundations and modus operandi. Over the years, the critique has shifted from being concerned primarily with the poor functioning of the humanitarian *system* to one targeted at basic humanitarian *values.*[39]

In light of this tradition, the recent documentary art film *Enjoy Poverty* (2008) by the Dutch artist Renzo Martens can be seen to act as a foil to

Hochschild's *King Leopold's Ghost*, particularly considering its exposure of the multiple complicities surrounding Western humanitarian action in the Democratic Republic of the Congo. Compared to *King Leopold's Ghost*, *Enjoy Poverty* presents an alternative strategy of commitment to exposing the human disaster in the Congo, one that explores the limits and complicities of humanitarian ideology and rejects conventional humanitarian narratives, despite the fact that it has Western humanitarian operations in the Democratic Republic of the Congo as its main theme.

Self-consciously staged as colonial heir, the director of *Enjoy Poverty* films himself on a journey through the Congo, where he gradually learns how Western philanthropy in the tropics has an economically profitable side to it and that humanitarian goals sometimes nourish the importation of guns, violence, or other forms of domination. Reporting on "the poverty industry" and realizing that the Congolese hardly profit from the amounts of money made from their imagery of poverty and starvation, Martens sets up an emancipation program that resonates with the former European mission to "uplift the natives." He teaches a group of Congolese wedding photographers that photographing malnourished children is a much more lucrative business than photographing weddings. However, when the group eventually tries to sell their photographs to Western news agencies, they are turned down. Subsequently Martens, too, abandons his emancipation program, having lost belief in progress, development, and reform. Eventually, he changes his humanitarian discourse by turning it inside out, as it were, and cynically "teaches" his Congolese interlocutors that their situation of poverty and starvation will not "improve" and that they should cultivate an attitude of resilience and resignation.

Translating the link between the humanitarian project and thriving commerce to contemporary geopolitical circumstances, *Enjoy Poverty* self-reflexively positions itself as complicit with perpetuating the structural inequalities that result from these circumstances. If it is true that Western global media cash in on the production of African doom and disaster for consumers in the West, the film cannot deny complicity with the very mechanism it uncovers. In so doing, the film poses its own ethical dilemmas, for instance about the extent to which acknowledging complicity could not also become a pretext for unnecessarily aggravating these inequalities, or the extent to which Congolese interlocutors are staged as speechless subalterns in a Western narrative for the purpose of voicing criticism. At the same time, however, *Enjoy Poverty* summons viewers, watching from their comfortable seats in a European arthouse cinema, to confront their situatedness as consumers of a spectacle of poverty which is being staged for them without offering them the solace of a humanitarian narrative.

The film thus presents us with an ethical vision based on commitment to uncovering multiple complicities and exposing how neither the protagonist, nor the Congolese, nor the Western viewers can abstract themselves from engaging with a system of domination and subjugation which encompasses everyone, be it past or present. From this perspective, *Enjoy Poverty* foregrounds the limits and contours of the moral tradition of liberal humanitarianism, which is revived in Hochschild's *King Leopold's Ghost* and which serves to define to a large extent the ideological framework of contemporary Belgian debates on the Congo atrocities held in the wake of its publication. In so doing, the film responds substantively to the Holocaust in a way *King Leopold's Ghost* does not, despite the latter's extensive citation and appropriation of the Holocaust vocabulary. In contrast with *King Leopold's Ghost*'s textual negotiation of Holocaust memory, *Enjoy Poverty* is a self-reflexive exploration of humanitarian traditions that conveys how ethics itself is not immune from failure, a point which has never manifested itself so clearly as in the aftermath of the Holocaust.

NOTES

Acknowledgments. This chapter is reprinted from "The Holocaust as a Paradigm for the Congo Atrocities: Adam Hochschild's *King Leopold's Ghost*" from *Criticism: A Quarterly for Literature and the Arts* 53, no. 4. Copyright © 2011 Wayne State University Press, with the permission of Wayne State University Press.

1. Michael Rothberg, *Multidirectional Memory: Remembering the Holocaust in the Age of Decolonization* (Palo Alto, CA: Stanford University Press, 2009).

2. Adam Hochschild, *King Leopold's Ghost: A Story of Greed, Terror, and Heroism in Colonial Africa* (Boston: Houghton Mifflin, 1998). All further references will be inserted parenthetically in the text.

3. Adam Hochschild, "Leopold's Congo: A Holocaust We Have Yet to Comprehend," *The Chronicle of Higher Education*, May 12, 2000, B4.

4. Steven Katz and Alan Rosen, ed., *Obliged by Memory: Literature, Religion, Ethics* (New York: Syracuse University Press, 2005).

5. "In the Heart of Darkness by Jean-Luc Vellut, Reply by Adam Hochschild, in Response to 'In the Heart of Darkness (October 6, 2005),'" *New York Review of Books* 53, no. 1 (January 12, 2006). http://www.nybooks.com/articles/18630. Accessed on February 26, 2010.

6. Echoes of Hochschild's thesis can be found in later publications, for instance, Jules Marchal's *Lord Leverhulme's Ghost: Colonial Exploitation in the Congo* (New York: Verso, 2008), which was originally published as *Travail forcé pour l'huile de palme de Lord Leverhulme, L'Histoire du Congo, 1910–1945* (Borgloon: Editions Paula Bellings, 2001).

7. Judith Butler, "Holocaust Analogies Demean Palestinian Suffering," *The Independent* September 26, 2005. http://www.independent.co.uk/opinion/commentators/judith-butler-holocaust-analogies-demean-palestinian-suffering-508366.html. Accessed February 26, 2010.

8. Referring to James Young, Michael Rothberg makes a similar argument in his discussion of Muhammad's reference to the "black holocaust," *Multidirectional Memory: Remembering the Holocaust in the Age of Decolonization*, 14.

9. Quoted in Andrew Osborn, "Belgium Exhumes Its Colonial Demons," *The Guardian* July 13, 2002, 18.

10. Jean-Luc Vellut departs from the assumption that comparative perspectives on the Jewish Holocaust and the Congo atrocities cannot render historically accurate representations nor do justice to the empirical particularities of both historical events. Considering that the irreducible particularities of two events in time—what happened, where, and why—can never be identical and are always subject to interpretation and evaluation, Rothberg proposes to shift attention away from the domain of empirical history, to take dissimilarity as a starting point instead, and to focus on questions of memory, representation, and the forms and functions of the narratives that shape our understanding of history. Michael Rothberg, *Multidirectional Memory: Remembering the Holocaust in the Age of Decolonization* (Palo Alto, CA: Stanford University Press, 2009), 10.

11. Andreas Huyssen, "Diaspora and Nation: Migration into Other Pasts," in *Diaspora and Memory: Figures of Displacement in Contemporary Literature, Art and Politics*, eds. M.-A. Baronian, S. Beder and Yolanse Jansen (Amsterdam: Rodopi, 2007), 81.

12. "In the Heart of Darkness by Jean-Luc Vellut, Reply by Adam Hochschild, in Response to 'In the Heart of Darkness (October 6, 2005).'"

13. Geert Castryck, "Whose History Is History? Singularities and Dualities of the Public Debate on Belgian Colonialism," in *Europe and the World in European Historiography*, ed. C. Lévai (Pisa: Edizione Plus—EC Sixth Framework Network of Excellence CLIOHRES.net, 2006), 71–88.

14. Geert Castryk, "Whose History Is History?"

15. Peter J. Haas, "Faith, Ethics and the Holocaust," in *Holocaust and Genocide Studies* 3, no. 4 (1988): 383.

16. John Roth, ed., *Ethics after the Holocaust: Perspectives, Critiques, and Responses* (St. Paul, MN: Paragon House, 1999).

17. Robert Burroughs, *Travel Writing and Atrocities: Eyewitness Accounts of Colonialism in the Congo, Angola and the Putumayo* (London: Routledge, 2010).

18. Mieke Bal, "Introduction," *Acts of Memory: Cultural Recall in the Present*, eds. Jonathan Crewe, Mieke Bal and Leo Spitzer (Hanover: University Press of New England, 1999), vii.

19. Kevin Grant, *A Civilised Savagery: Britain and the New Slaveries in Africa, 1884–1926* (London: Routledge 2005).

20. Kevin Grant, *A Civilised Savagery*, 9.

21. Robert Burroughs, *Travel Writing and Atrocities: Eyewitness Accounts of Colonialism in the Congo, Angola and the Putumayo* (London: Routledge, 2010).

22. Clarence Lusane, *Hitler's Black Victims*: *The Historical Experiences of Afro-Germans, European Blacks and African Americans in the Nazi Era* (London: Routledge, 2002), 71.

23. Louis Wm. Roger and Jean Stengers, ed., *E. D. Morel's History of the Congo Reform Movement* (Oxford: Clarendon, 1968), n.p. The epigraph presents itself as an echo of an earlier text also: Morel's inscription on John Holt's copy of "The Close of a Great Campaign," Supplement to the *African Mail*, June 27, 1913.

24. Louis Wm. Roger and Jean Stengers, ed., *E. D. Morel's History of the Congo Reform Movement*.

25. Hunt Hawkins, "Joseph Conrad, Roger Casement and the Congo Reform Movement," *Journal of Modern Literature* 9, no. 1 (1981/1982): 80.

26. Hunt Hawkins, "Joseph Conrad."

27. Louis Wm. Roger and Jean Stengers, ed., *E. D. Morel's History of the Congo Reform Movement*, 52.

28. Louis Wm. Roger and Jean Stengers, ed., *E. D. Morel's History of the Congo Reform Movement*, 4.

29. Adam Hochschild, "Leopold's Congo," B4.

30. This issue is explored in more detail in Bambi Ceuppens and Sarah De Mul, "De vergeten Congolees: Kolonialisme, postkolonialisme en multiculturalisme in Vlaanderen," in K. Arnaut et al., *Een leeuw in een kooi: De grenzen van het multiculturele Vlaanderen* (Antwerpen: Meulenhoff/Manteau, 2009), 48–67.

31. Jean-Luc Vellut, "Jan Vansina on the Belgian Historiography of Africa: Around the Agenda of a Bombing Raid. A reply to 'History Facing the Present: An Interview with Jan Vansina,'" in *Africaform*, January 31, 2002, http://www.h-net .org/~africa/africaforum/Vellut.htm. Accessed December 10, 2009.

32. Sarah De Mul, "Framing the Congo and the (Un)Bildung of the Imperial State: Cyriel Buysse's *De zwarte kost* (1898)," *Forum for Modern Language Studies* 45, no. 4 (2009): 390–400.

33. H. R. Fox Bourne, *The Other Side of the Emin Pasha Relief Expedition* (London, 1891) as quoted in F. Driver, "Henry Morton Stanley and His Critics: Geography, Exploration and Empire," *Past and Present* 133 (November 1991): 162.

34. Jules Marchal, *L'Etat libre du Congo: Paradis perdu. L'Histoire du Congo, 1876–1900, vol. 1* (Borgloon: Editions Paula Bellings, 1996); *L'Etat libre du Congo: Paradis perdu. L'Histoire du Congo, 1876–1900, vol. 2* (Borgloon: Editions Paula Bellings, 1996); *E. D. Morel contre Léopold II: L'Histoire du Congo, 1900–1910, vol. 1* (Borgloon: Editions Paula Bellings, 1996); *E. D. Morel contre Léopold II: L'Histoire du Congo, 1900–1910, vol. 2* (Borgloon: Editions Paula Bellings, 1996); Daniel Vangroenweghe, *Rood Rubber: Leopold II en zijn Kongo* (Brussels: Elsevier 1985).

35. Omer De Munck, "Kongo-gruwelen?" *Band* 16, no. 3 (1957): 101–14.

36. R. L. Derderian, *North-Africans in Contemporary France: Becoming Visible* (New York: Palgrave Macmillan, 2004), 158.

37. Judith Butler, *Precarious Life: The Powers of Mourning and Violence* (London: Verso, 2004), 4.

38. David Rieff, *A Bed for the Night: Humanitarianism in Crisis* (London: Vintage, 2002); Doug Mayhew, *The Dark Sides of Virtue: Reassessing International Humanitarianism* (Princeton, NJ: Princeton University Press, 2004); Richard Ashby and Richard Brown, eds., *Humanitarianism and Suffering: The Mobilization of Empathy* (New York: Cambridge University Press, 2009).

39. Joanna Macrae, "The Death of Humanitarianism? An Anatomy of the Attack," *Refugee Survey Quarterly* 17, no. 1 (1998): 24–32.

BIBLIOGRAPHY

Ashby, Richard, and Richard Brown, eds. *Humanitarianism and Suffering: The Mobilization of Empathy.* New York: Cambridge University Press, 2009.

Bal, Mieke. "Introduction." In *Acts of Memory: Cultural Recall in the Present*, edited by Jonathan Crewe, Mieke Bal and Leo Spitzer. Hanover: University Press of New England, 1999.

Butler, Judith. *Precarious Life: The Powers of Mourning and Violence.* London: Verso, 2004.

———. "Holocaust Analogies Demean Palestinian Suffering," *The Independent,* Monday, September 26, 2005. http://www.independent.co.uk/opinion/commenta tors/judith-butler-holocaust-analogies-demean-palestinian-suffering-508366.html. Accessed November 26, 2011.

Castryck, Geert. "Whose History Is History? Singularities and Dualities of the Public Debate on Belgian Colonialism." In *Europe and the World in European Historiography*, edited by C. Lévai, 71–88. Pisa: Edizione Plus, 2006.

Ceuppens, Bambi, and Sarah De Mul, "De vergeten Congolees: Kolonialisme, postkolonialisme en multiculturalisme in Vlaanderen." In *Een leeuw in een kooi: De grenzen van het multicuturele Vlaanderen*, edited by K Arnhaut, 48–67 (Antwerpen: Meulenhoff/Manteau, 2009).

De Mul, Sarah. "Framing the Congo and the (Un)Bildung of the Imperial State: Cyriel Buysse's *De zwarte kost* (1898)." *Forum for Modern Language Studies* 45, no. 4 (2009): 390–400.

De Munck, Omer. "Kongo-gruwelen?" *Band* 16, no. 3 (1957): 101–14.

Derderian, R. L. *North-Africans in Contemporary France: Becoming Visible.* New York: Palgrave Macmillan, 2004.

Driver, Felix. "Henry Morton Stanley and His Critics: Geography, Exploration and Empire." *Past and Present* 133 (November 1991): 134–66.

Grant, Kevin. *A Civilised Savagery: Britain and the New Slaveries in Africa, 1884–1926.* London: Routledge, 2005.

Haas, Peter J. "Faith, Ethics and the Holocaust . The Morality of Auschwitz: Moral Language and the Nazi Ethic." *Holocaust and Genocide Studies* 3, no. 4 (1988): 383–93.

Hawkins, Hunt. "Joseph Conrad, Roger Casement and the Congo Reform Movement." *Journal of Modern Literature* 9, no. 1 (1981/1982): 65–80.

Hochschild, Adam. *King Leopold's Ghost: A Story of Greed, Terror and Heroism in Colonial Africa.* Boston: Houghton Mifflin, 1998.

———. "Leopold's Congo: A Holocaust We Have Yet to Comprehend." *The Chronicle of Higher Education.* May 12, 2000, B4.

———. "In the Heart of Darkness by Jean-Luc Vellut, Reply by Adam Hochschild, in Response to 'In the Heart of Darkness (October 6, 2005).'" *New York Review of Books* 53, no. 1, January 12, 2006. http://www.nybooks.com/articles/18630. Accessed November 26, 2011.

Huyssen, Andreas. "Diaspora and Nation: Migration into Other Pasts." *New German Critique* No. 88, Contemporary German Literature (Winter 2003): 147–64.

Katz, Steven and Alan Rosen, ed. *Obliged by Memory: Literature, Religion, Ethics.* New York: Syracuse University Press, 2005.

Lusane, Clarence. *Hitler's Black Victims*: *The Historical Experiences of Afro-Germans, European Blacks and African Americans in the Nazi Era.* London: Routledge, 2002.

Macrae, Joanna. "The Death of Humanitarianism? An Anatomy of the Attack," *Refugee Survey Quarterly* 17, no. 1 (1998): 24–32.

Marchal, Jules. *L'Etat libre du Congo: Paradis perdu. L'Histoire du Congo, 1876–1900, 2 vols.* Borgloon: Editions Paula Bellings, 1996.

———. *E. D. Morel contre Léopold II: L'Histoire du Congo, 1900–1910, 2 vols.* Borgloon: Editions Paula Bellings, 1996.

———. *Travail forcé pour l'huile de palme de Lord Leverhulme, L'Histoire du Congo 1910–1945.* Borgloon: Editions Paula Bellings, 2001.

———. *Lord Leverhulme's Ghost: Colonial Exploitation in the Congo.* New York: Verso, 2008.

Mayhew, Doug. *The Dark Sides of Virtue: Reassessing International Humanitarianism.* Princeton, NJ: Princeton University Press, 2004.

Morel, E. D. *E. D. Morel's History of the Congo Reform Movement*, edited by Louis Wm. Roger and Jean Stengers. Oxford: Clarendon, 1968.

Osborn, Andrew. "Belgium Exhumes Its Colonial Demons." *The Guardian*, Saturday July 13, 2002.

Rieff, David. *A Bed for the Night: Humanitarianism in Crisis.* London: Vintage, 2002.

Roth, John, ed. *Ethics after the Holocaust: Perspectives, Critiques, and Responses.* St. Paul, MN: Paragon House, 1999.

Rothberg, Michael. *Multidirectional Memory: Remembering the Holocaust in the Age of Decolonization.* Palo Alto, CA: Stanford University Press, 2009.

Vangroenweghe, Daniel. *Rood rubber: Leopold II en zijn Kongo.* Brussels: Elsevier 1985.

Vellut, Jean-Luc. "Jan Vansina on the Belgian Historiography of Africa: Around the Agenda of a Bombing Raid. A reply to 'History Facing the Present: An Interview with Jan Vansina.'" *Africaform*, January 31, 2002. http://www.h-net.org/~africa/africaforum/Vellut.htm. Accessed November 10, 2011.

LITERATURE AND MULTICULTURALISM

Chapter Ten

Dutch Homonationalism and Intersectionality

Murat Aydemir

In the Netherlands, certain homosexual identities and lifestyles have gained recognition by government, the law, and the media. Same-sex marriage—if we are to accept that as a decisive benchmark—was legalized in 2001. A full appraisal of the possibilities and limitations of that recognition is beyond the scope of this essay.[1] Yet, what I want to point out is that the qualified emancipation of lesbians and gays in the country has run side by side with, been followed by, or in any case not prevented the emergence of a new collective subject of discipline, of power and knowledge: "Moroccan boys." Indeed, it does not require extensive exposure to Dutch television, newspapers, and magazines to conclude that just about everybody is now a recognized expert on the tortured psychology, tribal loyalties, inherent criminality, religious affectations, and sexual proclivities of young Moroccan men. Making up the third-generation offspring of the so-called guest workers Dutch corporations recruited in the 1970s, their appellation in political parlance presently ranges from "problem youth," to "kutmarokkanen" (literally, "cunt-Moroccans") to "Moroccan scum" to "street terrorists."[2]

I should perhaps caution that I assume no direct chronological or causal relationship between the Dutch advances in lesbian and gay emancipation and this more recent phenomenon; yet, neither do I want to foreclose the consideration of a possible surreptitious association between the two developments. That consideration is especially urgent, I contend, since received wisdom now has it that the relationship between Dutch gays and lesbians—because of *our* sexuality—and Moroccan young men—because of *their* culture or religion (read: race)—can only be antagonistic to the extent that the needs, wants, rights, interests, desires, and claims of the two groups can only ever be mutually exclusive. Of course, reality is considerably more complicated than

187

that. In order to convey the ambivalence of relations between the two groupings, it suffices to point to the following uncanny combination of facts: while
Moroccan young men are associated with rising numbers of gay bashing in
Amsterdam, they are also overrepresented in the numbers of sex workers and
victims of sexual abuse.[3] In 2006, the latter fact prompted Ahmed Marcouch,
then the social-democratic chair of the Slotervaart borough in Amsterdam, to
decry what he described as "domestic sex tourism"—a call remarkably less
well publicized than his enduring attempts to persuade Islamic immigrants to
accept sexual equality.

Nevertheless, the cultivated conflict between Dutch homosexuals and
immigrant teens arguably indicates a perceived rupture between interpella-
tions that are based on sex and those based on race, a rupture that is part of
the very way in which we think, experience, and live sex and race. Jasbir
K. Puar has commented on the "perpetual fissuring of race from sexuality
. . . the two dare not converge."[4] In *Terrorist Assemblages: Homonationalism in Queer Times* (2007), Puar further specifies the strategic parcelling
out of mutually exclusive domains of race and sexuality as "the Muslim or
gay binary."[5] The binary mandates that the homosexual other is usually understood as normatively white, while the racial other is most often regarded
as straight as well as axiomatically homophobic (32). This convenient
alignment accommodates the rhetorical production of a supposedly exceptional national and liberal sexuality, which Puar terms "homonationalism."
The term points at the uncanny "convergence" between the increasing (if
qualified, half-hearted, and opportunistic) inclusion of homosexual citizens
in the body politic with the increased exclusion of racial and class others
(1–2). Rather than persisting with a cherished sexual "outlaw" status or
the redolent trope of "transgression" while Western gays and lesbians are
increasingly mainstreamed as consumers and legal subjects, we would do
better, Puar argues, to "point to ourselves as accomplices of certain norma-
tivizing violences" (24). While Puar deals most extensively with the U.S.,
she also singles out Britain and the Netherlands as the country's homona-
tionalist counterparts (11).

In what follows, I give an account of what I regard as an exemplary case
of Dutch homonationalism, revolving on an activist's appeal protesting the
hanging of gay men in Iran. In the second part of this article, I reconsider the
notion of "intersectionality," an early and contested attempt to conceptualize
compounded or crossed identification. My purpose here is to inquire whether
and, if so, how the theory of intersectionality might help move beyond the
deadlock of the "gay or Muslim" binary. Is it possible to recognize sex and
race as located in the same place and the same time, or do they somehow
invariably end up in disparate symbolic universes?

MOROCCAN BOYS

In August of 2005, I was alerted to a petition posted on the Internet condemning the public hanging of Mahmoud Asgari and Ayaz Marhoni in the town of Mashhad, which is located in Northern Iran.[6] The two young men were reportedly executed for having sex with each other or, alternately, for raping a thirteen year old boy.[7] Nevertheless, the petition alleged a definitive "sexual orientation" as the men's "only crime." Those signing the appeal joined initiator Frank van Dalen, at that time the chair of the C.O.C., the oldest and largest lesbian and gay advocacy group in the Netherlands, in calling on Western political leaders to send "a strong signal towards the Iranian government." The signal would include public condemnation, political and economic sanctions, the granting of asylum to gay refugees from Iran, and/or the cessation of ongoing negotiations between the country and the European Union to establish an associative treaty.

Though unequivocal, the signal called for was so far couched in the relatively genteel language of international relations—consisting of statements, sanctions, and negotiations—which might potentially have appealed to members of the Iranian government and judiciary. That was not the case, however, for the stronger signal the petition also included, which foreclosed the very possibility of a political relationship between the West and Iran.

For, at one point, the text urged: "These barbarian and medieval events have to stop immediately." The phraseology instantly disqualified Iranian politicians and judges as potential partners in dialogue, relegating their existence to an irrelevant past and rendering their speech inarticulate (the Greek etymology of "barbarian" refers to people who talk incomprehensibly, uttering inarticulate sounds like "bar bar" or "blah blah"). In this way, the contemporary international context, in which politicians of Western states might call on their Iranian counterparts to forge agreement or to establish disagreement, was redistributed by the renewed dichotomy between the civilized and the barbarian, the modern and the archaic, laying down linguistic and temporal boundaries no appeal or signal could ever hope to cross. The only agreement the petition could now garner was between Western citizens and their representatives to the effect that Iranian justice is medieval and barbarian; a judgment that is easily extended (since Iran's theocracy is so often misunderstood as the essence of Islam, Islamic practice at its purest) to Islamic politics, culture, and law in general. The petition's terse and belated admission that "*even* the Iranian opposition" (emphasis added) had condemned the hangings merely registered a contemptuous surprise.

The same van Dalen who initiated the petition also manifested himself as a political ally of the Dutch anti-immigration and anti-Islam politician

Rita Verdonk.[8] Verdonk served as Secretary of Immigration and Integration from 2003 to 2007. Revealingly, she was installed at the Justice Department rather than the Ministry of the Interior. Following the executions of Asgari and Marhoni, Verdonk, caught in a perfect double bind between her pro-gay and anti-immigration agendas, initially continued extraditing homosexual asylum seekers from Iran, until parliamentary pressure enforced a temporary moratorium. In 2006, she instituted a special group policy for gay Iranians, acknowledging their risk of persecution and facilitating their acceptance as refugees, while stopping short of accepting sexual persecution as a legitimate ground for refugee status in general. The politics of Verdonk and her political associate van Dalen can be seen to connect international gay activism with national anti-Islam and anti-immigration politics.

My engagement with van Dalen here is meant only to highlight that link-age, and to flag its commonality and acceptability, which arose in the wake of Pim Fortuyn's intervention in Dutch politics. Invariably characterized as "unapologetically" and even "flamboyantly" gay, Fortuyn characterized Is-lam as an "achterlijke cultuur" (a "backwards" or "retarded" culture).[9] While the chosen adjective alleges Islam's historical and cultural lagging behind Western modernity, hence accounting for its supposedly medieval and bar-baric position, the more insidious and lasting gesture of Fortuyn's shorthand phraseology lies in characterizing Islam in terms of culture. As *one* culture, hence erasing the different histories, geo-economic developments, and Dutch policies that brought immigrants from Turkey, Morocco, Somalia, and Ghana to the country, as well as the differences between Muslim cultures; and as *a* culture to begin with, a move effectively cancelling out two pre-existing politi-cal vocabularies in one go: the one linked to the social-democratic principle of emphasizing the socio-economic position of immigrants, the other linked to the cherished Dutch tradition of "pillarization," that is, organizing and eman-cipating religious minorities, primarily Catholics.[10] Muslim immigrants in the Netherlands are no longer part of political discourse as a disenfranchised class or as a marginalized religious minority, but as a "culturalized" grouping.[11]

The global framing of the gay cause that van Dalen's politics epitomizes, accommodates the quick assimilation of different contexts. As a result, the Iranian henchmen hanging Asgari and Marhoni became all but equated with immigrant boys in the Netherlands; what distinguished them was merely a matter of degree, not kind. Disappearing through that approximation were and are crucial social and economic distinctions on both sides: between un-derclass immigrants and the Dutch white middle classes, between the West and other parts of the globe. One might well suspect that the national and international bracketing of socio-economic differences in the service of a putatively liberal cause is precisely one of the current uses of the kind of gay politics that van Dalen and others champion.

Significantly, van Dalen's contemporary orientalism enacts a double gesture. On the one hand, he condemns the Iranian judges who condemned to death Asgari and Marhoni, as well as Muslim immigrants in the Netherlands, presumably on the same or a similar footing. Yet, on the other hand, he beckons Iranian, Islamic, gay-identified asylum seekers, lobbying for their admittance and accommodation in the Netherlands. In that sense, this form of liberal orientalism is not immediately reducible to a reactionary nationalism or racism. It does not trade on the charged opposition between national or ethnic communities; rather, it welcomes people from Iran on the basis of their assumed sexual individuality, while rejecting Dutch-Islamic immigrants—who have been living in the country for three generations—on the basis of their culture. The expanded context of the cause provokes the redistribution of affiliation and repudiation at home and abroad, as well as a new parcelling out of the domains of sexuality and culture.

In both its global and domestic dimensions, that new mapping may be regarded differently. In "Unbearable Witness" (2009), Scott Long offers a sharp analysis of the implications and consequences of the international strategies of Western gay and lesbian advocacy groups. His central case, akin to that of Asgari and Marhoni, revolves on the 2007 Iranian hanging of Makwan Mouloudzadeh for the alleged rape of three boys. In the activism on Mouloudzadeh's behalf, Long observes the aggressive application of the Western autonomization of sexual identity, its separation from other identifications and socioeconomic circumstances. He concludes that activists risk imposing the Western identitarian model of sexuality where it might not be socio-culturally warranted and/or political productive.[12] The definitive "sexual orientation" that van Dalen ascribes to Asgari and Marhoni may well allow him to speak *for* them, but may not at all speak *to* them—let alone to their persecutors and executioners.

Moreover, by isolating that identity, Long continues, international gay human rights activists wittingly or unwittingly constrain the yield of potential political support. They effectively bracket the possibility of effective protest against the death penalty for any "crime"—either in Iran *or in the U.S.*—especially in the case of defendants who are minors, or who were minors when they committed their alledged crimes.[13] Finally, the "cosmopolitan oneness" that unites Western activists and Iranian gays under the same banner is inevitably accompanied by the discursive production of another other: "Outside is the murdering and intransigent world of the non-us, the Islamo-fascist, who cannot be co-opted into dialogue."[14] Revealingly, van Dalen's appeal can only tersely acknowledge that the Iranian opposition in fact shares his views (let alone invite Muslims or non-Westerners to join his cause).

In the domestic context, meanwhile, the politics that van Dalen voices assumes the congenital homophobia of Islamic immigrants, routinely calling on the state to safeguard the acquired rights of gays and lesbians against them. Yet, Chandan Reddy argues that culturalist claims about the sexual mores of immigrant populations "mask the state's role . . . in exactly engendering and enforcing the very immigrant homophobias that many claim are brought over by immigrants from their home countries."[15] According to Reddy, the U.S. partly relies on family reunification to maintain a low-wage work force, while the state's neoliberal policies, there as well as elsewhere, have increasingly shifted its social responsibilities onto community and familial life. The result has been the very strengthening of the patriarchal and heteronormative aspects of immigrant ways of life—aspects whose genealogies, one should immediately add, may include colonial legacies just as easily as native ones. As an added bonus, Reddy continues, the supposedly unenlightened sexual mores of immigrants helps justify "the exclusion of immigrant communities from state power" as well as their low socio-economic status.[16]

Long's and Reddy's arguments help to bring into relief the expedient instrumentalization of van Dalen's politics. Internationally, that politics helps shore up the geopolitical and geo-economic "war" that is nominally fought against the "Islamo-fascist"; domestically, it underwrites the disciplining of underclass immigrant subjects. Long offers two examples that make explicit the gay liberal endorsement of those vested interests. In the U.S., the figure of the "Islamo-fascist" has helped brand the "war on terror" a gay cause, prompting Andrew Sullivan, for one, to claim that "[t]his is our war, too."[17] In the U.K., in what Long describes as a "politics of provocation," activists have shifted their struggle against the religious homophobia institutionalized by the Anglican Church to Muslim immigrants, "who enjoy none of the authority Christianity could claim."[18]

Together, the figures of the gay asylum seeker from Iran and the homophobic Islamic immigrant form an ideological pair. On one side, the asylum seeker from faraway, the self-arrogated protection of whose threatened sexual individuality rhetorically enables Western countries to legitimate overriding dialogue and negotiation, facilitating violent intervention under the flag of sexual freedom. On the other side, the homophobic, gay-bashing immigrant nearby, whose culturalization enforces a qualified, conditional, and precarious citizenship. Hence, in what might be described as the liberal-imperial strategy of the tightly circumscribed sex-culture distribution that animates the entangled contexts of van Dalen's politics, the assumed sexuality of the asylum seeker makes him *already Western, already modern*, while the imposed culture of the Muslim immigrant insures he will *never be Western and modern enough*. The logic at play hinges on a strategic disarticulation of sexuality and culture, their measured parcelling out in order to forge mutually exclusive identifications.

Those identifications follow a familiar script, which pinpoints the modern sex/culture split. Arguably, modern individuation hinges on sexuality, based on the enunciation and exercise of desire in defiance of the shaming constrictions that are imposed by family, religion, community, and tradition. In that respect, homosexuality is not just exceptional, but paradoxically exceptional *and paradigmatic* at the same time. Asserting and enacting one's desire is understood to emancipate the individual from her or his cultural environment, enabling the inner or self-determination that transforms the subject into a true individual. In the same vein, culture designates the external determination of the subject, requiring the full observance of inchoate but coercive precepts, so that no free or autonomous individuality can emerge within its terms. Or, as Wendy Brown puts it: "'we' have culture while culture has 'them,' or we have culture while they are a culture."[19] For us, culture forms an extraneous background; for them, an authoritative essence.[20]

Merely by being sexualized as "gay," the Iranian asylum seeker is granted full individuality; by the same token, he becomes fully modern and Western. Whether avowed or imputed, "his" homosexuality instantly erases his cultural, ethnic, or religious identifications as Iranian, Muslim, or Eastern, amounting to a full transformation, his complete reconstitution in a different discursive universe. Personhood does not translate across the sex/culture divide. Meanwhile, the individuality of the culturalized immigrant is pre-empted, his pre-modern and non-Western station established.

In that tortuous set-up, the demand for sexual tolerance that is frequently imposed on immigrant populations can register as a form of forcible assimilation. Consequently, homophobia can emerge as a form of resistance that insists on a social, ethnic, and economic particularity. All the more so, since the discipline enacted by the cultural determination of the immigrant subject, pre-empting his or her individuality, has as its corollary a form of secondary sexualization. This supplement installs a sexuality that already culturalized subjects cannot themselves own, claim, or speak, a non-individuated, non-emancipated sexuality that is perverse, wild, frustrated, opportunistic, repressed, hysterical, and excessive. Therefore, the culturalization of immigrants goes hand in hand with a judicious fascination for phenomena such as "lover boys," gang rapes, "closeted" and oppressed Islamic gays, and so on.

The above notwithstanding, the cultivated conflict between Dutch gays and Moroccan boys cannot but force the two groups into a peculiar intimacy. After all, it is their very *relation* that supplies politicians and pundits with political capital. In "Imams and Homosexuality: A Post-Gay Debate in the Netherlands" (2002), Gert Hekma for example points to a surprising similarity and closeness between the two groups. After commenting on the stark irony that Eastern practices of pederasty used to supply Western imperialism with one of its legitimations just as effectively as Islamic homophobia does today, he writes:

> The pervasive homosexuality of Moroccan culture has another interesting result. Due to their sexual socialization, Moroccan youth are so much more aware of homosexual signs that many of them recognize the hidden gay radar of Dutch guys. Gay men and Moroccan male youngsters resemble each other closely in their street behavior, sexual alertness and fashion hunger. Between them, it is the fetishism of the small differences that might lead to violence as well as shared sexual desires.[21]

Hekma is right: just visit the fashionable Zara department store in Amsterdam on a Saturday afternoon, and witness the Moroccans and the gays get to business, while the straight boys stand by helplessly as their girlfriends shop for them!

Of course, the male-male eroticism that pervades Moroccan culture cannot be fully approximated to the Western understanding of "homosexuality." Interestingly, moreover, Hekma appears to substitute Freud's "narcissism of minor differences" with "the fetishism of small differences." That may be a typo or a mistake; if so, it is a particularly felicitous one. For, those small differences may well inspire a narcissistically fuelled hatred, but they may also be eroticized, cherished, and loved. Perhaps the desires shared by Dutch gays and Moroccan young men may be understood to include the utopian and queer potential of an eroticism that is unburdened by identity as much as by culture, an erotic situated tangentially in relation to the wily pressures of the sex/culture divide.

TRAFFIC SCENES

The notion of "intersectionality," one would assume, might serve as an effective antidote to what Puar describes as the "gay or Muslim" binary. After all, it literally imagines multiple avenues of interpellation and identification within a single spatial continuum, traversing the rupture installed between sex and race-culture. Yet, the legacies of the term seem more complex and more contentious than that. As it happens, Puar herself has sharply contested the concept. For, to the extent that it promises that the "messiness" of identity can be disarticulated, broken down into its components, as well as contained in a structural grid, she argues, the notion accords with liberal multicultural-ism and corporate diversity management.[22] Hence, the term warrants closer scrutiny. How can sex and race-culture, deposited on either side of the liberal split, be re-imagined to hang together in a spatial field? I begin with reflecting on what I see as a closely related rhetorical commonplace in the contempo-rary humanities and social sciences: the obligatory "etc." that follows ostensibly exhaustive listings of socio-politically relevant vectors of identity. As in: "gender, sexuality, race, ethnicity, class, age, disability, etc." What kind of ordering or distribution of identity does that "etc." betray?

According to Judith Butler, what she describes as the "embarrassed etc." signifies "the illimitable process of signification itself."[23] For Butler, the "etc." acts as an excess or supplement, which may be levered strategically for the resignification of identity through its citational reiteration. Nevertheless, other implications of the customary listing and the "etc." may hold as well.

For one, besides acting as a failsafe placeholder rhetorically immunizing the speaker against the opprobrium that would inevitably follow an inadver-tent oversight, the "etc." also denotes a totalization that is based on a con-sensus so compelling that the speaker can fully trust the reader or listener to complete the series with any remainder of alternative or future identifications. Those identifications may not be readily nameable as of yet, but are never-theless assumed to do little more than add more variables to the list rather than rearticulate the principle that strings them together. In that sense, the obligatory "etc." helps to prevent *other* or *different* differences from making an actual difference.

Furthermore, the "etc." retroactively equalizes the series as a set of vectors that can be organized within a single plane. In that way, the distinct relevance of class as an analytic of socio-economic position is effectively curtailed: it becomes but one identity on a par with others. Moreover, sex and race are effectively squared; only a minute comma now marks the large-scale structur-ing effects of the modern sex/culture divide.

In addition, the list breaks down identity into so many variables, which can only be measured and summarized from a position that is itself imagined as neutral, withdrawn from the field of diverging and competing identities. Arguably, that position is inevitably indicative of, or aligned with, that of the state, placing under surveillance the internal differentiation of the popu-lation. And finally, the list allows for the carving up and parcelling out of identity into discrete territories of scholarly expertise. Race-culture becomes the "etc." of queer theory, while sexuality becomes the "etc." of postcolonial studies. In sum, the commonplace of the "etc." can be taken to suggest the atomization, equalization, and totalization of what are ultimately divergent socio-historical experiences. And, while it hypothetically keeps open the possibility of other identifications emerging in the future, it reduces those to yet another set of variables in advance. So, to what extent and in what way can the notion of intersectionality help to alleviate this predicament?

The *locus classicus* of the concept is offered by Kimberlé Crenshaw, who is credited with coining the term:

> Intersectionality is what occurs when a woman from a minority group tries to navigate the main crossing in the city . . . The main highway is Racism Road. One cross street can be Colonialism, then Patriarchy Street. . . . She has to deal not only with one form of oppression but with all forms, those named as road signs, which link together to make a double, a triple, multiple, a many-layered blanket of oppression.[24]

The minority woman in Crenshaw's allegory faces a crowded intersection. At the very least, however, she knows where her oppression is coming from: she recognizes the names of the streets she is navigating, and she is familiar with their layout and intersections. In Crenshaw's model, the subject is capable of situating herself on the map of power in a nearly geometrically precise localization: "I am slotted into society here, where Racism Road, Patriarchy Street, and Colonialism Avenue meet." The epistemological mastery afforded by that localization allows for effective political identification and agency: "If this is where I am, I must march on this street and that street to forge my emancipation." In that sense, Crenshaw allows for the liberal possibility of a future of, say, fully realized pedestrian rights, universal rights of passage, in which every minority, every form of oppression, is identified, named, politicized, emancipated, and finally included. Oppression may well be multiple and many-layered, but its road signs are readable and totalizable; the streets add up and link together in a transparent and legible map of power relations.

A first line of criticism might address the absence of the larger contexts of power in Crenshaw's model. All stress is on the named streets rather than the organization of the map as a whole. What is missing from Crenshaw's crossroads are the High and Wall Street of capitalism—presumably because the economy organizes the map as a whole rather than a specific, and hence nameable, portion of it. The same goes for the framing and pervading of the scene of power by the bio-political state. Both capital and bio-power are too big to fit on the map; they *are* the map. Since Crenshaw's model of intersectionality restricts itself to the street signs, it misses the forms of power that organize the city as a whole, controlling the movement of bodies and goods.

Furthermore, Crenshaw's map situates variegated forms of interpellation and identification within a single spatial continuum. As a result, those forms of subjectivity easily become equalized with and reducible to each other. That tendency is arguably facilitated by two pervasive intellectual habits:

the structuralist tendency to situate differences as so many variables within a common grid, and the poststructuralist habit to link and reduce all differences to a capitalized but underspecified "Difference." Though various forms of oppression and contestation are all intertwined, that should not be taken to imply they are all similar, let alone amount to more or less the same thing. In her criticism of Crenshaw, Nira Yuval-Davis aptly argues that a careful differentiation between "different kinds of difference" is necessary: "To be Black or a woman is not another way of being working class, or even a particular type of working-class person."[25] Then again, Yuval-Davis' caution should not be taken to imply that respective identifications stand fully apart, either. Only a perspective in which sex and race are neither fully divorced from, nor fully reducible to, each other can help to counter the sex/culture split. That perspective requires us to observe the ways in which they shift in relation to each other through a spatiotemporal logic that is not fully comprehensible in a logical or Newtonian way. Analysing the intimate distance or proximate separation of sex and race calls for a different understanding of space than Crenshaw's two-dimensional traffic scene allows for: a space shot-through with impossible simultaneities, wormholes, and loops.

Intriguingly, Eve Kosofsky Sedgwick argues that the terrain of gender, sexuality and race is not entirely isotopic or smooth, but intricately textured. Peculiar portions of the map, she claims, are organized *orthogonally*, which means that they are independently or unpredictably variable.[26] To make matters even more complicated, Sedgwick also proposes that the map is filled with unexpected thresholds, places where "quantitative increments along one dimension can suddenly appear as qualitative differences somewhere else on the map entirely."[27] To Sedgwick's mind, it is entirely possible to move steadily in one direction on one street, and suddenly find yourself on another, moving in the opposite direction. Sedgwick's model goes some way in suggesting a non-continuous space, in which sex and race are articulated and disarticulated.

In a brilliant article called "Punk'd Theory" (2005), Tavia Nyong'o analyses a particular "intersection" that follows Sedgwick's model rather than Crenshaw's. According to Nyong'o, the word *punk* indicates an arrested dialectic between the late 1970s British subculture, primarily made up of white working class youth, and the use of the same term, from the 1950s onwards, as African-American slang for "queer." The connection hints at experiential identifications that closely entangle black homophobia with white anti-capitalism. That link is remembered in vernacular—or street—knowledge through the usage of the same term and its resonances, but is studiously forgotten by the academic forms of knowledge production that are beholden to disciplinary power, insisting on clear road signs and discrete territories.

Restoring the frozen dialectic between the two, Nyong'o claims, allows for a perspective in which the two to some extent start to switch places: the aggressive anti-capitalism of the British punks is *also* about a recuperative masculinity; African-American homophobia *also* expresses defiance in the face of socioeconomic domination (being "punked" means being "fucked" or "outwitted"). Punk, for Nyong'o, gestures at a larger and more intricate map, one on which class, race, and sexuality are unpredictably distributed. In his conclusion, Nyong'o offers a different picture of the intersectionality of power:

> An intersection is also a meeting of two streets, and in a landscape long given over to automotivity, it is a place of particular hazard for the pedestrian . . . The rights of the pedestrian . . . balance the right of way of the automobile. Yet, as any streetwalker will tell you, enforcing any of these rights against the legal and illegal incursions of car culture requires continuous tactics of everyday resistance . . . So, in the practice of everyday life, the vernacularly mobile are required to demand both their rights and more than their rights, simply to preserve a portion of the mobility they had prior to enclosure. Examples proliferate: workers become illegal immigrants; poor mothers become welfare queens; protestors become potential terrorists. All must attack the presumption of their criminality merely to preserve their way of life from the ongoing incursions of disciplinary power.[28]

Nyong'o's streetwalker must not only negotiate the named streets of Crenshaw's crossroads, but also the incursive power represented by the cars, the emissaries of a disciplinary power that works through identification, whether oppressive or emancipatory. Moreover, that power increases incrementally and flexibly, so that it is impossible simply to claim and hold your place on the grid. Merely protecting your rights of passage or your territory implies in time to lose them. Just maintaining a foothold, let alone moving ahead, requires a form of "punk" navigation that straddles familiar street names and well-trodden intersections, tracing nearly forgotten, ignored, or all but invisible alleyways. At those junctures, the dialectic between identity and difference may well be erratic and unpredictable.

Sedgwick and Nyong'o help us to reconceptualize intersectionality in a way that resonates with the contemporary realities of Dutch homonationalism. Rather than a static grid that allows for respective positions, they help us to imagine a space inhabited by temporality and motion. Power *moves,* and so does the distribution of identification and contestation: positions erratically stalling, flipping, bypassing, and approximating in close relation to each other. This implies that an established foothold on the map can only be a transient and equivocal blessing. While, in the contemporary political scene of the Netherlands, immigrant teens are disciplined as "street terrorists," Dutch gays might well be re-disciplined as "pedophiles" in an all too near future.

Moreover, closeness and distance can be thought as paradoxically simultaneous. On the one hand, Dutch homosexuals and Moroccan young men move through entirely different universes, deposited on either side of the sex-culture divide. On the other hand, now taking into account the cruisy, streetwise eroticism they share according to Hekma, they might as well be cast as close neighbours. From one perspective, the gay asylum seeker from Iran travels from an ethnic neighbourhood to the individualistic gay scene downtown; from another, he merely switches sides between two competing gangs. In the vein of Nyong'o's case, supposedly opposed camps can be seen to switch places: the political claims made on behalf of a mainstreamed homosexuality *also* channel the contempt of the Dutch middle classes for a largely immigrant underclass; immigrant "homophobia" *also* articulates defiance in the face of discrimination and exploitation.

NOTES

1. In the historical overview offered by Schuyf and Krouwel, lesbian and gay emancipation in the Netherlands is contextualized in the country's long tradition of consensus politics, through which marginal constituencies of the population are in time incorporated. They conclude: "The very superficial liberal ideology that characterizes the public debate in the Netherlands allows people to distinguish between groups of a specific ethnic, cultural, social, and sexual characters, yet the egalitarian culture prohibits a different treatment of these minorities. Government policies and financial grants to organized interests are allocated for the integration of minorities into mainstream society. Dutch lesbian and gays have been successful in taking advantage of the opportunities that arose in the political and social sphere as a result of consensual practices" (179). Notably, the same politics of consensus or accommodation do not at present extend to Islamic immigrants.

2. In 2002, the term "kutmarrokanen" was brought into circulation by the social-democratic politician Rob Oudkerk, who used the word in an off-camera conversation in a television study, thinking his mic was switched-off. The phrase stuck. In 2009, the mayor of Venray, Jan Waals, used the term in a public lecture (as reported by *De Telegraaf* on September 25, 2009). "Moroccan scum" and "street terrorists" are part of the everyday vocabulary of the PVV (Freedom Party), led by Geert Wilders. The party obtained 15.5% of the vote in the 2010 parliamentary elections.

3. The 2005 Amsterdam assault on Windows Media Editorial Director Chris Crain, allegedly by Moroccan teens, was widely publicized in the U.S. blogosphere. However, the numbers seem ambivalent. A 2008 national study, carried out by the Politieacademie ["Police Academy"], estimated that 14% of anti-gay incidents were caused by non-Western suspects. That same year, Laurens Buijs, Gert Hekma, and Jan

Willem Duyvendak published a study claiming that 57% of incidents in Amsterdam are attributable to immigrants (*Als ze maar van me afblijven*). In 2006, a study by the Amsterdam Centrum Buitenlanders alleged that immigrant boys are overrepresented among sex workers as well as victims of pedosexual abuse ("Jongens huilen niet").

4. Jasbir K. Puar, "Queer Times, Queer Assemblages," *Social Text* 23, nos. 84–85 (Fall/Winter 2005): 126.

5. Jasbir K. Puar, *Terrorist Assemblages: Homonationalism in Queer Times* (Durham, NC: Duke University Press, 2007), 19. Further page references are given in the text.

6. Frank van Dalen, "Gayteens Executions in Iran." Available at http://www .petitiononline.com/1021ir/petition.html.

7. Wikipedia offers the clearest account of the case and the controversy that followed, detailing the perspectives of a large range of actors, such as Amnesty International, Human Rights Watch, the International Gay and Lesbian Human Rights Commission, the U.S. Log Cabin Republicans, the journalist Andrew Sullivan, the U.K.-based OutRage!, and the Islamic Al-Fatiha Foundation. See http://en.wikipedia .org/wiki/Mahmoud_Asgari_and_Ayaz_Marhoni.

8. Van Dalen manifested himself as such in an episode of the television show *Pauw and Witteman*, which aired September 17, 2007.

9. Fortuyn made the claim in an interview published by the national newspaper de Volkskrant, February 9, 2002. See http://www.volkskrant.nl/den_haag/article153195 .ece/De_islam_is_een_achterlijke_cultuur.

10. For more on Dutch pillarization with respect to Islam, please refer to Boehmer and Gouda in the present volume.

11. That designation is in step with what Mahmoud Mahdami terms "culture talk," or the "culturalization" of political, social, and economic conflicts. Similarly, Slavoj Zizek observes that "[p]olitical differences—differences conditioned by political inequality or economic exploitation—are naturalized and 'neutralized' into 'cultural' differences, that is into different 'ways of life' which are something given, something that cannot be overcome" (119).

12. Scott Long, "Unbearable Witness: How Western Activists (Mis)Recognize Sexuality in Iran," *Contemporary Politics* 15, no. 1 (March 2009): 124.

13. Long, "Unbearable Witness," 125.

14. Long, "Unbearable Witness," 130.

15. Chandan Reddy, "Asian Diasporas, Neoliberalism, and Family: Reviewing the Case for Homosexual Asylum in the Context of Family Right," *Social Text* 23, nos. 84–85 (Fall/Winter 2005): 111.

16. Reddy, "Asian Diasporas," 122.

17. Quoted in Long, "Unbearable Witness," 124.

18. Long, "Unbearable Witness," 122, 130.

19. Wendy Brown, *Regulating Aversion: Tolerance in the Age of Identity and Empire* (Princeton, NJ: Princeton University Press, 2006), 150–51.

20. Brown, *Regulating Aversion*, 153.

21. Gert Hekma, "Imams and Homosexuality: A Post-Gay Debate in the Netherlands," *Sexualities* 5, no. 2 (2002): 245.

22. Jasbir K. Puar, "Queer Times," 127–28.

23. Judith Butler, *Gender Trouble: Feminism and the Subversion of Identity* (New York: Routledge, 1990), 182.

24. Quoted in Nira Yuval-Davis, "Intersectionality and Feminist Politics," *European Journal of Women's Studies* 13, no. 3: 196.

25. Yuval-Davis, "Intersectionality," 199–200.

26. Eve Kosofsky Sedgwick, "Gosh, Boy George, You Must Be Awfully Secure in Your Masculinity!" in *Constructing Masculinity*, ed. Maurice Berger, Brian Wallis, and Simon Watson (New York: Routledge, 1995), 15.

27. Sedgwick, "Gosh, Boy George," 16.

28. Tavia Nyong'o, "Punk'd Theory," *Social Text*, 23, nos. 84–85 (Fall/Winter 2005): 31.

BIBLIOGRAPHY

Amsterdams Centrum Buitenlanders. "Jongens huilen niet: Seksueel geweld tegen allochtone jongens." January 2006. Available at http://www.huiselijkgeweld.nl/doc/seksueel_misbruik/jongenshuilenniet.pdf.

Brown, Wendy. *Regulating Aversion: Tolerance in the Age of Identity and Empire*. Princeton, NJ: Princeton University Press, 2006.

Buijs, L., G. Hekma, and J. W. Duyvendak. *Als ze maar van me afblijven: Een onderzoek naar antihomoseksueel geweld in Amsterdam*. Amsterdam: Amsterdam University Press, 2009.

Butler, Judith. *Gender Trouble: Feminism and the Subversion of Identity*. New York: Routledge, 1990.

Hekma, Gert. "Imams and Homosexuality: A Post-Gay Debate in the Netherlands." *Sexualities* 5, no. 2 (2002): 237–48.

Long, Scott. "Unbearable Witness: How Western Activists (Mis)Recognize Sexuality in Iran." *Contemporary Politics* 15, no. 1 (March 2009): 119–36.

Mamdani, Mahmood. *Good Muslim/Bad Muslim: America, the Cold War, and the Roots of Terror*. New York: Pantheon, 2004.

Marcouch, Ahmed. "Marokaanse jongens: Pompe(n) of verzuipen?" Online column, published February 16, 2006. Available at http://www.amsterdam.pvda.nl/afdeling_nieuwsbericht/2866/nieuwwest.

Nyong'o, Tavia. "Punk'd Theory." *Social Text* 23, nos. 84–85 (Fall/Winter 2005): 19–34. Special Issue, "What's Queer about Queer Studies Now?" Edited by David L. Eng with Judith Halberstam and José Esteban Muñoz.

Politiecademie. *Rapportage homofood geweld: Politiegegevens Periode 1 januari–1 juli 2008. September 2008*. Available at http://www.rijksoverheid.nl/documenten-en-publicaties/kamerstukken/2008/11/17/rapportage-homofoob-geweld-politiegegevens-1-januari-1-juli-2008.html.

Puar, Jasbir K. "Queer Times, Queer Assemblages." *Social Text* 23, nos. 84–85 (Fall/Winter 2005): 120–40. Special Issue, "What's Queer about Queer Studies Now?" Edited by David L. Eng with Judith Halberstam and José Esteban Muñoz.

———. *Terrorist Assemblages: Homonationalism in Queer Times.* Durham, NC: Duke University Press, 2007.

Reddy, Chandan. "Asian Diasporas, Neoliberalism, and Family: Reviewing the Case for Homosexual Asylum in the Context of Family Rights." *Social Text* 23, nos. 84–85 (Fall/Winter 2005): 101–20. Special Issue, "What's Queer about Queer Studies Now?" Edited by David L. Eng with Judith Halberstam and José Esteban Muñoz.

Schuyf, Judith, and Andé Krouwel. "The Dutch Lesbian and Gay Movement: The Politics of Accommodation." In *The Global Emergence of Gay and Lesbian Politics: National Imprints of a Worldwide Movement*, edited by Barry D. Adam, Jan Willem Duyvendak, and André Krouwel, 158–83. Philadelphia, PA: Temple University Press, 1999.

Sedgwick, Eve Kosofsky. "Gosh, Boy George, You Must Be Awfully Secure in Your Masculinity!" In *Constructing Masculinity*, edited by Maurice Berger, Brian Wallis, and Simon Watson, 11–20. New York: Routledge, 1995.

van Dalen, Frank. "Gayteens Executions in Iran." Available at http://www.petition online.com/1021ir/petition.html.

Yuval-Davis, Nira. "Intersectionality and Feminist Politics." *European Journal of Women's Studies* 13, no. 3 (2006): 193–209.

Chapter Eleven

Becoming UnDutch:
"Wil je dat? Kun je dat?"

Mireille Rosello

The "Wil je dat? Kun je dat?" (Will you? Can you?) of my title are not real questions, they are quotations. I could write that I found them; but really they found me, they confronted me, challenged me. I heard them at the end of the documentary entitled "Naar Nederland" (Direction: Nederland), a set of complex narratives that future migrants must buy to prepare themselves for the Civic Integration Examination, the test that foreigners must pass before applying for an Authorization for temporary stay (mvv) in the Netherlands. "Wil je dat? Kun je dat?" are the very last words uttered by a female narrator, an actress, who plays the role of a guide throughout the story. But this guide is not here to welcome us, to show us the way. She is not into hospitality, she is not greeting us, she is telling us what we must know before we come. That the Netherlands are not paradise and that we are going to have to work very hard if we come. Hence the questions "Wil je dat? Kun je dat?"

If we have not learned the lesson properly, we will never have the opportunity to meet her on Dutch soil, we will have failed the test. The guide is a sort of teacher, but unlike the worst imaginable human teacher, she is a fictive character made of pixels, so that no dialogue is ever possible. What she tells us is not to be discussed or questioned. When she explains the Dutch educational system, she emphasizes that, in Dutch schools, "children have to discover a lot for themselves," to learn how to "ask questions and to form their own opinion." Yet, she treats us as completely passive auditors. Do as I say . . .

At times friendly, at times threatening, at times slightly tedious and at times entertaining, she is the link between all the disparate pieces of information that migrants who wish to immigrate must accept as the truth about the Netherlands and then memorize before applying for a residency permit. Of course, not all migrants are equal. Not everyone must take the test. As the website that introduces the documentary puts it, only "sommige mensen" (some people) must take it.[1] Must we, must I take the test or not? We do not know. It is our duty to doubt. We must find out. And the site tells us where to look: "Op de website van de Immigratie en Naturalisatie Dienst (IND) kunt u opzoeken of ook u het examen moet doen" [You can check whether you too have to take the examination on the website of the Immigration and Naturalisation Service (IND)].[2] The moment of uncertainty and perhaps slight worry that we experience as we try to find out whether we are exempt or not is a fraction of what we will go through if we determine that we must take the test. And if we discover that we don't, it is perhaps unavoidable to feel relief instead of remembering that the first encounter with our fears was representative of what anyone might feel and perhaps sharable with those who must take the test.

As it turned out, I did not have to take the test. I already live in the Netherlands. But I took the test. Not as an academic who sought an exotic object of inquiry, not as a privileged migrant who goes slumming, not as a paranoid "skilled migrant" who wanted to check that the high opinion that the government has of me was not, somehow, usurped, and not as a well-intentioned scholar who wanted to speak for those who will only have been able to speak into the telephone, to the computer, and then move on to the business of surviving in a strange, rainy land.[3] I did not even take the test to expiate the fact that, of course, I was relieved when I found out that I did not have to. Or because I understood that I should know better because, even if selfishness guides me, I am only relatively safe since "they" can, any time, be redefined to include "me."

I took it, really, because I had heard so much about it in the press and in academic articles that I was beginning to wonder if the cultural debate sparked by one very specific aspect of the test was not obscuring a whole set of other important issues. I became even more suspicious of what I would find if I did not concentrate on the obvious problem that so many voices were inviting me to focus on. Two shots in that film made the test both controversial and probably much more visible that it would have been otherwise: a topless woman on a beach, and two male lovers kissing in a field. I don't know how many times I saw these words written on a page or on a computer screen before I actually watched the film.[4] I could easily imagine a number of reasons why such images could infuriate different types of people and create new alliances and solidarities. Even if we want to avoid the simple equation between such images and Western sexual freedom or non-discrimination against gays, it is even more urgent to regret that the bitter struggles that led to the (far from perfect) political implementation of such ideals should now be used to intimidate future migrants into comparing their own sense of public etiquette with this display of nudity or passionate affection.[5]

The attention paid to the issue of sexual democracy in the film had, perhaps remarkably, an unexpected consequence. I started wondering if the images were scandalous in the etymological sense: a *skandalon*, in Greek, is a stumbling block and also a trap, something that stops you from going elsewhere, perhaps further. In a move that Eve Sedgwick would have been right to understand as "paranoid criticism,"[6] I suspected that the sexy images might well function as a screen: while my critical energy focused on the contradictions of "sexual democracies," I was watching something perhaps even more troubling if less visible. What did I learn or not learn while chasing the elusive titillation of the sexy images? What facial expressions of shock, pleasure or astonishment could have been recorded as I was viewing all the chapters of the documentary?

To avoid falling into the "trap" laid by the controversial definition of sexual democracy, I decided to watch the film again with new questions in mind: what other, seemingly more innocent proposals, were implicitly or explicitly presented as truths and deployed as mechanisms of exclusion? Which disciplinary discourses were invoked, which assumptions were we asked to take for granted? Examining the structure of the test, I noticed that by the end of the eight-part presentation, I, the migrant, was expected to have learned about 1. Geography, transportation and accommodation; 2. History; 3. Government, Politics and the Law; 4. The Dutch language and the importance of learning it; 5. Education; 6. Health; 7. Work and income and, finally, 8. How to take the test at the embassy.

The documentary includes different genres: testimonies of recently arrived migrants; interviews with doctors, workers, politicians; reconstructed historical scenes; close-ups on computer screens; and fictional scenes where a clumsy bad immigrant demonstrates what should not be done. But when all is said and done, and this is what strikes me as astonishing, someone who has not seen the documentary could easily pass the test because what matters, in the end, is not so much the documentary but the booklet that comes with the DVDs when you buy the preparation package.

The booklet is a photo-album that contains one hundred photographs, stills from the film. At the end, we find a list of one hundred questions that correspond to each of the pictures. And each question has an answer. Both questions and answers are in Dutch.[7] The goal is to memorize the answers, exactly. And having watched the film may help you connect the images and the questions (give you a context), but there is no guarantee that remembering the story will help you provide an answer acceptable by the computer because your role, during the test, is to repeat exactly the words as they appear on the page. In other words, even if you know a lot about Dutch (or world) culture, you may still fail the test. Question 33: "Waarom is Anne Frank beroemd? Ze schreef een dagboek" [Why is Anne Frank famous? She wrote a diary]. The more you know about Anne Frank, the more confused you will be: there are dozens of plausible answers. As far as I am concerned, "she wrote a diary" would not have been my first choice. On the other hand, nothing prevents you from memorizing the answers whether or not you believe in the values upheld by the quasi rhetorical questions ("Wanneer moet u werk gaan zoeken, zo snel mogelijk of later?" [When must you look for a job, right away or later?]. What do I demonstrate, I wonder, if I know that the correct answer is "zo snel mogelijk"? How do you say, in Dutch: "oh, I'd much rather be permanently unemployed and collect benefits" (not supplied by the questionnaire)?

Traditionally, as cultural critics, we watch a film and then analyze it. In this case, the film watches us, tells us how it sees us, migrants. It anticipates our surprises and our areas of ignorance, our differences and our future difficulties. I, the migrant, am looking at myself in this amazing mirror that performatively interpellates and subjectifies me.

I am also expected to believe that this mirror, this way of seeing me, is part of the country where I am going to reside, the nation and its national community's assumption that I will already be an insider-foreigner. The mirror expects me to listen and repeat the right answers, whether or not I agree, whether or not I understand more than the words that I have memorized, whether or not the life that I will lead once on Dutch soil is in any way predicted by or related to what I have answered, correctly or not.

What more do I understand at that point? The Netherlands, the DVD tells me, are in danger, they are a fragile, precarious land. I see a map. Green land, blue sea to the North and to the West. The invisible friendly guide says that the vast majority of the country is below sea level. Something ridiculous. I hesitate to believe that I have understood correctly. Six meters below sea level? And if the sea rose, a third of the land would "verdwijnen onder water" and that third is precisely the part of Holland where most urban centers are located. Amsterdam where I live would "verdwijnen" too. I really need to know what threatens me, them, us. I look up the word. I had guessed that verdwijnen was bad. But it is worse than I thought. "Disappear" says the impassible electronic dictionary. The country would purely and simply disappear. Not be hit by a hurricane and then become the object or hero of media coverage, plays or books such as Daniel Maximin's *L'Ile et une nuit*.[8] Not be devastated by a tsunami and have to pick up the pieces with or in spite of international help. Not be half destroyed by Katrina. And I wonder: don't I remember correctly that when New Orleans was submerged, Dutch water management experts and mobile water pumps were sent from the Netherlands to "de-water"?[9] I start picturing just how high the water would rise if the sea had its way. I look out the window. A pretty little canal, whose quiet brownish water is safely contained by old walls. What would happen? Would the water rise slowly but surely, or would it be like a devastating wave rushing through streets, uprooting trees, destroying bridges and whatever stands in its way. Would humans be safe if they happened to be on the first floor, the second floor? Still, "disappear" seems a bit grandiloquent. Most buildings in this area have four, five or six floors, not to mention the tall churches, towers and monuments. Something would stick out. Of course I understand that it would be a disaster whose magnitude I cannot fathom but would the country cease to exist? Why not tell me what might happen and what I could do if there were to be a major flood?

I wonder if the test book will teach me something different. I take a look. Picture 8. A new map of the Netherlands greets me. The picture is worth a thousand words. The Netherlands as it would look if the dikes broke. Lots of baby blue and still lots of green but a completely different shape. The funny little cape that makes the north of Holland as recognizable as French Brittany is gone. Islands are sprinkled along what used to be the shore, to the East. The rest is relentlessly blue. The Netherlands are an archipelago. This is a peaceful and static new map. All it took was a few clicks and the computer program obliged, quietly reorganizing the world as we know it, changing the colors of our universe. The computerized visual tragedy has swallowed up the victims. All that is left is a bird's eye view of the catastrophe. We have disappeared.

Something in me breathes an ambiguous sigh of relief. So, water is the enemy, not me, not the migrant. I feel compassion and sadness for the drowned blue land and for the quaint little mills that we saw as the helicopter filmed the countryside and the canals. I try to find ways of helping. Is this a national sea, a national story, a national stereotype, I ask myself. From one imaginary perspective, sea water is the same everywhere, it is as global as the air we all breathe.[10] But the globalizing of elements is a narrative too and the water-as-a-global-element story both clashes and happily coincides with locally constructed meanings so that another "we" now gets differently affected by what the sea can do to them. Both local and global narratives carry with them secret agendas, more or less acknowledged fears, and as long as we remember that our waters are not transparent Cartesian flows, we may be able to refrain from transforming our slightly neurotic images into political agendas. While critics have warned us against overstating "the cultural" over "the political" and against worshipping the new idols of hybridity and creolization without even realizing that we do so,[11] in this case, it seems to me as if the risk is the opposite one. If I fear my national sea because my recently acquired also-Dutch imagination is limited to a simple opposition between the global sea (which "we" all share), and the national sea (which another "we" must fear); am I not going to make supposedly rational decisions based on the kind of poetry that I would, if I identified it as poetry, dismiss as apolitical? And the opposition is not so much between global and local seas but between global and local narratives of global or local seas. Some narratives seem to have the ambition to function as global speech acts even as they focus on one local body of water.

For example, perhaps because I have my own active personal myths about the Mediterranean, I am always surprised by the rather peremptory way in which Edouard Glissant's *Introduction à une poétique du divers* (among other texts) insists that the Mediterranean sea is the other, even the opposite, of the preferred "diffracting" Caribbean sea.[12] The Caribbean sea opens, I am told, the Mediterranean "concentrates."[13] According to Glissant, the latter is the cradle of civilizations and monotheistic religions, it is powerful enough to "bend"[14] human thought towards the One and unity. He concedes, in a later interview, that there is "historic greatness"[15] in this concentrationary power, but that is obviously no compliment.

I don't believe that the Mediterranean deserves its reputation as "la mer de l'un."[16] When Glissant writes *"même à travers* des drames, des guerres et des conflits" [in despite of tragedies, wars and conflicts],[17] does he not push aside, as an irrelevant detail, the visible symptoms of a historically forgotten creolization of the Mediterranean basin? I feel like arguing that cities around the Mediterranean are not radically incommensurable with Caribbean islands if we remember that so many different peoples were sometimes forced to cohabit by imperial logic or postcolonial migrations. And that surely, only if we look at "civilizations" from a totalizing and homogenizing perspective can we forget their inherent hybridity. Of course, I am quick to point out to myself that it may be theoretically lame to claim that the Mediterranean has always already creolized when my secret agenda is to defend my favourite sea against accusations that I consider damning. After all, I want to rehabilitate the Mediterranean because I have internalized Glissant's implicitly negative judgment against a logic of the One, the Same. Still, in the end, Glissant's comparative reverie about water strikes me as rather inhospitable to his own poetics of creolization.

That said, if those theoretical passages make me attentive to the way in which such narratives about the sea work, each story is geographically specific and neither the concentrating nor creolizing Mediterranean is a good model for the relationship between the Dutch land and the Dutch sea. Those stories do not help me tame my, their fear of the water, make peace with a sea that means disappearance. And if I am to "integrate," shall I not be resubjectified as an "I" who is expected to be part of that terrifying Dutch narrative? Or should I bring other narratives that might profitably rewrite that Dutch vision (or highlight those narratives that already know that the Netherlands is part of a larger global imaginary that I, the migrant, complicate)?

Perhaps others can help us. I remember Richard Watts's reading of Patrick Chamoiseau's *Biblique des derniers gestes.* His analysis follows the main character's global and local narratives about bodies of water that are both transnational and unique in their specificity. He points out that even when water is used as a form of torture, the novel claims or helps us imagine, that the detestable act of violence misfires, and that the hero is healed by the dirty, unhealthy, contaminated water that should make him dirty, unhealthy, contaminated.[18] Watts notices that the bodies of waters described in the novel are transnational but he precisely does not reduce them to a universal, globalized element. They have different names, different identities and different relationships with the people who live close to them: the fresh-water spring of his native island is not confused with the Ganges. Of course, Watt's interpretation is theoretical and his critics are certainly right to remark "on the limitations of water as a figure for political resistance."[19] Yet I find his text most politically useful when he chooses to pay attention to apparently irrelevant details: he reads a footnote that seems to interrupt the novel's potentially idealizing cultural and literary stream and draws our attention to what Watts calls "a reflection on access to water in an era of economic globalization."[20] Attached to a passage that describes a fresh water spring as a supernatural and almost sacred place, the footnote reads:

> Il faut trouver ces lieux . . . les protéger, les garder libres pour tous! Car l'eau est en danger en ce monde à dollars nourri au CAC 40! Et les puissants vont se l'approprier pour la vendre en barils! Ils vont en faire une curée commerciale à laquelle les peuples pauvres n'auront jamais accès! Il nous laisseront les eaux à pesticides, bourrées de mercure ou d'uranium déchu, ou ces eaux désolées que d'obscurs alchimistes vont nous extraire du sel pour les vendre à prix d'or ! . . . Il faut écrire les *Droits universels de l'eau*, c'est le conseil que je vous donne![21]

> We must find those places . . . protect them, keep them free for all! For water is in danger in this dollar-world obsessed with the Dow Jones! The powerful will appropriate it and sell it in barrels. It will be a commercial water-rush and the poor will never have access. They will leave us pesticide-infested waters, full of mercury or fallen uranium, or those sorry waters that obscure alchemists will extract from salt and sell at an exorbitant price . . . We must write the "Universal Rights of Water," marks my words!

I want to take this passionate plea back to the Netherlands. My fragile land is worried about what the planet will do to it. And perhaps, it should consider what it is doing to the water. Perhaps, the nightmarish vision of a flood is precisely what the film is trying to teach me. That we, future and present, inhabitants of the Netherlands should take care of the sea; should learn how to respect not only its destructive power but its very existence as what could both make us disappear and what could itself disappear too. Another kind of nightmare. Let me see, perhaps I have understood the lesson. I should go back to the photo-album, to the list of questions and answers that I am supposed to memorize so that I can respond correctly to computerized cues when I see "picture 8," the image of Netherlands as an archipelago surrounded by a diffracting sea.

I flip to the end of the book. Perhaps the question that corresponds to the image contains the answer to the fear of disappearance. If I am to become Dutch enough for the immigration services, surely they will tell me what the solution is, what we must do, how we must we feel, who is the "we" that the water constantly threatens with annihilation? What must I say to them who will be us, me?

Question 8: "Wat gebeurt er als er geen dijken zijn?" or "What would happen if there were no dikes?" Answer: "staat Nederland onder water." Literally, the Netherlands are under water. No need here for a conditional ("would be"); "staat" is used in the present tense, that is how it works in my new non-native language. And so, we, they build *dijken*. That is the solution. We build walls.

The moment of empathy for the fragile land is gone and the question-answer irritates me. I am radically dissatisfied and frustrated. I am not quite sure what irks me but the celebration of great dikes, solid walls, waterproof borders as the only possible solution, as the obvious answer to the potentially delicate relationship between the land and the sea makes me suspicious. So that is what we-they do. We either erect an impenetrable wall or we disappear. I know that it is absurd, but I take it personally. What if the sea was a metaphor for something else, someone else? What if the selfish moment of relief that I experienced when I discovered that the migrant was not the worst enemy was an illusion. My reading of the whole episode becomes seriously paranoid. "How about protecting the sea instead?" I ask aloud, indignantly, as if the computer program could talk back, or rather could listen. Do you realize what you are doing to the planet?

I am not sure whom I mean by "you" exactly but whoever was responsible for the marketing and the packaging of the test in the Netherlands and abroad suddenly appears to me as ecologically irresponsible. I know that this is a moment of rash affective theorization due to the breaking down of some emotional and interdisciplinary boundary. I could put a stop to this train of thought that connects total strangers, or rather starts recognizing links where I used to see not even difference but no connection whatsoever. Yet I don't. I suddenly remember Stephen Frear's film, *Dirty Pretty Things.* Two undocumented migrants live or rather survive in London. Okwe has offered to cook dinner at Senay's flat (he is homeless). He tries to wash two glasses with hot water while he asks her questions about the organ traffic that goes on where they work. She storms out of the bathroom and demands that he stops. He does not understand: she can't fill her bathtub if he uses tap water in the kitchen. Glasses need "very very hot water" as Okwe puts it but "so do women," especially women whose job it is to clean all day and who end up having to scrub themselves as if they were dirty dishes. And Senay explains or rather proclaims her theory: "everything here is connected to everything there." If he uses water in the kitchen, she suffers in the bathroom, cleaning bodies and washing up is not radically different because Senay is reduced to a collection of organs by cynical traffickers. In the economy of the film, it is easy to read her anger as a critique of what globalization does to them. Everything is connected. For them, it means that whatever does not work (there is not enough water for two people in the flat) also becomes a network of misery and squalor; it turns their body into a collection of marketable parts. Her liver is connected to her passport and to someone else's body.

I look at the package that cost me €65. I try to convert into Moroccan dirhams (I imagine, why not, that I live in Oujda and that I want to join my spouse in the Netherlands). How much would the package cost me? 739.465 MAD says the currency converter. And that is assuming that I can buy the package there and that I don't have to rely on my Dutch relatives to send it. What else does Google tell me? What is my average income if I live in Oujda? If I want to emigrate, perhaps nothing. I may have to quit my job. I may never have had a job and that is the reason why I am trying to go elsewhere. One site suggests: $1,310.00, that is 10,046.52 MAD. By now, I am resigned: I know that I have to stretch so far out of my area of competence that my illiteracy is almost unbearable. And yet what choice do I have? I do not find that kind of information on the "Naar Nederland" site. Ten thousand dirhams. I divide by 12 to get a sense of how much I made last month: 837.21 dirhams. No comment. I am pretty much broke. I hate to think about how much it will cost me to register for the exam but, if I believe the site, it is of the order of €350. Good grief.

What does it have to do with *Dirty Pretty Things*, with protecting instead of fearing the sea, you'll ask? When I look at the package that I have in front of me and that just put me in the red, from an ecological point of view, it seems rather excessively wasteful. I can't help noticing that it is twelve times as thick as it could be. I am not very good at whatever involves figures, but it is actually even worse than that. Consider this: the instruction manual is written in Dutch, French, English, Spanish, Portuguese, Turkish, Standard Arabic, Moroccan Arabic, Chinese, Russian, Indonesian and Thai. At least that's what the website tells me since I was not literate enough to even recognize some of the alphabets that appear on the cover. User friendly, we think. But then again. There are more languages in here than there are brands of yoghurt in a Western supermarket. The book is not addressed to me, it is addressed to migrants, to no one, to everyone. Each individual reader must just find the language that he or she understands and thereafter pretend that the rest does not exist.

When I was in a generous and optimistic mood (before reading the question), I marveled at the beauty of the unknown alphabets. I deciphered the two Arabic scripts and wondered about what they meant in terms of imagined migratory flows. I was enchanted and disgusted by my ignorance (so much to learn, how is it possible to not even know which alphabet this is?). I looked forward to so many "becoming-Dutch," becomings that would all be different and yet similarly difficult and exciting. Now I simply resent that I had to acquire 11 useless versions of the same tedious list of instructions. What is this doing to the planet? The set of DVDs is also redundant, ecologically incorrect. Four disks in one package. You only need one. But each of us (and that's assuming we do have a DVD player), has been forced to be loyal to commercial networks that impose standards we sometimes know nothing about. People and goods may cross borders but a PAL/SECAM or NTSC DVD will not. I have watched one DVD, over and over again. The others will never be taken out of their plastic case unless I find a way of giving them to someone who does not have the same standard(s) as I have. What a waste. Four disks, 12 languages, and each eager learner needs a fraction of this material. In the bookstore, there were piles of packages. And I am forgetting that the manufacturer of this test also included giving the discerning or prude or indifferent consumer a choice between the "edited" or "unedited" version.

Of course I know that I am going through a full-blown connection-crazy episode. I make no sense to anyone that I can recognize, certainly not the bizarrely dutchified self that I have invented for myself. When we cut a tree in the Amazon forest, does the sea rise in Amsterdam? I should calm down, I tell myself. I can't afford chaos theory anyway (I don't have that type of computer). There must be another way of "relating" (as in telling the tale)[22] of why I am so disturbed by the way in which the connection is made, in the documentary, between the new land, the sea and the migrant.

This is the point at which I want to cross-examine the documentary. I refuse the narrative because I am already, partly, integrated. Integrated enough not only to have my views on "Dutch culture" but to feel responsible for how we-they share it with the world. The "friendly" guide, I find myself arguing, is of course not "typically" Dutch and what she says is not dictated by some God of Dutch culture. Not to mention that I don't like the way she dresses. Even "the Government" as a whole is probably not to blame. What the documentary says is as anonymous as a stereotype and it would probably offend many Dutch citizens if they were given a chance to watch it. The Dutch, of course, are the victims of this sad joke. And they cannot even mourn the fact that a voice that speaks on their behalf represents them as an ecologically inhospitable and irresponsible people because why would they watch this DVD?

Yes they, we-they proudly mobilize technology against the sea.[23] And on the one hand, it makes sense, doesn't it? After all, who wants to relive the 1953 catastrophic flood that killed almost two thousand people and caused massive evacuations.[24] It is just that the emphasis on dikes, in the documentary, strikes me as reductive poetically and politically disturbing. If migrants are put off because they think that, once they arrive, they will have to live according to those stories, the Dutch are being sorely misrepresented. The relationship between land and water, between us and them (us migrants, them Dutch people, us Dutch people, them migrants-to-be) is so much more complicated than that. Dikes are not walls that contain the sea. They are permeable border zones where diversity thrives, where oyster, mussel farmers and ecologists argue against closure. Even if you are not an engineer or a water management expert, it is easy to understand that even the great Deltawerken projects are a compromise between opening and closing, protecting against the sea and letting the sea be the source of our civilization.

And that is the trouble with the film. The narrator obviously thinks that you talk differently to a migrant and to an engineer, as if the two categories were a mutually exclusive pair. One speaks simply and plainly to barbarians. Moreover, one erects borders between disciplines, so that fields of expertise do not overlap. As the result, the DVD film admits of no public space for a discussion between mussel farmers and ecologists, historians and geographers. The film is divided into impermeable chapters and the separation between history and geography enables the narrator to block the connection between two radically different stories about the relationship between the Dutch and the sea.

The present situation is narrated via this simplistic geographical lesson. Computer-generated images construct the country as a frighteningly vulnerable land that can only adopt a defensive stance against the invader. The section on history, however, gives a completely different image of the same country. There, in a very different chapter, the narrator turns to her, our, their past, and/or relays a tale of mastery and power. She tells us about how in the 17th century "such a small land" conquered oceans, and sailed as far afield as Suriname and Japan. Bits of films show magnificent ships and remind us of a time when the Netherlands were "rich and powerful." At that time, the threatening ocean was as "diffracting" as Glissant's contemporary Caribbean sea. The Dutch sailed from a tiny island that they saw as the center; they did not protect themselves from what surrounded them. But this is history, the documentary tells us. It was the Golden Age, now locked like a precious relic in the distant past; it turns the contemporary period into a fallen and disgraced version of this beautiful past.

Of course it is difficult to talk about Europe's past without raising rather thorny issues. The Golden Age, for example, glorified colonization and treated slavery as the norm. Just as Western governments now know how to use and abuse the discourse of sexual freedom, as Aydemir also discusses in this collection, they usually avoid confronting a generally accepted postcolonial and anti-colonialist paradigm. The film includes a scene that represents barely clad fictional slaves (that image is obviously not considered as controversial), and although the commentary does not explicitly condemn slavery or link it to the level of wealth and power that the Netherlands enjoyed at the time, it is clear that the reference to such a glorious past is slightly ambivalent. The message does not seem to be "we know about the sea, we have a history of mastery that we can share with the world," but rather, "we were once a powerful seafaring nation and now we are a small country under threat." The unexplored quality of the relationship between colonization and seafaring expertise leads to an ambiguous non-condemnation and relegation of the past as a whole, as if no distinction could be made. As a result, a centuries-old history of how the Dutch have successfully mastered the liquid element is consigned to history books, while geography is entrusted with the preferred ideological narrative of vulnerability and dikes. Isn't this enough to turn me into a perpetually melancholic migrant? I don't know if I must mourn the absence of my newly acquired past either as a glorious but irrevocably lost heritage or as a disturbing legacy of violent practices that might well have victimized my own ancestors. In doubt, I could become melancholically schizophrenic and mourn both at the same time.

And yet, if the Dutch have a contemporary poetics and politics of water, it is surely more of the order of constant negotiation and intimate cohabitation than a clear inside-outside model. Before you land (the documentary simply assumes that your first encounter with the Netherlands will take place at Schiphol airport), you may already have been struck by the intricate network of elements, inland water, rivers, canals, fields and housing estates constantly encroaching upon each other. The Delta project is a masterpiece of negotiations between many different interests and competing forces. The Dutch know about canals, dredging, bridges, dikes, locks and the social control of resources. Water links science and industry, literature and painting, arts and politics. Amsterdam is "amphibious," as the author of *Building on Water* puts it.[25] When I walk around in Amsterdam, I marvel: we the Dutch seem to be building on or rather in water, anchoring houses as if they were crooked little boats. We build on polders as if we never believed in the myth of natural borders and the polders have since then leaked into our brains: we talk about our proverbial "Polder mentaliteit." We have played with dunes and islands, changing the shape of the shore, calculating how much water must go in or go out for both mussels and humans to cohabit. In the old days, we used to brew beer with the water from the canals, and now a constant ballet of pretty boats explain, in three or four languages, how the locks work and why we, the rich, stopped using the water when it became filthy. The poor, of course, continued to brew canal beer. Chamoiseau's fears in *Biblique des derniers gestes* are in the past as well as in our future. We live with the water, and if there is, one day, another disaster, it will not be a clash of civilizations, and the dead will have no opinion whatsoever about gay men kissing in the flooded meadows.

The test will not stop anyone. It will just make it more difficult, more discouraging, more humiliating, more time-consuming to cross the national border. And once we have crossed the borders, we will be more difficult, more discouraged, more humiliated and we will have less time to take the long, long time that people need to translate themselves in relation to and along with others. Not matter how well or how poorly we do on the test, we will probably feel slightly ashamed because we will have cheated: the goal is to prove that we are dumb enough to memorize one hundred questions by heart and we are obviously not that dumb since we have understood that the last thing we want to do is try to use intelligence to deal with this exercise. This is a performative ritual, not an examination. Everyone knows very well that the new dike that has been erected between the bad immigrant and the Netherlands is just as permeable as all the other water projects. But when I picked up the phone to start this absurd computer game, I knew that I was solemnly declaring: I do hereby recognize that I have been warned, that I am not welcome, and that I will not be helped by the Dutch. And although I may be dumb enough to learn one hundred questions and answers by heart, I am not dumb enough not to understand that a promise was made by the ritual: if anything bad happens to me, I and only I am accountable. And so, before I even meet my first Dutch person, I mourn the impossible friendship, the forbidden love that I could have had for the Dutch, because of course, as of now, all those, bless them, who will welcome me, who will help me, who will give me time and space and a broodje when I clumsily ask for one, all those people are really not Dutch because they do not correspond to what I have been taught and told to repeat about the Dutch. So I guess that as an immigrant, I have been lucky: by that standard, I have met very, very few Dutch people indeed. But if I were Dutch, and of course I am (in a certain way), I think that I would, at the very least, want to know what those forces emanating from my democratically elected government have done to me. And I would like to have a chance to be asked: Wilt u dat? Kunt u dat?

NOTES

1. See http://www.thiememeulenhoff.nl/documentenservice/pagina.asp?pagkey=53767 (accessed November 2007).

2. The phrase "Immigratie en Naturalisatie Dienst" is linked to http://www.immigratiedienst.nl/nl/index.asp (accessed November 2007).

3. The end of the documentary shows a migrant taking the test. Seated in front of a member of the Dutch embassy but separated by a thick pane of glass, she must pick up a phone and answer the questions that a computer will ask. The other human is only there to verify that she is not cheating. The glass partition and the telephone evoke images of prison parlors, except that there is no communication between the migrant and the employee, not even an obstructed form of dialogue.

4. See Gregory Crouch, "A Candid Dutch Film May Be Too Scary for Immigrants," *New York Times*, March 16, 2006, http://www.nytimes.com/2006/03/16/international/europe/16dutch.html (accessed June 2009); "Dutch Immigration Kit Offers a Revealing View," *Herald Tribune*, March 17, 2006, http://www.iht.com/articles/2006/03/16/news/dutch-5852942.php (accessed November 2007); Khaled Diab, "Testing Times: Across Europe, the Real Challenge When Dealing with Minority Groups Is Not Integration but Marginalisation," *Guardian*, June 7, 2007, http://www.guardian.co.uk/commentisfree/2007/jun/07/testingtimes (accessed June 2009); Jean-Pierre Stroobants, "Réalisme néerlandais et immigration," *Le Monde*, May 26, 2009, http://lemonde.fr; Nicola Smith. "Holland Launches the Immigrant Quiz," *The Sunday Times*, March 12, 2006, http://www.timesonline.co.uk/tol/news/world/article740148.ece (accessed November 2007).

5. See Eric Fassin, "Going Dutch," *Bidoun* 10 *Technology* (Spring 2007), http://www.bidoun.com/issues/issue_10/05a_all.html (accessed June 2009) and "La Démocratie sexuelle et le conflit des civilisations," *Multitudes* 26 (Fall 2006), http://multitudes.samizdat.net/spip.php?article2678 (accessed November 2007) and Judith Butler, "Politics, Torture, and Secular Time," *Frames of War* (London: Verso, 2009), 101–32.

6. Sedgwick defines paranoid readings as "anticipatory," generating a "unidirectionally future-oriented vigilance" (130). But she also points out that paranoia is "reflexive and mimetic" (131) and that it is "contagious tropism" (131). If I admit, here, that I suspect my own reading of being paranoid, it is to suggest that the documentary may create a very specific type of paranoid reader whose reaction ends up serving the ultimate agenda of the test: the goal is ultimately to include or exclude (me).

7. There is also an audio CD where we can listen to the list of questions and answers (these are in Dutch), and a third booklet explains where to register for the test, how to practice, how to take it. There is also a website linked to the equivalent of the NIS.

8. In which a woman weaves a tale of survival during the long night that she spends fighting the hurricane that is destroying her residence (Daniel Maximin, *L'Ile et une nuit* [Paris: Seuil, 1995]).

9. See the press release issued on November 30, 2005, by the Royal Netherlands Embassy in Washington ("Dutch Ambassador Visits New Orleans"), http://www .netherlands-embassy.org/article.asp?articleref=AR00001808EN(accessedNovember 2007). See also Martin Enserink and John Bohannon, "Hurricane Katrina: Questioning the 'Dutch Solution,'" *Science* 309, no. 5742 (September 16, 2005): 1809, http://www.sciencemag.org/cgi/content/full/309/5742/1809 (accessed November 2007).

10. See Patricia Pisters' analysis of Alejandro González Inarritu's *Babel* (2006) as a "mosaic film": "In *The Making of Babel* on the DVD of the film, Inarritu says he has always been fascinated by the air that we all breathe and travel through, that invisible entity that we all share. With this film he wants to show that although we are in different spaces and different time zones there is a literal cross-continental connection. Not only the same air that we breathe connects us, but also a Japanese gun, given as a present to a Berber shepherd in Morocco can have enormous consequences for people in Morocco, Mexico and the USA" ("The Mosaic Film: An Affair of Everyone: Becoming-Minoritarian in Transnational Media Culture," forthcoming).

11. See Anjali Prabhu, *Hybridity: Limits, Transformations, Prospects* (New York: SUNY, 2007) or Stephan Palmié, "Creolization and Its Discontents," *The Annual Review of Anthropology* 35 (2006): 433–56, http://www.annualreviews.org/journal/anthro (accessed November 2007).

12. "Est-ce que j'ai déjà parlé de mon opposition entre la Méditerranée et les Antilles? Je crois que la Méditerranée, c'est là sa grandeur historique, est une mer qui concentre. Ce n'est pas par hasard que les plus grandes religions monothéistes sont nées là, autour de la Méditerranée. C'est une mer de l'un. C'est la mer du gouffre fondamental, de l'abîme intérieur qui détermine toutes les philosophies de l'un" [Have I already mentioned the contrast I make between the Mediterranean and the Caribbean sea? I think that the Mediterranean, and its historic greatness, is a concentrating sea. It is not by chance that the greatest monotheistic religions emerged around the Mediterranean. It is the sea of the One, the sea of the fundamental chasm, of the internal abyss that inhabits all the philosophies of the One] (Leupin 2006).

13. Edouard Glissant, *Introduction à une poétique du divers* (Paris: Gallimard, 1996), 14.

14. Glissant, *Introduction.*

15. Alexandre Leupin, "Entretien inédit avec Edouard Glissant: 6. "Se séparer du lieu de l'énonciation pour y revenir," *Mondesfrancophones.com: Revue mondiale des francophonies* (2006) http://www.mondesfrancophones.com/interviews (accessed November 2007).

16. Leupin, "Entretien inédit."

17. Glissant, *Introduction*, 14.

18. Richard Watts, "'Toutes ces eaux!': Ecology and Empire in Patrick Chamoiseau's *Biblique des derniers gestes*," *MLN* 118, no. 4 (2003): 903.

19. Watts himself thanks Peter Hallward in a footnote for bringing this to his attention (see Peter Hallward, *Absolutely Postcolonial: Writing between the Singular and the Specific* [Manchester, UK: Manchester University Press, 2001]).

20. Watts, "'Toutes ces eaux!,'" 905.

21. Patrick Chamoiseau, *Biblique des derniers gestes* (Paris: Gallimard, 2001), 215, and quoted in Watts "'Toutes ces eaux!,'" 905.

22. See Glissant's unpacking of "Relation" as what is linked, relayed and narrated ("relié, relayé and relaté" in French [Glissant's *Poetics of Relation*, trans. Betsy Wing (Ann Arbor: University of Michigan Press, 1997), 169–79]).

23. The documentary teaches us the word "dijk" and also mentions what is known as "Deltawerken" [delta project], a large-scale water management project started after the 1953 catastrophic flood. It involved building massive dams to close off the mouths of rivers (Philips and Oester Dams) and, later, the construction of a gate that would both protect Zeeland against storms and remain partially open to preserve the natural environment of the sea-water estuary. See Harry Lintsen, "Two Centuries of Central Water Management in the Netherlands," *Technology and Culture* 43, no. 3 (2002): 549–68.

24. In January 1953, a flood killed almost 2,000 people, destroyed more than 4,000 houses and caused massive evacuations. Hectares upon hectares of fertile areas were flooded with salt water and livestock was swept away. Miles and miles of the great dikes that were supposed to protect the land were damaged. See Kees Slager, *De ramp: Een Reconstructie van de Watersnood van 1953* (Goes: De Koperen Tuin, 2003) and Herman Gerritsen, "What Happened in 1953? The Big Flood in the Netherlands in Retrospect," *Philosophical Transactions* 363, no. 1831 (June 15, 2005): 1271–91.

25. Salvatore Ciriacono, *Building on Water: Venice, Holland and the Construction of the European Landscape in Early Modern Times*, trans. Jeremy Scott (Oxford: Berghahn Books, 2006), 157.

BIBLIOGRAPHY

Butler, Judith. "Politics, Torture, and Secular Time." In *Frames of War.* London: Verso, 2009, 101–31.

Chamoiseau, Patrick. *Biblique des derniers gestes*. Paris: Gallimard, 2001.

Ciriacono, Salvatore. Building on Water. Venice, Holland and the Construction of the European Landscape in Early Modern Times. Trans. Jeremy Scott. Oxford and New York: Berghahn books, 2006.

Crouch, Gregory. "A Candid Dutch Film May Be Too Scary for Immigrants." *New York Times*, March 16, 2006. http://www.nytimes.com/2006/03/16/international/europe/16dutch.html. Accessed June 2009.

———. "Dutch Immigration Kit Offers a Revealing View." *Herald Tribune*, March 17, 2006. http://www.iht.com/articles/2006/03/16/news/dutch-5852942.php. Accessed November 2007.

Diab, Khaled. "Testing Times: Across Europe, the Real Challenge When Dealing with Minority Groups Is Not Integration but Marginalisation." *Guardian*, June 7, 2007. http://www.guardian.co.uk/commentisfree/2007/jun/07/testingtimes. Accessed June 2009.

Enserink, Martin, and John Bohannon. "Hurricane Katrina: Questioning the 'Dutch Solution.'" *Science* 309, no. 5742 (September 16, 2005): 1809. http://www.sciencemag.org/cgi/content/full/309/5742/1809. Accessed November 2007.

Fassin, Eric. "Going Dutch," *Bidoun* 10 *Technology* (Spring 2007), http://www.bidoun.com/issues/issue_10/05a_all.html. Accessed June 2009.

———. "La Démocratie sexuelle et le conflit des civilisations." *Multitudes* 26 (Fall 2006). http://multitudes.samizdat.net/spip.php?article2678. Accessed November 2007.

Gerritsen, Herman. "What Happened in 1953? The Big Flood in the Netherlands in Retrospect." *Philosophical Transactions* 363, no. 1831 (June 15, 2005): 1271–91.

Glissant, Edouard. *Introduction à une poétique du divers*. Paris: Gallimard, 1996.

———. *Poetics of Relation*. Translated by Betsy Wing. Ann Arbor: University of Michigan Press, 1997.

Hallward, Peter. *Absolutely Postcolonial: Writing between the Singular and the Specific*. Manchester, UK: Manchester University Press, 2001.

Leupin, Alexandre. "Entretien inédit avec Edouard Glissant: 6. "Se séparer du lieu de l'énonciation pour y revenir," *Mondesfrancophones.com: revue mondiale des francophonies* (2006). http://www.mondesfrancophones.com/interviews. Accessed November 2007.

Lintsen, Harry. "Two Centuries of Central Water Management in the Netherlands." *Technology and Culture* 43, no. 3 (2002): 549–68.

Maximin, Daniel. *L'Ile et une nuit*. Paris: Seuil, 1995.

Palmié, Stephan. "Creolization and Its Discontents." *The Annual Review of Anthropology* 35 (2006): 433–56. http://www.annualreviews.org/journal/anthro. Accessed November 2007.

Prabhu, Anjali. *Hybridity: Limits, Transformations, Prospects*. New York: SUNY, 2007.

Sedgwick, Eve. *Touching Feeling: Affect, Pedagogy, Performativity*. Durham, NC: Duke University Press, 2003.

Slager, Kees. *De ramp: Een Reconstructie van de Watersnood van 1953*. Goes: De Koperen Tuin, 2003.

Smith, Nicola. "Holland Launches the Immigrant Quiz." *The Sunday Times*, March 12, 2006. http://www.timesonline.co.uk/tol/news/world/article740148.ece. Accessed November 2007.

Stroobants, Jean-Pierre. "Réalisme néerlandais et immigration." *Le Monde*, May 26, 2009. http://www.lemonde.fr.

Watts, Richard. "'Toutes ces eaux!': Ecology and Empire in Patrick Chamoiseau's *Biblique des derniers gestes*," *MLN* 118, no. 4 (2003): 895–910.

Chapter Twelve

Unlike(ly) Home(s)

"Self-orientalisation" and Irony in Moroccan Diasporic Literature

Ieme van der Poel

In one of the essays in *Maghrébins en France: émigrés ou immigrés?*, a work that presents the state of knowledge on the sociology of immigration in the 1980s, A. Zahraoui questions how the way in which Maghrebian minorities settled in France relates to their country of origin.[1] First-generation immigrants left for France for the sole reason of improving the economic condition in their native communities; the only reason to leave was to return. For families immigrating in later years, the question of returning to the country of their ancestors has become less pronounced, but it has not disappeared altogether. In Zahraoui's own words:

> The question of returning (which, furthermore, seems more like *a departure* for children born in Europe) can be put on the back-burner, even though it is never absent from the *mental image* people have of their future.[2]

Having lost its material and concrete character, the return is now something that is left unsaid, a figment of the imagination even, just like the place from which the former immigrants came. As far as the texts that form the subject of this analysis are concerned, namely Moroccan diasporic literature, this consequently poses the question of how Morocco is portrayed as an imaginary homeland in the texts produced by Moroccan immigrant writers belonging to the second generation.

Family reunification has turned Maghrebian migration to Europe into a social and even political phenomenon, but it has also had a major impact on literary production in the four countries where the largest minority populations of Moroccan origin nowadays live: France, the Netherlands, Belgium, and Spain. Since the 1990s, family reunification is the force that drives migrant literature not only written in French or Spanish—European languages inherited from the colonial era and "bi-localised" in the sense that they are still spoken and written in Morocco today. It also drives that written in Dutch, Catalan, and even Italian.[3] Authors of this literature are second- or third-generation immigrants who have settled in Europe and have no thoughts about possibly returning to Morocco in any real, material sense. But that does not prevent them from revisiting the North African country where they have their roots in their works of fiction.

This essay proposes to determine the way in which the country of origin continues to haunt this relatively young literature, despite the vehemence with which its authors insist—and rightly so—that their works are indeed part of the literary history of the European country they now consider their own, in the language of which they have chosen to write.[4] As Leslie Adelson argues in relation to the German literature of migration, it is not a meeting of two cultures but an evolution that is taking place within European culture itself which affects our view of the relationship between past and present. Therefore, instead of trying to find "traces of 'home'" in diasporic writing, critics must consider these texts as "imaginary sites where cultural orientation is being radically rethought."[5] My aim is to substantiate Adelson's assertion by considering the narrative modes and literary devices used to this effect. But unlike Adelson, I will not dismiss the idea of "home" altogether. Given the overall presence of certain aspects of Morocco or "Moroccan-ness" in these novels, I will, instead, consider these as part of an imaginative geography, one in which the old clichés about the "Orient" are recycled, turned upside down, and disrupted. This leads me to the untranslatable notion of the French *le pays dépaysé*, of a home which has become unlike home and is both uncanny and enchanting.[6]

I have chosen two novels published during the past decade to illustrate my thesis. *L'últim patriarca* (2008), written in Catalan by Najat el Hachmi; and *Paravion* (2003), written in Dutch by Hafid Bouazza. I will compare these two texts with a third novel, *Au pays* (2009), by Tahar Ben Jelloun, a well-known author who, although he is part of the Moroccan Diaspora, also belongs to the first generation of immigrants. Furthermore, and in contrast to El Hachmi and Bouazza, Ben Jelloun's novels are written in French and read on both sides of the Mediterranean.

ORIENTALISM AND "SELF-ORIENTALISATION"

The question of the portrayal of Morocco and "Moroccan-ness" in texts aimed mainly at a European readership also poses the question of orientalism or, perhaps more precisely, of a particular type of "self-orientalisation."

Here, one may recall the film *The Secret of the Grain* (2007) by Abdellatif Kechiche in which the heroine, a young woman from Marseilles who is fully integrated into French culture, performs a belly dance in the purest oriental style in order to save her family's restaurant. In *Minnares van de duivel* [The devil's lover] (2002) by Naima El Bezaz, a novel written in Dutch in which the action takes place in Morocco, each chapter's heading is a verse from the Koran.[7] Moreover, as often happens in contemporary Euro-Moroccan literature, El Bezaz's text is peppered with Arabic words which are explained in a small glossary at the end.

At first glance, such attempts at self-exotisation may recall the spirit of the "ethnographic" literature of the colonial era in which the subaltern, following the example of the colonial novel, emphasised the picturesque and exotic aspects of his or her daily life to please a European readership, while at the same time trying to "explain" the Maghreb, indeed the Orient, to occidental readers. Today's postcolonial writers, too, tend at times to lapse into orientalist clichés in order to satisfy the expectations of a European public. A case in point is presented by the writing of Morocco's most famous author, Tahar Ben Jelloun. In spite of being extremely successful abroad, his writings provoke a certain uneasiness among the Moroccan public.[8] But as Ulrich Johannes Beil argues in an article entitled "Against exotism," it is not always a question of literary conformism in the colonialist vein.[9]

What initially appears as a form of submission to the tastes and feelings—not to say prejudices—of a European readership, may also conceal a strategic plan, a gesture of resistance. The above-mentioned belly dance scene in *The Secret of the Grain* illustrates this wonderfully, as the lascivious performance by the heroine is far from being an act of submission. The dancer "orientalises" herself in order to achieve a purely commercial goal: to make the customers of her family's newly opened restaurant forget that the traditional Maghrebian food they were expecting (couscous and mullet) has not yet been served. As a replacement for the couscous she "serves" them a belly dance, thus impersonating yet another icon of Maghrebian culture: the oriental dancer.[10] According to Anthony Shay and Barbara Sellers-Young, this kind of intercultural performance is quite common among belly dancers in the Middle East and the West: "Individuals native to a dance's place of origin utilize orientalist elements, often originating in Western sources, in their performances in both the East and the West, for they constitute a form of globalism uneasily circulating between the East and the West."[11]

It is worth noting that Shay and Sellers-Young stress the ambiguity involved in recycling orientalist stereotypes. So does Frank F. Scherer, who proposes to expand the notion of "orientalism" put forward by Said in order to include the different ways in which this concept has been "received, accepted, modified, rejected, or otherwise challenged" by the "Orientals" themselves.[12] It is thus possible to go beyond the single meaning of orientalism, as elaborated in *Orientalism*, to reach a plural and *dialectic* orientalism.[13] Without ignoring the risk of the double-sidedness of such a self-orientalizing discourse, Scherer draws attention to the fact that self-essentialization may also result in a "counterdiscourse to Euro-American orientalist positions," thus changing it into an active performative (Scherer, 163). The idea of an "inverted" and dialectic orientalism will serve as a point of departure in my analysis of the three texts in this essay. If my hypothesis proves to be true, then this narrative strategy will not only allow the authors concerned to shed traditional stereotypes, but will also breathe new life into worn-out exotic clichés.

BEN JELLOUN: THE RETURN TO THE OLD VILLAGE

Of the three novels I am interested in here, *A Palace in the Old Village* by Tahar Ben Jelloun is the only one that actually describes the definitive return to the country of origin.[14] The protagonist is an immigrant worker who has just taken retirement. Belonging to a generation for whom migration is justified only by work (or, at a pinch, by unemployment, which is its counterpart), he is shattered by his new retired status.[15] However, the realisation of his longstanding dream of returning to the old village—an action that, for men of his generation, represents the *sine qua non* of the initial departure—clashes with the inevitable fact that the country of his ancestors has also changed. And his own offspring, which now constitutes the part of the family that is most important and dear to him, has taken root in France and has become Frenchified. Although the ancestors' country initially seduces them with its strangeness or exotism, the children quickly become disappointed as soon as they discover there is none of the entertainment they were used to in France:

> Les paysages leur paraissent étranges, ils s'attendent à voir surgir un héros de *La Guerre des étoiles* une épée laser entre les mains. Ils attendent que quelque chose se passe. Rien, n'absolument rien n'arrive. Seuls les pierres, les figuiers de Barbarie et des chiens errants dans une chaleur suffocante.

> The landscapes appear strange to them. They expect to see a hero from *Star Wars* appear suddenly holding a lightsabre with both hands. They wait for something to happen. Nothing, absolutely nothing, happens; only rocks, Barbary fig trees and stray dogs in the suffocating heat.[16]

As a presentation of the problems of the first generation of immigrants, *A Palace in the Old Village* can be read as the sequel to *Solitary Confinement*, published 35 years earlier, in 1976. In this narrative, Ben Jelloun describes the alienation and sexual misery that was common among lonely Moroccan men when, still young, they arrived in Europe in the 1960s. *A Palace in the Old Village*, in which the action takes place in the 2000s, depicts the confusion and distress of this first generation of immigrants at the moment when they are approaching death: "This solitude smelt of medicine mixed with a stench from somewhere else, something that prowls around this population in which no one had envisaged how they would withdraw from life" (*Au pays*, 78). As the years go by, indifference towards the newcomers has been replaced by suspicion and hate.

Although Ben Jelloun's two novels reveal a comparable social commitment, *A Palace* differs from *Solitary Confinement* in that it is written in a more conventional mode.[17] It is for a large part a third-person narrative in which the main focalizer is Mohamed, an old, illiterate Moroccan. But this character's perception of the world—his psyche, if you like—is heavily "influenced" by that of the external, third-person narrator, who seems to be driven by the desire to depict the problem of Maghrebian immigration in its totality. In this respect, Ben Jelloun's novel illustrates the concept of the "impossible ubiquity" put forward by the sociologist Abdelmalek Sayad, a specialist in Maghrebian migration:

> So as not to be pure "absence," migration calls on a form of impossible "ubiquity," a way of being that affects the conditions of the absence it causes [. . .] only being partially absent from where one is absent [. . .] and, correlatively, not being totally present where one is present [. . .]—it is the condition or the paradox of the immigrant.[18]

But if Sayad is here giving a dynamic depiction of the migratory phenomenon, this type of transfer between the host country and the adopted country is absent from Ben Jelloun's novel. There are two very distinct worlds: Morocco, the retired immigrant worker's native country, emerges in his solitary daydreaming, while France comes up when he is talking with other immigrants or walking around the gloomy suburb, the setting for his wanderings.

The novel is a comprehensive and well-informed social and political critique of both France and Morocco. But from the reader's point of view it is sometimes difficult to associate these informed commentaries with the character of an old, illiterate immigrant worker. Moreover, they give the work an explanatory and didactic character that is reminiscent of the ethnographic novel of the early twentieth century.[19] Marc Gontard describes this as "hesitation between interiority and exteriority, authenticity and exotism."[20] *A Palace in the Old Village* therefore gives a perfect illustration of the impossible ubiquity idea but without the work exceeding, transcending or deconstructing what we have learned from sociology. In this respect the final pages of the novel where the narrative adopts the register of the marvellous real, bring about a notable change. In the description of the old man's very last days on earth, where Maraboutism and Christian passion come together, Ben Jelloun's work finally succeeds in bringing about a synthesis of all the contradictions of the immigrant's fate and to turn Sayad's dynamics of an impossible ubiquity into fiction.

BOUAZZA AND EL HACHMI: SPIRIT OF BURLESQUE AND IRONY

Au pays by Ben Jelloun acts as a foil for the analysis of two texts written by authors of Moroccan origin who at the same time consider themselves new Europeans, as described above. *Paravion*, written by the Dutch author Hafid Bouazza, was published in 2002 and won the *Gouden Uil* [Golden Owl], one of the most prestigious literary prizes in the Netherlands and Flanders. The action takes place in two fictitious countries: Morea and Paravion.[21] The latter country, which is described as being very similar to the City of Amsterdam, appears in the text as a mirage inciting Moreans to take to their flying carpets and travel northwards. The text presents the emigrational experience as a modern-day chivalric novel in which a great deal belongs to the realm of fantasy and magical realism.

Najat El Hachmi also belongs to the second generation of Moroccan migrants. Her family, like that of Bouazza, is originally from the Rif. *The Last Patriarch*, her first novel, was published in Catalan by Planeta, Barcelona, in 2008, and won the Ramon Llull literary prize.[22] The book consists of two parts, the first being made up of the story of Mimoun, the last patriarch to whom the title refers. The account of his departure from his village in the Rif to go and work in Spain, or, more precisely, in Catalonia, is given, or organised and assembled, by an external narrator who, as we gradually find out, is the patriarch's only daughter. The second part of the novel tells the story of the latter's successful integration into Catalan society, which at the same time marks the total disintegration of the last patriarch and his authority. It is the presence of this falsely naïve narrator that gives *The Last Patriarch* its burlesque and caustic spirit.

Although the world of immigrants evoked by Bouazza is a lot more fanciful than the rural Moroccan and Spanish city environments depicted by El Hachmi, the two narratives are equivalent in terms of extravagance and originality. Self-referentiality and apostrophes are frequent, which confirms a literariness that manifests itself from the first pages onwards; and the beginnings of these two novels, which reference a much older European literary tradition, are strongly similar. While the first words of El Hachmi's text refer to the epic tradition as well as biblical texts, albeit in the mood of parody, Bouazza is inspired by medieval Dutch literature.[23] Used ironically, this medieval literature is conspicuous in *Paravion* and even involves the use of some quite unusual vocabulary. Using a clever mix of archaic words, neologisms and terms borrowed from medieval Dutch, the author has created a writing style that is both archaic and original, and in this way—and this to me is key—the text appears to underline once again that it is part of Dutch literature—in short it announces its Dutchness.[24]

This desire to become an integral part of the local literary tradition is also very present in El Hachmi's novel, but it reveals itself in a different way. She does not explicitly appropriate the "other" language through the voice of her character in order to try to carve out a place in her country's national literary history; rather, she explicitly refers to other contemporary Catalan authors, or more precisely, the works and person of Mercè Rodoreda, the *grande dame* of Catalan literature. I will return to this metatextual link in my conclusion.[25]

Let us first return to the very particular way in which these young authors have succeeded in incorporating Morocco into Europe and Europe into Morocco in their respective novels. In Bouazza's work, the immigration country, Paravion, bursts into Morea, the native country, in a recurring mirage. Its apparitions are more or less punctuated by the coming of the postman, who, by delivering the pale blue airmail envelopes (*par avion*) to which the adopted country owes its name, creates the link between the two places:

> De postbode verliet het dorp. Omdat iedereen siësta hield, zag niemand dat elke middag in de mirage Paravion zichtbaar werd: grijze koepels van oude kerken, verweerde kerktorens waar klokken glansden maar zwegen, hoewel ze ooit lang en welluidend moesten hebben geklonken [. . .] overal in dit zalige oord ademde de rijke lommer, een groen antwoord op het katoen dat aan de hemel groeide. De postbode huiverde door de mirage alsof hij door wapperende sluiergewaden reed [. . .] knikte de poortwachters toe en betrad Paravion.

> The postman left the village. As everyone was taking their siesta, no one noticed that every afternoon Paravion revealed itself in a mirage: the grey domes of the old churches, the weather-beaten church towers in which once gleaming bells had now been reduced to silence, though their ring must have formerly been melodious and deep [. . .] undulating greenery would breathe everywhere in this blessed place, a green retort to the cotton that grew in the sky. The postman crossed the mirage in a shiver as if moving among veils floating in the wind. He greeted the gatekeepers and entered Paravion.[26]

But it also happens that the inhabitants of the North African village are transplanted, as if by a miracle, to this Paravion that impels them to dream so much. This happens in particular to the protagonist, Baba Baloek. While absorbed in his frolicking with the nymph Quadrige, he surreptitiously goes from a Mediterranean Arcadia to a garden landscape, a paradise which in its own way closely resembles Amsterdam's Vondelpark on a beautiful summer's day.

Impossible ubiquity can also be achieved using metaphoric style rather than drawing on the substance of magical realism. This can be seen in the character of the immigrant carter who, suffering from deafness, perceives his new Dutch environment using synaesthesia:

> Hij bewoog zich gelukkig voort in zijn gewatteerde doofheid. Het was niet zo dat hij niets hoorde, maar wat hij hoorde hield niet altijd verband met wat hij zag. Zijn gehoor was nog vervuld van geluiden van voorheen: vrouwengelach, gerinkel van armbanden, het schokken en ratelen van de kar.

> He strolled around joyously in his muffled deafness. Although he was not totally deaf, the sounds he perceived were not automatically linked to the images his eyes registered. His ears were still filled by noises of old: women's laughter, the rattling of bracelets, and the jolts and squeaking of the cart.[27]

Finally, and less surprisingly, perhaps, there is the satellite dish that brings Morocco into Europe by transmitting images of the country to customers at a Moroccan café in Amsterdam. Grouped around the television set, the café regulars watch a report on the drama of drowned stowaways that is unfolding on the same shores they left behind. It is thus via the media that the first wave of immigrants is confronted with the victims of the second. The literary text here deftly illustrates Arif Dirlik's argument that "the thirld world, far from being confined to its assigned space, has penetrated the inner sanctum of the first world in the process of being 'third-worlded'—arousing, inciting, and affiliating with the subordinated others in the first world."[28]

But at the same time, the idea of a possible "affiliation" between subalterns of the third and the first world is deconstructed. Instead of pitying the sad fate of these victims, to "affiliate" with them, as Dirlik has it, the character on whom the narrative focuses here and who in his former life was a fisherman in this same area, scrutinises these images with the sole hope of seeing himself on the screen (*Paravion*, 143). Yet the idea that the periphery has now positioned itself at the very heart of Europe, stays intact. Or, as Ahmed Boubeker argues in his very insightful essay on Sayad's work: "Leaving its peripheral position with regard to the French [or, in this case, Dutch] society, immigration now positions itself at the centre of current developments as a telltale sign of social, political and cultural changes and a foreclosure in a history of misunderstandings." A similar stance is taken by anthropologist Caroline B. Brettell: "The act of migration brings populations of different backgrounds into contact with one another and hence creates boundaries. It is the negotiation across such boundaries, themselves shifting, that is at the heart of ethnicity and the construction of migrant identities."[29]

As the satellite dish example shows, in *Paravion*, the interpenetration of the two worlds is above all tied to images, to the visual world. In El Hachmi's text, however, this interpenetration, which more often resembles a shock or confrontation, is dominated by smells. The first thing the young narrator observes on arriving in Catalonia is that it is full of an execrable odour: "And everywhere this stench. A stench that had started in the town, in the canton, in the department, in the entire country" (*LP*, 179–80). There is only one way of getting rid of this stench, namely using the aromas given off by Moroccan food: "The apartment was no longer the same when we returned. Instead, it was full of the smell of the country we had left, as my mother had done the cooking" (*LP*, 183).

Later, when the heroine has no doubt that Spain is her true country, her attachment to her ancestors' country seems to boil down to the aromas of the country she left: "In spite of everything, I wanted to return to this far-off place that was no longer my home but which was home to the scents of my childhood" (*LP*, 301). While the North-African aromas are not specified beyond being linked "to cooking," they are totally different from the almost general stench covering Spain—the vile smell coming off pigs. This animal becomes something of a symbol of Spain in Najat El Hachmi's writing and, in the immigrants' view, turns the host country into a huge pigsty: the tanneries polluting its rivers; the excessive consumption of pork and pork charcuterie making its people ugly, men as well as women; the innumerable animal carcasses polluting its towns and cities and the countryside around about.

But if the hyperbolic presence of the pig at first reinforces the burlesque character of the narrative, the fact that this presence is used in the context of Maghrebian immigration is not without significance. Firstly, it draws our attention to Morocco (without naming it specifically) as a country that smells good because there are no pigs there. Then, by launching into the (perhaps unpredictable) discourse about pigs, the narrator recalls another discourse that is more real: the incriminations (within a certain European and xenophobic context) in relation to halal meat and the smells spread by exotic cooking—Maghrebian cooking, in fact. This is explicit in Ben Jelloun's text where the protagonist, in a bid to be noticed as little as possible in order to avoid racism, advises his wife "not to cook with our spices that give off disturbing odours" (*AP*, 69).

THE ROLE OF IRONY

The latter comparison draws our attention to the important role of ellipsis and irony in El Hachmi's text. A striking exemple of this can be found in the passage where the narrator alludes to the "strange disappearances" of young Moroccan immigrant girls from her classroom when school starts again after the long summer break (*LP*, 296). Another example is provided by the following description of domestic violence: "We [the narrator and her two class mates] had all witnessed strange and extraordinary things at home: like flying plates or glasses" (*LP*, 299).

At first sight, the narrator in "orientalising" a sordid reality which is the opposite of a *Thousand and One Nights*–tale, takes up a recognizably western discourse on "Orientals." The strength of these passages is that the subaltern narrator takes as true her own words which are subsequently deconstructed by the way in which they are presented by the author.[30] In this particular case, the role of irony is all the more interesting as it targets both Spanish and Moroccan societies. Spanish society is criticised between the lines for closing its eyes to certain abuses taking place in it, while the Moroccan government is under attack for tolerating the continued existence of arranged marriages. And ultimately El Hachmi's criticism is also aimed at those consenting Moroccan mothers who do nothing to oppose this sudden interruption in their daughters' schooling. Backing both horses, the narrator here clearly does more than simply repeat a Western discourse on "Orientals" (described by Bhabha as "almost the same, *but not entirely*"[31]). He is an interlocutor who, thanks to the double perspective that results from being both inside and outside the two societies at stake here, makes use of this ubiquity (absence that is also presence) in order to judge them better.[32] Fiction makes it possible to bridge the gap that exists between here and there. It is the presence of this deceptively naïve narrator that gives El Hachmi's narrative its unity and removes all ambiguity in terms of the target of her irony. Her ethical judgement is crystal clear.

This brings us to *Paravion,* Hafid Bouazza's novel where irony as a discursive strategy is not always unambiguous. As Linda Hutcheon confirms in *Irony's Edge*:

> Irony's intimacy with the dominant discourses it contests—it uses their very language as it is said—is its strength [. . .]. But intimacy can also be seen as complicity: one is always "vulnerable to being reassimilated to the modes of power and knowledge which one seeks to disrupt.[33]

It can be argued, therefore, that irony forms the textual or stylistic counterpart of the equally double-sided narrative strategy of self-orientalisation or self-exotisation. The ambiguity of these strategies is also their great strength.

The risk that irony runs of being misread, and therefore understood wrongly, is illustrated by the response to Bouazza's book when it first came out in 2004. Instead of making the distinction between the two Bouazzas, the novelist and the intellectual, critics only saw in this work the affirmation of Bouazzas ideas on Islam that he had expressed shortly before in press articles.[34] But it is wrong to want to reduce a novel as complex as *Paravion* to a simple refutation of Islam.

In reality, Bouazza's irony, like El Hachmi's, functions as a double-edged discursive strategy that targets, in equal measure, the hypocrisy of Moroccan fundamentalists, and the fears, as unfounded as they are irrational, of Low Countries' islamophobes. An example of this is the passage in which a convoy of Moroccan immigrants sitting comfortably on their flying carpets approach the region, recognising as soon as they see them its innumerable minarets:

> Dit is Paravion—zie, zijn minaretten zijn al zichtbaar! Zij rijzen fier als opgeheven vingers zenithwaarts, streven de deemoedige kerktorens voorbij [. . .]. Nog even, zo ging het gerucht in het theehuis, en ook alle kerken zouden moskeeën worden.

> Paravion ahead—look, we can already see its minarets! They dart proudly into the sky, passing high above the humble church bells. [. . .] According to the rumours going around in the teahouse, it wouldn't be long before all the churches were to be changed into mosques.[35]

The same reversal of perspective takes place when one of the immigrants, the carpet seller, foresees the abolition of the Dutch language in the not too distant future: "Remember what I tell you: one day everyone here will speak our language."[36] And what should one think of the regulars of an Amsterdam mosque who complain that the last church still standing in the district spoils their view and that the noise of its bells disturbs them?[37]

In describing the enthusiasm of Moroccan immigrants when they see the Low Countries with minarets spiked along the horizon, Bouazza's narrator anticipates the creation of the "no to minarets" lists in several European countries from 2009 onwards. For example, in March 2010, the Christian fundamentalist party (GPV) tried, in vain, to get parliament to pass legislation in order to ban the construction of minarets in the Netherlands.[38]

The three passages quoted therefore formulate a fanciful discourse that echoes one that is much more real. By emphasising the religious identity of the immigrants, Bouazza turns our attention towards islamophobes, but without mentioning them specifically. If his irony sometimes goes unnoticed, it is because his position is less pronounced than El Hachmi's. This "vagueness" comes mainly from the absence of any unequivocal narrative authority in the text. Pierre Schoentjes states that, in similar cases, "the irony, rather than

being a counter-discourse, is understated," or, as I have suggested, is not always devoid of a certain ambiguity or doublesidedness.[39] In this respect there
is indeed a resemblance between self-orientalisation and irony.

CONCLUSION

The contrast between the native country and the host country is at the centre
of the two texts discussed in this essay: *The Last Patriarch* and *Paravion*. But
instead of spelling out the contrasts between the two countries, as is the case
with Ben Jelloun, the authors of these two works, Bouazza and El Hachmi,
manage to incorporate one country into the other. In doing so, their writings
illustrate the idea that fiction has the power to overcome the immigrant's
predicament of impossible ubiquity.

In Bouazza's text, the notion of impossible ubiquity which we borrowed
from the work of the Franco-Algerian sociologist Abdelmalek Sayad, dis-
solves into an Arcadia that oscillates between a Mediterranean country—
although originally set in ancient Greece, the "Arcadian" landscape is also
proper to the Maghreb—and a public park in Amsterdam where, on hot
summer days, the joyous and "playful" spirit of May 1968 still persists. The
author therefore mixes the nostalgia of a permissive and above all hospitable
Dutch society with the image of a Moroccan society in full change, where,
little by little, women allow themselves to be overcome by a spirit of revolt
comparable to what could be described as "the Vondelpark spirit":

> De vrije omgang tussen de meisjes en de jongens was hem niet ontgaan. Dat was
> in zijn tijd wel anders geweest, en als hij in staat was zijn starre tijden mee te
> verhuizen naar verre oorden zoals Paravion, zou het niet moeilijk zijn de tijden
> hier te doen herleven.

> The free morals that existed between boys and girls had not escaped the carpet
> seller's attention. It had been very different in his time and age, and if he was
> capable of bringing with him his rigid past to far-away places, such as Paravion, it
> would not prove to be difficult to revive the days of old in this part of the world.[40]

The narrator's double perspective also sheds a new light on the Dutch past,
given that in Dutch public discourse there is a tendency to forget that the
arrival of the first Moroccan immigrants to the Netherlands coincided with
the hippy movement of the 1970s. The nostalgia of these splendid years is
therefore shared not only by the Dutch but also by the new arrivals amazed
by a society devoid of the racism they had sometimes witnessed in France and
the severe political repression that they had experienced in their homeland
during the reign of King Hassan II.[41] The absence of racism towards the first

wave of immigrant workers in the Netherlands can perhaps also be explained by the fact that there were never any colonial ties between the Netherlands and the countries of the Maghreb. For Dutch people at this time, these young Moroccans represented a wholly unknown and exotic world, while in France the unequal relationship between colonizers and colonized was transplanted from the former Maghrebian colonies to the *métropole*.[42] We also find this idea in *Ik, Driss* [I, Driss], a fictional narrative that relates the adventures of a young immigrant worker who arrives in Amsterdam in the early 1970s having lived in Lille, France, for a few years.[43]

The narrator of *The Last Patriarch* destroys patriarchy as an emblem of Rifian traditionalism by transgressing the number one taboo: she allows herself to be seduced by her uncle, the brother of her tyrannical father. But this subversive action allows her to assert, by means of intertextuality, her double Catalan and Mediterranean identity. In the first instance, she reminds us that the first lady of Catalan literature, Mercè Rodoreda, had also married her uncle. Secondly, the narrator is alluding, somewhat provocatively, to the famous scene in Bernardo Bertolucci's film *Last Tango in Paris* (1972) in which the heroine, played by Maria Schneider, is sodomised by Marlon Brando: "He asked me to use olive oil, not butter like Marlon Brando, as we are Mediterraneans after all!" And there you have Spain incorporated into Morocco in the most intimate fashion possible.

In the texts written by these young authors who belong to the second generation of immigrants, we witness a reconstitution of the European cultural heritage alongside a notable modification of certain literary and stylistic practices inherited from the past, such as irony, orientalism, and the ethnographic novel. It is a cultural and multi-lingual phenomenon that alters both the content and form of European literature today.

NOTES

1. A. Zahraoui, "Le retour: Mythe ou réalités?," in *Maghrébins en France: Émigrés ou immigrés?*, ed. Larbi Talha et al. (Paris: CNRS, 1983), 230.

2. "La question du retour (qui, par ailleurs, apparaît plutôt comme *un départ* pour les enfants nés en Europe) peut être reléguée au second plan, bien qu'elle ne soit jamais absente de la *représentation* que les uns et les autres se font du futur" (A. Zahraoui, "Le retour," 231). Unless stated otherwise, all translations from the French are my own. Italics added.

3. The Casablance International Book Fair 2010 was dedicated, in part, to authors of Moroccan origin who write in Italian.

4. The two immigrant authors discussed in this chapter have both published essays in which they claim to belong to the literary and cultural world of their adopted

country. See Hafid Bouazza, *Beer in bontjas* [A Bear in a Fur Coat] (2001) and Najat El Hachmi, *Jo també soc catalana* [I Too Am Catalan] (2004).

5. See Leslie A. Adelson, "Against Between: A Manifesto," in *Zafer Senocak*, eds. Tom Cheesman and Karin Yesilada (Cardiff: University of Wales Press, 2003), 133–34.

6. For an illustration of this ambiguity that cannot be translated into English, see Tzvetan Todorov, *L'Homme dépaysé* (Paris: Seuil, 1996). This topic is also discussed by Réda Bensmaïa in *Experimental Nations: Or, the Invention of the Maghreb* (Princeton, NJ: Princeton University Press, 2003).

7. Naima El Bezaz, *Minnares van de duivel* (Amsterdam: Contact, 2002). Curiously, the picture that appears on the cover of the paperback edition (2009) has been taken from *L'Histoire de Merlin* (14th century) and shows a sleeping woman visited by an incubus, a Christian homologue of the Maghrebian *djinn* portrayed in the novel.

8. In this respect the position of Ben Jelloun, the only Moroccan author considered a "cosmopolitan celebrity," resembles that of the Indo-Anglian writers discussed by Graham Huggan in the second chapter of *The Post-Colonial Exotic*. But since the focus of my article is on two writers who have adopted a European minority language, whether Catalan or Dutch, the question of literary commodification does not seem to apply, at least not on a global scale. See Graham Huggan, *The Post-Colonial Exotic: Marketing the Margins* (London: Routledge, 2001), 58–83.

9. Ulrich Johannes Beil, "Wider den Exotismus: Zafer Senocaks west-östliche Moderne," in *Zafer Senocak*, eds. Tom Cheesman and Karin Yesilada (Cardiff: University of Wales Press, 2003), 32.

10. For the role of food and flavours in migrant literature today, see my essay, "Lorsque Combray s'appelle Alger ou Saigon: Pour une 'déterritorialisation' des saveurs," in *Savoirs, saveurs*, ed. Jean-Christophe Delmeule (Lille: Presses de l'Université Lille III, 2010), 239–51.

11. Anthony Shay and Barbara Sellers-Young, "Belly Dance: Orientalism—Exoticism—Self-Exoticism," *Dance Research Journal* 35, no. 1 (Summer 2003): 18.

12. Frank F. Scherer, "Sanfancón: Orientalism, Self-Orientalization, and 'Chinese Religion' in Cuba," in *Nation Dance: Religion, Identity and Cultural Difference in the Caribbean*, ed. Patrick Taylor (Bloomington: Indiana University Press, 2001), 157.

13. Scherer, "Sanfancón," 167.

14. Tahar Ben Jelloun, *Au pays* (Paris: Gallimard, 2009). The quotations in this article derive from the French original.

15. I take the idea that migration is legitimated either by work or unemployment from Abdelmalek Sayad, "Le phénomène migratoire: Une relation de domination?," in *Maghrébins en France: Emigrés ou immigrés?*," 380.

16. Ben Jelloun, *Au pays*, 35.

17. For the innovative nature of *Solitary Confinement*, see Charles Bonn, "L'exil et la quête d'identité: Fausses portes pour une approche des littératures de l'immigration?," in *Cultures transnationales de France des "Beurs" aux . . . ?*, ed. Hafid Gafaïti (Paris: l'Harmattan, 2001), 40–41. Bonn's essay gives a very relevant analysis of three major works of Maghrebian literature that were published in the

1970s and whose authors can be considered the founders of immigration novels: Rachid Boudjedra, *Topographie idéale pour une agression caractérisée* (1975; Tahar Ben Jelloun, *La Réclusion solitaire* (1976); and Mohammed Dib, *Habel* (1977).

18. Abdelmalek Sayad, "Le Phénomène migratoire: Une relation de domination?' *Maghrébins en France: Emigrés ou immigrés?*, 381.

19. As far as Morocco is concerned, the commentaries relate to the *Makhzen* (Moroccan governing elite) and the near absence of medical care for elderly and handicapped people. France is described as a country in which racism flourishes and individualism is pushed to the extreme. The latter point is illustrated for example by means of an allusion to August 2003 when many old people died as a result of the excessive heat. They had been abandoned by their children during the summer holidays "like animals abandoned on the roadside," as Ben Jelloun puts it (*A.P.*, 36).

20. Marc Gontard is here referring to the work of the first Moroccan author writing in French, Ahmed Séfrioui. See *Littérature francophone*, ed. Charles Bonn and Xavier Garnier, vol. 1 ("le roman") (Paris: Hatier, 1997), 211.

21. Hafid Bouazza, *Paravion* (Amsterdam: Prometheus, 2004).

22. Najat El Hachmi, *Le Dernier Patriarche* (2008), translated from the Catalan by Anne Charlon (Arles: Actes Sud, 2009). All further references are to the French edition of this text.

23. Bouazza's novel opens with "Luister" ("Listen") and ends with a chapter in which the narrator again addresses a narratee, this time multiple, and represented by the Dutch "mijne heren de poortwachters," meaning the "gatekeepers" of a medieval city. But these refuse to open the gate to Paravion (*Paravion*, 9 and 219–20). El Hachmi starts her narrative as follows: "This is the story of Mimoun, son of Driouch, son of Allal, son of Mohammed, son of Mohand, son of Bouziane, whom we shall simply call Mimoun." This turn of phrase is repeated at the start of the first chapter: "On that day, after three daughters, a first son was born to Driouch of Allal of Mohammed of Mohand of Bouziane, etc." (*The Last Patriarch*, 8 and 11).

24. This also confirms the argument developed by Liesbeth Minnaard, following on from Leslie Adelson, which considers migrant literature as largely constitutive of European national identities today. I return to this subject in my conclusion. See Liesbeth Minnaard, *New Germans, New Dutch: Literary Interventions* (Amsterdam: Amsterdam University Press, 2008), 54. In her insightful monograph on Bouazza, Henriëtte Louwerse also stresses the Dutchness of Bouazza's unconventional writing style, especially in connection with the nineteenth-century literary movement of the so-called *Tachtigers* [the 1880s mouvement]. See Henriëtte Louwerse, *Homeless Entertainment: On Hafid Bouazza's Literary Writing* (Oxford: Peter Lang, 2007), 39–48.

25. According to Anouar Ouyachchi, the references to Catalan authors throughout the text "show the importance of school in constructing the identity of the novelist." I prefer to see here an effort by the author to appropriate a literary and cultural heritage that might be denied to her. See Anouar Ouyachchi, "La tyrannie du patriarche," *Le Magazine littéraire du Maroc* 1 (Autumn 2009): 34.

26. Bouazza, *Paravion*, 71.

27. Bouazza. *Paravion*, 146.

28. Arif Dirlik, "The Postcolonial Aura: Third World Criticism in the Age of Global Capitalism," *Critical Inquiry* 20, no. 2 (Winter 1994): 335.

29. "De sa position périphérique par rapport à la société francaise, l'immigration s'impose ainsi au coeur de l'actualité comme un révélateur des mutations sociales, politiques ou culturelles et une forclusion dans une histoire de malentendus." Ahmed Boubeker, "Abdelmalek Sayad, pionnier d'une sociologie de l'immigration postcoloniale," in Nicolas Bancel, Florence Bernault et al., eds., *Ruptures postcoloniales* (Paris: La Découverte, 2010), 47; Caroline B. Brettell, "Theorizing Migration in Anthropology," *Migration Theory: Talking Across Disciplines*, eds. Caroline B. Brettell and James F. Hollifield (New York: Routledge, 2008), 132.

30. Pierre Schoentjes, *Silhouettes de l'ironie* (Geneva: Droz, 2007), 174. Linda Hutcheon described the same phenomenon in the literature of African Americans. See *Irony's Edge: The Theory and Politics of Irony* (London: Routledge, 1995), 29–31.

31. Homi Bhabha, *The Location of Culture* (London: Routledge, 1994), 86.

32. "Because the intellectual sees things both in terms of what has been left behind and what is actual here and now, there is a double perspective that never sees things in isolation," in Edward W. Said, *Representations of the Intellectual* (London: Vintage, 1994), 44.

33. R. Siegle, *The Politics of Reflexivity: Narrative and the Constitutive Poetics of Culture* (1986), quoted by Linda Hutcheon, 30.

34. For a relevant analysis of the reception of *Paravion* in the Netherlands, see Liesbeth Minnaard, *New Germans, New Dutch*, 124.

35. Bouazza. *Paravion*, 139.

36. "Let op mijn woorden: eens zal iedereen hier onze taal spreken" (*Paravion*, 145).

37. *Paravion*, 151 and 144.

38. By doing so, the GPV followed the example of the Swiss who organised a referendum on the banning of minarets in December 2009. *Le Monde* reported the creation of "no to minarets" lists in Lorraine and Franche-Comté during the regional elections of March 15, 2010.

39. Pierre Schoentjes, "Séduction de l'ironie," in *L'ironie aujourd'hui, lectures d'un discours oblique*, ed. Mustapha Trabelsi (Clermont-Ferrand: Presses Universitaires Blaise Pascal, 2006), 297.

40. Bouazza, *Paravion*, 214.

41. Some of the first Moroccan migrant workers who arrived in the Netherlands were indeed political activists who felt threatened by the political repression under Hassan II during the so-called years of lead.

42. This point of view is adopted, among others, by the militants of the so-called *Mouvement des indigènes de la République*. See http://indigenes-republique.org, accessed October 21, 2008.

43. "My older brother wanted me to leave France [. . .] He told me that work in the Netherlands would be cleaner. He also told me that the Dutch are nicer than the French. They often called us 'dirty Arabs.'" Driss Tafersiti, *Ik, Driss* (Amsterdam: Atlas, 2010), 9. Translation mine.

BIBLIOGRAPHY

Adelson, Leslie A. "Against Between: A Manifesto." In *Zafer Senocak.* Edited by Tom Cheesman and Karin Yesilada, 131–41. Cardiff: University of Wales Press, 2003.

Beil, Ulrich Johannes. "Wider den Exotismus: Zafer Senocaks west-östliche Moderne." In *Zafer Senocak.* Edited by Tom Cheesman and Karin Yesilada, 31–42. Cardiff: University of Wales Press, 2003.

Ben Jelloun, Tahar. *Au pays*. Paris: Gallimard, 2009.

Bhabha, Homi. *The Location of Culture*. New York: Routledge, 1994.

Bonn, Charles. "L'exil et la quête d'identité: Fausses portes pour une approche des littératures de l'immigration?" In *Cultures transnationales de France des "Beurs" aux . . . ?* Edited by Hafid Gafaïti, 37–55. Paris: l'Harmattan, 2001.

Bouazza, Hafid. *Paravion*. Amsterdam: Prometheus, 2004.

Boubeker, Ahmed. "Abdelmalek Sayad, pionnier d'une sociologie de l'immigration postcoloniale." In *Ruptures postcoloniales*. Edited by Nicolas Bancel, Florence Bernault, et al., 37–49. Paris: La Découverte, 2010.

Brettell, Caroline B. "Theorizing Migration in Anthropology." In *Migration Theory: Talking Across Disciplines*. Edited by Caroline B. Brettell and James F. Hollifield, 113–61. New York: Routledge, 2008.

Dirlik, Arif. "The Postcolonial Aura: Third World Criticism in the Age of Global Capitalism." *Critical Inquiry* 20, no. 2 (Winter 1994): 328–56.

El Hachmi, Najat. *Le dernier patriarche*. Translated from the Catalan by Anne Charlon. Arles: Actes Sud, 2009 (2008).

Gontard, Marc. "Maroc." In *Littérature francophone, Vol. 1, "le roman"*. Edited by Charles Bonn and Xavier Garnier, 211–28. Paris: Hatier, 1997.

Hutcheon, Linda. *Irony's Edge: The Theory and Politics of Irony*. London: Routledge, 1995.

Minnaard, Liesbeth. *New Germans, New Dutch*. Amsterdam: Amsterdam University Press, 2008.

Ouyachchi, Anouar. "La tyrannie du patriarche." *Le Magazine littéraire du Maroc*, 1 (Autumn 2009): 34.

Poel, Ieme van der. "Lorsque Combray s'appelle Alger ou Saigon: Pour une 'déterritorialisation' des saveurs." In *Savoirs, saveurs*. Edited by Jean-Christophe Delmeule, 239–51. Lille: Presses de l'Université Lille III, 2010.

Sayad, Abdelmalek. "Le phénomène migratoire: Une relation de domination?" In *Maghrébins en France: Émigrés ou immigrés?* Edited by Larbi Talha et al., 365–407. Paris: National Centre for Scientific Research, 1983.

Scherer, Frank F. "Sanfancón: Orientalism, Self-Orientalization, and 'Chinese Religion' in Cuba." In *Nation Dance: Religion, Identity and Cultural Difference in the Caribbean*. Edited by Patrick Taylor, 153–70. Bloomington: Indiana University Press, 2001.

Schoentjes, Pierre. "Séduction de l'ironie." In *L'Ironie aujourd'hui, lectures d'un discours oblique*. Edited by Mustapha Trabelsi, 295–314. Clermont-Ferrand: Presses Universitaires Blaise Pascal, 2006.

———. *Silhouettes de l'ironie*. Geneva: Droz, 2007.

Zahraoui, A. "Le retour: Mythe ou réalités?" In *Maghrébins en France: Émigrés ou immigrés?* Edited by Larbi Talha et al., 229–47. Paris: National Centre for Scientific Research, 1983.

Chapter Thirteen

"Games of Deception" in Hafid Bouazza's Literary No Man's Land

Henriette Louwerse

In June 2008 the literary journal *de revisor* devoted a special issue to what has since become known as "genre collapse": the blurring of the clear distinctions between what were traditionally regarded as discreet genres. The writer Atte Jongstra contributed a cartoon to the journal in the form of an old-fashioned poster depicting a contorted hand alongside the warning "Do be careful with literary non-fiction; the writing hand maimed for the rest of his life, for while writing he did twist the truth." The archaic language and spelling is mirrored in the background image: men in rows working lathes in a dark environment, a gloomy half-light falling through small factory windows. The enigmatic warning, the industrial setting and the gesture towards the perils of manual labour appear to confirm the notion of non-fiction as a craft or skill. Yet a pointed irony lies in the suggestion that mixing craftsmanship with art—or in other words, non-fiction with fictional elements—will inflict irreversible disfigurement on the craftsman, and most likely the materials of his craft. Jongstra's image amounts to a wry call for a renewed attention to safety: namely a strict division of the literary and the non-literary.

In the editorial of the same issue the state of literature in Dutch is summarized as follows: "Actually, we are all confused. Novels are increasingly read and judged on whether they are true-to-life, while the preferred adjective for non-fiction is 'literary,' which conveniently appears to cover all untruths."[1] The contributions cover a varied set of observations on the relationship between fact, fiction, non-fiction and the literary. Even though the editorial promises to reinstitute the old order—non-fiction for journalism and academic writing, literary writing for the novel—the contributions illustrate that strict divisions between these categories are a thing of the past. Some contributors express regret; others are angry; some argue that there was never a clear distinction in the first place.

Figure 13.1. Atte Jongstra, "Do be careful with literary non-fiction." Courtesy of Atte Jongstra.

In his contribution entitled "De waarheid, de halve waarheid en alles be-halve de waarheid" [The truth, the half truth and everything but the truth] the novelist Jonathan Coe defines the distinction between fiction and non-fiction in terms of an implied author-reader contract, an unwritten agreement between writer and reader. Non-fiction is like journalism, according to Coe, the contract between writer and reader rests on the assumption that non-fiction writers promise to stick to the factual truth to the best of their ability. They may fail to do so due to deficient memory or poor investigative qualities, but that does not alter the shared understanding that what is offered is real: that is, based on facts. [2] In contrast to this truth-agreement Coe postulates the fiction-agreement: beautiful in its simplicity, immune to misinterpretation and difficult to break, "The author simply places the book in the hands of the reader and says: 'I promise you that everything in this book is a lie. There is not a true word to be found.' And the reader agrees and reads the book according to that strict agreement."[3] Coe calls this a "pure contract" that leads to an "honest form of writing," because the reader knows and accepts that the novelist is "a liar."[4] The reader cannot claim truths based on the book; the author relinquishes responsibility.

Though rather unsophisticated in its representation of the complex relationship between the literary work, its creator, the reader and the context, the contract image may work if the author is of the run-of-the-mill type, white male middle-class European. However, I would argue that in the case of an author who is somehow "marked," a "deviation from the norm" such as the migratory or diasporic author, that same relationship between author and work is not naturally assumed. Even in a poststructuralist world of decentred subjectivity it is still often expected that the specific circumstances of these authors will dominate, or at least impact on, their literary choices. They are destined—or doomed—to make their specific position in society the driving force behind their writing. Equally, the reader cannot ignore the exotic name on the cover; the inevitable intrusion of the extra-literary illustrates the predicament of both author and reader. The unwritten contract, "all this is a lie," which according to Coe is the "strict agreement" under which the reader reads the work, is under siege.

Clearly the literary text is always part of a wider field of cultural production in which an important contributory factor is the extra-literary image of the author created in the media or by marketing departments, but in case of an "extra-ordinary" writer, the relationship between the literary and the extra-literary can become genuinely critical. The reader's knowledge of the authors' circumstances penetrates the text, even if the authors themselves do not explicitly seek to activate the specificity of their personal circumstances. Their work appears somehow caught between fiction and non-fiction; it hovers in a no man's land in which Coe's "beautifully simple contract" does not apply.

In Britain and the Netherlands today the post-migratory author is still remarkable enough to be considered a divergence from the standard, born-and-bred author. In this contribution I will focus on the response of one "marked author" in particular, the Dutch author of Moroccan descent, Hafid Bouazza. I will look at Bouazza's strategies of outmanoeuvring the overriding focus on his background as an author, and to claim the freedom to choose his own subject away from his personal circumstances. I will look in particular at the construct in his work of an all-encompassing vision, the "land of the imagination," a no man's land in which commercial concerns and reader expectations can be left behind. But before I move to Bouazza I will briefly focus on a recent publication in the British context, *Too Asian, Not Asian Enough*; a collection of short stories by a new generation of British Asian authors with as its central concern a similar desire to move away from author biography and reader expectations.

In the foreword to *Too Asian, Not Asian Enough* (2011), the editor of the collection Kavita Bhanot suggests that the success of Asian British writing, films and sit-coms have forged a British Asian genre with as main characteristics the generational conflict, cultural differences between home- and outside-world, generally delivered with a tragicomic tone. Not only is the expectation of the British public geared towards these stock ingredients, but the authors themselves are also affected by it: "the existing narratives are so pervasive that they form a barrier between us and the world; they bleed into our imaginations and influence how we write about our lives."[5] The "reality" of British Asian life portrayed in the existing representations is, in addition to a commercially attractive formula, an imposing force that shapes or at least impacts on the writing of British Asian authors. Bhanot herself concludes that she, unwittingly, adopted what she refers to as a "white middle-class or bourgeois Indian" gaze that shaped her writing, reducing it to a *performance* of their supposedly torn condition, a paralyzing repetition of stock ingredients produced under the license of the white literary establishment and an Indian elite.

In spite of Bhanot's triumphant pronouncement of the end of the clichés of the British Asian narrative, one of the contributors Gautam Malkani underscores the condition rather than offering a cure. Malkani's short story, "Asian of the Month," records the events behind the scenes of an X-factor style reality show to crown the most authentic Asian. Cast in a highly artificial set-up on a stage in bright spotlights, the contestants are challenged to act out an authentic Asianness. In addition to the impossible task of proving one's authenticity, the contestants find themselves faced with unpredictable panels of judges and are thus forced to spend their energy on trying to anticipate what type of assumed Asian authenticity will find favour in their eyes. For their first outing, their guess is that the panel will consist of "white middle-class marketing professionals," so they all tailor their appearance and presentation according to the stock "white" perception of Asian authenticity; demonstrating "street cred" and downplaying their educational achievements and material success.[6] When the judges turn out to be of Asian origin, however, the gulf between the ideas of what a "proper" Asian is like from an Asian perspective and the authentic Asian as seen through white eyes is painfully exposed: the contestants are scolded for dressing too sloppily, for not showing enough respect for their elders and for lacking in allegiance towards fellow Asians.

When, for the third and final test, the contestants not only have to prove that they are authentically Asian, but also that they are "a sustainable version" of the authentic Asian, the conflicting demands multiply. All aim for a mixed approach, a palatable version of Asianness acceptable to the wider public: "ethnic dress, but clean-shaven and secular above the neck."[7] One of the contestants makes what at first appears a convincing and definitive statement:

> I am not Asian, [. . .] I am a free man. A metrosexual, metropolitan man [. . .] My metropolitan identity consigns to history all your dead-beat debates about whether I am torn between being British and being Asian. In my metropolitan identity, I am not even a minority. I do not suffer from racial discrimination or economic deprivation. I do not get lost in dreams of the motherland or work with my mother in a corner shop or her family's flock-papered Indian restaurant. I do not support India at cricket *or* England—I support whichever team has the best looking female fans. I do not hear sitars in my head and dream of my mother in her favourite sari. I do not have any angst about an arranged or a semi-arranged marriage. I do not do terrorism, fundamentalism or Bollywood films. Because, frankly, I'm too busy building my own brand of Britishness; trying to get into the record business; spending my parents' hard-earned income on designer trainers, designer clothes and designer smartphones; driving around in an un-stolen Audi and spending my evenings trying to get laid by fit-looking women.[8]

On closer inspection, however, it appears that this declaration of cultural independence and individuality is cast in highly commercial terms and ambitions: self-definition is reduced to branding, building a *brand* of Britishness, based on a pursuit of fame and designer goods. Malkani does not offer a triumphant way out of the popular, bankable formula; on the contrary, he reiterates the inevitable subjugation to the pressure of the masses and the inescapability of market principles. Echoing Bhanot's complaint in the introduction to the collection, it is the extra-diegetic narrator who formulates the effect: "creative paralysis."[9] Joining the game, adhering to the rules, can only end in defeat. It appears that creative paralysis can only be lifted by changing the game, and changing the game into "a game of deception" as suggested by Hafid Bouazza, may point to a way out of the straitjacket of existing narratives.

A BEAR IN A FUR COAT

Hafid Bouazza burst onto the literary scene in the Netherlands in the mid 1990s.[10] In his early years a striking feature of his work—apart from the literary quality of his writing—was his explicitly advertised resistance to the ways in which he and his novels were received and to the labels attached to his writing. He strongly objected to being considered a migrant author, an "ethnic" author or even a "Moroccan-Dutch" author. He argued that since he wrote in Dutch, he was a Dutch writer and that no further qualifications were required. Moreover, he insisted that his art had nothing to do with his personal background, not even if most of the stories of *De voeten van Abdullah* were set in an imaginary Moroccan village Bertollo, which carried the same name as the actual village from which the Bouazzas had emigrated in 1977.

Bouazza also stressed repeatedly that he neither felt he was a spokesperson for the Dutch-Moroccan community nor did he aim to further understanding between cultural groups. He positioned himself as an "ordinary," autonomous author giving expression to a highly individual artistic drive through literary texts. In an interview in 1997 he stated clearly:

> Ik schrijf omdat ik wil schrijven, niet omdat ik de bedoeling heb om meer begrip tussen culturen te kweken. Hou toch op. En ik schrijf al helemaal niet omdat ik me de tolk voel van de tweede generatie allochtonen. Ik ben geen maatschappelijk werker. Schrijft een Nederlandse schrijver soms ook namens anderen?

> I write because I want to write, not because I aim to further intercultural relations. Get over it. And I certainly don't write because I feel a spokesperson for second-generation migrants. I am not a social worker. Does a Dutch author write in the name of others?[11]

He confirms this position in the publication I would like to look at in more detail. *Een beer in Bontjas* [Bear in a Fur Coat], is a short work published in March 2001, followed by an extended and revised edition in 2004.[12] *Een beer in bontjas* was commissioned by the CPNB, the *Collective Promotion of the Dutch Book,* to support the annual promotional Book Week in the Netherlands. In 2001, the CPNB had chosen a very topical theme for their promotional week: *Land van herkomst. Schrijven tussen twee culturen* ("Country of origin: Writing between two cultures"). With 70,000 copies sold, *Een beer in bontjas,* Bouazza's personal view on the "country of origin" theme, was the bestselling publication of Book Week 2001.[13]

Een beer in bontjas is neither a conventional essay nor a straightforward autobiography. In this artistic manifesto-cum-memoir, Bouazza combines autobiographical details about this migration from Morocco to the Netherlands in 1977 with commentary on the reception of his writing, his position as an author "between two cultures," and his personal views on literature and the literary world. Various characters appear including an author called Hafid Bouazza, who is not, however, a straightforward representation of the *persona practica* Hafid Bouazza. This Bouazza is simply one character among others in the text, which also features Mrs Split, a woman in her fifties with a penchant for the exotic; Haaris Boelfachr, another author "between two cultures"; and a first-person narrator. *Een beer in bontjas* in its entirety drafts Bouazza's informal poetics set against, or amidst, stories of the biographical Hafid Bouazza.

Een beer in bontjas opens with a parable based on a 1946 children's book by Frank Tashlin.[14] It is the story of a bear who, on coming out of hibernation, finds himself in the middle of a big factory built on top of his hiding place while he was asleep. As soon as he is discovered by the workers, he is kitted out with a helmet, a cigarette and a cup of coffee. Now he is expected to work, like all the others. When the bear refuses to comply—"I can't work. I am a bear"—he is accused of laziness and taken to various supervisors of increasingly higher rank, who all repeat the same misconception: "You are a silly man who needs a shave and wears a fur coat." In the face of such unwavering opposition, the bear begins to doubt his hitherto unchallenged identity and begins to believe that he is indeed a "silly man." In his confusion, the bear wonders what a "silly man" would do to keep warm.

The metaphor is clear: humans do not recognise the bear's individuality, they do not want to listen to his version of himself, but they are keen to make him fit *their* perception and expectations. The bear is not allowed to be just a bear, but is forced to think of himself as a "silly man" in a fur coat. The reader is quick to make the link with Bouazza himself, who, like the bear, has repeatedly stated that he is a *Dutch* author and not the oriental-occidental amalgam widely seen as popular and commercially attractive. However, his audience seemingly cannot be colour blind and accordingly labels the author a migrant writer. This theme runs as a thread through *Een beer in bontjas*: the literary establishment's expectation that the background of the author—with the two cultures of which he or she is expected to have intimate knowledge— is a crucial, if not determining, factor in his or her artistic expression. As Bouazza says:

Als ik de meeste critici mag geloven, ben ik een Marokkaanse schrijver. Maar ik geloof de meeste critici niet. Volgens andere, welwillende mensen ben ik een Marokkaans-Nederlandse schrijver. Deze aanduiding klinkt echter ongemakkelijk. Zij loopt tegelijkertijd op muil en klomp—en dat loopt verdomd moeilijk. Dan heb je nog de voorzichtige mensen (die zijn in de minderheid), voor wie ik de titel N.S.M.A.N.N. heb verzonnen. Dat is, maatschappelijk gezien, de

enige juiste aanduiding, maar je maakt er geen vrienden mee. Het klinkt als een
zeldzame ziekte.

If I were to believe most critics then I am a Moroccan writer. But I do not believe
most critics. According to other, well-disposed people, I am a Moroccan-Dutch
author. But that label sounds uncomfortable. It hobbles around in a slipper and
a clog—and that makes walking bloody tricky. Then there are the careful people
(they are a minority) for whom I have coined the title D.A.M.D.D.N. [Dutch
Author of Moroccan Descent with Dutch Nationality]. That is the only politically correct designation, but it will not make you very popular. It sounds like
a rare disease.[15]

Bouazza rejects the special category that has been reserved for him as a
Moroccan-born author or a Dutch-Moroccan author and he points out that, although he recognises that these labels should not be seen as deliberately mali-
cious attempts to keep the author in his or her place, he considers his assigned
space as a migrant author to be undeserved and restrictive: "What is wrong
with just 'author' or 'writer' without the weight of a topographical hump?"[16]
Bouazza consistently demands, whether in the Dutch literary world or more
broadly, to be read without regard for his social and personal circumstances.
He energetically states that real art can only be inspired and born from art,
not from personal trauma, "authorship does not arise from the first trauma,
but from the first discovery of literature."[17] The background of the author, his
or her social environment, religious beliefs, sexual preference or skin colour
are all irrelevant when it comes to producing literature because an author is a
creature of language and not a biographical person: "It is the world he creates
in language that concerns us [...] we do not require private information."[18]
This world of language is for Bouazza not simply a conceptual alternative to
the biased reality of everyday existence: it is a *home*, a homeland provided by
language and narrative. The traditional connotations of home and homeland,
such as homogeneity, contiguity and familiarity, are exactly those elements
that are assumed to be destabilised in the case of the migrant, Bouazza. His
response is to turn the idea of home into a "literary homeland" created by the
author who shapes and colours the landscape according to his or her own will:

"Onze kindertijd is een land waaruit wij allemaal emigreren," heeft de schrijver
Salman Rushdie gezegd, beroemd vanwege de prijs die op zijn hoofd staat. Al
zouden immigranten dat verlies sterker voelen. "En de taal," voeg ik eraan toe,
"is het enige land waarin de schrijver zich thuis voelt. De taal is zijn identiteit,
stijl zijn paspoort."

"Our childhood is a country from which we all emigrate," said the author
Salman Rushdie, famous for the price on his head. Although immigrants would
feel this loss more strongly. "And language," I add, "is the only place where the
writer feels at home. Language is his identity, style his passport."[19]

This home in language, Bouazza argues in *Een beer in bontjas*, is opened up by the artist's creative powers. These give access to a "land of the imagination," an alternative to the real world of everyday worries, entirely non-topographical, open to all and strictly egalitarian. Due to its position above the realities of everyday existence, worldly differences are effaced and harmony rules:

> In de kloof die hem [de auteur] van de lezer scheidt, strekt zich het land van de verbeelding uit. Daar wordt geen onderscheid gemaakt naar afkomst. Daar rust de leeuw naast de hinde en, inderdaad, de kameel naast de koe. Waar de verbeelding regeert, daar is vereniging.

> Along the gap that separates him [the author] from the reader stretches the land of the imagination. No distinction based on descent is made here. The lion rests alongside the hind and, indeed, the camel next to the cow. Where the imagination rules, there is unity.[20]

The evocation of an imaginary land of equality away from the specific circumstances of the author and the reader is an understandable textual strategy under the circumstances. *Een beer in bontjas* was after all a commissioned piece to discuss "Writing between Two Cultures." However, Bouazza has rejected the idea of being caught between two cultures from the word go. He even strategically denies any link between biography and artistic output. Thus Bouazza, in *Een beer in bontjas*, has a clear mission: he wants, once and for all, to shed his "topographical hump," reject the niche of migrant writer to which he has been assigned based on his cultural background, and claim his artistic individuality and independence. However, there is more to Bouazza's poetic craft than this advocated, radical separation of the private circumstances of the author and his writing might suggest.

Remarkably, the plea to disregard biographical knowledge appears in a publication with the subtitle *Autobiografische beschouwingen* (*Autobiographical Reflections*). A paradox appears: Bouazza articulates his call for a strict division between the author as an ordinary member of society and the author as an artist in a publication featuring the story of the author's migration and early authorship. In other words, *Een beer in bontjas* is (also) an autobiography designed to underline that the author's life-story is irrelevant when it comes to writing or reading literature. We had better be on our guard: "*do* be careful with literary non-fiction."

At this point, let us revisit the parable of the bear from which *Een beer in bontjas* derives its title. As I mentioned earlier, the metaphor seems obvious: the bear is not allowed to be himself; instead he is expected to act according to the expectations of his environment. Bouazza confirms this interpretation: "The question the story so beautifully raises is whether identity is a matter of personal choice or determined by the environment."[21] "The environment" that persistently desires to catch glimpses of the authentically "other" culture appears to refer to the Netherlands' literary scene, or even the Netherlands' society at large. Translated in terms of the Malkani's story discussed above, the author is expected to perform his otherness along the expectations of his white Dutch set of judges. But Bouazza does not stop here and he continues: "there are increasingly more people who discover that there are Arabs and ever more Arabs who discover that they are Arabs.'"[22] With this enigmatic addition, the context of Bouazza's reference is destabilised. The easy and seemingly obvious assumption that Bouazza was referring to a Dutch context proves unfounded. With his sarcastic comment on the recent trend of "identity discovery," Bouazza reaches beyond the particular context, Dutch or Arab, to *identity* as a political construct. No longer is it simply Dutch society that keeps the author locked up in his exotic cage. It is not even the "original" or "home" culture that is under attack from restricted freedom of movement in a new environment. On closer inspection, the bear parable does not simply criticise the insider-outsider opposition, but it outmanoeuvres and undermines this polarised construct. Bouazza rejects the assumption that underpins the opposition, namely that there is such a thing as a "stable" identity *at all*. Instead he demands "bloederige vrijheid," bloody freedom: "But if I were that bear, I would take my fur coat off, no matter the blood and pain involved; no stubble, no fur coat, bloody freedom."[23] Naked and bleeding, Bouazza is neither bear nor madman; identification with either has the same result: compromised freedom. Bouazza thus gives the bear parable an unexpected twist. After lulling the reader into pity for the bear, denied the space to act out his "bear identity," Bouzza makes a critical addition. What is involved here is indeed an "acting out," a performance. And then, in a final gesture, Bouazza exposes the truth behind the fundamental truth: there is no bear, and certainly no such thing as a bear identity.[24]

The insight the bear parable offers is not the obvious call for the recognition of difference, which upholds the us-them opposition. Rather, the bear parable is a call for a crushing of the ideology of difference, an ideology that under the guise of tolerance is set to maintain the status quo.[25] Against the expectation of difference, Bouazza pitches the demand for uncompromised artistic freedom and defends that freedom in a society that has become more open, more varied, more global, and, as a result, more fragmented and more unsure about its (perceived) essence. Bouazza rejects social or moral responsibilities as authorial obligations and vehemently defends the right of the artist (and the reader) to escape into a world of the imagination. However, he or she is, in Rushdie's words, "obliged to accept that he [or she] is part of the crowd, part of the ocean, part of the storm."[26] Bouazza and Malkani are part of the multicultural reality in the Netherlands and Britain today and their writing reflects this particular predicament.

Finally, the paradox Bouazza sets up in *Een beer in bontjas*—the use of autobiography to dismiss the biographical factor—is in fact typical of his writing more broadly. Bouazza refers to this as "the game of deception."[27] This "deception" relies on his readers' extra-literary knowledge of the biographical circumstances of the author, which he then dismisses as irrelevant. The question arises, then: does this game of deception not render his call for artistic autonomy and his evocation of an identity-neutral "land of the imagination" insincere? Not necessarily. By endorsing conflicting ideas simultaneously, he forces his readers to take seriously background as a significant component in the complex author-text-reader relationship. He challenges both the easy biographical reading as well as the undesirable return to New Critical orthodoxy with its strictures on the biographical fallacy. Instead he forces us to restructure the way we think about text and context—he demands a series of distinct, yet intertwined domains of freedom—freedom to be everything and nothing at the same time. So just as he writes between *two* cultures, he writes between *none*. Just as he writes autobiography, essay and fiction, he writes none of the above. Just as strict dividing lines between genres have lost their relevance, so have any simplistic distinctions between us and them, fiction and reality, authentic and the exotic. What both Bouazza and Malkani illustrate is the inevitable intrusion of the extra-literary that lays bare the predicament of both author and reader. We are subjects in but also subject to our specific time and place with its focus on difference and urge for authenticity. Their work summons the readers to take seriously the very notion of background and to recognise that, at least as far as literature is concerned, *con*text is also text and consequently requires reading.

NOTES

1. "Eigenlijk zijn we allemaal in de war. Romans worden steeds vaker gelezen en beoordeeld op herkenbaarheid, terwijl non-fictie inmiddels liefst 'literair' heet, waarmee de eventuele onwaarheden die erin staan onmiddellijk gedekt zijn." Editorial, *De Revisor* 34, nos. 2–3 (June 2008): 4. All translations are by this author.

2. Jonathan Coe, "De waarheid, de halve waarheid en alles behalve de waarheid," *De Revisor* 34, nos. 2–3 (June 2008): 55.

3. "Het contract tussen de schrijver en de lezer van fictie is mooi in zijn eenvoud, laat geen verkeerde interpretatie toe en valt uiterst moeilijk te verbreken. De schrijver legt het boek simpelweg in de handen van de lezer en zegt: 'Ik beloof je dat alles in dit boek gelogen is. Er is geen waar woord in te vinden.' En de lezer stemt ermee in het boek te lezen volgens de strikte afspraak." Coe, "De waarheid," 56.

4. Coe, "De waarheid," 57.

5. Kavita Bhanot, ed., *Too Asian, Not Asian Enough* (Birmingham: Tindal Street Press, 2011), x.

6. Gautam Malkani, "Asian of the Month," in *Too Asian, Not Asian Enough*, ed. Kavita Bhanot (Birmingham: Tindal Street Press, 2011), 16.

7. Malkani, "Asian of the Month," 18.

8. Malkani, "Asian of the Month," 20.

9. Malkani, "Asian of the Month," 19.

10. For an extensive study on the works of Hafid Bouazza, see Henriette Louwerse, *Homeless Entertainment: On Hafid Bouazza's Literary Writing* (Oxford: Peter Lang, 2007).

11. Wilma Kieskamp, "Bekroonde Hafid Bouazza gebruikt archaïsch Nederlands in sprookjesachtige verhalen," *Trouw*, January 21, 1997.

12. Hafid Bouazza, *Een beer in bontjas: Autobiografische beschouwingen* (Amsterdam: Prometheus, 2004).

13. "Boek Bouazza best verkocht in de Boekenweek," *NRC Handelsblad*, March 27, 2001. The Book Week Essay was introduced in 1987 as a second annual publication commissioned by the CPNB when they decided to introduce a theme for their yearly event. Unlike the Book Week Gift, the essay is expected to support the theme of the Book Week. Since its introduction, the essay (which, unlike the gift, is not free) has been written by well-known Dutch writers such as Rudy Kousbroek, Jeroen Brouwers, Jan Wolkers, Gerrit Komrij and Geert Mak.

14. Frank Tashlin's 1946 children's book *The Bear That Wasn't* was made into a Looney Tunes cartoon in 1967. Tashlin himself was involved in the production of the short film. Bouazza translated the book in 2004, *De beer die geen beer was*, trans. Hafid Bouazza (Amsterdam: Van Goor, 2004).

15. Bouazza, *Beer in bontjas*, 14–15.

16. Bouazza, *Beer in bontjas*, 15.

17. "Het schrijverschap ontstaat echter niet bij het eerste trauma, maar bij de eerste ontdekking van literatuur." Bouazza, *Beer in bontjas*, 16.

18. "En het is de wereld die hij in taal schept die ons aangaat [. . .] Private informatie hebben we niet nodig." Bouazza, *Beer in bontjas*, 94–95.

19. Bouazza, *Beer in bontjas*, 67.

20. Bouazza, *Beer in bontjas*, 73.

21. "Wat het verhaal zo mooi aan de orde stelt, is of identiteit een kwestie van persoonlijke keuze is, of van de omgeving." Bouazza, *Beer in bontjas*, 14.

22. "Ik bedoel, er zijn steeds meer mensen die ontdekken dat er Arabieren zijn en steeds meer Arabieren die ontdekken dat zij Arabieren zijn." Bouazza, *Beer in bontjas*, 14.

23. "Maar als ik de beer was, dan zou ik mijn bontjas, met alle bloed en pijn van dien uittrekken; geen stoppelbaard, geen bontjas, bloederige vrijheid." Bouazza, *Beer in bontjas*, 13.

24. Significantly, this is the literal title of Tashlin's book, *A Bear That Wasn't*, which Bouazza translated in 2004 as *De beer die geen beer was*.

25. For a critical discussion of the "ideologie van het verschil," see, for instance, Rudi Visker, *Vreemd gaan en vreemd blijven: Filosofie van de multiculturaliteit* (Amsterdam: Sun, 2005), 34–40.

26. Salman Rushdie, *Imaginary Homelands: Essays and Criticisms, 1981–1991* (London: Granta Books, 1992), 100.

27. Bouazza, *Beer in bontjas*, 66.

BIBLIOGRAPHY

Bhanot, Kavitha, ed. *Too Asian, Not Asian Enough.* Birmingham: Tindal Street Press, 2011.

Bouazza, Hafid. *Een beer in bontjas: Autobiografische beschouwingen.* Amsterdam: Prometheus, 2004.

Coe, Jonathan. "De waarheid, de halve waarheid en alles behalve de waarheid." *De Revisor* 34, nos. 2–3 (June 2008): 4–57.

Kieskamp, Wilma. "Bekroonde Hafid Bouazza gebruikt archaïsch Nederlands in sprookjesachtige verhalen," *Trouw*, January 21, 1997

Louwerse, Henriette. *Homeless Entertainment: On Hafid Bouazza's Literary Writing.* Oxford: Peter Lang, 2007.

Malkani, Gautam. "Asian of the Month." In *Too Asian, Not Asian Enough.* Edited by Kavita Bhanot, 13–21. Birmingham: Tindal Street Press, 2011.

Rushdie, Salman. *Imaginary Homelands: Essays and Criticisms, 1981–1991.* London: Granta Books, 1992.

Tashlin, Frank. Een beer die geen beer was. Translated by Hafid Bouazza. Amsterdam: Van Goor, 2004.

Visker, Rudi. *Vreemd gaan en vreemd blijven: Filosofie van de multiculturaliteit.* Amsterdam: Sun, 2005.

Wagenaar, Bert. "Een goed verhaal." *De Revisor* 34, nos. 2–3 (June 2008): 27–32.

Index

About the Contributors

Elleke Boehmer is professor of world literature in English at the University of Oxford. Bilingual in Dutch and English, she is interested in the postcolonial debates that draw together Britain and the Netherlands. Besides being an acclaimed novelist and short story writer, Boehmer's books include *Colonial and Postcolonial Literature* (1995, 2005), *Empire, the National and the Postcolonial, 1890–1920* (2002), *Stories of Women* (2005), and the biography *Nelson Mandela* (2008). She edited Robert Baden-Powell's *Scouting for Boys* (2004) and the anthology *Empire Writing* (1998) and coedited *JM Coetzee in Writing and Theory* (2009), *Terror and the Postcolonial* (2009), and *The Indian Postcolonial* (2010). She is currently working on a memoir fiction partly set in the Netherlands.

Frances Gouda is professor of history and gender studies at Amsterdam University. Her dissertation and first research project focused on the social and intellectual history of nineteenth century France and the Netherlands, which resulted in a book entitled *Poverty and Political Culture: The Rhetoric of Social Welfare in the Netherlands and France* (1994). Her later scholarly work has analysed the Dutch colonial history of Indonesia, which produced the books *Dutch Culture Overseas: Colonial Practice in the Netherlands-Indies, 1900–1942* (1995) and *American Visions of the Dutch East Indies/Indonesia: US Foreign Policy and Indonesian Nationalism, 1920–1949* (2002). She has coedited a collection of essays with Julia Clancy-Smith on *Domesticating the Empire: Race, Gender, and Family Life in French and Dutch Colonialism* (1998, 1999).

Isabel Hoving is affiliated with the Department of Film and Literary Studies of Leiden University, where she teaches postcolonial theory, cultural analysis, gender studies and ecocriticism. Her study on Caribbean migrant women writers, *In Praise of New Travellers*, was published in 2001 by Stanford UP. She has coedited several books on (Dutch) migration, Caribbean literatures, African literature and art, and has just completed a monograph on the intersections of postcolonial theory and ecocriticism. She is a member of the editorial board of *Thamyris/Intersecting: Place, Sex, and Race*, and *Ecozon@: The European Journal of Literature, Culture and the Environment*. In addition to her academic work, she is an award-winning youth writer.

Theo D'haen is professor of English and comparative literature at KU Leuven, and earlier held the Chair of English Literature at Leiden. He has published numerous books and articles on (post)modernism, (post)colonialism, popular genres, and world literature. Recent publications include *The Routledge Concise History of World Literature*, *The Routledge Companion to World Literature* (ed., with David Damrosch and Djelal Kadir) and *The Routledge Reader in World Literature* (ed., with César Domínguez and Mads Rosendahl Thomsen).

Sarah Bracke is assistant professor of sociology of religion and culture at the Katholieke Universiteit Leuven. Her work engages with questions of modernity, religion and secularism, with particular attention to questions of subjectivity, agency and gender, and is specifically situated in the context of (the construction of) Europe. She has published in *Theory, Culture and Society*, the *European Journal of Women's Studies*, and *Feminist Review* and coauthored a book investigating the "multicultural debate" in Flanders (*Een leeuw in een kooi*, 2009, Meulenhof/Manteau).

Nadia Fadil studied sociology and anthropology at the Catholic University of Leuven, Belgium and holds a PhD in social sciences from the same university. She was a Jean Monnet Postdoctoral Fellow at the European University Institute in Florence and currently holds a Postdoctoral Fellowship of the Research Foundation Flanders (FWO) at the Center for Sociological Research of the University of Leuven. Her research interests revolve around questions of subjectivity and embodiment, secular governmentality, liberalism and multiculturalism, focused in particular on the case of Islam in Belgium and Europe.

Pamela Pattynama is Indisch Huis Professor of Colonial and Postcolonial Literature and Culture, specifically the Netherlands-Indies. She teaches film studies and Dutch colonial literature in the departments of Media Studies, Dutch Modern Literature and Literary Studies at the University of Amsterdam. She has published widely on (post)colonial discourse, cultural memory and the representation of gender and "mixed race" in postcolonial films and literature. Currently, she is working on a book on cultural memory and colonial photographs, literature and films. She is Professor of Dutch East-Indies Literature and Culture at the University of Amsterdam.

Liesbeth Minnaard is assistant professor in comparative literature at Leiden University. Her main fields of expertise are interculturality in literature, cultural effects of migration and globalisation, and postcolonial studies. She has published widely on the literature of migration, as well as on exoticism in literature. She is the author of the monograph *New Germans, New Dutch. Literary Interventions* (Amsterdam University Press, 2008) and coeditor of *Literature, Language and Multiculturality in Scandinavia and the Low Countries* (forthcoming at Rodopi 2012).

Louise Viljoen is professor in the Department of Afrikaans and Dutch at the University of Stellenbosch, South Africa. Her field of research is Afrikaans literature and literary theory with a special focus on postcolonialism, gender, identity and (auto-)biographical writing. She has compiled an anthology of Afrikaans poetry, *Poskaarte. Beelde van die Afrikaanse poësie sedert 1960* (1998) with colleague Ronel Foster, as well as a selection of poetry by Barend Toerien, *Om te onthou* (2006). She has also published a book on the work of Antjie Krog, *Ons ongehoorde soort. Beskouings oor die werk van Antjie Krog* (2009).

Sarah De Mul is FWO-postdoctoral fellow at K.U. Leuven University and lecturer at the Open University, the Netherlands. She is the author of *Colonial Memory* (2011) and coauthor of a Dutch-language monograph on multiculturalism in Flanders (2009). She coedited *Commitment and Complicity in Cultural Theory and Practice* (2009) and *Literature, Language, and Multiculturalism in Scandinavia and the Low Countries* (2012).

Murat Aydemir is associate professor in comparative literature and cultural analysis at the University of Amsterdam. He is the author of *Images of Bliss: Ejaculation, Masculinity, Meaning* (2007) and the (co)editor of *Migratory Settings: Transnational Perspectives on Place* (2008) and *Indiscretions: At the Intersection of Queer and Postcolonial Theory* (2011).

Mireille Rosello teaches at the University of Amsterdam. Her research focuses on diasporic voices (Europe, North Africa and the Caribbean) and gender constructions (queer theories and performativity). She is the author of *The Reparative in Narratives: Works of Mourning in Progress* (2010) and is coediting two volumes on "What's Queer about Europe?" and on "Multilingual Europe, Plurilingual Europeans."

Ieme van der Poel is professor of French literature and the director of the College of Humanities at the University of Amsterdam. She has published widely on (post) colonial literature in French, and is the author of *Congo-Océan (1921-1934): Un chemin de fer colonial controversé* (2006). Her book on migrant literature, *Diasporic Writing: New Moroccan Voices in French, Spanish, Catalan and Dutch*, will be published by Liverpool UP in 2013.

Henriette Louwerse is senior lecturer and director of studies in Dutch in the School of Modern Languages of the University of Sheffield. Her research focuses on postcolonial and migration literature and her publications include the monograph *Homeless Entertainment: On Hafid Bouazza's Literary Writing* (Oxford: Peter Lang, 2007).

Lightning Source UK Ltd.
Milton Keynes UK
UKHW010727160819
348071UK00002B/184/P